THEATRE WORLD

by

JOHN WILLIS

1967-68 SEASON

Volume 24

CROWN PUBLISHERS, INC.
419 Park Avenue South
New York, N. Y.

Copyright © 1968, by John Willis. Manufactured in the U.S.A.

Library of Congress Catalog Card No. 46-13321

Published simultaneously in Canada by
General Publishing Company Limited

To

EDITH S. BLYDENBURGH

Maureen Stapleton and George C. Scott
in
"PLAZA SUITE"

Martha Swope Photo

CONTENTS

EDITOR: JOHN WILLIS
Assistant Editor: Harold Stephens
Staff: Frances Crampon, Stanley Reeves, Evan Romero
Staff Photographers: Louis Mélançon, Friedman-Abeles, Bert Andrews, Van Williams

REVIEWING THE SEASON

Artistically and financially, this season was the best in several years for Broadway, Off-Broadway, and touring companies. Surprisingly, straight plays were more successful than musicals for the first time in a number of seasons. There were 73 Broadway productions, more than in any season since 1950-51, according to Hobe Morrison, the statistical genius of *Variety*. However, the quality this season did not seem worthy of a prize from the Pulitzer committee. Likewise, the Drama Critics Circle decided not to select any American play for citation, although it did select a British import "Rosencrantz and Guildenstern Are Dead." This was also the recipient of an Antoinette Perry Award ("Tony") for best play of the season. The "Tony" for best musical went to "Hallelujah, Baby!" that opened last season, but too late to be considered for the 1966-67 awards.

Again, some of the best productions of the season were either imports or revivals: "The Birthday Party," "After The Rain," "A Day In The Death of Joe Egg" (generally referred to as "Joe Egg"), "The Prime of Miss Jean Brodie," "There's A Girl In My Soup," "Exit The King," "The Show-Off," and "The Little Foxes." Other noteworthy productions were "Plaza Suite," "More Stately Mansions" (Eugene O'Neill's unfinished last play), "Everything In The Garden," "Spofford," "I Never Sang For My Father," "The Price," "The Seven Descents of Myrtle," "The Only Game In Town," "George M!," "The Happy Time," and the Broadway debut of the incomparable Marlene Dietrich in her solo performance. The APA once again presented some of the best theatre on Broadway, and the Lincoln Center Repertory Theater had its best season to date.

Actors who gave memorable performances were Maureen Stapleton, Zoe Caldwell, Colleen Dewhurst, George C. Scott, Ingrid Bergman, Albert Finney, Estelle Parsons, John Colicos, Melvyn Douglas, Ellis Rabb, George Rose, Joel Grey, Patricia Routledge, Robert Goulet, Zena Walker, Marian Seldes, Harold Gary, James Patterson, Pert Kelton, Rosemary Murphy, Margaret Leighton, Brenda Vaccaro, Alice Playten, Julie Gregg, Ruth White, Milo O'Shea, Eli Wallach, Barbara Ferris, Alan Webb, Lillian Gish, Hal Holbrook, Kate Reid, Dorothy Tutin, David Wayne, Tammy Grimes, Barry Nelson, Pearl Bailey, Helen Hayes, Anne Jackson, Hiram Sherman, Jack Crowder, Linda Lavin, and Claudia McNeil. Actors Equity increased its picketing against productions using imported actors, but with very little success. However, it will probably be a prime issue at negotiations when Equity contracts expire.

Off-Broadway had the most successful season in its history, both in quantity (12 more productions than last year) and in quality. The so-called "new wave" of writing and staging produced several imaginative and stimulating evenings in the theatre. However, the seeming lack of censorship this season apparently nurtured the increase of bad taste in some productions, and helped to reduce the shock-value of their vulgarity and complete nudity on stage. The failure of some such plays would indicate that the public is not willing to pay for a few seconds of voyeurism in a bad play with an amateurish cast. Some of the best presentations were "Scuba Duba," "Arms and The Man," "Stephen D.," "Now Is The Time For All Good Men," "The Trials of Brother Jero" and "The Strong Breed," "Iphigenia In Aulis," "Jacques Brel Is Alive and Well and Living In Paris," "In Circles," "The Concept," "Summertree," "The Boys In The Band," "Tom Paine," "Curley McDimple," "The Indian Wants The Bronx," "Saturday Night," "Muzeeka" and "Red Cross," "Ceremony of Innocence," "The Electronic Nigger and Others," "Endecott and The Red Cross," and all four of the Negro Ensemble Company's plays. This organization's premiere season was very impressive and gave promise of a bright future. Also, the first season for the New York Shakespeare Festival's Public Theater proved a welcomed and talented addition for the theatregoer. Its up-dated "Hamlet" with music, as well as its "Ergo," "The Memorandum," and "Hair" were well done and well received. The latter, however, was revised, a nudity scene added, and moved to Broadway where it proved commercially successful but less impressive than in its original version. The delightful "Your Own Thing" was the first Off-Broadway production ever to win an award over Broadway musicals from the Drama Critics Circle.

Some Off-Broadway's outstanding performers were Moses Gunn, David Birney, Kenneth Haigh, Irene Papas, Stephen Joyce, Kenneth Nelson, Al Pacino, Pamela Burrell, Brenda Smiley, Mari Gorman, Peggy Pope, Rusty Thacker, Harold Scott, Jerry Orbach, Hermione Baddeley, Sam Waterston, Zina Jasper, April Shawhan, Martin Sheen, Cynthia Belgrave, Michael O'Sullivan, Marcia Rodd, Elly Stone, James Coco, Gene Hackman, Paul Roebling, Donald Madden, and Sandy Duncan.

Professional Resident Theatres throughout the United States continued to thrive and increase in number. It is very encouraging that they are taking more chances on new scripts and helping to develop talented new playwrights as well as actors and audiences.

Robert Goulet

Pearl Bailey

BROADWAY CALENDAR

June 1, 1967 through May 31, 1968

Ingrid Bergman

Joel Grey

Albert Finney

Marlene Dietrich

PALACE THEATRE

Opened Monday, July 31, 1967.°
Sid Luft presents a Group V Ltd. Production:

JUDY GARLAND
At Home At The Palace

with
John Bubbles
Jackie Vernon
Francis Brunn
and
Lorna and Joey Luft

Staged by Richard Barstow; Costumes, Bill Smith, Travilla; Lighting, Ralph Alswang; Musical Director, Bobby Cole; Assistant to the Producer, Vern Alves; Hair Styles, Frank Buscarello.

Presented in two parts.

Company Manager: Emanuel Azenberg
Press: Bill Doll & Co., Midori Lederer, Ted Goldsmith, Virginia Holden
Stage Manager: Paul Phillips

° Closed August 26, 1967. (32 performances) Same program was repeated in The Felt Forum of the New Madison Square Garden for 3 performances on Dec. 25, 26, 27, 1967.

Right: Judy Garland, and below with her children Lorna Luft and Joey Luft

PALACE THEATRE

Opened Monday, August 28, 1967.°

BUDDY HACKETT
EDDIE FISHER

Musical Director, Colin Romoff
A two-man revue presented in two parts.

Manager: Philip Adler
Press: Frank Goodman, Martin Shwartz, Fred Weterick
Stage Manager: Bunny Fisher

° Closed October 7, 1967. (42 performances)

Eddie Fisher, Buddy Hackett

8

BELASCO THEATRE

Opened Monday, September 25, 1967.°
Saint-Subber presents:

DR. COOK'S GARDEN

Written and Directed by Ira Levin; Set
and Lighting, David Hays; Costumes, Noel
Taylor; Associate Producers, Frank Prince,
Manuel Seff; Production Assistants, James
Turner, R. T. Ingham.

CAST

Dr. Jim Tennyson	Keir Dullea
Bea Schmidt	Bette Henritze
Dora Ludlow	Lee Sanders
Elias Hart	Bob Berger
Dr. Leonard Cook	Burl Ives

UNDERSTUDIES: Cook and Hart, Seymour
Penzner; Tennyson, Peter Haig; Bea and
Dora, Jen Jones

A Melodrama in three acts. The action
takes place in the home and office of Dr.
Leonard Cook in the village of Greenfield
Center, Vermont on a Friday in the fall of
1966.

General Manager: C. Edwin Knill
Press: Harvey B. Sabinson, Lee Solters,
Bob Ullman
Company Manager: Helen Richards
Stage Managers: Mortimer Halpern,
Tom Leith

° Closed Sept. 30, 1967, after 8 performances
and 6 previews.

Friedman-Abeles Photos

Burl Ives, Keir Dullea
(also top right)

PLYMOUTH THEATRE

Opened Wednesday, September 27, 1967.°
David Merrick by arrangement with Allan
Davis, Ltd. and Michael Medwin presents:

KEEP IT IN THE FAMILY

By Bill Naughton; Director, Allan Davis;
Designer, Lloyd Burlingame; Costumes, Mary
McKinley; Associate Producer, Samuel Liff.

CAST

Daisy Brady .... Maureen O'Sullivan
Florence Brady .... Marian Hailey
Betsy Jane .... Sudie Bond
Billy Brady .... Jeff Siggins
Michael Brady .... Burt Brinckerhoff
Hilda Brady .... Karen Black
Frank Brady .... Patrick Magee
Arthur .... Tom Atkins

UNDERSTUDIES: Daisy and Betsy, Elizabeth
Parrish; Frank, William Chambers; Michael,
Arthur, Ed Garrabrandt; Florence, Hilda,
Louise Shaffer; Billy, Edmund Gaynes

A Comedy in two acts and three scenes.
The action takes place in the Brady home in a
town in Massachusetts in autumn almost 20
years ago.

General Manager: Jack Schlissel
Company Manager: Harold Kusell
Press: Harvey B. Sabinson,
Lee Solters, Leo Stern
Stage Managers: Gerald O'Brien,
William Chambers, Ed Garrabrandt

° Closed Sept. 30, 1967, after 5 performances
and 2 previews. Original London production
presented under title "Spring and Port Wine."

Maureen O'Sullivan, Jeff Siggins, Burt Brinckerhoff, Patrick Magee,
Marian Hailey, Karen Black. Top Right: Sudie Bond, Maureen O'Sullivan

ANTA THEATRE

Opened Thursday, September 28, 1967.°
Gene Dingenary, Miranda d'Ancona,
Nancy Levering present:

SONG OF THE GRASSHOPPER

By Alfonso Paso; Adapted from the Spanish
by William Layton and Agustin Penon; Director, Charles Bowden; Scenic Production, Oliver
Smith; Lighting, Martin Aronstein; Costumes,
Noel Taylor; Associate Producer, Eugenie
Snell; Assistant to Producers, William Heins.

CAST

Bisbiana	Diana Davila
Euphemia	Robin Ponterio
Aristobulo	Alfred Drake
Pepe	Michael Enserro
Alfredo	Ben Piazza
Elena	Jan Farrand

STANDBY for Bisbiana and Elena: Verna
Bloom

A Comedy in two acts. The action takes
place in the house of Aristobulo Rivas on the
outskirts of Madrid.

General Manager: Norman Maibaum
Press: Ben Kornzweig, Reginald Denenholz,
Tom Trenkle
Stage Managers: Tom Sawyer, Gene Nye

° Closed Sept. 30, 1967, after 4 performances
and 4 previews.

Friedman-Abeles Photos

Diana Davila, Ben Piazza, Jan Farrand, Alfred Drake
Top Right: Michael Enserro, Alfred Drake

BOOTH THEATRE

Opened Tuesday, October 3, 1967.°
Haila Stoddard, Mark Wright, Leonard S.
Field present:

THE BIRTHDAY PARTY

By Harold Pinter; Director, Alan Schneider;
Setting and Costumes, William Ritman; Light-
ing, Tharon Musser; Associate Producer, Duane
Wilder; Assistant to Producers, John Toland;
Production Assistant Peter Skolnik; Hair Styles,
Nino Raffaelo.

CAST

Petey	Henderson Forsythe
Meg	Ruth White
Stanley	James Patterson†
Lulu	Alexandra Berlin
Goldberg	Ed Flanders
McCann	Edward Winter

STANDBYS: Petey, James Karen; Meg and
Lulu, Marilyn Chris; Stanley, McCann, Jordan
Charney; Goldberg, Jack Hollander

A Drama in three acts. The action takes
place at the present time in the living room of
a house in a seaside town in England.

Manager: Victor Samrock
Company Manager: Ben Rosenberg
Press: David Rothenberg,
Lawrence Schneider

° Closed Jan. 20, 1968. (126 performances)
† Succeeded by Jordan Charney.

Henry Grossman Photos

James Patterson ("Tony" Award for supporting
actor), Ruth White, Edward Winter, Alexandra
Berlin. Top: Ruth White with James Patterson
(L), Henderson Forsythe (R)

BROOKS ATKINSON THEATRE
Opened Friday, October 6, 1967.°
Edwin and Robert F. Mirvish present:

A MINOR ADJUSTMENT

By Eric Nicol; Director, Henry Kaplan; Scenery, Leo B. Meyer; Costumes, Saul Bolasni; Lighting, Jules Fisher; Production Assistant, Evelyn Page; Hair Styles, Henri Bendel.

CAST

Ron Webster	William Redfield
Cameron Clark	Austin Willis
Mary Clark	Margaret Draper
Cam Clark, Jr.	Paul Collins
Gilian Walsh	Joan Darling

UNDERSTUDIES: Ron, Carleton Carpenter; Clark, Casey Walters; Gilian, Arleen Lorrance; Mary, Evelyn Paeper; Cam Jr., Kenneth Carr.

A Comedy in two acts and six scenes. The action takes place in the library-den of the Clark home in a suburb of Vancouver, British Columbia, in May of the present time.

General Manager: Allentuck,
Azenberg & Wolsk
Company Manager: Peter Neufeld
Press: Frank Goodman, Martin Shwartz
Stage Managers: Murray Gitlin,
Kenneth Carr

° Closed Oct. 7, 1967, after 3 performances and 13 previews.

Friedman-Abeles Photos

Austin Willis, William Redfield, and top with Joan Darling

13

CORT THEATRE

Opened Sunday, October 8, 1967.°
Theater 1968 (Richard Barr, Clinton Wilder, Charles Woodward, Jr.) present:

JOHNNY NO-TRUMP

By Mary Mercier; Director, Joseph Hardy; Scenery, Lighting, and Costumes, William Ritman; Executive Assistant, Seth Dansky; Production Assistant, James Prideaux.

CAST

Harry Armstrong	Pat Hingle
Mrs. Franklin	Barbara Lester
John Edwards	Don Scardino
Florence Edwards	Sada Thompson
Alexander Edwards	James Broderick
Bettina	Bernadette Peters

STANDBYS: Harry, Alexander, James Noble; Florence, Barbara Lester; John, Richard Thomas; Bettina, Deborah White

A Comedy-Drama in two acts and three scenes. The action takes place in the Armstrong home on Long Island in February of the present time.

General Manager: Michael Goldreyer
Business Manager: Michael Kasdan
Press: Howard Atlee, Bill Cherry
Stage Managers: D. W. Koehler,
Charles Kindl

° Closed Oct. 8, 1967, after one performance and 5 previews.

Bert Andrews Photos

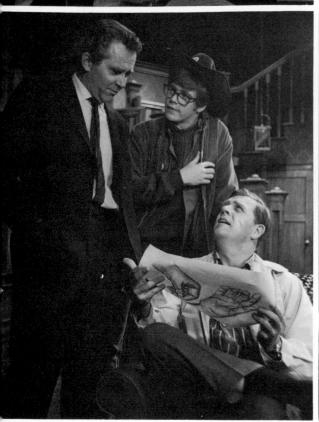

James Broderick, Don Scardino, Pat Hingle and top with Sada Thompson

Don Scardino, Sada Thompson

14

JOHN GOLDEN THEATRE

Opened Monday, October 9, 1967.*
Helen Jacobson by arrangement with
John Roberts presents:

AFTER THE RAIN

By John Bowen; Director, Vivian Matalon;
Scenic Designs, Brian Currah; Sets Executed
by Paul Morrison; Lighting, Tharon Musser
Costumes, Domingo A. Rodriguez; Production
Assistant, Valgene Massey; Hair Styles, Mr.
Vincent of Enrico Caruso.

CAST

The Lecturer	Paul Sparer
His Assistants	Edward J. Moore, Alan Rachins
Captain Hunter	Anthony Oliver
Arthur Henderson	Alec McCowen
Gertrude Forbes-Cooper	Nancy Marchand
Tony Batch	Bill Burns
Wesley Otterdale	John Carpenter
Muriel Otterdale	Maureen Pryor
Harold Banner	Alan MacNaughtan
Alan Armitage	John Colenback
Sonya Banks	Gretchen Corbett

UNDERSTUDIES: Arthur, Hunter, Wesley,
Colgate Salsbury; Gertrude, Muriel, Joyce
Reed; Lecturer, Banner, John Carpenter; Armi-
tage, Alan Rachins; Batch, Edward J. Moore

A Drama in two acts. The action takes
place continuously in a university lecture hall
200 years after the rain of 1969.

General Manager: Edward H. Davis
Press: Sol Jacobson, Lewis Harmon
Stage Managers: Ben Janney,
Nelle Nugent

* Closed Dec. 2, 1967. (64 performances)

Friedman-Abeles Photos

Gretchen Corbett, John Colenback, Nancy Marchand, Alec McCowen,
Alan MacNaughtan, Maureen Pryor, Bill Burns, Anthony Oliver.
Top: Maureen Pryor, Paul Sparer, Bill Burns, Alec McCowen, Anthony Oliver

15

LUNT-FONTANNE THEATRE

Opened Monday, October 9, 1967.°
Alexander H. Cohen presents:

MARLENE DIETRICH

Arrangements, and Orchestra Conducted by
Burt Bacharach; Lighting, Joe Davis; Production Supervisor, Jerry Adler; Assistant to Producer, Davina Crawford; Production Assistants,
Jan Monkhouse, Gloria Banta, Beth Uffner;
A Nine O'Clock Theatre Production.

A one-woman show presented without intermission.

General Manager: Roy A. Somlyo
Company Manager: Clayton Coots
Press: John Springer Associates,
Louise Weiner
Stage Managers: Tony Chardet,
Daniel Broun

° Closed Nov. 18, 1967, after a limited engagement of 48 performances.

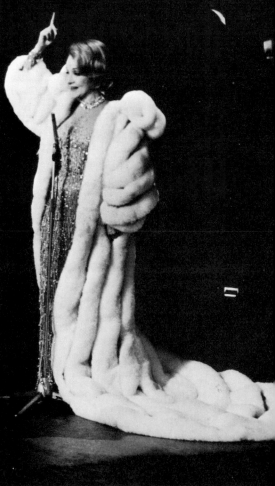

Right: Marlene Dietrich, Burt Bacharach

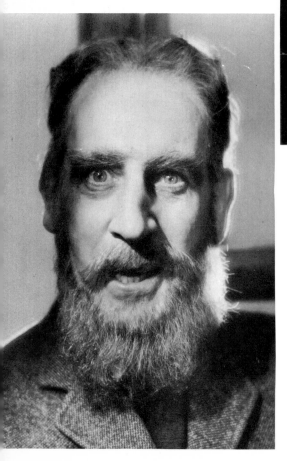

LYCEUM THEATRE

Opened Thursday, October 12, 1967.°
Arthur Cantor and Nicholas Vanoff, Ltd.
present:

"BY GEORGE"

Devised by Michael Voysey; Production
Supervisor, Ed Julien; Production Assistants,
Kathy Garvey, Janice Knowlton; Produced in
association with Santa Fe Productions, Inc.;
Recorded by Angel Records.

with

MAX ADRIAN

as

Bernard Shaw

A one-man show presented in three parts:
The Search, The Arrival, and The Eminence.

General Manager: Richard Osorio
Company Manager: Martin Cohen
Press: Artie Solomon
Stage Manager: Paul A. Foley

° Closed Oct. 22, 1967, after 13 performances
and 3 previews.

Max Adrian as Bernard Shaw

LONGACRE THEATRE

Opened Sunday, October 15, 1967.°
Robert Leder and Michael Productions
present:

DAPHNE IN COTTAGE D

By Stephen Levi; Director, Martin Fried;
Scenery and Lighting, Jo Mielziner; Costumes,
Theoni V. Aldredge; Associate Producer, Porter
Van Zandt; Production Supervisor, Ralph O.
Willis; Production Assistant, Richard Foltz; As-
sociate Designer, Paul Trautvetter.

CAST

Daphne _____ Sandy Dennis
Joseph _____ William Daniels

STANDBYS: Rose Gregorio, John P. Ryan

A Comedy in two acts. The action takes
place in the living room of a cottage in a
resort hotel on the New England coast on a
summer night at the present time.

General Manager: Edward H. Davis
Company Manager: Oliver W. Nicoll
Press: Harvey B. Sabinson, Lee Solters,
Robert Larkin
Stage Managers: Philip Mandelker,
John Actman

° Closed Nov. 18, 1967, after 41 performances
and 7 previews.

Friedman-Abeles Photos

William Daniels, Sandy Dennis
Top: Sandy Dennis

ALVIN THEATRE

Opened Monday, October 16, 1967.°
(Moved Jan. 8, 1968 to Eugene O'Neill Theatre)

David Merrick Arts Foundation by arrangement with The National Theatre of Great Britain presents:

ROSENCRANTZ AND GUILDENSTERN ARE DEAD

By Tom Stoppard; Director, Derek Goldby; Associate Director, Claude Chagrin; Scenery and Costumes, Desmond Heeley; Lighting, Richard Pilbrow; Music, Marc Wilkinson; Associate Producer, Samuel Liff; Musical Supervisor, Robert Mandell.

CAST

Rosencrantz	Brian Murray
Guildenstern	John Wood
The Player	Paul Hecht
Tragedians:	
Alfred	Douglas Norwick
The King	Roger Kemp
The Poisoner	Dino Laudicina
The Spies	B. J. DeSimone, Roy Lozano
Hamlet	Noel Craig
Ophelia	Patricia McAneny
Claudius	Roger Hamilton
Gertrude	Anne Meacham
Polonius	Ralph Drischell
Soldier	Alexander Courtney
Ambassador	Carl Jacobs
Horatio	Michael Holmes
Musicians	Bruce Levine, Bernard Karl, Jack Knitzer, Don Arol

Courtiers, Ambassadors, Soldiers, Attendants: Walter Beery, Stephen Bernstein, Gaetano Bongiovanni, Margaret Braidwood, Esther Buffler, Elizabeth Eis, Elizabeth Franz, William Grannell, John Handy, Mary Hara, Edward Marshall, Ted Pezzulo

Standbys: Rosencrantz, Jonathan Reynolds; Guildenstern, Garnett Smith

A Comedy in three acts. The action is set within and around the action of "Hamlet."

General Manager: Jack Schlissel
Company Manager: Richard Osorio
Press: Harvey B. Sabinson, Lee Solters, Robert Larkin
Stage Managers: Mitchell Erickson, Andre St. Jean, John Handy

° Still playing May 31, 1968. Winner of "Tony" and Drama Critics Awards.

Martha Swope Photos

Brian Murray, Roger Hamilton, Anne Meacham, John Wood
Top Left: John Wood, Brian Murray

John Wood, Paul Hecht, Brian Murray. Top: Roger
Kemp, B. J. DeSimone, Paul Hecht, Douglas
Norwick, Roy Lozano

Brian Murray, John Wood, Patricia McAneny,
Noel Craig

19

THE MUSIC BOX

Opened Wednesday, October 18, 1967.°
Saint-Subber and Michael Codron in association with Columbia Pictures Corp.
present:

THERE'S A GIRL IN MY SOUP

By Terence Frisby; Director, Robert Chet-
wyn; Designed by Hutchinson Scott; Costumes,
Stanley Simmons; Lighting, Lloyd Burlingame;
Production Assistants, James Turner, R. T. Ingham; Produced by Nancy Enterprises I· .

CAST

Robert Danvers	Gigi Young†1
Clare	Rita Gam
Andrew	Jon Pertwee†2
Porter	George Hall
Paola	Erica Fitz†3
Marion	Barbara Ferris†4
Jimmy	Gawn Grainger

STANDBYS: Marion, Marie Masters; Clare,
Judith Searle; Andrew, Porter, Steven Scott;
Jimmy, Wisner Washam.

A Comedy in two acts. The action takes
place in Robert Danvers' flat in London, in late
summer of the present time.

General Manager: C. Edwin Knill
Company Manager: William Craver
Press: Harvey B. Sabinson, Lee Solters,
Harry Nigro
Stage Managers: Harvey Medlinsky,
Wisner Washam

° Still playing May 31, 1968.

† Succeeded by: 1. Laurence Hugo, 2. Wil-
liam Larsen, 3. Billie Dixon during Miss
Fitz illness, 4. Marie Masters during Miss
Ferris' illness, then permanently by Amanda
Reiss.

Friedman-Abeles Photos

Barbara Ferris, Jon Pertwee

Gig Young, Barbara Ferris
Top: Barbara Ferris, Rita Gam

BILLY ROSE THEATRE

Opened Thursday, October 19, 1967.°
Harold Leventhal and Marie Desmarais present The Jewish State Theatre of Poland (Ida Kaminska, Artistic Director) in:

MIRELE EFROS

By Jacob Gordin; Adaptation and Direction, Ida Kaminska; Scenery, Marian Stanczak; Lighting Consultant, Charles Elson; Accompanying English translation by Raphael Rothstein; Production Manager, Eugenia Blumenfeld-Lauterpacht; Technical Director, Joe Pasmanik.

CAST

Mirele Efros	Ida Kaminska
Josele	Juliusz Berger
Donie	Karol Latowicz
Machle	Maria Fridman
Reb-Szalmen	Marian Melman
Nuchemtse	Michael Szwejlich
Chane Dwojre	Ruth Kowalska
Szejndele	Ruth Kaminska
Szlojmele	Harry Gold
Cantor	Marian Rudenski
Jurke	Henryk Grynberg
Oksana	Dina Fijalkowska

A Drama in four acts. The action takes place in Sluck and Grodno.

General Manager: Richard Seader
Company Manager: Lawrence Rothman
Press: Ben Kornzweig, Reginald Denenholz, Benjamin Rothman
Stage Manager: Mieczyslaw Bram

° Closed Dec. 17, 1967, after 54 performances in repertory with "Mother Courage."

BILLY ROSE THEATRE

Opened Thursday, November 16, 1967.°
Harold Leventhal and Marie Desmarais present the Jewish State Theatre of Poland (Ida Kaminska, Artistic Director) in:

MOTHER COURAGE

By Bertolt Brecht; Adaptation and Direction, Ida Kaminska; Scenery, Zenobius Strzelecki; Music, Paul Dessau; Technical Director, Joe Pasmanik; English Translations, Erika Rosner; Accompanying English translations, Raphael Rothstein; Production Manager, Eugenia Blumenfeld-Lauterpacht.

CAST

Feldfebel	Samuel Rettig
Recruiting Soldier	Michael Szwejlich
Mother Courage	Ida Kaminska
Eilif	Karol Latowicz
Szwejcerkez	Juliusz Berger
Katrin	Ruth Kaminska
The Cook	Seweryn Dalecki
The Commander	Szymon Szurmiej
The Chaplain	Marian Melman
Armorer	Marian Rudenski
Ivette	Dina Fijalkowska
Soldier	Abraham Rozenbaum
Man with eye patch	Jozef Retik
Sergeant Major	Herman Lercher
Colonel	Michael Szwejlich
Copyist	Izaak Dogim
Elder Soldier	Herman Lercher
Younger Soldier	Marian Rudenski
Drunken Soldier	Samuel Rettig
Young Artisan	Henryk Grynberg
His Mother	Ruth Kowalska
Escorting Soldier	Mieczyslaw Bram
Standard Bearer	Abraham Rozenbaum
Soldier 1	Szymon Szurmiej
Soldier 2	Herman Lercher
Peasant	Izaak Dogim
His Wife	Maria Fridman
Their Son	Jozef Retik

A Chronicle Play of the Thirty Years' War in 2 parts and 11 scenes.

General Manager: Richard Seader
Company Manager; Lawrence Rothman
Press: Ben Kornzweig, Reginald Denenholz, Benjamin Rothman
Stage Manager: Mieczyslaw Bram

° Played in repertory with "Mirele Efros," and closed Dec. 17, 1967 after 54 performances for both.

Ida Kaminska, Dina Fijalkowska in "Mother Courage". Top Right: Ida Kaminska, Marian Melman in "Mirele Efros"

HELEN HAYES THEATRE

Opened Sunday, October 22, 1967.°
Michael Myerberg and Donald Flamm present:

WHAT DID WE DO WRONG?

By Henry Denker; Director, Sherwood Arthur; Settings, Albert Johnson; Costumes, Jack Edwards; Lighting, Leo B. Meyer; Music, Paul Martin; Executive Producer, Paul Jacobson; Production Assistant, James E. Shields.

CAST

Norma Davis	Philippa Bevans
Walter Davis	Paul Ford
Walter Davis, Jr.	Russell Horton
Scott	Gregory Rozakis
Cindy	Heidi Vaughn
Woody	Roy Providence
Clarence Cahill	Hugh Franklin
Charlotte Cahill	Enid Markey

UNDERSTUDIES: Walter Davis, Hugh Franklin; Junior and Scott, Christopher Strater

A comedy in two acts and four scenes. The action takes place at the present in the living room of the Davis home in White Plains, N.Y.

General Manager: E. Anthony Myerberg
Manager: Daniel Melnick
Press: Bill Doll & Co.
Stage Managers: Herman Magidson, Christopher Strater

° Closed Dec. 2, 1967. (48 performances and 14 previews)

Friedman-Abeles Photos

Russell Horton, Heidi Vaughn, Roy Providence, Gregory Rozakis, Paul Ford
Top Right: Paul Ford, Philippa Bevans

PALACE THEATRE

Opened Monday, October 23, 1967.°
Edward Specter Productions and Norman Twain present:

HENRY, SWEET HENRY

Book, Nunnally Johnson; Music and Lyrics, Bob Merrill; Based on "The World of Henry Orient" by Nora Johnson; Director, George Roy Hill; Scenery and Lighting, Robert Randolph; Costumes, Alvin Colt; Choreography, Michael Bennett; Musical Direction and Vocal Arrangements, Shepard Coleman; Orchestrations, Eddie Sauter; Dance Music, William Goldenberg and Marvin Hamlisch; Hair Styles, Ernest Adler; Associate Producer, Joseph H. Shoctor; Production Assistants, Ann Kempner, Louis Sica; Original cast album by ABC Records.

CAST

Kafritz	Alice Playten
Valerie Boyd	Robin Wilson
Miss Cooney	Barbara Beck
Marian Gilbert	Neva Small
Henry Orient	Don Ameche
Stella	Louise Lasser
Mrs. Gilbert	Trudy Wallace
Usherette	Julie Sargant
Mrs. Boyd	Carol Bruce
Russ	John Mineo
Captain Kenneth	George NeJame
Hal	Robert Iscove
Policeman	Gerard Brentte
Mr. Boyd	Milo Boulton
Policeman	Charles Rule
Big Val	K. C. Townsend

NORTON SCHOOL STUDENTS: Chris Bocchino, Lori Cesar, Terry Forman, Joyce James, Baayork Lee, Gina Page, Ilene Schatz, Joy Stark, Rebecca Urich, Pia Zadora.

KNICKERBOCKER GREYS: Paul Charles, Robert Iscove, Joe Mazzello, Kim Milford, John Mineo, George NeJame, Craig Wineline.

ADULT ENSEMBLE: Robert Avian, Barbara Beck, Gerard Brentte, Gene Castle, Robert Fitch, Marvin Goodis, Neil Jones, Mary Ann Kerrick, Priscilla Lopez, Lee Lund, Laried Montgomery, Charles Rule, Julie Sargant, Mary Ann Snow, Trudy Wallace.

UNDERSTUDIES: Henry, Joseph Leon; Stella, Leila Martin; Mrs. Boyd, Mary Ann Snow; Val, Rebecca Urich; Gil, Pia Zadora; Kafritz, Lori Cesar; Big Val, Mary Ann Kerrick; Mrs. Gilbert, Barbara Beck.

MUSICAL NUMBERS: "Academic Fugue," "In Some Little World," "Pillar To Post," "Here I Am," "Whereas," "I Wonder How It Is To Dance With A Boy," "Nobody Steps On Kafritz," "Henry, Sweet Henry," "Woman In Love," "The People Watchers," "Weary Near To Dyin'," "Poor Little Person," "I'm Too Blue," "To Be Artistic," "Forever," "Do You Ever Go To Boston," Finale.

A Musical in 2 acts and 20 scenes. The action takes place at the present time in New York City.

General Manager: Sherman Gross
Company Manager: Virginia Snow
Press: Harvey Sabinson, Lee Solters, David Powers
Stage Managers: William Dodds, Harry Clark, Neil Jones

° Closed Dec. 31, 1967. (80 performances and 12 previews)

Sam Siegel Photos

Top: (L) Robin Wilson, Neva Small. (R) Alice Playten. **Below:** Neva Small, Don Ameche

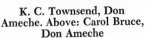

K. C. Townsend, Don Ameche. Above: Carol Bruce, Don Ameche

Robin Wilson, Neva Small

23

BROADHURST THEATRE

Opened Tuesday, October 31, 1967.°,
Elliot Martin in association with Center
Theatre Group of Los Angeles presents:

MORE STATELY MANSIONS

By Eugene O'Neill; Director, Jose Quintero; Scenery, Ben Edwards; Costumes, Jane Greenwood; Lighting, John Harvey; Production Associate, Marjorie Martin; By arrangement with Quinto Productions.

CAST

Jamie Cregan	Barry Macollum
Mickey Maloy	Vincent Dowling
Nora Melody	Helen Craig
Sara	Colleen Dewhurst
Simon Harford	Arthur Hill
Cato	John Marriott
Deborah	Ingrid Bergman
Nicholas Gadsby	Fred Stewart
Joel Harford	Lawrence Linville
Benjamin Tenard	Kermit Murdock

UNDERSTUDIES: Deborah, Sara, Jacqueline Brookes; Simon, Lawrence Linville; Joe, Jamie, William Goodwin; Nicholas, Mickey, Alfred Hinckley; Benjamin, Vincent Dowling

A Drama in 2 acts and 9 scenes. The action takes place in and near a Massachusetts city between 1832 and 1841.

General Manager: Al Goldin
Press: Nat and Irvin Dorfman, Marcia Katz
Stage Managers: William Weaver,
Alfred Hinckley

° Closed March 2, 1968 after a limited engagement of 150 performances and 4 previews. Opened at the Ahmanson Theatre, Los Angeles, for 48 performances from Sept. 12, through Oct. 21, 1967.

Fred Stewart, Ingrid Bergman, Lawrence Linville
Above: Helen Craig, Colleen Dewhurst, Arthur Hill

Arthur Hill, Ingrid Bergman. Above: Colleen Dewhurst
Arthur Hill, and top with Ingrid Bergman

ANTA THEATRE

Opened Sunday, November 5, 1967.°
Gene Persson presents:

THE TRIAL OF
LEE HARVEY OSWALD

By Amram Ducovny and Leon Friedman;
Based on idea by Harold Steinberg and Am-
ram Ducovny; Director, Tunc Yalman; Light-
ing, Jules Fisher; Settings, Robin Wagner;
Costumes, Theoni V. Aldredge; Art Director,
Lewis Zacks; Associate Producer, Jay Fuchs;
Bruitage, Joseph Raposo; Production Assistants,
Karen Lippolt, Joan Alperin; Projectionist,
Henry Perlman.

CAST

Lee Harvey Oswald	Peter Masterson
Judge Hammond Morton	Dan Priest
Prosecuting Attorney Phelps	Clifton James
Defense Counsel Rogers	Ralph Waite
Jesse Bellknapp	John Gerstad
Daniel Gibbon	Glenn Kezer
Carl Turner	Douglas Stark
Governor John B. Connally	Barton Stone
Dr. Paul Dettering	Glenn Kezer
George Robinson	John Gerstad
Lincoln King	Garrett Saunders
Sanford Alexander	Charles Randall
Capt. Frank McQueen	Douglas Stark
Steve Barton	William Leach
Harry Stevens	Garrett Saunders
Abner Finchlea	Barton Stone
Elbert Briggs	John Gerstad
Mrs. Sally Newfield	Anne Shropshire
Norman Astor	William Leach
Elizabeth Rote	Anne Shropshire
Philip Markfield	Barton Stone
Clyde Landers	Charles Randall
Harrison Edwards	John Gerstad
Alice Williams	Louise Stubbs
Harold Lane	Garrett Saunders
Bruce Currie	Douglas Stark
Dr. Ray Jones	William Leach
Victoria Mavis	Louise Stubbs

UNDERSTUDIES: Oswald, William Leach;
Ralph Waite, Barton Stone, Charles Randall—
Michael Miller; Douglas Stark, William Leach,
Garrett Saunders—Will Gregory

A Drama in two acts. The action takes
place in a courtroom trial at the present
time. All evidence is based on actual evidence
uncovered in the investigation of the assassi-
nation of President John F. Kennedy.

General Manager: Richard Osorio
Company Manager: Marty Cohen
Press: Max Eisen, Carl Samrock,
Jeanne Gibson Merrick
Stage Managers: Del Hughes,
Fred Reinglas

° Closed Nov. 11, 1967. (9 performances
and 5 previews)

Ralph Waite, Peter Masterson, Clifton James

BILTMORE THEATRE
Opened Monday, November 6, 1967.°
Philip Rose, David Wilde and Neder-
lander-Steinbrenner Productions present:

THE NINETY-DAY MISTRESS

By J. J. Coyle; Director, Philip Rose; Set-
ting, Leon Munier; Costumes, Pearl Somner;
Lighting, Clarke Dunham; Associate Producer,
Selma Leichtling: Technical Adviser, John
Higgins.

CAST

Leona Hastings	Dyan Cannon
Danny Liken	Martin Milner
Phyllis	Doris Belack
Alan	Nicolas Coster
Judith Hastings	Ruth Ford
Bill Hastings	Walter Abel
Rudy Avarian	Tony LoBianco

UNDERSTUDIES: Leona, Beverly Ballard;
Danny, Joe Ponazecki; Judith, Mary Cooper;
Bill, John Wardwell; Phyllis, Rose Arrick;
Alan, Rudy, Gregory Sierra

A Comedy in 2 acts and 5 scenes. The
action takes place at the present time in the
apartment of Leona Hastings on the East
Side of Manhattan.

General Manager: Walter Fried
Company Manager: Helen Richards
Press: Merle Debuskey, Faith Geer,
Violet Welles
Stage Managers: Leonard Auerbach,
Norman Shelly

° Closed Nov. 25, 1967. (24 performances)

Friedman-Abeles Photos

Walter Abel, Ruth Ford. Top: Martin Milner,
Dyan Cannon

Dyan Cannon

BROOKS ATKINSON THEATRE

Opened Tuesday, November 7, 1967.°
Alexander H. Cohen presents:

HALFWAY UP THE TREE

By Peter Ustinov; Directed by Mr. Ustinov; Scenery and Lighting, Ralph Alswang; Costumes, James Hart Stearns; Associate Producer, Hildy Parks; Production Supervisor, Jerry Adler; Production Assistants, Jan Monkhouse, Gloria Banta.

CAST

Lady Fitzbuttress	Eileen Herlie
Helga	Hanne Bork
General Sir Mallalieu Fitzbuttress	Anthony Quayle
Robert	Sam Waterston
Lesley	Charles Austin
Judy	Margaret Linn
Tiny Gilliatt-Brown	William Larsen
Basil Utterwood	John Tillinger
The Vicar	Graham Jarvis

UNDERSTUDIES: Fitzbuttress, Tiny, Vicar, Rufus Smith; Lady Fitzbuttress, June Prud'Homme; Helga, Judy, Kristin Helmore, Barbara Blair; Robert, Basil, Franklin Kiser

A Comedy in 3 acts. The action takes place at the present time in a cottage in Hampshire, England.

General Manager: Roy A. Somlyo
Company Manager: Seymour Herscher
Press: James D. Proctor,
David Roggensack, Ruth Cage
Stage Managers: Jake Hamilton,
Charles Austin

° Closed Dec. 31, 1967. (63 performances and 9 previews)

•: (L) Anthony Quayle, Eileen Herlie. (R) John
inger, Margaret Linn, Graham Jarvis, Eileen
Herlie, Hanne Bork, Sam Waterston

Sam Waterston, Hanne Bork, and above with
Anthony Quayle, Eileen Herlie

27

ST. JAMES THEATER

Opened Sunday, November 12, 1967.°
David Merrick presents:

HELLO, DOLLY!

Book, Michael Stewart; Based on "The Matchmaker" by Thornton Wilder"; Music and Lyrics, Jerry Herman; Director, Gower Champion; Re-Staged by Lucia Victor; Dance Assistant, Jack Craig; Settings, Oliver Smith; Costumes, Freddy Wittop; Lighting, Jean Rosenthal; Dance and Incidental Music Arrangements, Peter Howard; Orchestrations, Philip J. Lang; Musical Direction, Saul Schechtman; A David Merrick and Champion-Five Inc. Production; Staff Associates, Sylvia Schwartz, Lynn Middleton, Linda Patton; Original cast album by RCA Victor.

CAST

Mrs. Dolly Gallagher Levi	Pearl Bailey
Ernestina	Mabel King
Ambrose Kemper	Roger Lawson
Horse	Dianne Conway, Barbara Harper
Horace Vandergelder	Cab Calloway
Ermengarde	Sherri "Peaches" Brewer
Cornelius Hackl	Jack Crowder
Barnaby Tucker	Winston DeWitt Hemsley
Irene Molloy	Emily Yancy
Minnie Fay	Chris Calloway
Mrs. Rose	Marie Bryant
Rudolph	Morgan Freeman
Judge	Walter P. Brown
Court Clerk	James Kennon-Wilson

TOWNSPEOPLE, WAITERS, ETC.: Marki Bey, Edloe R. Brown, Dianne Conway, Merle Derby, Dolores Easty, Demarest Gray, Lavinia Hamilton, Barbara Harper, Pattie Harris, Lolli Hinton, Ernestine Jackson, Laverne Ligon, Joni Palmer, Saundra Sharp, Freda Turner, Guy Allen, Bryant Baker, Fred Benjamin, Walter P. Brown, Donald Coleman, Peter Colly, Dowlin Davis, Clifton Davis, Sargent Faulkner, Larry Ferrell, Julius Fields, Ray Gilbert, Olon Godare, Reginald Jackson, Don Jay, Bob Johnson, James Kennon-Wilson, Peter Norman, E. B. Smith, Joe Williams

UNDERSTUDIES: Dolly, Marie Bryant, Bibi Osterwald; Vandergelder, Walter P. Brown; Irene, Saundra Sharp; Cornelius, Clifton Davis; Minnie Fay, Marki Bey; Barnaby, Olon Godare; Ermengarde, Edloe R. Brown; Ernestina, Laverne Ligon; Ambrose, Donald Coleman; Judge, Don Jay

MUSICAL NUMBERS: "I Put My Hand In," "It Takes A Woman," "Put On Your Sunday Clothes," "Ribbons Down My Back," "Motherhood," "Dancing," "Before The Parade Passes Me By," "Elegance," "Waiters' Gallop," "Polka Contest," "It Only Takes A Moment," "So Long, Dearie," "Hello, Dolly!"

A Musical Comedy in 2 acts and 15 scenes. The action takes place in the past in Yonkers and New York City.

General Manager: Jack Schlissel
Press: Lee Solters, Harvey Sabinson, Leo Stern, Muffy Newman
Stage Managers: Frank Dudley, Toni Manzi, Walter P. Brown

° Still playing May 31, 1968. For original production with Carol Channing and David Burns, see THEATRE WORLD, Vol. 20.

Friedman-Abeles Photos

Top Left: Pearl Bailey, Cab Calloway. Below: Jack Crowder, Winston DeWitt Hemsley, Emily Yancy, Chris Calloway

Pearl Bailey

HENRY MILLER'S THEATRE

Opened Tuesday, November 14, 1967.°
Helen Bonfils, Morton Gottlieb and Peter
Bridge present:

THE PROMISE

By Aleksei Arbuzov; Translated by Ariadne
Nicolaeff; Director, Frank Hauser; Scenery,
William Ritman; Lighting, Tharon Musser;
Production Assistant, David Wiltse.

CAST

Lika	Eileen Atkins
Marat (Marik)	Ian McShane
Leonidik	Ian McKellen

STANDBYS: Lika, Nancy Acly; Marat, Leon
Russom; Leonidik, DeVeren Bookwalter

A Drama in 3 acts. The action takes place
in 1942, 1946, and 1959 in a room in a
Leningrad apartment.

General Manager: Richard Seader
Press: Dorothy Ross
Stage Managers: Warren Crane,
Wayne Carson

° Closed Dec. 2, 1967. (23 performances
and 12 previews)

Bert Andrews Photos

Ian McShane, Ian McKellen, Eileen Atkins
Top: Ian McKellen, Ian McShane

Eileen Atkins, Ian McShane, Ian McKellen

CORT THEATRE

Opened Tuesday, November 28, 1967.°
King/Hyman/Wolsk/Azenberg present:

SOMETHING DIFFERENT

By Carl Reiner; Directed by Mr. Reiner;
Scenery and Lighting, Will Steven Armstrong;
Costumes, Ann Roth; Associate Producers, Jack
Edreich, Doris Kuller, Jane Cohen; Production
Supervisor, Jose Vega; Production Assistant,
Paula Lorge.

CAST

Sheldon "Bud" Nemerov ---------------- Bob Dishy
Beth Nemerov -------------------------- Linda Lavin
Phil Caponetti ------------------------- Gabriel Dell
Kevin and Bevin ------------------- Messrs Starkman
and Battle
Mrs. Kupferman --------------------- Victoria Zussin
Rose Keller ----------------------------- Helena Carroll
Ida Schwartz ----------------------- Maureen Arthur
Sarah Goldfine ------------------------ Claudia McNeil
The Players -------- Messrs. Jones and Mansfield
UNDERSTUDIES: Bud, Phil, Richard Schaal;
Beth, Ida, Zina Jasper; Sarah, Helen Martin;
Mrs. Kupferman, Rose, Mina Kolb; Starkman
and Battle, Jones and Mansfield

A Comedy in 2 acts and 4 scenes. The
action takes place at the present time in the
den of the Nemerov's suburban home.

General Manager: Max Allentuck
Company Manager: Peter Neufeld
Press: Mike Merrick, Barry Kobrin
Stage Manager: Charles Gray

° Closed Feb. 24, 1968. (111 performances)

Friedman-Abeles Photos

Gabriel Dell, Linda Lavin

Victoria Zussin, Claudia McNeil. Top: Maureen
Arthur, Bob Dishy, Linda Lavin

30

PLYMOUTH THEATRE

Opened Wednesday, November 29, 1967.°
Theater 1968 (Richard Barr, Clinton
Wilder) present:

EVERYTHING IN THE GARDEN

By Edward Albee; Adapted from the Play
by Giles Cooper; Director, Peter Glenville;
Setting and Costumes, William Ritman; Lighting, Tharon Musser; Executive Assistant, Seth
Dansky; Production Assistant, James Prideaux.

CAST

Jenny	Barbara Bel Geddes
Richard	Barry Nelson
Jack	Robert Moore
Mrs. Toothe	Beatrice Straight
Roger	Richard Thomas
Beryl	Mary K. Wells
Chuck	Whitfield Connor
Louise	M'El Dowd†
Gilbert	Tom Aldredge
Perry	Charles Baxter
Cynthia	Augusta Dabney

UNDERSTUDIES: Richard, Mark O'Daniels;
Roger, Steve Skiles; Beryl, Louise, Cynthia,
Delphi Harrington

A Drama in 2 acts. The action takes place
at the present time in the suburban home of
Jenny and Richard.

General Manager: Michael Goldreyer
Business Manager: Michael Kasdan
Press: David Rothenberg, Barry Plaxen
Stage Managers: Gerald O'Brien,
Joseph Cali

° Closed Feb. 10, 1968. (86 performances)
† Succeeded by Diana Douglas.

Henry Grossman Photos

arry Nelson, Beatrice Straight. Top Right:
Barbara Bel Geddes, Richard Thomas,
Barry Nelson

Barry Nelson, Barbara Bel Geddes. Above:
Robert Moore, Barry Nelson

31

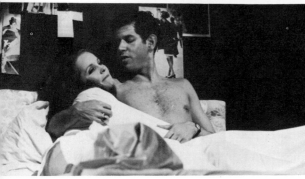

Marlyn Mason, Anthony Roberts. Above:
Marlyn Mason, Brenda Vaccaro

LUNT-FONTANNE THEATRE

Opened Thursday, December 7, 1967.°
David Merrick by arrangement with Edwin H. Morris & Co., Inc. presents:

HOW NOW, DOW JONES

Book, Max Shulman; Based on an idea by Carolyn Leigh; Lyrics, Carolyn Leigh; Music, Elmer Bernstein; Director, George Abbott; Scenic Production, Oliver Smith; Costumes, Robert Mackintosh; Lighting, Martin Aronstein; Musical Direction, Dance and Vocal Arrangements, Peter Howard; Orchestrations, Philip J. Lang; Dances and Musical Numbers Staged by Gillian Lynne; Associate Producer, Samuel Liff; Staff Associates, Sylvia Schwartz, Lynn Middleton, Juliet Taylor; Hairstylist, Joe Tubens; Original cast album by RCA Victor.

CAST

Cynthia	Brenda Vaccaro
Herbert	James Congdon
Broker	Joe McGrath
Kate	Marlyn Mason
Wingate	Hiram Sherman
Nichols	Bob Gorman
Judy Evans	Patti Davis
Wally	Alexander Orfaly
Charley	Anthony Roberts
Sue Ellen	Jennifer Darling
Bradbury	Rex Everhart
Waiter	Tommy Tune
Senator McFetridge	Barnard Hughes
Dow	Stanley Simmonds
Jones	Martin Ambrose
Tycoons	Frank DeSal, Bob Gorman, John Joy, Alexander Orfaly
Lion	Ron Schwinn
Customers' Men	Bob Gorman, Frank DeSal, John Joy, Doug Spingler
Dr. Gilman	Sammy Smith
Mrs. Ragosa	Francesca Smith
Mrs. Klein	Fran Stevens
Mrs. Harris	Sally DeMay
Mrs. Callahan	Lucie Lancaster
Mrs. Millhauser	Charlotte Jones
A. K.	Arthur Hughes

DANCERS: Oscar Anthony, Linnea Chandler, Joel Conrad, Patricia Cope, Frank DeSal, Lois Etelman, Cyndi Howard, Yanco Inone, Eileen Lawlor, Debra Lyman, Diana Quijano, Sally Ransone, George Ramos, Ron Schwinn, Doug Spingler, Ron L. Steinbeck, Pat Trott

SINGERS: Martin Ambrose, Leigh Curran, Patti Davis, Bill Gibbens, Bob Gorman, Maria Hero, John Joy, Joe McGrath, Jack Murray, Alexander Orfaly, Anna Pagan, Dixie Stewart, Mara Worth

UNDERSTUDIES: Charley, Lester James; Kate, Maria Hero; Cynthia, Leigh Curran; Sue Ellen, Patricia Cope; Wingate, Alexander Orfaly; Gilman, Stanley Simmonds; Mrs. Millhouser, Fran Stevens; Bradbury, Martin Ambrose; Widows, Patricia Cope

MUSICAL NUMBERS: "A-B-C," "They Don't Make 'em Like That Anymore," "Live A Little," "The Pleasure's About To Be Mine," "A Little Investigation," "Walk Away," "Goodbye, Failure, Goodbye," "Step To The Rear," "Shakespeare Lied," "Big Trouble," "Credo," "One Of Those Moments," "He's Here!," "Panic," "Touch and Go," "That's Good Enough For Me."

A Musical Comedy in 2 acts and 18 scenes. The action takes place at the present time in New York City.

General Manager: Jack Schlissel
Company Manager: Richard Highley
Press: Lee Solters, Harvey Sabinson, David Powers, Muffy Newman
Stage Managers: Charles Blackwell, Henry Velez, Kenneth Porter

° Still playing May 31, 1968.

Friedman-Abeles Photos

Top Left: Hiram Sherman ("Tony" Award featured musical actor), Brenda Vaccaro. Belo Francesca Smith, Lucie Lancaster, Sally DeMa Anthony Roberts, Charlotte Jones, Fran Steve

ANTA THEATRE

Opened Thursday, December 14, 1967.°
Zev Bufman in association with James Riley presents:

SPOFFORD

By Herman Shumlin; Based on novel "Reuben, Reuben" by Peter DeVries; Director, Mr. Shumlin; Scenery and Lighting, Donald Oenslager; Costumes, Winn Morton.

CAST

Spofford	Melvyn Douglas
George	Alan North
Mare	Tresa Hughes
First Customer	Carole Ann Lewis
Mrs. Punck	Pert Kelton
Mrs. Beausigneur	Barbara Britton
Geneva	Penelope Windust
Tad	Jeffrey Weiss
Second Customer	Oceana Briggs
Pycraft	Wallace Rooney
Mrs. Springer	Audra Lindley
Gromler	Joseph Boland
Hopwood	Ian Martin
Gowan McGland	Jerome Dempsey
Maid	Jan DeVries
Mrs. Crane	Joen Arliss
Committee Members	Ian Martin, Charles Maggiore

UNDERSTUDIES: Spofford, Wallace Rooney; Punck, Oceana Briggs; Beausigneur, Carole Ann Lewis; McGland, Charles Maggiore; Springer, Mare, Joen Arliss; George, Ian Martin; Geneva, Jan DeVries; Tad, Robert Tananis

A Comedy in two acts. The action takes place at the present time in a town in Connecticut.

General Manager: Diana Krasny
Company Manager: Irving Cone
Press: Bill Doll & Co., Midori Lederer, Ted Goldsmith, Virginia Holden
Stage Managers: Edward Julien, Lola Shumlin, Jan DeVries

° Still playing May 31, 1968.

Friedman Abeles Photos

Melvyn Douglas, Audra Lindley. Above: Penelope Windust, Jerome Dempsey, Melvyn Douglas. Top: Barbara Britton, Melvyn Douglas

Melvyn Douglas, Pert Kelton

JOHN GOLDEN THEATRE

Opened Monday, December 18, 1967.°
David Susskind and Daniel Melnick present:

BRIEF LIVES

By Patrick Garland; Adapted from the works of John Aubrey; Designed by Julia Trevelyan Oman; Lighting Design and Set Supervision, Lloyd Burlingame; Directed by Patrick Garland; Production Assistant, Nancy Simmons.

CAST

John Aubrey _____ Roy Dotrice

An "Evening of Theatre" presented in two parts. The action takes place in Mistress Byerley's lodgings in Dirty Lane, Bloomsbury, in 1697, the year of Aubrey's death.

General Managers: Joseph Harris,
Ira Bernstein, Seth Schapiro
Press: Frank Goodman, Martin Shwartz
Stage Managers: Porter Van Zandt,
Lynn Montgomery

° Closed Dec. 30, 1967 after 16 performances, but gave an additional performance on Jan. 7, 1968 for Actors' Fund.

Roy Dotrice as John Aubrey

Molly Picon, Godfrey Cambridge

HUDSON THEATRE

Opened Thursday, December 28, 1967.°
Jon-Lee and Seymour Vall present;

HOW TO BE A JEWISH MOTHER

Conceived by Seymour Vall; Based on book by Dan Greenburg; Director, Avery Schreiber; Music, Michael Leonard; Lyrics, Herbert Martin; Scenery, Robert Randolph; Costumes, Michael Travis; Lighting, John J. Moore; Musical Staging, Doug Rogers; Musical Direction and Arrangements, Julian Stein; Associate Producers, Rick Mandell, Margaret Aldrich; Production Assistant, Ann Hopkins.

CAST

Molly Picon
Godfrey Cambridge

STANDBYS: Naomi Riseman, Riger Haynes

MUSICAL NUMBERS: "Once The Man You Laughed At," "Laugh A Little," "Since The Time We Met," "The Wedding Song," "Child You Are."

A revue presented in two acts.

General Manager: Edward H. Davis
Press: Seymour Krawitz, Ruth Cage,
Clint Atkinson
Stage Managers: William Krot,
John Glennon

° Closed Jan. 13, 1968. (21 performances)

Friedman-Abeles Photos

34

BILTMORE THEATRE

Opened Wednesday, January 10, 1968.°
Bill Freedman and Charles Kasher present:

STAIRCASE

By Charles Dyer; Director, Barry Morse;
Scenery and Costumes, Michael Annals; Lighting, Gil Wechsler.

CAST

Charles Dyer _____ Eli Wallach
Harry Leeds _____ Milo O'Shea

A Comedy in two acts. The action takes
place at the present time in a barber's shop in
a suburb of London.

General Manager: Victor Samrock
Company Manager: Ben Rosenberg
Press: Mike Merrick, Barry Kobrin
Stage Managers: Thomas Bohdanetzky,
Wayne Carson

° Closed March 3, 1968. (61 performances
and 20 previews)

Friedman-Abeles Photos

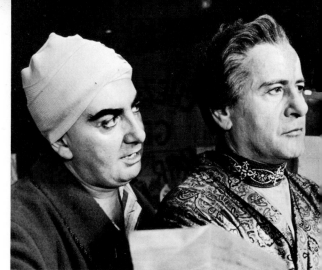

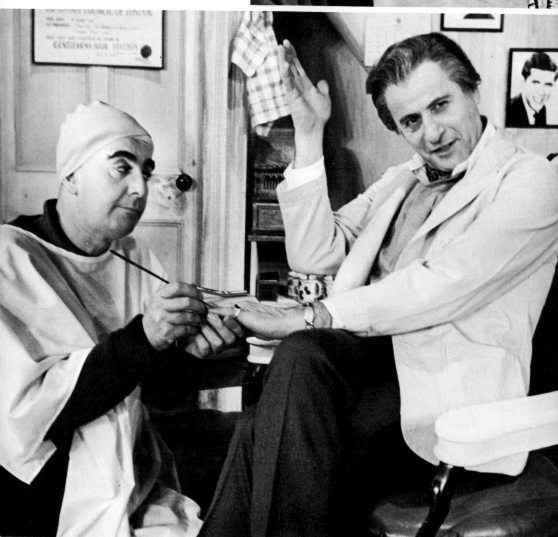

Milo O'Shea, Eli Wallach, also at top

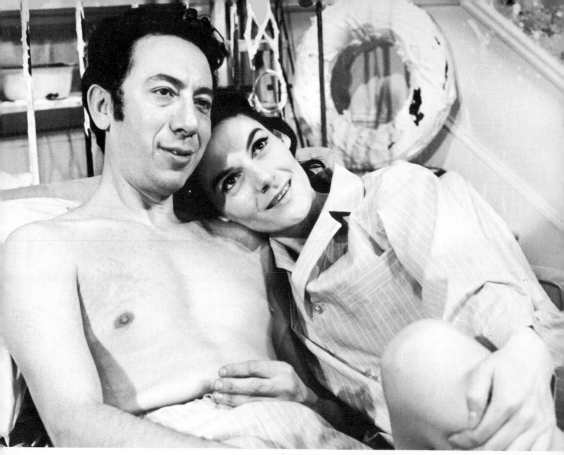

HENRY MILLER'S THEATRE

Opened Thursday, January 11, 1968.°
Peregrine Productions, Inc. presents:

BEFORE YOU GO

By Lawrence Holofcener; Director, Mark Gordon; Scenery, Ed Wittstein; Costumes, Theoni V. Aldredge; Lighting, Jules Fisher; Producer, Peter Moreau; Associate Producer, S. Walter Epstein; Technical Adviser, John Higgins.

CAST

Man	Gene Troobnick
Woman	Marian Seldes
Dog	L. P.

A Comedy in 2 acts and 3 scenes. The action takes place at the present time in the Greenwich Village apartment of Stanley Fish in New York City.

General Manager: Walter Fried
Company Manager: Oliver W. Nicoll
Press: Merle Debuskey, Violet Welles, Faith Geer
Stage Managers: Stephen Gardner, Gill Dennis

° Closed Feb. 3, 1968. (28 performances and 11 previews)

Friedman-Abeles Photos

Marian Seldes, Gene Troobnick, also above

HELEN HAYES THEATRE

Opened Tuesday, January 16, 1968.°
Robert Whitehead in association with
Robert W. Dowling presents:

THE PRIME OF MISS JEAN BRODIE

By Jay Allen; Adapted from novel by
Muriel Spark; Director, Michael Langham;
Scenery and Lighting, Jo Mielziner; Costumes,
Jane Greenwood; Incidental Music Composed
and Arranged by John Cook; Production Assistant, Doris Blum.

CAST

Sister Helena	Denise Huot
Mr. Perry	Douglas Watson
Jean Brodie	Zoe Caldwell
Sandy	Amy Taubin
Jenny	Diana Davila
Monica	Catherine Burns
Mary MacGregor	Kathryn Baumann
Miss MacKay	Lennox Milne
Gordon Lowther	Joseph Maher
Teddy Lloyd	Roy Cooper
McCready	Brooks Morton
Miss Campbell	Sheila Coonan

CITIZENS, GIRL GUIDES, SCHOOL GIRLS:
Roberta Maxwell, Celia Watson, Nora Heflin,
Mady Heflin, Jane Actman, Doreen Miller,
Donna Conforti, Stephanie Sheppard, Jami
Fields, Jim Oyster, Brooks Morton, Janice
Mars, Jack Knight

UNDERSTUDIES: Brodie, Denise Huot;
Mackay, Sheila Coonan; Helena, Sandy, Roberta Maxwell; Jenny, Jane Actman; Monica,
Mary, Nora Heflin; Perry, Jim Oyster; Campbell, Janice Mars

A Comedy in two acts. The action takes
place in Edinburgh, Scotland, now, and from
1931 to 1933.

General Manager: Oscar E. Olesen
Company Manager: James Walsh
Press: Seymour Krawitz, Ruth Cage
Stage Managers: Harry Young,
William Webster, Jim Oyster

° Still playing May 31, 1968.

Friedman-Abeles Photos

Caldwell ("Tony" Award for dramatic ...ess). Top Right: Kathryn Baumann, Diana Davila, Zoe Caldwell, Amy Taubin, Catherine Burns

Zoe Caldwell, and above with Amy Taubin, Kathryn Baumann, Joseph Maher

Julie Gregg, Robert Goulet ("Tony" Award for musical star)

BROADWAY THEATRE

Opened Thursday, January 18, 1968.°
David Merrick presents:

THE HAPPY TIME

Book, N. Richard Nash; Suggested by characters in stories by Robert L. Fontaine; Music, John Kander; Lyrics, Fred Ebb; Directed, Filmed, and Choreographed by Gower Champion; Settings, Peter Wexler; Costumes, Freddy Wittop; Lighting, Jean Rosenthal; Film Sequences Created by Christopher Chapman; Film Technical Direction, Barry O. Gordon; Orchestrations, Don Walker; Musical Direction and Vocal Arrangements, Oscar Kosarin; Associate Choreographer, Kevin Carlisle; Dance and Incidental Music Arrangements, Marvin Laird; Production Manager, Michael Thoma; Associate Producer, Samuel Liff; Staff Associates, Sylvia Schwartz, Lynn Middleton, Juliet Taylor; Original cast album by RCA Victor.

CAST

Jacques Bonnard	Robert Goulet
Suzanne Bonnard	Jeanne Arnold
Philippe Bonnard	George S. Irving
Bibi Bonnard	Mike Rupert
Louis Bonnard	Charles Durning
Annabelle Bonnard	Kim Freund
Gillie Bonnard	Julane Stites
Nanette Bonnard	Connie Simmons
Felice Bonnard	June Squibb
Grandpere Bonnard	David Wayne

The Six Angels:

Lizette	Jacki Garland
Dorine	Mary Gail Laverenz
Sylvie	Tammie Fillhart
Monique	Mary Ann O'Reilly
Bella	Vicki Powers
Grace	Susan Sigrist
Laurie Mannon	Julie Gregg
Foufie	Jeffrey Golkin
Ganache	Dallas Johann
Swing Dancer	Sammy Williams

DANCERS: Ron Abshire, Jovanni Anthony, Quinn Baird, Andy Bew, Blake Brown, Leonard Crofoot, Ron Crofoot, Wayne Dugger, Joe Giamalva, Dallas Johann, Gene Law, Steve Reinhart, Jon Simonson, Michael Stearns

SINGERS: Marc Anthony, Alan Blight, George Connolly, Tom De Mastri, Paul Dwyer, Scott Gandert, Eric Hamilton, Gary Hamilton, Jeffrey Hamilton, Kevin Hamilton, Mark Lonergan, Brian Shyer, Brandy Wayne, Teddy Williams, Marc Winters

UNDERSTUDIES: Jacques, Philippe, John Gabriel; Grandpere, Louis, Ben Kapen; Suzanne, Felice, Iva Withers; Laurie, Vicki Powers; Bibi, Leonard Crofoot.

MUSICAL NUMBERS: "The Happy Time," "He's Back," "Catch My Garter," "Tomorrow Morning," "Please Stay," "I Don't Remember You," "St. Pierre," "Without Me," "Among My Yesterdays," "The Life of The Party," "Seeing Things," "Ballet," "A Certain Girl," "Being Alive."

A Musical in two acts. The action takes place in the past in Jacques Bonnard's studio, and earlier still in his home in a small town in Canada.

General Manager: Jack Schlissel
Company Manager: Fred Cuneo
Press: Harvey Sabinson, Lee Solters,
David Powers, Muffy Newman
Stage Managers; Bob Bernard,
Jeff Chambers

° Still playing May 31, 1968.
Had World Premiere at Ahmanson Theatre, Los Angeles, where it played from Nov. 13, through Dec. 23, 1967.

Friedman-Abeles Photos

Top Left: Mike Rupert, Robert Goulet, David Wayne. Below: David Wayne, Jeanne Arnold, Kim Freund, Robert Goulet, Charles Durning, Julane Stites, Connie Simmons

LONGACRE THEATRE

Opened Thursday, January 25, 1968.°
Gilbert Gates in association with Doris Vidor presents:

I NEVER SANG FOR MY FATHER

By Robert Anderson; Director, Alan Schneider; Scenery and Lighting, Jo Mielziner; Costumes, Theoni V. Aldredge; Production Associate, Bilee Steinberg; Production Assistants, Peter L. Skolnik, Jane Cates.

CAST

Gene Garrison	Hal Holbrook
Porter	Earl Sydnor
Tom Garrison	Alan Webb
Margaret Garrison	Lillian Gish
Mary	Sloane Shelton
Nurse	Laurinda Barrett
Reverend Pell	Allan Frank
Marvin Scott	Matt Crowley
Waiter	James A. Spearman
Dr. Mayberry	Daniel Keyes
Alice	Teresa Wright

UNDERSTUDIES: Gene, Thomas Coley; Margaret, Lois Wilson; Tom, Daniel Keyes; Alice, Laurinda Barrett; Pell, Mayberry, Scott, William Callan; Nurse, Sloane Shelton.

A Drama in two acts. The action takes place in the present and past, in New York City and a town in Westchester County.

General Manager: Robert Kamlot
Company Manager: James Preston
Press: Lee Solters, Harvey Sabinson, Harry Nigro, Muffy Newman
Stage Managers: Paul A. Foley, William Callan, Earl Sydnor

° Closed May 11, 1968. (124 performances and 1 preview)

Martha Swope Photos

Alan Webb, Lillian Gish. Above: Lillian Gish, Hal Holbrook. Top: Hal Holbrook, Alan Webb

Hal Holbrook, Teresa Wright

39

GEORGE ABBOTT THEATRE

Opened Saturday, January 27, 1968.°
The Theatre Guild and Joel Schenker
present:

DARLING OF THE DAY

Music, Jule Styne; Lyrics, E. Y. Harburg;
Based on Arnold Bennett's "Buried Alive";
Director, Noel Willman; Choreography, Lee
Theodore; Scenery, Oliver Smith; Costumes,
Raoul Pene duBois; Lighting, Peggy Clark;
Musical Director and Vocal Arrangements, Buster Davis; Dance Music, Trude Rittman; Orchestrations, Ralph Burns; Hair Styles, D.
Rusty Bonaccorso; Staff Assistant, Julie Morgan; Original cast album by RCA Victor.

CAST

Oxford	Peter Woodthorpe
Priam Farll	Vincent Price
Henry Leek	Charles Welch
Old Gentleman	Carl Nicholas
Lady Vale	Brenda Forbes
Cabby	Ross Miles
Doctor	Leo Leyden
Alice Challice	Patricia Routledge
Daphne	Joy Nichols
Alf	Teddy Green
Bert	Marc Jordan
Rosalind	Beth Howland
Sydney	Reid Klein
Attendant	Larry Brucker
Frame Maker	Paul Eichel
Duncan	Mitchell Jason
Equerry	John Aman
The King	Charles Gerald
Constable	John Aman
Mrs. Leek	Camila Ashland
Curates	Herb Wilson, Fred Siretta
Pennington	Michael Lewis
Judge	Leo Leyden

SINGERS: Marian Haraldson, Kay Oslin,
Jeannette Seibert, Maggie Task, Maggie Worth,
John Aman, Larry Brucker, Paul Eichel, Reid
Klein, Carl Nicholas, Albert Zimmerman.

DANCERS: Bonnie Ano, Reby Howells, Beth
Howland, Georgianne Thon, Phyllis Wallach,
Denise Winston, Christopher Chadman, George
Lee, Jim May, Ross Miles, Fred Siretta, Herb
Wilson

UNDERSTUDIES: Priam, Mitchell Jason;
Alice, Joy Nichols; Lady Vale, Jeannette
Seibert; Oxford, Michael Lewis; Alf, Ross
Miles; Duncan, Pennington, Charles Gerald;
Doctor, Zale Kessler; Daphne, Maggie Worth;
Leek, Marc Jordan; Bert, Charles Welch; Mrs.
Leek, Maggie Task; for Charles Gerald,
Paul Eichel

MUSICAL NUMBERS: "Mad For Art," "He's
A Genius," "To Get Out Of This World
Alive," "It's Enough To Make A Lady Fall
In Love," "A Gentleman's Gentleman,"
"Double Soliloquy," "Let's See What Happens," "Panache," "I've Got A Rainbow Working For Me," "Money, Money, Money," "That
Something Extra Special," "What Makes A
Marriage Merry," "Not On Your Nellie,"
"Sunset Tree," "Butler In The Abbey."

A Musical Comedy in 2 acts and 14 scenes.
The action takes place in London in 1905.

General Manager: Victor Samrock
Company Manager: Ralph Roseman
Press; Arthur Cantor, Arthur Solomon
Stage Managers: Phil Friedman,
Michael Sinclair, Phil King

° Closed Feb. 24, 1968. (31 performances)

Patricia Routledge ("Tony" Award for best musical
star), Teddy Green. Top: Vincent Price,
Patricia Routledge

BOOTH THEATRE

Opened Wednesday, January 31, 1968.°
Morris Jacobs and Jerome Whyte in association with Richard Rodgers present:

AVANTI !

By Samuel Taylor; Director, Nigel Patrick; Scenery and Lighting, Donald Oenslager; Costumes, Winn Morton; Fashion Consultant, Geoffrey Beene.

CAST

John Wesley	Rik Pierce
Alexander Ben Claiborne	Robert Reed
A Waiter	Frank Nastasi
Baldassare Pantaleone	Keith Baxter
Alison Ames	Jennifer Hilary
A Porter	Loreto Caringi
Helen Claiborne	Betsy Von Furstenberg

UNDERSTUDIES: Alison, Helen, Susan Sullivan; Alexander, Vince Carroll; Baldassare, Loreto Caringi; John, Steven Meyer

A Comedy in 2 acts and 4 scenes. The action takes place during Spring of the present time, in the sitting room of an apartment hotel in Rome.

Business Manager: Maurice Winters
Press: Betty Lee Hunt, Henry Luhrman
Stage Managers: Randall Brooks, Steven Meyer

° Closed Feb. 17, 1968. (21 performances)

Friedman-Abeles Photos

ght: Frank Nastasi, Robert Reed, Rik Pierce
op: Robert Reed, Keith Baxter, Betsy Von Furstenberg, Jennifer Hilary

Jennifer Hilary, Robert Reed, Keith Baxter

Robert Reed, Jennifer Hilary

41

Zena Walker ("Tony" Award for supporting
actress), Albert Finney

Elizabeth Hubbard, John Carson, Albert Finney

BROOKS ATKINSON THEATRE

Opened Thursday, February 1, 1968.°
Joseph Cates and Henry Fownes,
Michael Medwin (for Memorial Ltd.)
presents:

A DAY IN THE DEATH OF
JOE EGG

By Peter Nichols; Director, Michael Blakemore; Designed by Robin Pidcock; Lighting
and Set Supervision, Lloyd Burlingame; Music, Andy Park.

CAST

Bri	Albert Finney †1
Sheila	Zena Walker
Joe	Susan Alpern
Pam	Elizabeth Hubbard
Freddie	John Carson †2
Grace	Joan Hickson †3

UNDERSTUDIES: Sheila, Pam, Jo Henderson;
Freddie, Dan Hogan, John Tillinger; Joe,
Moni Ferguson; Grace, Kate Tomlinson

A Comedy in two acts. The action takes
place at the present time in Bristol, England.

General Manager: Bill Levine
Press: Max Eisen, Carl Samrock,
Jeanne Gibson Merrick,
Cheryl Sue Dolby
Stage Managers: Ben Janney, Nelle Nugent

° Still playing May 31, 1968.

† Succeeded by: 1. Donal Donnelly, 2. Ed
Zimmermann, 3. Nancy R. Pollock.

Ed Zimmerman, Elizabeth Hubbard, Zena Walker,
Donal Donnelly. Above: Elizabeth Hubbard, John
Carson, Zena Walker, Albert Finney, (L) Albert
Finney, Joan Hickson

SAM S. SHUBERT THEATRE

Opened Sunday, February 4, 1968.°
Joseph P. Harris and Ira Bernstein present:

GOLDEN RAINBOW

Book, Ernest Kinoy; Based on play "A Hole In The Head" by Arnold Schulman; Music and Lyrics, Walter Marks; Director, Arthur Storch; Choreography, Tom Panko; Scenery and Lighting, Robert Randolph; Costumes, Alvin Colt; Musical Direction and Vocal Arrangements, Elliot Lawrence; Orchestrations, Pat Williams, Jack Andrews; Dance Music Arranged by Marvin Hamlisch and Luther Henderson; Associate Choreographer, Martin Allen; Hair Styles, Ernest Adler; A Diplomat Production. Original cast album by Calendar Records, distributed by RCA Victor.

CAST

Mr. Novotny	Alan Kass
Ally	Scott Jacoby
Mr. Hausknecht	Howard Mann
Eloise	Linda Jorgens
Laundryman	Charles Karel
Henry	Will Hussung
Mr. Diamond	Sid Raymond
Larry Davis	Steve Lawrence
Mrs. Magruder	Fay Sappington
Lou Garrity	Joseph Sirola
Jerome Stone	Gene Foote
Rosemary Garrity	Marilyn Cooper
Gordon	John Anania
Mr. Korngold	Sam Kressen
Reporters	Charles Karel, Lanier Davis
Lead Dancer	Diana Saunders
Judy Harris	Eydie Gorme
Georgia	Carol Conte
Stripper	Thelma Sherr
Sam	Frank Pietri
Umbawa	Larry Merritt
Persian Girl	Linda Jorgens
Cat Girl	Carole Bishop
Nebuchadnezzar	John Anania
Virgin	Diana Saunders
Hero	Antony DeVecchi
Stage Manager	Charles Karel
Victor	Lanier Davis
Gambler	Michael Vita

DANCERS: Carole Bishop, Carol Conte, Susan Donovan, Antony DeVecchi, Tina Faye, Alice Glenn, Linda Jorgens, Maralyn Miles, Jean Preece, Wayne Boyd, Gene Foote, Blair Hammond, Larry Merritt, Frank Pietri, Tom Rolla, Michael Shawn, Michael Vita

SHOWGIRLS: Betty Jo Alvies, Bernadette Brookes, Rae Samuels, Thelma Sherr

UNDERSTUDIES: Larry, Mace Barrett; Judy, Marilyn Cooper; Novotny, Gene Foote; Ally, Dewey Golkin; Hausknecht, Diamond, Korngold, John Anania; Eloise, Carole Bishop; Henry, Lanier Davis; Mrs. Magruder, Carole Conte; Garrity, Charles Karel; Rosemary, Tina Faye; Gordon, Frank Pietri

MUSICAL NUMBERS: "Golden Rainbow," "We Got Us," "He Needs Me Now," "Kid" "For Once In Your Life," "Taking Care Of You," "I've Got To Be Me," "The Fall of Babylon," "Taste," "Desert Moon," "All In Fun," "It's You Again," "How Could I Be So Wrong."

A Musical Comedy in 2 acts and 13 scenes. The action takes place at the present time in Las Vegas.

Business Manager: Sam Pagliaro
Press: Mike Merrick, Barry Kobrin, Karl Bernstein
Stage Managers: George Thorn, Peter Stern

° Still playing May 31, 1968.

Henri-Dauman, Friedman-Abeles Photos

Eydie Gorme, Steve Lawrence, also above
and at top

PALACE THEATRE

Opened Tuesday, February 6, 1968.°
Lee Guber and Shelly Gross by arrangement with Bruno Coquatrix present:

THE GRAND MUSIC HALL OF ISRAEL

Staged and Choreographed by Jonathan Karmon; Musical Direction and Arrangements, Itzchak Graziani; Assistant Director, Gavri Levi; Costumes, Hovav Kruvi; Lighting, Jules Fisher; Assistant Conductor, Ami Gilad; Production Assistant, Julie Hughes.

CAST

Helena Hendel, Geula Gill and The High Willows, Ilan and Ilanit, The Carmelim, Nishri, Boaz and Nechemia, Alice and Hannan, and The Karmon Histadruth Ballet

PROGRAM

ACT I: "Israeli Rhapsody," "Songs of Youth," "Dance of The Fisherman," "Oriental Rhythms," "The New Sound of Israel's Hit Parade," "Hassidic."

ACT II: "Desert Rhythms," "The Story of Her People In Song," "In A Kibbutz On The Border," "Music In A Novel Manner," "The New Spirit of A People In Their Singing Style," "The Feasts of The Kibbutz," "Shalom."

Company Manager: Marvin A. Krauss
Press: Saul Richman
Stage Manager: John Actman

° Closed Mar. 31, 1968 after a limited engagement of 63 performances to tour.

Barry Kramer Photos

The Carmelin
Top: Ilan and Ilanit

Nishri. Above (L & R) Karmon Histadruth Dancer

MOROSCO THEATRE

Opened Wednesday, February 7, 1968.°
Robert Whitehead in association with
Robert W. Dowling presents:

THE PRICE

By Arthur Miller; Director, Ulu Grosbard;
Setting and Costumes, Boris Aronson; Light-
ing, Paul Morrison; Production Assistant, Doris
Blum.

CAST

Victor Franz	Pat Hingle
Esther Franz	Kate Reid
Gregory Solomon	Harold Gary
Walter Franz	Arthur Kennedy

STANDBYS: Esther, Joan Copeland; Victor,
Eugene Roche; Walter, Paul Sparer.

A Drama presented without intermission. The
action takes place at the present time on the
attic floor of a Manhattan brownstone.

General Manager: Oscar E. Olesen
Press: James D. Proctor, David Roggensack
Stage Managers: Del Hughes,
Howard Fischer

° Still playing May 31, 1968.

Inge Morath Photos

**Kate Reid, Pat Hingle, Harold Gary, Arthur
Kennedy (also at top). Above: Pat Hingle,
Arthur Kennedy. Right: Kate Reid, Pat Hingle**

PLYMOUTH THEATRE

Opened Wednesday, February 14, 1968.°
Saint-Subber presents:

PLAZA SUITE

By Neil Simon; Director, Mike Nichols;
Scenic Production, Oliver Smith; Costumes,
Patricia Zipprodt; Lighting, Jean Rosenthal;
Hair Styles, Ernest Adler; Production Assistants, James Turner, R. T. Ingham; Produced
by Nancy Enterprises, Inc.

CAST

"Visitor From Mamaroneck"

Bellhop _____ Bob Balaban
Karen Nash _____ Maureen Stapleton
Sam Nash _____ George C. Scott †
Waiter _____ Jose Ocasio
Jean McCormack _____ Claudette Nevins

"Visitor From Hollywood"

Waiter _____ Jose Ocasio
Jesse Kiplinger _____ George C. Scott †
Muriel Tate _____ Maureen Stapleton

"Visitor From Forest Hills"

Norma Hubley _____ Maureen Stapleton
Roy Hubley _____ George C. Scott †
Borden Eisler _____ Bob Balaban
Mimsey Hubley _____ Claudette Nevins
STANDBYS: Miss Stapleton, Elizabeth Wilson; Mr. Scott, Alfred Sandor; Miss Nevins,
Judith Barcroft; Messrs. Balaban and Ocasio,
Wisner Washam

These three one-act plays take place at the
present time in a suite of the Plaza Hotel.

General Manager: C. Edwin Knill
Company Manager: William Craver
Press: Harvey B. Sabinson, Lee Solters,
Harry Nigro, Muffy Newman
Stage Managers: Harvey Medlinsky,
Wisner Washam

° Still playing May 31, 1968.

† During Mr. Scott's illness, played by Alfred
Sandor, then Nicol Williamson.

Martha Swope Photos

George C. Scott, Maureen Stapleton

George C. Scott, Maureen Stapleton, also above

JOHN GOLDEN THEATRE

Opened Tuesday, February 27, 1968.°
Saint-Subber in association with Harold
Loeb presents:

CARRY ME BACK TO MORNINGSIDE HEIGHTS

By Robert Alan Aurthur; Director, Sidney
Poitier; Designed by Kert Lundell; Lighting,
Gil Wechsler; Production Assistant, R. T.
Ingham.

CAST

Willie Nurse	Louis Gossett
Seymour Levin	David Steinberg
Henry Hardy	Johnny Brown
Myrna Jessup	Cicely Tyson †
Alma Sue Bates	Diane Ladd

STANDBYS: Willie, Spencer Holden; Seymour, Richard Blair; Myrna, Beverly Todd; Alma Sue, Marilyn Madderom; Henry, Douglas Johnson.

A Comedy in 3 acts and 4 scenes. The action takes place at the present time in an apartment on Morningside Heights in New York City.

General Manager: C. Edwin Knill
Company Manager: Irving Cooper
Press: Harvey B. Sabinson, Lee Solters,
Robert Ullman, Muffy Newman
Stage Managers: Victor Straus,
Douglas Johnson

° Closed Mar. 2, 1968. (7 performances and 1 preview)

† Succeeded by Beverly Todd.

Friedman-Abeles Photos

David Steinberg, Cicely Tyson, Louis Gossett, Diane Ladd, Johnny Brown. Above: Louis Gossett, Cicely Tyson. (L) Diane Ladd, David Steinberg

47

HENRY MILLER'S THEATRE

Opened Wednesday, February 28, 1968.°
H. Clay Blaney, Albert W. Selden and
Hal James present:

PORTRAIT OF A QUEEN

Edited and arranged as a play by William
Francis; Director, Val May; Settings and
Lighting, Marvin Reiss; Costumes, Theoni V.
Aldredge; Ballads selected and arranged by
William Francis and Charles Chilton; Miss
Tutin's costumes, Jane Helder; Executive As-
sistant, Wendy Mackenzie; Associate Producer,
Richard Waring; Technical Adviser, John Hig-
gins.

CAST

Balladsinger	Nicholas Smith
King Leopold of Belgium	Richard Waring
Victoria	Dorothy Tutin
Lord Melbourne and other ministers	Michael Barrington
Bishop of Durham	Frederic Warriner
First Lady-in-Waiting	Nancy Acly
Second Lady-in-Waiting	Holly Brooke
Archbishop of Canterbury	Thomas Barbour
Prince Albert	Derek Waring
Editor of the "Times"	Thomas Barbour
Gentlemen of the Press	Frederic Warriner, Michael Bradshaw
Viscount Palmerston	Richard Waring
Benjamin Disraeli	Dennis King
William Gladstone	James Cossins
Footmen	Michael Bradshaw, Christopher Flavell, John Milligan, Harlan Cary Poe, Bernard Taylor

Presented in 3 acts. The action takes place
in London and elsewhere between 1837 and
1900. Dialogue spoken by Queen Victoria
consists of her own words drawn from her
diaries and letters. That of her contemporaries,
only words written or spoken by them.

General Manager: Walter Fried
Company Manager: James Awe
Press: Merle Debuskey, Faith Geer,
Violet Welles
Stage Managers: James Gelb,
Frank Hamilton, Ernest Austin

° Closed Apr. 20, 1968. (60 performances)

Friedman-Abeles Photos

Nicholas Smith, Michael Barrington, Dennis King,
Dorothy Tutin. Above: Derek Waring, Dorothy
Tutin. (L) Michael Barrington, Dorothy Tutin

BILLY ROSE THEATRE
Opened Sunday, March 3, 1968.°
Mitch Miller presents:

HERE'S WHERE I BELONG

Book, Alex Gordon; Based on novel "East of Eden" by John Steinbeck; Music, Robert Waldman; Lyrics, Alfred Uhry; Director, Michael Kahn; Dances and Musical Staging, Tony Mordente; Scenery, Ming Cho Lee; Costumes, Ruth Morley; Lighting, Jules Fisher; Musical Direction and Vocal Arrangements, Theodore Saidenberg; Dance Music, Arnold Goland; Orchestrations, Glenn Osser, Norman Leyden, Jonathan Tunick; Produced in association with United Artists; Production Assistant, Charles Willard; Staff Assistants, Paula Lorge, Terry Spierer; Hair Styles, Steve Atha; Original cast album by United Artists Records.

CAST

Adam Trask	Paul Rogers
Caleb Trask	Walter McGinn
Aron Trask	Ken Kercheval
Lee	James Coco
Will Hamilton	Casper Roos
Mrs. Bacon	Bette Henritze
Mrs. Tripp	Dena Dietrich
Mrs. Heink	Patricia Kelly
Abra Bacon	Heather MacRae
School Children	Lee Wilson, Tod Miller
Miss Ida	Barbara Webb
Rabbit Holman	Scott Jarvis
Faith	Graciela Daniele
Eva	Aniko Morgan
Della	Dorothy Lister
Kate	Nancy Wickwire
Joe	Joseph Nelson
Juana	Joetta Cherry
Newspaper Man	Taylor Reed
British Purchasing Agent	Darrell Askey

TOWNSPEOPLE, FIELD WORKERS, DENIZENS OF CASTROVILLE STREET: Darrell Askey, Joetta Cherry, Graciela Daniele, Elisa De Marko, Larry Devon, John Dickerson, Bud Fleming, John William Gardner, Gene Gavin, John Johann, Ray Kirchner, Jane Laughlin, Dorothy Lister, Andy Love, Richard Marr, David McCorkle, Joyce McDonald, Tod Miller, Aniko Morgan, Joan Nelson, Joseph Nelson, Donald Norris, Taylor Reed, Clifford Scott, Joy Serio, Michele Simmons, David Thomas, Barbara Webb, Lee Wilson

UNDERSTUDIES: Kate, Rita Morley; Cal, Scott Jarvis; Lee, Taylor Reed; Aron, Tod Miller; Abra, Joan Nelson; Mrs. Bacon, Den Dietrich; Mrs. Tripp, Mrs. Heink, Joyce McDonald; Will, Richard Marr; Rabbit, John Johann

MUSICAL NUMBERS: "We Are What We Are," "Cal Gets By," "Raising Cain," "Soft Is The Sparrow," "Where Have I Been," "No Time," "Progress," "Good Boy," "Ballet," "Act Like A Lady," "The Send-Off," "Top Of The Train," "Waking Up The Sun," "Pulverize The Kaiser," "You're Momma's," "Here's Where I Belong," "We're A Home."

A Musical in 2 acts and 17 scenes. The action takes place in Salinas, California in 1915.

General Manager: Allentuck, Azenberg & Wolsk
Company Manager: Peter Neufeld
Press: Frank Goodman, Martin Shwartz, Abby Hirsch
Stage Managers: William Dodds, D. W. Koehler, Gene Gavin

° Closed Mar. 3, 1968. (1 performance and 20 previews)

Friedman-Abeles Photos

Top Right: Heather MacRae, Ken Kercheval, Nancy Wickwire, Paul Rogers, James Coco, Walter McGinn. Below: Paul Rogers, Nancy Wickwire

Walter McGinn, Heather MacRae

HUDSON THEATRE
Opened Wednesday, March 6, 1968.°
Noel Weiss presents:

THE GUIDE

By Harvey Breit and Patricia Rinehart;
Based on novel by R. K. Narayan; Director,
George L. Sherman; Designed by William
Pitkin; Lighting, Martin Aronstein; Temple
Dance Staged by Matteo; Music supervised
by Ravi Shankar.

CAST

Raju	Zia Mohyeddin
Bhabani	Titos Vandis
Velan	Michael Kermoyan
Devi	Madhur Jaffrey
Boy	Jerry Ram
Chandra	Peter DeAnda
Muthu	Richard Dmitri
Soma	Martin Meyers
Ramu	Vikas
Shopkeeper	Ian Edward
Police Officer	John Branon

VILLAGERS: Vincente Elias, John Patrick
Hart, Shireen Subramanya, Osceola Archer,
Angela D'Ambrosia
UNDERSTUDIES: Raju, Peter DeAnda; Bhabani, Martin Meyers; Velan, Ian Edward; Devi,
Angela D'Ambrosia; Boy, Vincente Elias;
Shopkeeper, Muthu, Vikas; Chandra, Richard
Dmitri

A Drama in three acts. The action takes
place at the present time before a neglected
temple on the bank of a river in South India.

General Managers: Allentuck,
Azenberg & Wolsk
Press: Harvey B. Sabinson, Lee Solters,
Jay Russell
Stage Managers: Roger Johnson, Jr.,
Donald King

° Closed Mar. 9, 1968. (5 performances and
12 previews)

Titos Vandis, Michael Kermoyan, Zia Mohyeddin
Top: Zia Mohyeddin

BROADHURST THEATRE

Opened Wednesday, March 13, 1968.°
Saint-Subber and Lester Osterman present:

WEEKEND

By Gore Vidal; Director, Joseph Anthony; Scenic Production, Oliver Smith; Costumes, Theoni V. Aldredge; Lighting, Jean Rosenthal; Associate Producer, Simon L. Saltzman; Production Assistant, R. T. Ingham.

CAST

Roger	John Marriott
Miss Wilson	Kim Hunter
Norris Blotner	Gene Blakely
Senator MacGruder	John Forsythe
Senator Andrews	Staats Cotsworth
Mrs. Andrews	Eleanor Wilson
Estelle MacGruder	Rosemary Murphy
Beany MacGruder	Marco St. John
Louise Hampton	Carol Cole
Mrs. Hampton	Zaida Coles
Dr. Hampton	Graham Brown
First Photographer	John Newton
Second Photographer	Robert Lawson
Reporter	Norma Darden

UNDERSTUDIES: MacGruder, Gene Blakely; Estelle, Wilson, Mrs. Andrews, Virginia Robinson; Louise, Norma Darden; Andrews, Blotner, John Newton; Beanie, Robert Lawson; Mrs. Hampton, Javotte Sutton Greene; Roger, Dr. Hampton, Stanley Greene.

A Comedy in two acts. The action takes place at the present time in the MacGruder home in Washington, D.C.

General Manager: C. Edwin Knill
Company Manager: Helen Richards
Press: Harvey B. Sabinson,
Lee Solters, Ken L. Hinaman,
Edie Kean
Stage Managers: William Ross,
Bernard Pollock

° Closed March 30, 1968 after 22 performances.

Martha Swope Photos

Marco St. John, Graham Brown, Carol Cole, Rosemary Murphy, John Forsythe, Zaida Coles. Top: John Forsythe, Rosemary Murphy, Kim Hunter

51

BILTMORE THEATRE
Opened Monday, March 18, 1968.°
Losal Productions Inc. by arrangement with Oscar Lewenstein and Michael White presents:

LOOT

By Joe Orton; Director, Derek Goldby; Scenery and Lighting, William Ritman; Costumes, Patton Campbell; Song by Paul Evans and Paul Parnes.

CAST

McLeavy	Liam Redmond
Fay	Carole Shelley
Hal	Kenneth Cranham
Dennis	James Hunter
Truscott	George Rose
Meadows	Norman Barrs
Policeman	William MacAdam

STANDBYS: Truscott, McLeavy, Norman Barrs; Fay, Joan Bassie; Hal, William McAdam; Dennis, John Horn.

A Comedy in two acts. The action takes place at the present time in a room in McLeavy's house.

General Manager: Allen Whitehead
Company Manager: David Hedges
Press: Sol Jacobson, Lewis Harmon,
Ellen Levene
Stage Managers: Warren Crane,
William MacAdam

° Closed April 6, 1968 after 22 performances.

Liam Redmond, Carol Shelley. Top: James Hunter, Carole Shelley, Norman Barrs (kneeling), Kenneth Cranham, George Rose

Bert Andrews Photos

ETHEL BARRYMORE THEATRE

Opened Wednesday, March 27, 1968.°
David Merrick presents:

THE SEVEN DESCENTS OF MYRTLE

By Tennessee Williams; Director, Jose Quintero; Setting and Lighting, Jo Mielziner; Costumes, Jane Greenwood; Associate Producer, Samuel Liff; Staff Associates, Sylvia Schwartz, Suzanne Lamarre, Lynn Middleton, Juliet Taylor.

CAST

Chicken ------------------------------ Harry Guardino
Myrtle ------------------------------------ Estelle Parsons
Lot -- Brian Bedford

STANDBYS: Myrtle, Marilyn Chris; Lot, Michael Stoddard; Chicken, Don Barnett.

A Comedy-Drama in three acts. The action takes place in Lot's house on the banks of a Southern river.

General Manager: Jack Schlissel
Company Manager: Hugh McGauley
Press: Lee Solters, Harvey B. Sabinson, Robert Larkin
Stage Managers: Charles Blackwell, Michael Stoddard, Don Barnett

° Closed April 20, 1968 after 29 performances.

Martha Swope Photos

**Harry Guardino, Estelle Parsons (also top left)
Above: Brian Bedford, Estelle Parsons**

53

ALVIN THEATRE

Opened Thursday, April 4, 1968.°
Andre Goulston/Jack Farren and Stephen Mellow present:

THE EDUCATION OF H*Y*M*A*N K*A*P*L*A*N

Book, Benjamin Bernard Zavin; Based on stories by Leo Rosten; Music and Lyrics, Paul Nassau and Oscar Brand; Director, George Abbott; Settings, William and Jean Eckart; Costumes, Winn Morton; Lighting, Martin Aronstein; Musical Direction and Vocal Arrangements, Julian Stein; Orchestrations, Larry Wilcox; Dance Music Arranged by Lee Holdridge; Associate Producer, David W. Sampliner; Assistant to Producers, Vivian Farren; Dances and Musical Numbers Staged by Jaime Rogers; Production Assistant, Neil Israel; Hair Styles, Ronald DeMann.

CAST

Jimmy	Stephen Bolster
Pushcart Vendor	Dick Ensslen
Old Clothes Man	Cyril Murkin
Kathy McKenna	Donna McKechnie
Sam Pinsky	Nathaniel Frey
Reuben Plonsky	David Gold
Giovanni Pastora	Dick Latessa
Mrs. Moskowitz	Honey Sanders
Sarah Moskowitz	Susan Camber
Mr. Parkhill	Gary Krawford
Fanny Gidwitz	Maggie Task
Rose Mitnick	Barbara Minkus
Hyman Kaplan	Tom Bosley
Eileen Higby	Dorothy Emmerson
Marie Vitale	Beryl Towbin
Mrs. Mitnick	Mimi Sloan
Officer Callahan	Wally Engelhardt
Yissel Fishbein	Hal Linden
Guard	David Ellin
Judge Mahon	Rufus Smith

DANCERS: Pamela Barlow, Mickie Bier, Susan Camber, Joanne DiVito, Andrea Duda, Lee Lund, Kuniko Narai, Eileen Woliner, Takeshi Hamagaki, Tanco Inone, Pat Matera, Barry Preston, George Ramos, Steven Ross.

SINGERS: Alice Cannon, Martha Danielle, Trudy Wallace, Edward Becker, David Ellin, Jack Fletcher

UNDERSTUDIES: Hyman, Hal Linden; Rose, Alice Cannon; Yissel, Sam, David Ellin; Mrs. Mitnick, Mrs. Moskowitz, Maggie Task; Reuben, Pat Matera; Giovanni, Dick Ensslen; Parkhill, Stephen Bolster; Jimmy, Jack Fletcher; Kathy, Lee Lund; Judge, Wally Engelhardt; Callahan, Rufus Smith; Sarah, Joanne DiVito

MUSICAL NUMBERS: "Strange New World," "OOOO-EEEE," "A Dedicated Teacher," "Lieben Dich," "Loving You," "The Day I Met Your Father," "Anything Is Possible," "Spring In The City," "Old Fashioned Husband," "Julius Caesar," "I Never Felt Better In My Life," "When Will I Learn," "All American."

A Musical Comedy in 2 acts and 13 scenes. The action takes place on the Lower East Side of New York City in 1919-20.

General Manager: Norman Maibaum
Company Manager: Al Jones
Press: Harvey B. Sabinson, Lee Solters, Leo Stern
Stage Managers: Edward Preston, Edward Julien, Wally Engelhardt, Jack Fletcher

° Closed April 27, 1968 after 28 performances.

Friedman-Abeles Photos

Top Right: Gary Krawford (L), Donna McKechnie (C), Tom Bosley (R). Below: Donna McKechnie, Honey Sanders, Hal Linden, Barbara Minkus

Tom Bosley, Barbara Minkus

Opened Wednesday, April 10, 1968.°
David Black, Konrad Matthaei and Lorin
E. Price present:

GEORGE M !

Book, Michael Stewart, John and Fran Pascal; Music and Lyrics, George M. Cohan; Lyric and Musical Revision, Mary Cohan; Direction and Choreography, Joe Layton; Musical Supervision, Laurence Rosenthal; Scenery, Tom John; Costumes, Freddy Wittop; Lighting, Martin Aronstein; Musical Direction and Vocal Arrangements, Jay Blackton; Orchestrations, Philip J. Lang; Production Supervisor, Jose Vega; Hair Styles, Ronald DeMann; Original cast album on Columbia Records.

CAST

Loni Ackerman	Dog Trainer, Second Pianist, Fay Templeton's maid Rose
Jonelle Allen	Living Statue, Secretary in Cohan & Harris office
Jacqueline Alloway	Fay Templeton, Draper's Assistant, Wardrobe Lady
Karin Baker	Living Statue, Pushcart Girl
Susan Batson	First Little Girl, Mrs. Red Deer, Sharpshooter's Assistant, Little Girl with Fay Templeton
Bill Brandon	Acrobat, Boy in Pushcart
Roger Braun	Dr. Webb, E. F. Albee, Living Statue, Ben, Mayor
Danny Carroll	Louis Behman, Bell Ringer, Vendor, Fay Templeton's Manager
Gene Castle	Willie, Sharpshooter, Walt (Stage Manager)
Jerry Dodge	Jerry Cohan
Jamie Donnelly	Ethel Levey
James Dybas	Stagehand, Dog Trainer, Louie, Congressman Burkhardt, Actor
Harvey Evans	Sam Harris, Violinist, Bell Ringer
Joel Grey	George M. Cohan
Betty Ann Grove	Nellie Cohan
Patti Mariano	Second Little Girl, Acrobat
Angela Martin	Ventriloquist, Ma Templeton
John Mineo	Archie, Draper, Dockhand, Judge Anspacher, First Policeman, Man on Street
Jill O'Hara	Agnes Nolan
Bernadette Peters	Josie Cohan
Scotty Salmon	First Pianist, Acrobat, Bell Ringer, Piano Player in Cohan office
Kathie Savage	Living Statue, Pushcart Girl
Janie Sell	Madame Grimaldi, Mrs. Baker, Flamethrower's Assistant
Alan Weeks	Buck and Winger, Designer's Assistant, Sailor, Frankie
Ronald Young	Saxophonist, Flamethrower, Bell Ringer, Ship's Captain, Alderman Hailey, Accordionist, Director

UNDERSTUDIES: George M., Jerry Dodge; Josie, Patti Mariano; Jerry, Danny Carroll; Nellie, Agnes, Karin Baker; Ethel, Kathie Savage; Albee, Bill Brandon; Harris, Behman, Willie, John Mineo; Fay Templeton, Jonelle Allen; Grimaldi, Angela Martin; Director, Roger Braun; Walt, James Dybas; Swing Girl, Katherine Hull

MUSICAL NUMBERS: "Musical Moon," "Oh, You Wonderful Boy," "All Aboard For Broadway," "Musical Comedy Man," "I Was Born In Virginia," "Twentieth Century Love," "My Town," "Billie," "Push Me Along In My Pushcart," "Ring To The Name of Rose," "Popularity," "Give My Regards To Broadway," "45 Minutes From Broadway," "So Long, Mary," "Down By The Erie," "Mary," "All Our Friends," "Yankee Doodle Dandy," "Harrigan," "Nellie Kelly I Love You," "Over There," "You're A Grand Old Flag," "The City," "I'd Rather Be Right," "Dancing Our Worries Away," "The Great Easter Sunday Parade," "Hannah's A Hummer," "Barnum and Bailey Rag," "The Belle of The Barber's Ball," "American Ragtime," "All In The Wearing," "I Want To Hear A Yankee Doodle Tune."

A Musical Comedy in 2 acts and 16 scenes with prologue and epilogue. The action takes place between 1878 and 1937.

General Managers: Allentuck, Azenberg & Wolsk
Company Manager: R. Tyler Gatchell, Jr.
Press: Frank Goodman, Martin Shwartz, Abby Hirsch
Stage Managers: Tony Manzi, Lee Welling
° Still playing May 31, 1968.

Friedman-Abeles Photos

Joel Grey, above with Bernadette Peters, Betty Ann Grove, Jerry Dodge

HUDSON THEATRE

Opened Thursday, April 18, 1968.°
Zev Bufman, Abe Margolies, Edward A.
Franck present:

MIKE DOWNSTAIRS

By George Panetta; Director, Donald Driver;
Scenery, Edward Burbridge; Costumes, Hal
George; Lighting, Thomas Skelton; Music Ar-
ranged by Peter Matz; Associate Producer,
Philip Turk.

CAST

Mike	Dane Clark
Lupo	William Daprato
Joe	Leonardo Cimino
First Authority	John Tormey
Second Authority	Alan Peterson
Donna Maria	Loretta Fury
Paul	Tom Pedi
Minnie Picarella	Eleni Kiamos
Patsy	Arnold Soboloff
Sam	Richard Castellano
Josie Spero	Kay Michaels
Big Authority	Russell Baker
Priest	David Ellis
Uncle	Lloyd Harris
First Soldier	Johnny Evans
Second Soldier	Edmond Varrato

CITIZENS: Barbara Beckley, John Bentley,
Louise Clay, Michael Enserro, Roxee Graziano,
Antonia Rey, Helen G. Ross

UNDERSTUDIES: Mike, Arnold Soboloff;
Lupo, Paul, Patsy, Big Authority, John Bentley; Joe, Priest, Edmond Varrato; First &
Second Authority, Johnny Evans; Donna Maria, Antonia Rey; Sam, Uncle, Michael Enserro

A Comedy in two acts. The action takes
place on Mulberry Street, near City Hall, in
New York City.

General Manager: Jeff Britton
Company Manager: Edward H. Davis
Press: Betty Lee Hunt, Henry Luhrman
Stage Managers: William Krot,
Carol Raymont

° Closed April 20, 1968 after 4 performances.

Friedman-Abeles Photos

Leonardo Cimino, Dane Clark, Russell Baker,
Alan Peterson. Top: Leonardo Cimino, Dane
Clark, Kay Michaels, Richard Castellano

Opened Tuesday, April 23, 1968.°
Zvi Kolitz, Solomon Sagall, Abe Margolies present:

I'M SOLOMON

Book, Anne Croswell, Dan Almagor; Based on play "King Solomon and The Cobbler" by Sammy Gronemann; American Adaptation in collaboration with Zvi Kolitz; Music, Ernest Gold; Lyrics, Anne Croswell; Directed and Supervised by Michael Benthall; Settings, Rouben Ter-Arutunian; Costumes, Jane Greenwood; Lighting, Martin Aronstein; Musical Direction and Vocal Arrangements, Gershon Kingsley; Orchestrations, Hershy Kay; Special Material, David Finkle, Bill Weeden; Dance Arrangements, Dorothea Freitag; Dances and Musical Numbers Staged by Donald McKayle; Associate Producers, Philip Turk, Kalman Ginzburg; Production Assistant, Helene Spinner; Hairstylist, Frank Bianco.

CAST

Meir, the Drummer	Meir Alon
Ali, the Flutist	Al DeSio
Issac, Tavern Keeper	John Dorrin
Tavern Dancer	Sally Neal
Yoni, a Cobbler	Dick Shawn
Na'Ama, his wife	Karen Morrow
Yoel, Temple Building Supervisor	Kenneth Scott
Mago, Architect	Johnny La Motta
Lemech, a Dyer	Ed Ericksen
Aviva, a Harlot	Alice Evans
Bruria, a Harlot	Lynn Archer
Officer of the Royal Guard	Gordon Cook
Ben Hesed, Commander	Paul Reed
Princess Nofrit	Barbara Webb
F'htar, her Slave	Mary Barnett
Solomon	Dick Shawn
Bathsheba	Carmen Mathews
Ambassador	Nat Horne
Ranor	Fred Pinkard
Aide to Ranor	Garrett Morris
Rachel	Caryl Tenney
Makedah	Salome Jens

SOLOMON'S CONCUBINES: Jeri Barto, Connie Burnett, Miriam Ehrenberg, Carol Flemming, Mary Jane Houdina, Nina Janik, Carol Manning, Sally Neal, Martha Pollak, Renee Rose, Joan Tannen, Nina Trasoff, Myrna White
OTHER WIVES: Lynn Archer, Chris Callan, Jacque Dean, Alice Evans, Carol Flemming, Marsha Hastings, Mary Jane Houdina, Sherry Lambert, Carol Manning, Sally Neal, Joan Tannen

PEOPLE OF JERUSALEM, GUARDS, SLAVES, ETC. Clifford Allen, Meir Alon, Jeri Barto, Connie Burnett, Chris Callan, Al Cohen, Gordon Cook, Nikolas Dante, Jacque Dean, Esteban DeLeon, Al DeSio, John Dorrin, Miriam Ehrenberg, Ed Ericksen, Carol Flemming, Stokely Gray, Rodney Griffin, Jerry Grimes, Marsha Hastings, Nat Horne, Mary Jane Houdina, Jason Howard, Nina Janik, Sherry Lambert, Johnny La Motta, Carol Manning, Garrett Morris, Sally Neal, Keith Perry, Martha Pollak, Ken Richards, Renee Rose, Jeffrey Shawn, Clay Taliaferro, Joan Tannen, Caryl Tenney, Nina Trasoff, Kyle Weaver, Bruce Wells, Myrna White

UNDERSTUDIES: Solomon, Alfred Toigo; Na'Ama, Alice Evans; Bathsheba, Lynn Archer; Ranor, Nat Horne; Nofrit, Makedah, Carol Flemming; Aviva, Joan Tannen; Bruria, Jacque Dean; Rachel, Myrna White; Ben-Hesed, John Dorrin; F'hta, Renee Rose; Yoel, Lemech, Garrett Morris; Mago, Al Cohen; Dancer, Martha Pollak.

MUSICAL NUMBERS: "David and Bathsheba," "Hail The Son of David!," "Preposterous," "Have You Heard?," "The Citation," "In Love With A Fool," "Someone Like Me," "In Someone Else's Sandals," "The Three Riddles," "Once in 2.7 Years," "Have You Ever Been Alone With A King Before?," "Lord I Am But A Little Child," "I Am What I Am," "Something In His Eyes," "That Guilty Feeling," "Time To Let Go," "With Your Hand In My Hand."

A Musical Fable in two acts. The action takes place in various locales in and around Jerusalem from the morning of one day to noon of the next, about 100 B.C.

General Manager: Al Goldin
Company Manager: Oscar Berlin
Press: Max Eisen, Carl Samrock, Cheryl Sue Dolby
Stage Managers: Mortimer Halpern, Norman Shelly, Bert Wood

° Closed April 27, 1968 after 7 performances and 9 previews.

Carmen Mathews, Dick Shawn

Dick Shawn (C)

JOHN GOLDEN THEATRE

Opened Wednesday, April 24, 1968.*

Lyn Austin, Oliver Smith, Jay J. Cohen, and Leslie J. Stark present:

THE EXERCISE

By Lewis John Carlino; Director, Alfred Ryder; Setting, Oliver Smith; Lighting, Jean Rosenthal; Sound, Teiji Ito; Associate Producer, Ann McIntosh; Assistant to Producers, Lisa Stamm; Production Assistant, Edith M. P. Wehle.

CAST

The Actor ------------------------------- Stephen Joyce
The Actress ----------------------------- Anne Jackson
STANDBYS: Peggy Feury, Tony LoBianco

A Drama in two acts. The action takes place at the present time on an empty stage in a theatre.

General Manager: Oscar Olesen
Company Manager: James Awe
Press: Samuel Lurie, Stanley F. Kaminsky
Stage Managers: Wayne Carson, Darryl Wells

* Closed Apr. 27, 1968, after 5 performances and 10 previews.

Henry Grossman Photos

Anne Jackson, Stephen Joyce

Anne Jackson, Stephen Joyce, also above

BILTMORE THEATRE

Opened Monday, April 29, 1968.°
Michael Butler presents the Natoma Production of:

HAIR

Book and Lyrics, Gerome Ragni and James Rado; Music, Galt MacDermot; Director, Tom O'Horgan; Executive Producer, Bertrand Castelli; Dance Director, Julie Arenal; Musical Director, Galt Mac Dermot; Costumes, Nancy Potts; Scenery, Robin Wagner; Lighting, Jules Fisher; Sound Robert Kiernan; Production Assistant, Lani Ball; Production Coordinator, Cara Robin; Production Supervisor, Mike Montell; Hairpieces and Hairstyles, Wig City; Hairstylist, Roberto Vega.

CAST

Claude	James Rado
Ron	Ronald Dyson
Berger	Gerome Ragni
Woof	Steve Curry
Hud	Lamont Washington
Sheila	Lynn Kellogg
Jeanie	Sally Eaton
Dionne	Melba Moore
Crissy	Shelley Plimpton
Mother	Sally Eaton, Jonathan Kramer, Paul Jabara
Father, Principal	Robert I. Rubinsky, Suzannah Norstrand, Lamont Washington
Tourist Couple	Jonathan Kramer, Robert I. Rubinsky
Waitress	Diane Keaton
Young Recruit	Jonathan Kramer
General Grant	Paul Jabara
Abraham Lincoln	Lorri Davis
Sergeant	Donnie Burks
Parents	Diane Keaton, Robert I. Rubinsky
Standby for Claude	Seth Allen

THE TRIBE: Donnie Burks, Lorri Davis, Leata Galloway, Steve Gamet, Walter Harris, Diane Keaton, Hiram Keller, Marjorie LiPari, Emmaretta Marks, Natalie Mosco, Suzannah Norstrand, Robert I. Rubinsky

MUSICAL NUMBERS: "Aquarius," "Donna," "Hashish," "Sodomy," "Colored Spade," "Manchester," "Ain't Got No," "I Believe In Love," "Air," "Initials," "I Got Life," "Going Down," "Hair," "My Conviction," "Easy To Be Hard," "Hung," "Don't Put It Down," "Frank Mills," "Hare Krishna," "Where Do I Go," "Electric Blues," "Black Boys," White "Boys," "Walking In Space," "Abie Baby," "Prisoners In Niggertown," "What A Piece of Work Is Man," "Good Morning Starshine," "The Bed," "The Flesh Failures."

The American Tribal Love-Rock Musical in two acts.

General Manager: Richard Osorio
Company Manager: Virginia Snow
Press: Robert Ganshaw,
Michael F. Goldstein, Inc.
Stage Managers: Fred Reinglas,
Michael Maurer, Donnie Burks

° Still playing May 31, 1968.

Dagmar Photos

James Rado, Gerome Ragni

Above: (L) Lamont Washington. (R) Lynn Kellogg

BILLY ROSE THEATRE

Opened Wednesday, May 1, 1968.°
Herman Shumlin, Zev Bufman and
Raphael Silver by arrangement with Kenneth Tynan present:

SOLDIERS

By Rolf Hochhuth; Translated by Robert
D. MacDonald; Director, Clifford Williams;
Designed by Ralph Koltai; Scenery Supervision, James Riley; Costume Supervision,
Richard Anderson.

CAST

Dorland	Colin Fox
The Sculptor	Muni Seroff
Dorland's Son	Richard Monette
An Actor (Kocjan)	James Luisi
Helen MacDonald	Patricia Wheel
Churchill	John Colicos
Lord Cherwell	Joseph Shaw
General, Sir Alan Brooke	Basil Langton
General Sikorski	Eric House
Group Captain Clark	Michael Lewis
Messenger	David Thomas
Bell, Bishop of Chichester	Tony Church

UNDERSTUDIES: Cherwell, Michael Lewis;
Brooke, Dorland, Clark, Leslie Redford; Bishop,
Sculptor, David Thomas; Sikorski, Muni Seroff;
Kocjan, Messenger, Edmund Williams; Helen,
Catherine Ellis

A Drama in three acts. The action takes
place in St. Michael's Cathedral, Coventry,
England, at the dress rehearsal of a play
marking the 100th anniversary of The Geneva
Convention. The play in rehearsal takes place
in 1943.

General Manager: Diana Shumlin
Company Manager: Michael Goldreyer
Press: Joe Wolhandler Associates,
Marianne Mackay
Stage Managers: Daniel Broun,
Edmund Williams

° Closed May 19, 1968 after 21 performances
and 3 previews.

Friedman-Abeles Photos

John Colicos, also above with Joseph Shaw

BOOTH THEATRE

Opened Thursday, May 2, 1968.°
Jack Rollins presents Leonard Sillman's:

NEW FACES OF 1968

Words and Music, Ronny Graham, June Carroll, Arthur Siegel, Clark Gesner, Sam Pottle, David Axelrod, Jerry Powell, David Shire, Richard Maltby, Jr., Murray Grand, Paul Nassau, Hal Hackady, Alonzo Levister, Kenny Solms, Gail Parent, Gene P. Bissell, Carl Friberg, Fred Hellerman, Fran Minkoff, Michael McWhinney, Sydney Shaw, Michael Cohen, Tony Geiss; Sketches, Ronny Graham, Peter DeVries, William F. Brown, Kenny Solms, Gail Parent, Jack Sharkey, David Axelrod, Robert Klein, Norman Kline; Continuity and additional dialogue, William F. Brown; Entire Production Conceived and Staged by Leonard Sillman; Choreographed and Directed by Frank Wagner; Settings and Costumes, Winn Morton; Lighting, Paul Sullivan; Production Coordinator, Jacqueline Adams; Orchestrations, Lanny Meyers; Musical Direction, Ted Simons; Production Assistant, Leslie Werner; Original cast album by Warner Bros.-7 Arts.

CAST

Michael K. Allen	Madeline Kahn
Suzanne Astor	Robert Klein
Rod Barry	Joe Kyle
Gloria Bleezarde	Robert Lone
Trudy Carson	Brandon Maggart
Marilyn Child	George Ormiston
Dottie Frank	Rod Perry
Elaine Giftos	Nancie Phillips

Leonard Sillman
Standbys: Kelly Britt, F. David Halpert

PROGRAM

ACT I: "Illustrated Overture," "Definitions," "Welcome," "Opening," "Audition," "By The Sea," "Where Is The Waltz?," "A New Waltz," "Happy Landings," "The Girl In The Mirror," "The American Hamburger League," "Love Songs," "Something Big," "Love In A Tempo," "Hungry," "Luncheon Ballad," "The Underachiever," "You're The One I'm For," "Where Is Me?," "Gospel According To Jack," "Mama Doll," "Toyland"

ACT II: "Hullabaloo At Thebes," "#X9RL-220," "You Are," "Evil," "The Refund," "Prisms," "Tango," "Philosophy," "The Pile-Up," "Das Chicago Song," "Missed America," "Die Zusammenfügung," "The Girl of The Minute."

General Manager: Richard Osorio
Company Manager: Martin Cohen
Press: Sol Jacobson, Lewis Harmon
Stage Managers: Jack Timmers, Paul Sullivan, Rod Barry

° Still playing May 31, 1968.

Frank Derbas, Friedman-Abeles Photos

Top Right: Front Row: Robert Lone, Rod Barry, Michael K. Allen, Joe Kyle. 2nd: Dottie Frank, Suzanne Astor, Leonard Sillman, Trudy Carson, Elaine Giftos. 3rd: Gloria Bleezarde, Brandon Maggart, Robert Klein, Nancie Phillips. Top: Rod Perry, Marilyn Child, Madeline Kahn, **George Ormiston**

Brandon Maggart, Gloria Bleezarde, Leonard Sillman, Robert Klein. Above: (L) Madeline Kahn

61

ETHEL BARRYMORE THEATRE

Opened Saturday, May 11, 1968.°
Anamark Productions presents:

HAPPINESS IS JUST A LITTLE THING CALLED A ROLLS ROYCE

By Arthur Alsberg and Robert Fisher; Director, David Alexander; Scenery, Larry Rehling; Costumes, Ann Roth; Lighting, John Harvey; Production Assistant, Donna Gray.

CAST

Myra Bagley	Hildy Brooks
Walter Bagley	Pat Harrington
Chuck Kinsey	Marvin Lichterman
Karen Kinsey	Phoebe Dorin
Andrew McIntire	John McGiver
Phil Gorshin	Lee Bergere
Jerry Ramsey	Ray Fulmer
Sanford Rutchik	Shimen Ruskin
Andrea Clithero	Alexandra Berlin

A Comedy in two acts. The action takes place in New York in the Past, the Present, and the Future.

General Managers: Azenberg, Allentuck and Wolsk
Press: Bernard Simon
Stage Managers: Don Doherty, Joe Calvan, Simm Landres

° Closed May 11, 1968 after 1 performance and 4 previews.

Friedman-Ables, Bob Golby Photos

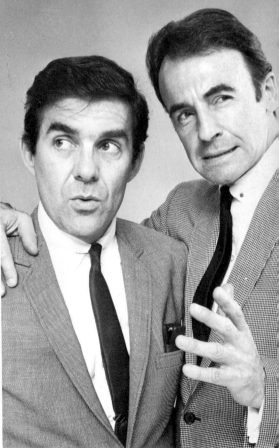

Pat Harrington, Alexandra Berlin, Hildy Brooks Above: Pat Harrington, Hildy Brooks, Marvin Lichterman, Phoebe Dorin

Pat Harrington, Lee Bergere. Above: Pat Harrington Alexandra Berlin, John McGiver

BROADHURST THEATRE

Opened Thursday, May 23, 1968.°
Edgar Lansbury presents:

THE ONLY GAME IN TOWN

By Frank D. Gilroy; Director, Barry Nelson;
Scenery, George Jenkins; Costumes, Theoni
V. Aldredge; Lighting, Jules Fisher; Incidental
Music, Dan Elliot; Produced in association with
TDJ Productions Inc.; Production Assistant,
Pat Johnston.

CAST

Fran Walker .... Tammy Grimes
Joe Grady .... Barry Nelson
Thomas Lockwood .... Leo Genn
Standby: James Karen

A Comedy in 2 acts and 9 scenes. The
action takes place two years ago and tonight
in Fran Walker's second-floor garden apartment just off the Strip in Las Vegas, Nevada.

General Manager: Joseph Beruh
Press: Samuel J. Friedman,
Jane Friedman
Stage Managers: Ben D. Kranz,
Curt Dempster

° Still playing May 31, 1968.° Opened at the
Mechanic, Baltimore, Jan. 16, 1968 with
Carolan Daniels, Richard Mulligan, and Al-
bert Paulsen, but closed for revisions after
Feb. 24, 1968 performance in Boston.

Henry Grossman Photos

Leo Genn, Tammy Grimes, Barry Nelson
Top: Barry Nelson, Tammy Grimes

HENRY MILLER'S THEATRE

Opened Tuesday, May 28, 1968.°
Arthur Cantor and Zenon R. Mocarski, Inc. present The Theatre of Genoa (Artistic Directors, Ivo Chiesa and Luigi Squarzina) in:

THE VENETIAN TWINS

By Carlo Goldoni; Director, Luigi Squarzina; Scenery and Costumes, Gianfranco Padovani; Music, Giancarlo Chiaramello; Production Associate, Henry Popkin; Production Coordinator, Gianfranco Padovani.

CAST

Dr. Balanzoni	Mario Bardella
Rosaura	Silvia Monelli
Pancrazio	Camillo Milli
Zanetta and Tonino	Alberto Lionello
Lelio	Eros Pagni
Beatrice	Lucilla Morlacchi
Florindo	Giovanni DeLellis
Brighella	Omero Antonutti
Colombina	Margherita Guzzinati
Arlecchino	Giancarlo Zanetti
Tiburzio	Luigi Carubbi
Chief Constable	Enrico Ardizzone
Constables	Marcello Aste, Vittorio Melloni
Porter	Gianni Fenzi
Footman	Marcello Aste

A Comedy in three acts. The action takes place in Verona in 1754.

General Manager: Richard Seader
Press: Arthur Solomon
Stage Managers: Giorgio Catani,
William Chambers

° Still playing May 31, 1968.°

Camillo Milli, Alberto Lionello
Top: Silvia Monelli, Alberto Lionello

ASSOCIATION OF PRODUCING ARTISTS

LYCEUM THEATRE

Opened Thursday, November 30, 1967.°
APA-Phoenix (a project of Theatre Inc.)
T. Edward Hambleton, Managing Director, presents the APA Repertory Company (Ellis Rabb, Artistic Director) in:

PANTAGLEIZE

By Michel de Ghelderode; Directed by John Houseman and Ellis Rabb; Assistant, Jack O'Brien; Scenery and Lighting, James Tilton; Costumes, Nancy Potts; Music, Bob James; Incidental Lyrics, Jack O'Brien.

CAST

Pantagleize	Ellis Raab
Bamboola	Nat Simmons
Innocenti	Sydney Walker
A Poet	Nicholas Martin
Policeman	Richard Easton
Anarchist	Keene Curtis
Rachel Silbershatz	Patricia Conolly
General MacBoom	Joseph Bird
Bank Managers	Kermit Brown, George Addis
First Soldier	George Pentecost
Second Soldier	James Whittle
Distinguished Counsel	Richard Woods
Generalissimo	Gordon Gould
An Officer	Alan Fudge

SOLDIERS, WAITERS, JURYMEN: George Addis, Dan Bly, Kermit Brown, Alan Fudge, Reuben Greene, Gil Michaels, Gastone Rossilli.

A Farce to make you sad presented in two parts. The action takes place in a city on the eve of one war and the morrow of another.

General Manager: Norman Kean
Press: Ben Kornzweig, Reginald Denenholz
Stage Managers: George Darveris, Nikos Kafkalis

° Presented in repertory and still playing May 31, 1968.

Graphic House, Van Williams Photos

Patricia Conolly, Ellis Rabb. Top Right: Keene Curtis, Nat Simmons, Nicholas Martin, Sydney Walker

Keene Curtis, Nat Simmons, Ellis Rabb, Sydney Walker. Above: Joseph Bird, Richard Woods, Gordon Gould

LYCEUM THEATRE

Opened Tuesday, December 5, 1967.°
APA-Phoenix (a project of Theatre Inc.)
T. Edward Hambleton, Managing Director, presents the APA Repertory Company (Ellis Rabb, Artistic Director) in:

THE SHOW-OFF

By George Kelly; Director, Stephen Porter; Scenery and Lighting, James Tilton; Costumes, Nancy Potts.

CAST

Clara	Gwyda DonHowe
Mrs. Fisher	Helen Hayes
Amy	Pamela Payton-Wright
Frank Hyland	Alan Fudge
Mr. Fisher	Joseph Bird
Joe	George Pentecost
Aubrey Piper	Clayton Corzatte
Mr. Gill	James Greene
Mr. Rodgers	Gordon Gould

A Comedy in three acts. The action takes place in the home of the Fisher family in North Philadelphia in 1924.

General Manager: Norman Kean
Press: Ben Kornzweig, Reginald Denenholz
Stage Managers: R. Derek Swire,
Harley Hackett

° Presented in repertory and still playing May 31, 1968. Original production opened at The Playhouse on Feb. 5, 1924 with Helen Lowell, Louis John Bartels, and Lee Tracy and ran for 571 performances. It was revived Dec. 12, 1932 at the Hudson and ran for 119 performances with Jean Adair, and Raymond Walburn.

Van Williams Photos

Joseph Bird, Helen Hayes, George Pentecost
Above: Helen Hayes, Gwyda DonHowe

Pamela Payton-Wright, Clayton Corzatte
Top Left: Helen Hayes, Clayton Corzatte

LYCEUM THEATRE

Opened Tuesday, January 9, 1968.°
APA-Phoenix (a project of Theatre Inc.)
T. Edward Hambleton, Managing Director, presents the APA Repertory Company
(Ellis Rabb, Artistic Director) in:

EXIT THE KING

By Eugene Ionesco; Translated by Donald Watson; Director, Ellis Rabb; Scenery, Rouben Ter-Arutunian; Costumes, Nancy Potts; Lighting, James Tilton; Music, Conrad Susa.

CAST

Berenger the First .... Richard Easton
Queen Marguerite .... Eva Le Gallienne
Queen Marie .... Patricia Conolly
The Doctor .... Richard Woods
Juliette .... Pamela Payton-Wright
The Guard .... Clayton Corzatte

A Drama presented without intermission.
Press: Ben Kornzweig, Reginald Denenholz
Stage Managers: R. Derek Swire,
Harley Hackett

° Presented in repertory and still playing May 31, 1968.

Van Williams Photos

Richard Woods, Richard Easton, Patricia Conolly, Pamela Payton-Wright
Top: Eva Le Gallienne, Richard Easton

LYCEUM THEATRE

Opened Tuesday, March 19, 1968.°
APA-Phoenix (a project of Theatre Inc.)
T. Edward Hambleton, Managing Director, presents the APA Repertory Company (Ellis Rabb, Artistic Director) in:

THE CHERRY ORCHARD

By Anton Chekov; Translated and Directed by Eva LeGallienne; Assistant Director, Jack O'Brien; Scenery and Lighting, James Tilton; Costumes, Nancy Potts; Music Supervision, Conrad Susa; Wigs, Dorman Allison.

CAST

Lopahin (Yermolay Alexeyevitch)	Donald Moffat
Dunyasha	Patricia Conolly
Epihodov (Semyon Pantaleyevitch)	Keene Curtis
Firs	Clayton Corzatte
Charlotta Ivanovna	Nancy Walker
Semyonov-Pishtchik	Sidney Walker
Anya	Pamela Payton-Wright
Madame Ranevskaya	Uta Hagen
Gaev (Leonid Andreyevitch)	Richard Woods
Varya (Varvara Mihailovna)	Betty Miller
Yasha	George Pentecost
Trofimov (Pyotr Sergeyvitch)	Richard Easton
A Tramp	Alan Fudge
Maid	Jennifer Harmon
Station Master	Kermit Brown
Post Office Clerk	Michael Durrell
Servants	Kermit Brown, Harley Hackett
Visitors	Alan Fudge, Harley Hackett, Nikos Kafkalis. Etain O'Malley, James Whittle

A Drama in 2 acts and 4 scenes. The action takes place on the estate of Madame Ranevskaya.

Press; Ben Kornzweig, Reginald Denenholz
Stage Managers: George Darveris, Dan Bly, Harley Hackett

° Presented in repertory and still playing May 31, 1968.

Van Williams Photos

George Pentecost, Patricia Conolly. Above: Donald Moffat, Betty Miller, Uta Hagen

Uta Hagen, Clayton Corzatte. Top: Donald Moffat, Nancy Walker, Uta Hagen

ST. JAMES THEATRE

Opened Thursday, January 16, 1964.°
David Merrick presents:

HELLO, DOLLY!

Book, Michael Stewart; Based on play "The Matchmaker" by Thornton Wilder; Music and Lyrics, Jerry Herman; Director-Choreographer, Gower Champion; Settings, Oliver Smith; Costumes, Freddy Wittop; Lighting, Jean Rosenthal; Musical Direction, Dance and Incidental Music Arrangements, Peter Howard; Orchestrations, Philip J. Lang; Vocal Arrangements, Shepard Coleman; A David Merrick and Champion-Five Inc. Production; Special Assistant, Marge Champion; Staff Associate, Sylvia Schwartz; Original cast album by RCA Victor Records.

CAST

Mrs. Dolly Gallagher Levi	Betty Grable†1
Ernestina	Patricia Sauers
Ambrose Kemper	Richard Hermany†2
Horse	Patti Pappathatos†3, Elisa DeMarko
Horace Vandergelder	Max Showalter
Ermengarde	Alice Playten†4
Cornelius Hackl	Will Mackenzie†5
Barnaby Tucker	John Mineo†6
Irene Molloy	June Helmers
Minnie Fay	Alix Elias†7
Mrs. Rose	Yolanda Poropat
Rudolph	Dan Merriman
Court Clerk	Keith Kaldenberg
Judge	Gordon Connell

TOWNSPEOPLE, WAITERS: Linda Bonem, Eileen Casey, Joyce Dahl, Elisa DeMarko, Caryl Hinchee, Debra Lyman, Kay Oslin, Janice Painchaud, Yolanda Poropat, Bonnie Schon, Bettiane Shumska, Mary Ann Snow, Pat Trott, George Blackwell, Wayne Boyd, Dick Crowley, Wayne Dugger, David Evans, Tony Falco, Gene Gebauer, Ben Gillespie, Jerry Gotham, Joe Helms, Jim Hovis, Scott Hunter, Keith Kaldenberg, J. David Kirby, Joe McGrath, Ed Mastin, Michael Podwal, Bob Remick

UNDERSTUDIES: Dolly, Bibi Osterwald; Horace, George Blackwell, Gordon Connell; Hackl, Gene Gebauer, Richard Hermany; Irene, Joyce Dahl, Mary Ann Snow; Minnie, Bonnie Schon; Barnaby, Joe Helms, J. David Kirby; Kemper, Gene Gebauer, David Evans; Ernestina, Yolanda Poropat; Mrs. Rose, Ellie Rogers; Ermengarde, Debra Lyman; Judge, Keith Kaldenberg, Ed Mastin

MUSICAL NUMBERS: "I Put My Hand In," "It Takes A Woman," "Put On Your Sunday Clothes," "Ribbons Down My Back," "Motherhood," "Dancing," "Before The Parade Passes By," "Elegance," "Waiters' Gallop," "Hello, Dolly!," "It Only Takes A Moment," "So Long, Dearie."

A Musical in 2 acts and 15 scenes. The action takes place in the past in Yonkers and Manhattan.

General Manager: Jack Schlissel
Press: Lee Solters, Harvey B. Sabinson, David Powers
Stage Managers: Frank Dudley, Tony Manzi

° Closed Nov. 9, 1967 for opening of Pearl Bailey company.
For original cast, see THEATRE WORLD, Vol. 20.

† Succeeded by: 1. Bibi Osterwald for the last 4 performances before the Pearl Bailey company opened, 2. David Evans, 3. Debra Lyman, 4. Andrea Bell, 5. Richard Hermany, 6. Harvey Evans, 7. Leland Palmer.

Friedman-Abeles Photos

Betty Grable, also top center with Max Showalter

IMPERIAL THEATRE

Opened Tuesday, September 22, 1964.°
(Moved Feb. 27, 1967 to Majestic)
Harold Prince presents:

FIDDLER ON THE ROOF

Book, Joseph Stein; Based on Sholom Aleicheim's stories; Music, Jerry Bock; Lyrics, Sheldon Harnick; Direction and Choreography, Jerome Robbins; Settings, Boris Aronson; Costumes, Patricia Zipprodt; Lighting, Jean Rosenthal; Orchestrations, Don Walker; Musical Direction and Vocal Arrangements, Milton Greene; Dance Music Arrangements, Betty Walberg; Hairstylist, D. Rusty Bonaccorso; Original cast album by RCA Victor Records.

CAST

Tevye	Harry Goz
Golde	Maria Karnilova[1]
Tzeitel	Bette Midler
Hodel	Mimi Turque
Chava	Tanya Everett
Shprintze	Peggy Longo
Bielke	Leslie Silvia
Yente	Florence Stanley
Motel	David Garfield
Perchik	Gordon Gray[2]
Lazar Wolf	Paul Marin[3]
Mordcha	Zvee Scooler
Rabbi	Gluck Sandor
Mendel	Larry Ross
Avram	Dutch Miller[4]
Nachum	David Masters
Grandma Tzeitel	Duane Bodin[5]
Fruma-Sarah	Carol Sawyer[6]
Constable	Joseph Sullivan
Fyedka	Don Atkinson
Shandel	Helen Verbit
The Fiddler	Ken LeRoy

THE VILLAGERS: Bagel Man, John C. Attle; Streetsweeper, Marc Scott; Fishmonger, Lorenzo Bianco; Seltzer Man, Ben Gillespie; Surcha, Sarah Felcher; Woodsman, Tony Gardell; Potseller, Victor Pieran; Grocer, Ross Gifford; Baker, Dan Jasinsky; Knifeseller, Thom Koutsoukos; Fredel, Marta Heflin; Bluma, Jan Myers; Berille, Adrienne Barbeau; Mirala, Charlet Oberley; Sima, Judith Doren; Rivka, Ann Tell; Cobbler, Del Franklin; Anya, Susan Feldon; Hatmaker, Mel Auston; Vladimir, Frank Coppola; Sasha, Robert Berdeen.

UNDERSTUDIES: Tevye, Lazor, Joe Cusanelli; Golde, Yente, Helen Verbit; Tzeitel, Ann C. Davies; Hodel, Adrienne Barbeau; Chava, Peggy Longo; Perchik, Thom Koutsoukos; Shprintze, Bielke, Fruma, Judith Doren; Rabbi, Avram, David Masters; Motel, Nachum, John C. Attle; Constable, Ross Gifford; Mendel, Dan Jasinsky; Mordcha, Thom Koutsoukos; Grandma, Marta Heflin; Fiddler, Marc Scott; Fyedka, Robert Berdeen; Shandel, Charlet Oberley

MUSICAL NUMBERS: "Tradition," "Matchmaker, Matchmaker," "If I Were A Rich Man," "Sabbath Prayer," "To Life," "Miracles of Miracles," "The Tailor," "Sunrise, Sunset," "Bottle Dance," "Wedding Dance," "Now I Have Everything," "Do You Love Me?," "I Just Heard," "Far From The Home I Love," "Anatevka," "Epilogue."

A Musical in two acts. The action takes place in Anatevka, a village in Russia in 1905 on the eve of the revolutionary period.

General Manager: Carl Fisher
Company Manager: Clarence Jacobson
Press: Sol Jacobson, Lewis Harmon
Stage Managers: Ruth Mitchell, Edmund Baylies, Edward Preston

° Still playing May 31, 1968. For original cast see THEATRE WORLD, Vol. 21.

† Succeeded by: 1. Martha Schlamme during vacation, 2. Richard Morse, 3. Boris Aplon, 4. Joe Cusanelli, 5. Jan Myers, 6. Ann C. Davies.

Friedman-Abeles Photos

70 Harry Goz (also above), Maria Karnilova, Bette Midler, Mimi Turque, Tanya Everett, Gordon Gray, Peggy Longo, David Garfield Leslie Silvia

Top Left: Ken LeRoy, Leslie Silvia, Harry Goz
Maria Karnilova, Mimi Turque

urence Guittard, Eleanore Knapp, Robert Rounseville,
ane Barton, Irving Jacobson, David Atkinson (also top)
Above: Bernice Massi

ANTA WASHINGTON SQUARE
THEATRE
Opened Monday, November 22, 1965.°
(Moved to Martin Beck March 19, 1968)
Albert W. Selden and Hal James present:

MAN OF LA MANCHA

Book, Dale Wasserman; Music, Mitch Leigh.
Lyrics, Joe Darion; Book and Musical Staging,
Albert Marre; Choreography, Jack Cole; Set-
tings and Lighting, Howard Bay; Costumes,
Howard Bay, Patton Campbell; Musical Direc-
tion and Dance Arrangements, Neil Warner;
Musical Arrangements, Music Makers, Inc.;
Hairstylist, Charles LoPresto; Technical Ad-
viser, John Higgins; Production Assistant,
Dwight Frye; An ANTA-Goodspeed Presen-
tation; Original cast album by Kapp Records.

CAST

Don Quixote (Cervantes)	Jose Ferrer†1
Sancho	Irving Jacobson
Aldonza	Marian Marlowe†2
Aldonza (matinees)	Patricia Marand†3
Innkeeper	Wilbur Evans†4
Padre	Robert Rounseville
Dr. Carrasco	David Atkinson†5
Antonia	Dell Brownlee†6
Barber	Taylor Reed†7
Pedro, Head Muleteer	Shev Rodgers†8
Anselmo	Ted Forlow
Housekeeper	Eleanore Knapp
Jose	Will Carter
Juan	John Aristides†9
Paco	Antony De Vecchi†10
Tenorio	Carlos Macri
Romero	Louis Criscuola
Horses	Antony De Vecchi†10, Will Carter
Maria	Marceline Decker†11
Fermina	Gerrianne Raphael†12
Captain of The Inquisition	Renato Cibelli
Guitarist	Karl Herreshoff

GUARDS AND MEN OF THE INQUISITION:
Ray Dash, Jonathan Fox, Charles Leipart,
John Fields, Robert Cromwell

UNDERSTUDIES: Quixote, Laurence Guit-
tard, Renato Cibelli; Sancho, Louis Criscuola;
Aldonza, Marcia Gilford; Innkeeper, Bruce
MacKay, Renato Cibelli; Padre, Ralph Farn-
worth; Carrasco, Pedro, Renato Cibelli; Barber,
Louis Criscuola, Ted Forlow; Antonia, Mar-
cia Gilford, Janet Gaylord; Maria, Fermina,
Janet Gaylord; Housekeeper, Rita Metzger;
Captain, Ray Dash

MUSICAL NUMBERS: "Man Of La Mancha,"
"It's All The Same," "Dulcinea," "I'm Only
Thinking Of Him," "I Really Like Him,"
"What Does He Want Of Me?," "Little
Bird, Little Bird," "Barber's Song," "Golden
Helmet of Mambrino," "To Each His Dul-
cinet," "The Quest" (The Impossible Dream),
"The Combat," "The Dubbing," "The Ab-
duction," "Moorish Dance," "Aldonza," "The
Knight Of The Mirrors," "A Little Gossip,"
"The Psalm."

A Musical Play suggested by the life and
works of Miguel de Cervantes y Saavedra,
and presented without intermission. All the
characters in the play are imprisoned in a
dungeon in Seville at the end of the six-
teenth century. The entire action takes place
there and in various other places in the imagin-
ation of Cervantes.

General Manager: Walter Fried
Company Manager: Gino Giglio
Press: Merle Debuskey, Violet Welles,
Faith Geer
Stage Managers: Marnel Sumner,
Michael Turque, Renato Cibelli,
Alfred Leberfeld

° Still playing May 31, 1968. For original
NY production, see THEATRE WORLD, Vol.
22.

† Succeeded by: 1. David Atkinson, Hal Hol-
brook during vacation, 2. Bernice Massi, 3.
Carolyn Maye, 4. Ray Middleton, 5. Lau-
rence Guittard, 6. Marcia Gilford, Dianne
Barton, 7. Howard Girven, 8. Bruce MacKay,
9. Mark Ross, 10. Bill Stanton, 11. Rita
Metzger, 12. Marcia Gilford, 13. Stephen
Sahlein.

Friedman-Abeles Photos

ROYALE THEATRE

Opened Wednesday, December 8, 1965.°
David Merrick presents:

CACTUS FLOWER

By Abe Burrows; Based on Play by Pierre
Barillet and Jean Pierre Gredy; Director, Abe
Burrows; Scenic Production, Oliver Smith; Costumes, Theoni V. Aldredge; Lighting, Martin
Aronstein; Associate Producer, Samuel Liff;
Staff Associates, Sylvia Schwartz, Lynn Middleton; Produced in association with Beresford
Productions Ltd.

CAST

Toni	Ethelyne Dunfee†1
Igor	Burt Brinckerhoff†2
Stephanie	Lauren Bacall†3
Mrs. Durant	Diana Douglas†4
Julian	Barry Nelson†5
Harvey	Robert Moore†6
Senor Sanchez	Arny Freeman
Music Lover	Rick Lenz†7
Botticelli's Springtime	Marjorie Battles†8
Waiter	Rick Lenz†7

UNDERSTUDIES: Stephanie, Joan Eastman;
Julian, Donald Barton; Toni, Marsha Mason;
Igor, Michael Norell.

A Comedy in 2 acts and 15 scenes.
The action takes place at the present time in
uptown and downtown Manhattan.

General Manager: Jack Schlissel
Company Manager: Vince McKnight
Press: Harvey B. Sabinson, Lee Solters,
Bob Ullman, Edith Kean
Stage Managers: May Muth,
Geoffrey Johnson, Donald Barton,
Michael Norell

° Still playing May 31, 1968. For original
cast, see THEATRE WORLD, Vol. 22.

† Succeeded by: 1. Lee Lawson, Skye Aubrey,
2. Rich Lenz, 3. Betsy Palmer, 4. Joan
Eastman, 5. Lloyd Bridges, 6. William Bogert,
7. Michael Norell, 8. Betsy Durkin, Marsha
Mason.

Friedman-Abeles Photos

Arny Freeman, Betsy Palmer

Betsy Palmer, William Bogert
Top: Lloyd Bridges, Betsy Palmer

WINTER GARDEN

Opened Tuesday, May 24, 1966.°
Fryer, Carr and Harris present:

MAME

Book, Jerome Lawrence and Robert E. Lee; Music and Lyrics, Jerry Herman; Based on Novel "Auntie Mame" by Patrick Dennis, and Play by Jerome Lawrence and Robert E. Lee; Director, Gene Saks; Dances and Musical Numbers Staged by Onna White; Settings, William and Jean Eckart; Costumes, Robert Mackintosh; Lighting, Tharon Musser; Musical Direction and Vocal Arrangements, Donald Pippin; Orchestrations, Philip J. Lang; Dance Music Arranged by Roger Adams; Hairstylist, Ronald DeMann; Associate Producer, John Bowab; Production Assistants, Maxine Fox, Danny Banks; Original cast album by Columbia Records.

CAST

Patrick Dennis, age 10	Stuart Getz†1
Agnes Gooch	Jane Connell†2
Vera Charles	Anne Francine†3
Mame Dennis	Angela Lansbury†4
Ralph Devine	Ron Young†5
Bishop	Jack Davison†6
M. Lindsay Woolsey	Ray MacDonnell
Ito	Sab Shimono†7
Doorman	Art Matthews
Elevator Boy	Stan Page
Messenger	Gene Kelton
Dwight Babcock	Willard Waterman†8
Art Model	Jo Tract
Dance Teacher	Johanna Douglas
Leading Man	Jack Davison†6
Stage Manager	Art Matthews
Madame Branislowski	Charlotte Jones†9
Gregor	John Taliaferro
Beauregard Jackson Pickett Burnside	Charles Braswell†10
Uncle Jeff	Clifford Fearl
Cousin Fan	Ruth Ramsey†11
Sally Cato	Margaret Hall†12
Mother Burnside	Charlotte Jones†9
Patrick Dennis (19-29)	Jerry Lanning†13
Junior Babcock	Tommy Karaty†14
Mrs. Upson	Johanna Douglas
Mr. Upson	John C. Becher
Gloria Upson	Laurie Franks†15
Pegeen Ryan	Diane Coupé
Peter Dennis	Michael Maitland†16

MAME'S FRIENDS: Sean Allan, Diana Baffa, Henry Brunjes, Pat Cummings, Casper Roos, Robert Fitch, Luigi Gasparinetti, Jerri Harris, Gene Kelton, Diane Blair, Art Matthews, Stan Page, Roger Allan Raby, Susan Walther, Carol Richards, Betty Rosebrock, Belle Shalom, John Taliaferro, Jo Tract, Eleonore Treiber, Merrill Leighton, Kathy Wilson, Jerry Wyatt.

UNDERSTUDIES: Mame, Sheila Smith, Agnes, Laurie Franks; Fan, Merrill Elighton; Babcock, Upson, Clifford Fearl; Beau, Art Matthews; Older Patrick, Sean Allan; Sally, Madame, Jo Tract; Woolsey, Gregor, Casper Roos; Ito, Eleonore Treiber; Gloria, Pegeen, Betty Rosebrock; Jeff, Stage Manager, Stan Page; Junior, Pat Cummings; Younger Patrick, Danny Show

MUSICAL NUMBERS: "St. Bridget," "It's Today," "Open A New Window," "The Man In The Moon," "My Best Girl," "We Need A Little Christmas," "The Fox Hunt," "Mame," "Bosom Buddies," "Gooch's Song," "That's How Young I Feel," "If He Walked Into My Life Today."

A Musical in 2 acts and 16 scenes. The action takes place between 1928 and 1946 in Mame's Beekman Place apartment in New York, and wherever she becomes involved.

General Manager: Joseph P. Harris
Company Manager: Richard Grayson
Press: David Lipsky, Lisa Lipsky, Marian Graham
Stage Managers: Terry Little, Ralph Linn, Stan Page, Nancy Lynch

° Still playing May 31, 1968. For original cast, see THEATRE WORLD, Vol. 22.
† Succeeded by: 1. David Manning, 2. Helen Gallagher, 3. Audrey Christie, 4. Celeste Holm during vacation, Janis Paige, 5. Henry Brunjes, 6. Casper Roos, 7. Tom Matsusaka, 8. Ed Herlihy, 9. Ruth Jaraslow, 10. Randy Phillips, 11. Laurie Franks, 12. Sheila Smith, 13. Joseph Gallison, David Chaney, 14. David Chaney, Roger Allan Raby, 15. Susan Walther, 16. Danny Snow.

Friedman-Abeles Photos

Ed Herlihy, David Manning. Above: David Chaney, John C. Becher, Johanna Douglas, Susan Walther Top: David Manning, Janis Paige

73

BROADHURST THEATRE

Opened Sunday. November 20, 1966.°
(Moved March 7, 1967 to Imperial)
Harold Prince in association with Ruth
Mitchell presents:

CABARET

Book, Joe Masteroff; Based on Play by John
Van Druten and Stories by Christopher Isher-
wood; Music, John Kander; Lyrics, Fred Ebb;
Director, Harold Prince; Dances and Cabaret
Numbers, Ronald Field; Scenery, Boris Aronson;
Costumes, Patricia Zipprodt; Lighting, Jean
Rosenthal; Musical Direction, Harold Hastings;
Orchestrations, Don Walker; Dance Arrange-
ments, David Baker; Hairstylist, D. Rusty
Bonaccorso; Original cast album by Columbia
Records.

CAST

Master of Ceremonies	Joel Grey†1
Clifford Bradshaw	Bert Convy†2
Ernst Ludwig	Edward Winter†3
Custom Official	Howard Kahl
Fraulein Schneider	Lotte Lenya†4
Herr Schultz	Jack Gilford
Fraulein Kost	Peg Murray†5
Telephone Girl	Tresha Kelly
Kit Kat Klub Kittens	Maryann Burns,

Janice Mink, Nancy Powers, Viola Smith

Maitre D'	Frank Bouley
Max	John Herbert
Bartender	Ray Baron
Sally Bowles	Jill Haworth†6
Two Ladies	Mary Ehara, Rita O'Connor
German Sailors	Bruce Becker†7,

Steven Boockvor, Roger Briant,
Edward Nolfi

Frau Wendel	Mara Landi
Herr Wendel	Eugene Morgan
Herr Erdmann	Sol Frieder
Frau Kruger	Miriam Lehmann-Haupt
Maria	Pat Gosling
Lulu	Lynn Winn†8
Rosie	Bonnie Walker†9
Fritzie	Marianne Selbert
Texas	Kathie Dalton
Frenchie	Barbara Alston
Marlene	Carol Berea
Hulda	Bonnie Walker
Bobby	Jere Admire
Victor	Bert Michaels
Greta	Jayme Mylroie
Felix	Robert Sharp

UNDERSTUDIES: Sally, Penny Fuller;
Schultz, Sol Frieder; Bradshaw, George Rein-
holt; Schneider, Peggy Murray; M.C., Bert
Michaels; Kost, Mara Landi; Ludwig, John
Herbert

MUSICAL NUMBERS: "Willkommen," "So
What?," "Don't Tell Mama," "Telephone
Song," "Perfectly Marvelous," "Two Ladies,"
"It Couldn't Please Me More," "Tomorrow
Belongs To Me," "Why Should I Wake Up?,"
"Money Song," "Married," "Meeskite," "If
You Could See Her," "What Would You Do,"
"Cabaret."

A Musical in two acts. The action takes
place in Berlin, Germany before the start of
the Third Reich in 1929-30.

General Manager: Carl Fisher
Company Manager: Warren O'Hara
Press: Mary Bryant, Leslie Coven
Stage Managers: Ruth Mitchell,
James Bronson, Ed Aldridge

° Still playing May 31, 1968. For original
cast, see THEATRE World, Vol. 23.

† Succeeded by: 1. Martin Ross, 2. John Cunningham, 3. George Reinholt, 4. during vacation by Signe Hasso, Peg Murray, Despo,
5. Mara Landi during vacation, 6. Penny
Fuller during vacation, 7. Ray Chabeau,
Curtis Hood, 8. Susanne Carroll, 9. Sandra
Brewer.

Friedman-Abeles Photos

**Top Left: Bert Convy, George Reinholt,
Jill Haworth**

Lotte Lenya, Peg Murray. Above: Martin Ross (C)

Opened Monday, March 13, 1967.°
(Moved to Broadhurst Monday, June 24, 1968)
Jack Farren and Gilbert Cates present:

YOU KNOW I CAN'T HEAR YOU WHEN THE WATER'S RUNNING

By Robert Anderson; Director, Alan Schneider; Scenery, Ed Wittstein; Costumes, Theoni V. Aldredge; Lighting, Jules Fisher; Production Assistant, Vivian Farren.

CAST

"The Shock Of Recognition'

Jack Barnstable .... George Grizzard†1
Herb Miller .... Joe Silver†2
Dorothy .... Melinda Dillon†3
Richard Pawling .... Martin Balsam†4

The action takes place at the present time in a producer's office.

"The Footsteps Of Doves"

Salesman .... George Grizzard†1
Harriet .... Eileen Heckart†5
George .... Martin Balsam†4
Jill .... Melinda Dillon†3

The action takes place at the present time in a basement showroom of a bedding store.

"I'll Be Home For Christmas"

Chuck .... Martin Balsam†4
Edith .... Eileen Heckart†5
Clarice .... Melinda Dillon†3

The action takes place at the present time in their apartment living room and kitchen.

"I'm Herbert"

Herbert .... George Grizzard†1
Muriel .... Eileen Heckart†5

STANDBYS: Frances Sternhagen, Jeremiah Morris, Robert Darnell, Linda Selman

The action takes place at the present time on a side porch

General Manager: Robert Kamlot
Company Manager: Maurice Schaded
Press: Lee Solters, Harvey B. Sabinson, Harry Nigro, Muffy Newman
Stage Managers: Martin Gold, Robert Darnell, Jeremiah Morris

° Still playing May 31, 1968. For original production, see THEATRE WORLD, Vol. 23.

† Succeeded by: 1. William Redfield, 2. Jeremiah Morris for 1 week, 3. Kathleen Dabney for vacation, Linda Selman, 4. Joe Silver for 1 week, Larry Blyden, 5. Irene Dailey. Martin Balsam was awarded a "Tony" as best actor for his performance in this production.

Friedman-Abeles Photos

Top Left: Larry Blyden, Irene Dailey in "I'll Be Home For Christmas" Center: Larry Blyden, Irene Dailey, William Redfield

rene Dailey, William Redfield in "I'm Herbert"

Carol Lawrence, Gordon MacRae

FORTY-SIXTH STREET THEATRE
Opened Monday, December 5, 1966.°
David Merrick presents:

I DO! I DO!

Book and Lyrics, Tom Jones; Based on play "The Fourposter" by Jan de Hartog; Music, Harvey Schmidt; Scenic Production, Oliver Smith; Costumes, Freddy Wittop; Lighting, Jean Rosenthal; Director, Gower Champion; Musical Direction, John Lesko; Orchestrations, Philip J. Lang; Production Supervisor, Lucia Victor; Staff Associates, Sylvia Schwarz, Lynn Middleton, Juliet Taylor; Hairstylist, Vincent J. Nasso; At the pianos, Woody Kessler and Jack Holmes; A David Merrick and Champion-Six Inc. Production; Original cast album by RCA Victor Records.

CAST

She (Agnes) .... Mary Martin†1
He (Michael) .... Robert Preston†2
STANDBYS: Dran Hamilton, Stephen Douglass

MUSICAL NUMBERS: "Prologue," "All The Dearly Beloved," "Together Forever," "I Do! I Do!," "Good Night," "I Love My Wife," "Something Has Happened," "My Cup Runneth Over," "Love Isn't Everything," "Nobody's Perfect," "A Well Known Fact," "Flaming Agnes," "The Honeymoon Is Over," "Where Are The Snows," "When The Kids Get Married," "Another Wedding," "The Father of The Bride," "What Is A Woman?," "Someone Needs Me," "Roll Up The Ribbons," "This House."

A Musical in two acts. The action takes place in a bedroom and covers fifty years of a marriage, beginning just before the turn of the century.

General Manager: Jack Schlissel
Company Manager: Richard Highley
Press: Harvey B. Sabinson,
Lee Solters, Jay Russell
Stage Managers: Wade Miller,
Henry Sutton, Robert Vandergriff

° Still playing May 31, 1968. For original production, see THEATRE WORLD, Vol. 23.

† Succeeded by: 1. Carol Lawrence, 2. Gordon MacRae.

Friedman-Abeles Photos

BROADWAY PRODUCTIONS FROM OTHER SEASONS THAT CLOSED DURING THIS SEASON

Title	Opened	Closed	Performances
Barefoot In The Park	Oct. 23, 1963	June 25, 1967	1532
Funny	Mar. 26, 1964	July 1, 1967	1348
The Odd Couple	Mar. 10, 1965	July 2, 1967	966
Sweet Charity	Jan. 29, 1966	July 15, 1967	608
Don't Drink The Water	Nov. 17, 1966	Apr. 20, 1968	598
The Apple Tree	Oct. 18, 1966	Nov. 25, 1967	463
Black Comedy	Feb. 12, 1967	Dec. 2, 1967	338
The Homecoming	Jan. 5, 1967	Oct. 14, 1967	325
Illya, Darling	Apr. 11, 1967	Jan. 13, 1968	320
Hallelujah, Baby!	Apr. 26, 1967	Jan. 13, 1968	293
Star Spangled Girl	Dec. 21, 1966	Aug. 5, 1967	262
APA in repertory	Nov. 21, 1966	June 17, 1967	218
Galileo (Lincoln Center)	Apr. 13, 1967	June 17, 1967	76
Wonderful Town (City Center)	May 17, 1967	June 4, 1967	23

NEW YORK STATE THEATER

Opened Monday, June 12, 1967.°
Music Theater of Lincoln Center,
Richard Rodgers, President and Producing Director, presents:

SOUTH PACIFIC

Music, Richard Rodgers; Lyrics, Oscar Hammerstein 2nd; Book, Oscar Hammerstein 2nd and Joshua Logan; Adapted from "Tales of The South Pacific" by James A. Michener; Director, Joe Layton; Scenery and Costumes, Fred Voelpel; Lighting, Jules Fisher; Orchestrations, Robert Russell Bennett; Musical Director, Jonathan Anderson; Cast Album by Columbia Records.

CAST

Ngana	Dana Shimizu
Jerome	Keenan Shimizu
Henry	Robert Ito
Ensign Nellie Forbush	Florence Henderson
Emile de Becque	Giorgio Tozzi
Bloody Mary	Irene Byatt
Abner	Judd Jones
Stewpot	Brad Sullivan
Luther Billis	David Doyle
Professor	Mickey Karm
Lt. Joseph Cable	Justin McDonough
Capt. George Brackett	Lyle Talbot
Cmdr. William Harbison	Bob Monroe
Yeoman Herbert Quale	Ted Story
Sgt. Kenneth Johnson	William Lutz
Seabee Richard West	Frank Scannelli
Seabee Morton Wise	Alexander Orfaly
Pvt. Tom O'Brien	James O'Sullivan
Radio Operator Bob McCaffrey	Roger Brown
Marine Cpl. Hamilton Steves	Dick Ensslen
Seabee Thomas Hassinger	Phil Lucas
Seabee James Jerome	Joseph della Sorte
Pvt. Sven Larsen	Don Dolan
Pvt. Jack Walters	Bob Barbieri
Pvt. Dick Sederholm	Jess E. Richards
Seabee Roger Pitt	Marvin Camillo
Seabee John Nathan	David Jarratt
Seabee Keith Moore	Laried Montgomery
Lt. Genevieve Marshall	Jane Coleman
Ensign Lisa Manelli	Lisa Damon
Ensign Connie Walewska	Martha Danielle
Ensign Janet McGregor	Susan Campbell
Ensign Bessie Noonan	Joyce Maret
Ensign Pamela Whitmore	Patti Davis
Ensign Rita Adams	Anne Nathan
Ensign Sue Yaeger	Judy Case
Ensign Cora MacRae	Lynn Dovel
Ensign Dinah Murphy	Bobbi Baird
Liat	Eleanor Calbes
Lt. Buzz Adams	Jack Knight

UNDERSTUDIES: Emile, Gene Hollmann; Nellie, Bobbi Baird; Bloody Mary, Jane Coleman; Luther, Brad Sullivan; Cable, David Jarratt; Brackett, Howard Fischer; Harbison, Dick Ensslen; Liat, Joyce Maret; Stewpot, Don Dolan; Professor, Laried Montgomery; Ngana, Jerome, Nancy Asai

MUSICAL NUMBERS: Dites-moi Pourquoi, A Cockeyed Optimist, Twin Soliloquies, Some Enchanted Evening, Bloody Mary Is The Girl I Love, There Is Nothin' Like A Dame, Bali Ha'i, I'm Gonna Wash That Man Right Outa My Hair, I'm In Love With A Wonderful Guy, Younger Than Springtime, 'Happy Talk, Honey Bun, You've Got To Be Carefully Taught, Finale

A Musical in two acts. The action takes place on two islands in the South Pacific during World War II. There is a week's lapse of time between acts.

General Manager: Morris Jacobs
Company Manager: Ronald Bruguiere
Press: Frank Goodman, Martin Shwartz
Stage Managers: Harry Young, Howard Fischer, Phil King

° Closed Sept. 9, 1967. (104 performances) Original production opened at the Majestic Theatre Apr. 7, 1949 with Mary Martin, Ezio Pinza, Juanita Hall, Betta St. John, and William Tabbert, and played 1925 performances. See THEATRE WORLD Vol. 5.

Friedman-Abeles Photos

Eleanor Calbes, Justin McDonough
Above: Giorgio Tozzi, Florence Henderson

VIVIAN BEAUMONT THEATER

Opened Thursday, July 6, 1967.°
(Moved Sept. 18, 1967 to George Abbott
Theatre)
Alexander H. Cohen presents:

THE UNKNOWN SOLDIER
AND HIS WIFE

By Peter Ustinov; Director, John Dexter;
Music, David Shire; Scenery and Costumes,
Motley; Lighting, Jules Fisher; Associate Pro-
ducer, Hildy Parks; Production Supervisor,
Jerry Adler; Production Assistants, Jan Monk-
house, Gloria Banta.

CAST

Sergeant	W. B. Brydon
35914	Don Scardino†1
General	Brian Bedford
Rebel	Marco St. John†2
Wife	Melissa C. Murphy
Archbishop	Howard Da Silva
14768	Andrew Johns
71696	William Dolive
Unknown Soldier	Christopher Walken
94343	James Storm†3
Enemy Leader	Alan Mixon
Inventor	Bob Dishy†4
Woman	M'el Dowd†5
Reinforcements	Andrew R. Amic-Angelo,

Gary Barton, B. J. DeSimone, Larry Swanson
Musicians _____ Robert Rogers, Bernard Berger,
William Kirby, Irwin Farberman

UNDERSTUDIES: General and 14768, Larry
Swanson; Unknown Soldier, James Storm;
Woman and Wife, Kathleen Dabney; Enemy
Leader and 71696, B. J. DeSimone; Inventor,
William Dolive; Rebel and 94343, Andrew R.
Amic-Angelo; Sergeant, Andrew Johns; 35914,
Gary Barton

Two acts of war separated by a truce for
refreshment.

General Manager: Roy A. Somylo
Company Manager: Seymour Herscher
Press: James D. Proctor,
David Roggensack, Lila King
Stage Managers: Ben Janney,
Robert L. Borod, B. J. DeSimone,
Bennet Thomson

° Closed Nov. 11, 1967 after 11 previews and
84 performances at the Beaumont Theater,
and 64 at the Abbott Theatre.
† Succeeded by: 1. David-Rhys Anderson†6,
2. James Storm, 3. Palmer Deane, 4. Zale
Kessler, 5. Nancy Reardon, 6. Gary Barton.

Friedman-Abeles Photos

Melissa C. Murphy, Christopher Walken
Top Right: Howard Da Silva, Brian Bedford

Brian Bedford, Howard Da Silva,
Melissa C. Murphy. Above: Melissa C. Murphy,
Howard Da Silva

VIVIAN BEAUMONT THEATER

Opened Thursday, October 26, 1967.°
The Repertory Theater of Lincoln Center
(Jules Irving, Director) presents a special
invitational production under the supervision of Saint-Subber of:

THE LITTLE FOXES

By Lillian Hellman; Director, Mike Nichols;
Setting and Lighting, Howard Bay; Costumes,
Patricia Zipprodt; Hair Styles, Ernest Adler.

CAST

Addie	Beah Richards
Cal	Andre Womble
Birdie Hubbard	Margaret Leighton†1
Oscar Hubbard	E. G. Marshall†2
Leo Hubbard	Austin Pendleton
Regina Giddens	Anne Bancroft†3
William Marshall	William Prince†4
Benjamin Hubbard	George C. Scott†5
Alexandra Giddens	Maria Tucci†6
Horace Giddens	Richard A. Dysart

UNDERSTUDIES: Birdie, Regina, Elizabeth
Wilson; Ben, Robert Symonds; Oscar, Mar-
shall, John Braden; Alexandra, Kathleen Eric;
Horace, Ray Fry; Leo, Frank Bayer; Cal,
George Carter; Addie, Ruth Attaway

A Drama in three acts. The action takes
place in 1900 in the living room of the Gid-
dens' house in a small town in the South.

General Manager: C. Edwin Knill
Production Manager: Robert D. Currie
Press: Harvey B. Sabinson, Lee Solters,
Harry Nigro, Susan Bloch
Stage Managers: Tom Porter,
Frank Bayer, Brent Sutton

° Closed Dec. 17, 1967 and re-opened Dec.
19, 1967 at the Ethel Barrymore with cast
changes listed below. Closed to tour on
Jan. 20, 1968 after 100 performances.

† Succeeded by: 1. Felicia Montealegre, 2.
Scott McKay, 3. Margaret Leighton, 4. Liam
Sullivan, 5. E. G. Marshall, 6. Geraldine
Chaplin.

Original production opened at the National
on Feb. 15, 1939 and ran for 410 performances with Tallulah Bankhead, Patricia Collinge, Florence Williams, and Carl
Benton Reid.

Martha Swope Photos

**Top Left: George C. Scott, Richard A.
Dysart, Anne Bancroft, Margaret Leighton,
E. G. Marshall**

Richard A. Dysart, Beah Richards, Maria Tucci
Above: Geraldine Chaplin, Margaret Leighton

Austin Pendleton, E. G. Marshall,
Scott McKay

VIVIAN BEAUMONT THEATER

Opened Thursday, January 4, 1968.°
The Repertory Theater of Lincoln Center
(Jules Irving, Director) presents:

SAINT JOAN

By George Bernard Shaw; Director, John
Hirsch; Settings, David Hays; Costumes, Michael Annals; Sighting, John Gleason; Music,
Stanley Silverman.

CAST

Bertrand de Poulengy	John Braden
Steward	Nicholas Kepros
Joan	Diana Sands
Robert de Beaudricourt	Ted D'Arms
Archbishop of Rheims	Roger DeKoven
Mgr. de la Tremouille	Ronald Bishop
Court Page	Tom Fuccello
Gilles de Rais	Richard Clarke
Captain La Hire	Earle Hyman
The Dauphin	Edward Zang
Duchess de la Tremouille	Shirley Jac Wagner
Dunois	Philip Bosco
Dunois' Page	Northern Calloway
Richard de Beauchamp	William Hutt
Chaplain de Stogumber	Robert Symonds
Peter Cauchon	Tony van Bridge
Warwick's Page	Ryan Listman
The Inquisitor	John Heffernan
D'Estivet	Earl Montgomery
Brother Martin Ladvenu	Stephen Joyce
Executioner	Ronald Weyand
English Soldier	Ted D'Arms
Gentleman of 1920	Richard Clarke

MEMBERS OF THE FRENCH COURT:
Charles Burks, Roberta Callahan, Jane Karel,
Stephen Lemberg, Barbara Thurston, William
Walsh

ENGLISH SOLDIERS: John Dorrin, Robert
Haswell, Robert Phalen, Edmond Varrato
FRENCH SOLDIERS: Christopher Bernau,
John Felton, Jon Froscher, Chris Kelly, Michael Maurer, Fred Seagraves

UNDERSTUDIES: Joan, Rae Allen; Beaudricourt, Cauchon, Ronald Bishop; Steward, Ryan
Listman; Poulengy, Martin, Bluebeard, Robert Phalen; Archbishop, Stogumber, Earl
Montgomery; Tremouille, Ronald Weyand;
Dauphin, Nicholas Kepros; Duchess, Roberta
Callahan; Dunois, 20's Gentleman, John Braden; Warwick, Richard Clarke; Inquisitor, Ray
Fry; D'Estivet, Executioner, Robert Haswell

A Drama in 6 scenes with an epilogue, presented in two parts.

Press: Susan Bloch
Stage Managers: Brent Sutton,
Ronald Schaeffer, Christopher Bernau,
John Felton, Jon Froscher, Chris Kelly,
Michael Maurer, Barbara Mae Phillips,
Fred Seagraves
° Closed Feb. 10, 1968. (44 performances)

Martha Swope Photos

Roger DeKoven, Diana Sands, Earle Hyman
Above: (C) Diana Sands, Stephen Joyce

Diana Sands, Edward Zang
Top Left: Philip Bosco, Diana Sands

VIVIAN BEAUMONT THEATER

Opened Thursday, February 29, 1968.°
The Repertory Theater of Lincoln Center,
Jules Irving, Director, presents:

TIGER AT THE GATES

By Jean Giraudoux; Adapted by Christopher
Fry; Director, Anthony Quayle; Settings, David
Hays; Costumes, Fred Voelpel; Lighting, John
Gleason; Music, Stanley Silverman; Musical
Director, Roland Gagnon.

CAST

Cassandra	Diana Sands
Andromache	M'el Dowd
Laundress	Diane Kagan
Hector	Philip Bosco
Attendant	Northern Calloway
Paris	Dennis Cooney
Abneos	Edgar Daniels
Anchises	Al Corbin
Priam	Roger DeKoven
Demokos	Robert Symonds
Hecuba	Aline MacMahon
Polyxene	Eileen Dolphin or Gail Honig
Mathematician	Ray Fry
Maids-in-Waiting	Janet League, Sandy Rochelle
Helen	Jennifer West
Oneah	Lloyd Hollar
Minos	Robert Phalen
Troilus	Bruce Davison
Old Man	Robert Haswell
Busiris	Richard Clarke
Priests	Earl Montgomery, Charles Burks
Ajax	Ronald Weyand
Ulysses	Tony van Bridge
Topman	John Braden
Olpides	Ted D'Arms
Third Soldier	Christopher Kelly

TROJANS: Charles Burks, Ryan Listman, El-
vira Lockwood, Winifred Mann, Fred Sea-
graves, Daniel Sullivan, Shirley Jac Wagner.
UNDERSTUDIES: Hector, John Braden; Cas-
sandra, Hecuba, Shirley Jac Wagner; An-
dromache, Winifred Mann; Paris, Richard
Clarke; Abneos, Demokos, Earl Montgomery;
Anchises, Topman, Olpides, Daniel Sullivan;
Priam, Busiris, Robert Haswell; Helen, Diane
Kagan; Ajax, Ulysses, Ted D'Arms; Oneah,
Fred Seagraves; Laundress, Janet League;
Minos, Christopher Kelly; Troilus, Ryan List-
man; Mathematician, Al Corbin.

A Drama presented in two acts. The action
takes place in Troy.

Press: Susan Bloch
Stage Managers: James Kershaw,
Barbara-Mae Phillips,
Christopher Kelly, Fred Seagraves

° Closed Apr. 6, 1968 after limited engagement of 44 performances.

Martha Swope Photos

'el Dowd, Ronald Weyand, Diana Sands,
Philip Bosco

Ray Fry, Al Corbin, Robert Symonds, Edgar Daniels,
Eileen Dolphin, Aline MacMahon, Dennis Cooney
Top: Jennifer West, Diana Sands, Philip Bosco

Joseph Palmieri, Suzanne Grossmann, Robert Symonds,
John Braden. Above: Robert Symonds (L), Dennis
Cooney, Suzanne Grossmann. Top: (L) Robert Symond,
Philip Bosco

82

VIVIAN BEAUMONT THEATER

Opened Thursday, April 25, 1968.*
The Repertory Theater of Lincoln Center
(Jules Irving, Director) presents:

CYRANO DE BERGERAC

By Edmond Rostand; English version by
James Forsyth; Director, Carl Weber; Settings, David Hays; Costumes, James Hart
Stearns; Lighting, John Gleason, Music, William Bolcom; Swordplay, Albert Cavens; Musical Director, Roland Gagnon.

CAST

Jodelet	Roger DeKoven
Orange Girl	Sasha von Scherler
Porter	Robert Haswell
Citizen	Earl Montgomery
His Son	Donnie Melvin or Kim Michaels
Musketeer	Ted D'Arms
Cavalier	Robert Benson
Pickpocket	Robert Levine
Cutpurse	Northern Calloway
Apprentice Thieves	Gary Barton, Eileen Dolphin, Gail Honig
Pages	Ryan Listman, Bryan Marks, Jerry Mayer
Footmen	Tom Atkins, Jack Ryland
Tradesmen,	Thomas Costello, Christopher Kelly, Fred Seagraves
Drunkard	Robert Phalen
Cuigy	Richard Buck
Brissaille	Leon Russom
Marquis de Tremblay	Richard Clarke
Fop	Larry Pine
Bald Fop	David Vilner
Lightsmen	Howard Green, Brent Sutton
Christian de Neuvillette	Dennis Cooney
Ligniere	Ray Fry
Barthenoide	Shirley Jac Wagner
Urimedonte	Janet League
Cassandace	Maeve McGuire
Felixerie	Winifred Mann
Roxane	Suzanne Grossmann
Duenna (Sister Claire)	Nancy Marchand
Comte de Guiche	Philip Bosco
Valvert	Albert Cavens
Le Bret	John Braden
Ragueneau	Joseph Palmieri
Montfleury	Edgar Daniels
Cyrano de Bergerac	Robert Symonds
Whores	Dorothy Chace, Barbara-Mae Phillips, Sandy Rochelle
Jodelet's Troupe	Roberta Callahan, James Cook, Pamela Fife, Lloyd Hollar, Ronald Weyand
Bakers, Apprentices, Scullions	Gary Barton, Northern Calloway, Dorothy Chace, Ryan Listman, Earl Montgomery, Barbara-Mae Phillips, Sandy Rochelle, David Vilner
Lise	Winifred Mann
Children	Donnie Melvin, Kim Michaels, Eileen Dolphin, Gail Honig
Poets	Thomas Costello, Howard Green, Robert Haswell, Bryan Marks, Jerry Mayer
Carbon de Castel-Jaloux	Ronald Weyand
Cadets	Tom Atkins, Robert Benson, James Cook, Lloyd Hollar, Christopher Kelly, Robert Levine, Robert Phalen, Jack Ryland
Lute Player	Northern Calloway
Capuchin	Ray Fry
Spanish Officer	Roger DeKoven
Spanish Soldiers	Gary Barton, Richard Buck, Northern Calloway, Thomas Costello, Ted D'Arms, Howard Green, Ryan Listman, Bryan Marks, Jerry Mayer, Leon Russom, David Vilner
Sister Marthe	Blythe Danner
Mother Marguerite	Aline MacMahon
Nuns	Roberta Callahan, Dorothy Chace, Janet League, Maeve McGuire, Sandy Rochelle, Shirley Jac Wagner
Musicians	Karl Kraber, James Pedrick

UNDERSTUDIES: Roxane, Maeve McGuire;
Christian, Leon Russom; deGuiche, Richard
Clarke; Orange Girl, Sandy Rochelle; Valvert,
Howard Green; Duenna, Shirley Jac Wagner;
Lise, Sasha von Scherler

A Comedy-Drama in 3 acts and 5 scenes.
The action takes place in Paris and at the Siege
of Arras in 1640, and Paris in 1655

Press: Susan Bloch
Stage Managers: Timothy Ward,
Christopher Kelly, Barbara-Mae Phillips,
Fred Seagraves, Brent Sutton
* Still playing May 31, 1968.

Martha Swope Photos

LIBRARY & MUSEUM OF PERFORMING ARTS AUDITORIUM

Opened Monday, September 11, 1967.°
The Company of Twelve (C. K. Alexander, Artistic Director) presents in repertory:

FRANCESCA DA RIMINI

By George Henry Boker; Adapted by Barnabas Bailey; Director, C. K. Alexander; Sets, John Patrick Hart; Costumes, Sara Covalt; Lighting, Garry Harris; Production Supervisor, Elissa Lane; Original Music, Mario Quimber; Arranged and Conducted by Hale Smith.

CAST

Pepe	Arthur Berwick
Malatesta	Coe Norton
Lanciotta	Jeff David
Paolo	Dino Narizzano
Francesca	Deborah Steinberg
Ritta	Shirley Guy
Guido	Mel Boudrot
Carmella	Elizabeth Lawrence
Knight and Captain	David Piel

Presented in two acts. The action takes place about 1300 in the towns of Rimini and Ravenna, Italy.

THE CAMPBELLS OF BOSTON

By William Dean Howells; Adapted by J. Plunkett Harmon; Director, C. K. Alexander.

CAST

Jane	Deborah Steinberg
Amy	Elizabeth Lawrence
Willis	Coe Norton
Reverend Bemis	Jeff David
Agnes Roberts	Shirley Guy
Edward Roberts	Arthur Berwick
Mrs. Curwen	Janis Young
Dr. Lawton	Mel Boudrot
Mrs. Crashaw	Fay Sappington
Mr. Miller	Dino Narizzano
Mrs. Miller	Edith Renaud
Mr. Curwen	David Piel

Presented in three acts. The action takes place in Boston in 1895.

Stage Managers: Frank Melfo, Ruth Edwards, Sharon Manley

° Closed Sept. 16, 1967 after limited engagement of 6 performances.

Fay Sappington, Janis Young, David Piel, Mel Boudrot, Jeff David, Elizabeth Lawrence, Coe Norton, Dino Narizzano, Edith Renaud, Deborah Steinberg, Shirley Guy, Arthur Berwick in "The Campbells of Boston" Above: Jeff David, Coe Norton, Mel Boudrot, Deborah Steinberg, Dino Narizzano, David Piel, Shirley Guy in "Francesca Da Rimini"

Hugh Hurd, Alek Primrose, Gloria James, Judd Jones, Robert Lesser

THEATER-IN-THE-SCHOOLS

Opened Monday, October 2, 1967.°
The Repertory Theater of Lincoln Center under the direction of Jules Irving, presents:

IN WHITE AMERICA

By Martin B. Duberman; Directed by Daniel Sullivan.

CAST

Hugh Hurd	Judd Jones
Gloria James	Robert Lesser
Alek Primrose	

The material in this production, except for connecting narration, consists entirely of authentic documents. They are presented exactly as originally written or spoken, but none are used in their entirety.

Press: Susan Bloch, Charlene Slivnick
Stage Manager: Mitch Kessler

° Presented alternately with "Repertory In Action" in NYC schools through May 29, 1968.

Martha Swope Photo

THE FORUM

Opened Friday, November 10, 1967.°
The Repertory Theater of Lincoln Center
(Jules Irving, Director) presents:

WALKING TO WALDHEIM

By Mayo Simon; Director, George L. Sherman; Scenery, Peter Harvey; Costumes, Melly Eigsti; Lighting, John Gleason.

CAST

H. Goldblatt	Roger DeKoven
Mina	Aline MacMahon
Ralph	George Bartenieff
Eddie Bromberg	Jacob Ben-Ami
Yetta Sher	Sylvie Straus
Zelda	Mari Gorman

and

HAPPINESS

Old Lady	Lili Darvas
Old Man	Jacob Ben-Ami

Understudies: Shirley Jac Wagner, Ray Fry
Production Manager: Robert D. Currie
Press: Susan Bloch, Charlene Slivnick
Stage Managers: James Kershaw,
Ronald Schaeffer

° Closed Dec. 16, 1967 after 43 performances.

Martha Swope Photos

Front: Aline MacMahon, Jacob Ben-Ami, Roger DeKoven. Rear: Mari Gorman, Sylvie Straus, George Bartenieff in "Walking To Waldheim" Top: Lili Darvas, Jacob Ben-Ami in "Happiness"

THE FORUM
Opened Sunday, March 3, 1968.°
The Repertory Theater of Lincoln Center
(Jules Irving, Director) presents:

SUMMERTREE

By Ron Cowen; Director, David Pressman;
Setting and Costumes, James A. Taylor; Lighting, John Gleason.

CAST

Young Man .... David Birney
Little Boy .... Barry Symonds
                                   or Donnie Melvin
Mother .... Priscilla Pointer
Father .... Philip Sterling
Girl .... Blythe Danner
Soldier .... Tom Fuccello

UNDERSTUDIES: Young Man, Tom Fuccello;
Mother, Winifred Mann; Girl, Roberta Callahan;
Father, William Myers; Soldier, Christopher
Kelly

A Drama in three acts.

Press: Susan Bloch
Stage Managers: Ronald Schaeffer,
                  Seth Glassman

° Still playing May 31, 1968.

Martha Swope Photos

Barry Symonds, Tom Fuccello, David Birney, Philip Sterling, Blythe Danner,
Priscilla Pointer. Top: Priscilla Pointer, David Birney, Philip Sterling

85

NEW YORK CITY CENTER

Opened Thursday, October 19, 1967.°
The City Center Drama Company (Jean Dalrymple, Director) presents:

LIFE WITH FATHER

By Howard Lindsay and Russel Crouse; Based on book by Clarence Day; Director, Gus Schirmer; Scenery, Stewart Chaney; Costumes, Edith Lutyens Bel Geddes; Production Assistant, Madge D. Graves; Hair Styles, Jene Chandler.

CAST

Vinnie	Dorothy Stickney
Annie	Emily Peden
Clarence	Rusty Thacker
John	Gary Enck
Whitney	Jeff Stuart
Harlan	Jimmie Grubman
Father	Leon Ames
Margaret	Abby Lewis
Cousin Cora	Jean Sincere
Mary Skinner	Sandy Duncan
Rev. Dr. Lloyd	William Le Massena
Delia	Ann Freeman
Nora	Toni Darnay
Dr. Humphreys	Alexander Clark
Dr. Sommers	John D. Seymour
Maggie	Marta Heflin

UNDERSTUDIES: Clarence Jr., John, George Coleman; Mary, Emily Peden; Vinnie, Muriel Kirkland; Father, Alexander Clark; Margaret, Cora, Toni Darnay; Lloyd, Humphrey, John D. Seymour; Annie, Marta Heflin; Harlan, Whitney, Mark Kearney

A Comedy in three acts and six scenes. The entire action takes place in the morning room of the Day house on Madison Avenue in New York in the late 1880's.

General Manager: Homer Poupart
Company Manager: George Zorn
Press: John Clugstone
Stage Managers: Herman Shapiro, Forrest Carter, Jeff Chambers

° Closed Sunday, Nov. 5, 1967, after 22 performances and 2 previews. Original production opened Nov. 8, 1939 at the Empire Theatre with Dorothy Stickney and Howard Lindsay and ran for 3224 performances.

Friedman-Abeles Photos

Dorothy Stickney, Jean Sincere, Rusty Thacker, Sandy Duncan, Gary Enck
Above: Rusty Thacker, Sandy Duncan. Top: Leon Ames, Dorothy Stickney

NEW YORK CITY CENTER

Opened Wednesday, November 8, 1967.°
The City Center Drama Company (Jean
Dalrymple, Director) presents:

THE TENTH MAN

By Paddy Chayefsky; Director, Arthur Cantor; Setting and Lighting, David Hays; Costumes, Frank Thompson; Assistant to Mr. Cantor, Donald Buka; Hairstylist, Jene Chandler;
Production Assistant, Madge D. Graves.

CAST

Hirschman	Muni Seroff
Sexton	Jon Silo
Schlissel	Lou Polan
Zitorsky	Joseph Mell
Alper	Boris Tumarin
Foreman	Michael Gorrin
Evelyn Foreman	Pamela Kingsley
Arthur Landau	John Kerr
Harris	Sam Nudell
Rabbi	Gene Gross
Kessler Boys	Sol Serlin, Haig Chobanian
Policeman	Daniel P. Hannafin

UNDERSTUDIES: Arthur, Donald Buka; Eve-
lyn, Linda Washburn; Hirschman, Foreman,
Sol Serlin; Alper, Kesslers, Haig Chobanian;
Schlissel, Seaton, Sam Nudell; Policeman,
Kesslers, William Chambers

A Drama in 3 acts. The action takes place
at the present time in an Orthodox Synagogue
in Mineola, Long Island, N.Y.

General Manager: Homer Poupart
Company Manager: George Zorn
Press: John Clugstone
Stage Managers: Herman Shapiro,
William Chambers

° Closed Sunday, Nov. 26, 1967 after a limited engagement of 23 performances and 1
preview. The original production opened at
the Booth on Nov. 5, 1959 with Donald
Harron, Risa Schwartz, Lou Jacobi, Jack
Gilford, and George Voskovec, and ran for
623 performances. See THEATRE WORLD
Vol. 16.

Friedman-Abeles Photos

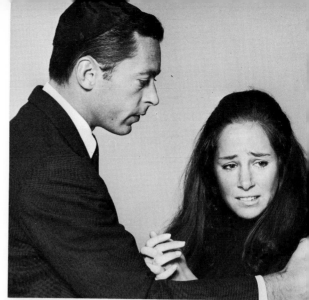

Pamela Kingsley, Joseph Mell, Boris Tumarin, Michael Gorrin. Above: Joseph Mell,
Lou Polan, Muni Seroff, Boris Tumarin, Michael Gorrin. Top: John Kerr, Pamela Kingsley

NEW YORK CITY CENTER

Opened Wednesday, December 13, 1967.°
The City Center Light Opera Company,
Jean Dalrymple, Director, presents:

BRIGADOON

Book and Lyrics, Alan Jay Lerner; Music,
Frederick Loewe; Director, Gus Schirmer; Musical Director, Jonathan Anderson; Original
Dances and Musical Numbers Staged by
Agnes de Mille; Re-staged for this production
by Gemze de Lappe and Dennis Cole; Settings, Oliver Smith; Costumes, Stanley Simmons; Lighting, Peggy Clark; Production Assistant, Madge D. Graves; Hairstylist, Jene
Chandler.

CAST

Tommy Albright	Bill Hayes
Jeff Douglas	Russell Nype
Sandy Dean	Henry Lawrence
Meg Brockie	Karen Morrow
Archie Beaton	Earl McDonald
Harry Beaton	Edward Villella or Frank André
Andrew MacLaren	Alexander Clark
Jean MacLaren	Sarah Jane Smith
Fiona MacLaren	Margot Moser
Angus McGuffie	Gordon Cook
Charlie Dalrymple	Evan Thomas
Maggie Anderson	Leslie Franzos
Sword Dancers	Dennis Cole, Wilfred Schuman
Mr. Lundi	William LeMassena
Bagpiper	Maurice Eisenstadt
Frank	Paul Adams
Jane Ashton	Jeanne Murray Vanderbilt

TOWNSFOLK: Chris Callen, Phyllis Bash,
Jane Coleman, Peggy Cooper, Mona Elson,
Marta Heflin, Oksana Iweszczenko, Mina
Jo King, Barbara Miller, Roberta Vatske, Paul
Adams, Donald Brassington, Edward Becker,
Peter Clark, Gordon Cook, Henry Lawrence,
Ken Richards, Robert Monteil, Don Wonder

DANCERS: Anita Arnell, Joanna Crosson,
Chele Graham, Jane Jaffe, Nicole Karol, Karen
Kristin, Lucia Lambert, Toodie Wittmer, Marget Wyeth, Paul Berne, Scott Hunter, J. David
Kirby, William Koch, Dick Korthaze, Wilfred
Schuman, Bud Spencer, Ron Tassone, Duane
Taylor

UNDERSTUDIES: Harry, Frank André;
Tommy, Angus, Jeff, Paul Adams; Jane, Betty
Hyatt Linton; Archie, Edward Becker; Andrew, Henry Lawrence; Fiona, Roberta Vatske;
Jean, Toodie Wittmer; Meg, Marta Heflin;
Charlie, Ken Richards; Maggie, Nicole Karol

MUSICAL NUMBERS: "Once In The Highlands," "Brigadoon," "Down On MacConnachy Square," "Waitin' For My Dearie,"
"I'll Go Home With Bonnie Jean," "Heather
On The Hill," "Love Of My Life," "Jeannie's
Packin' Up," "Come To Me, Bend To Me,"
"Almost Like Being In Love," "Wedding
Dance," "Sword Dance," "The Chase," "There
But For You Go I," "My Mother's Wedding
Day," "Funeral Dance," "From This Day
On."

A Musical in 2 acts and 11 scenes. The
action takes place in May of last year, in the
Scottish Highlands, and New York City.

General Manger: Homer Poupart
Company Manager: Catherine Parsons
Press: Jean Dalrymple, John Clugstone
Stage Managers: Herman Shapiro,
Forrest Carter, Paul Philips

° Closed Dec. 31, 1967 after a limited engagement of 23 performances and 1 preview.
Original production opened at the Ziegfeld
on Mar. 13, 1947 and ran for 581 performances with David Brooks, George Keane,
James Mitchell, Virginia Bosler, and Pamela
Britton. See THEATRE WORLD, Vol. 3.

Friedman-Abeles Photos

Top Left: Bill Hayes, Russell Nype,
Karen Morrow

Karen Morrow, Russell Nype
Above: Sarah Jane Smith, Edward Villella

NEW YORK CITY CENTER

Opened Monday, May 20, 1968.º
City Center Light Opera Company (Jean
Dalrymple, Director) presents:

THE KING AND I

Book and Lyrics, Oscar Hammerstein 2nd;
Based on "Anna and The King of Siam"
by Margaret Landon; Music, Richard Rodgers;
Director, John Fearnley; Music Director, Jonathan Anderson; Choreography, Jerome Robbins;
Reproduced by Yuriko; Scenery, Paul Mc
Guire; Costumes, Irene Sharaff; Supervised by
Frank Thompson; Lighting, Feder; Production
Assistants, Madge D. Graves, Esteban A. Chalbaud, Hairstylist, Jene Chandler.

CAST

Captain Orton	Sam Kirkham
Louis Leonowens	Eric Hamilton
Anna Leonowens	Constance Towers
The Interpreter	Paul Flores
The Kralahome	Ted Beniades
The King	Michael Kermoyan
Phra Alack	Robert Lenn
Lun Tha	Stanley Grover
Tuptin	Eleanor Calbes
Lady Thiang	Anita Darian
Prince Chululongkorn	Michael Thom
Princess Ying Yoalwalk	Dana Shimizu
Sir Edward Ramsey	Christopher Hewett

PRINCESSES, PRINCES: Caryn Chow, Sonja
Furiya, Dana Shimizu, Rachel Ticotin, Nancy
Ticotin, Russell Chow, Lewis Gerardo, Lawrence Kikuchi, Jaime Roque, Jason Rosen,
Keenan Shimizu, Marcus Ticotin.

ROYAL DANCERS: Diane Adler, Paula
Chin, Carol Fried, Linda Gumiela, Joann Ogawa, Margot Parsons, Kathleen Pierini, Susan
Platt, Juanita Londono, Wonci Lui, Stephanie
Satie, Britt Swanson, Margot Travers, Jaclynn
Villamil, Rebecca West, Lazar Dano, Gary
Dutton, Vito Durante, Rodger Gerhardstein,
Tim Ramirez.

SINGERS: Joan diDonato, Lee Hooper, Charlotte Marcheret, Betsy Norden, Barbara Reisman, Rebecca West, Maggie Worth, Larry Devon, Beno Foster, Richard Kie Wye Khan.

UNDERSTUDIES: Anna, Virginia Vestoff;
King, Ted Beniades; Kralahome, Lun Tha,
Paul Flores; Interpreter, Phra Alack, Richard
Kie Wye Kahn; Tuptin, Betsy Nordern; Thiang,
Lee Hooper; Louis, Phillip Nichols; Chululongkorn, Lawrence Kikuchi; Ramsey, Sam Kirkham

MUSICAL NUMBERS: "I Whistle A Happy
Tune," "My Lord and Master," "Hello, Young
Lovers," "March of The Siamese Children,"
"A Puzzlement," "Getting To Know You,"
"We Kiss In A Shadow," "Shall I Tell You
What I Think of You?," "Something Wonderful," "Western People Funny," "I Have
Dreamed," "The Small House of Uncle
Thomas," "Shall We Dance?"

A Musical in two acts. The action takes
place in the 1860's in and around the King's
Palace in Bangkok, Siam.

General Manager: Homer Poupart
Company Manager: Catherine Parsons
Press: Jean Dalrymple, John Clugstone
Stage Managers: Herman Shapiro,
Sean S. Cunningham, James Struthers

º Closed June 9, 1968 after a limited engagement of 24 performances. For original
Broadway production with Gertrude Lawrence
and Yul Brynner, see THEATRE WORLD,
Vol. 7.

Friedman-Abeles Photos

**Top Right: Eleanor Calbes, Stanley Grover
Center: Anita Darian, Constance Towers**

Anita Darian (L), Eric Hamilton,
Constance Towers (C), Michael Kermoyan (R)   89

NEW YORK CITY CENTER

Opened Tuesday, March 19, 1968.°
The Association for International Theatrical Exchange (Gert von Gontard, President) and The City Center of Music and Drama, Inc. present The Vienna Burgtheater (Ernst Haeusserman, Managing Director) in:

PROFESSOR BERNHARDI

By Arthur Schnitzler; Staged by Kurt Meisel; Scenery, Lois Egg; Costumes, Maxi Tschunko; Producer, Gert von Gontard; Narrators, Iris Merlis, Maria Pelikan, Eva Schulz.

CAST

Hochroitzpointner	Michael Janisch
Ludmilla	Lona Dubois
Dr. Oskar Bernhardi	Heinrich Eis
Professor Bernhardi	Ernst Deutsch
Dr. Kurt Pflugfelder	Curth A. Tichy
Dr. Ebenwald	Kurt Meisel
Dr. Tugendvetter	Richard Eybner
Dr. Adler	Edd Stavjanik
Dr. Cyprian	Paul Horbiger
Rev. Franz Reder	Wolfgang Gasser
Man-servant	Walter Stumvoll
Dr. Feuermann	Otto Kerry
Dr. Filitz	Andreas Wolf
Dr. Lowenstein	Fritz Lehmann
Prof. Dr. Flint	Fred Liewehr
Dr. Schreimann	Achim Benning
Prof. Pflugfelder	Heinz Moog
Dr. Wenger	Peter Schratt
Dr. Goldenthal	Manfred Inger
Dr. Winkler	Josef Meinrad
Servants	Hans Brand, Max Pfeiler

A Drama in 5 acts presented in 2 parts. The action takes place in Vienna circa 1910.

"Professor Bernhardi"

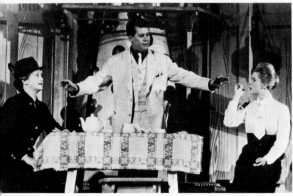

Opened Saturday, March 23, 1968.°

DAS KONZERT
(The Concert)

By Hermann Bahr; Staged by Josef Meinrad; Scenery, Lois Egg; Costumes, Ernie Kniepert; Producer, Gert von Gontard.

CAST

Gustav Heink	Axel von Ambesser
Mrs. Fanny Mell	Lona Dubois
Mrs. Claire Floderer	Jane Tilden
Miss Selma Meier	Sylvia Lukan
Eva Gerndl	Eva Kerbler
Mrs. Kann	Lotte Ledl
Miss Garden	Franziska Tilden
Miss Wehner	Trude Ackermann
Marie Heink	Susi Nicoletti
Dr. Franz Jura	Peter Weck
Pollinger	Hugo Gottschlich
Mrs. Pollinger	Gusti Wolf
Delfine Jura	Johanna Matz
Johann	Max Pfeiler

A Comedy in three acts, presented in two parts. The action takes place in and near Vienna circa 1910.

Susi Nicoletti, Peter Weck, Johanna Matz
Above: Gusti Wolf, Hugo Gottschlich
in "Das Konzert"

MARIA STUART

Opened Tuesday, March 26, 1968.°

By Friedrich von Schiller; Staged by Rudolf Steinbock; Scenery, Lois Egg; Costumes, Ronny Reiter; Technical Direction and Lighting, Sepp Nordegg; Producer, Gert von Gontard.

CAST

Hanna Kennedy	Hilde Wagener
Amias Paulet	Heinz Moog
Drury	Walter Stumvoll
Maria Stuart	Aglaja Schmid
Mortimer	Klaus Jurgen Wussow
William Cecil	Paul Hoffmann
Duke of Kent	Peter Schratt
Davison	Achim Benning
Elizabeth, Queen of England	Hilde Krahl
Aubespine	Andreas Wolf
Bellievre	Curth A. Tichy
George Talbot	Ewald Balser
Robert Dudley	Sebastian Fischer
Okelly	Heinz Ehrenfreund
Melvil	Wolfgang Gasser
Margareta Kurl	Lona Dubois
Burgoyn	Hans Brand
Ladies-in-Waiting	Franziska Tilden, Sylvia Lukan
Officer of the Guard	Heinrich Eis

An Historical Tragedy in 5 acts and 7 scenes presented in two parts. The action takes place in London and Fotheringhay in 1587.

Right: Sebastian Fischer, Hilde Krahl, Ewald Balser in "Maria Stuart"

age Konradi, Jane Tilden, Lotte Ledl, Josef einrad. Above: Josef Meinrad, Adrienne Gessner, age Konradi in "Einen Jux Will Er Sich Machen"

Opened Tuesday, April 2, 1968.°

EINEN JUX WILL ER SICH MACHEN
(He Wants To Have A Good Time)

By Johann Nestroy; Staged by Axel von Ambesser; Musical Direction, Alexander Steinbrecher; Scenery, Lois Egg; Costumes, Ernie Kniepert; Producer, Gert von Gontard.

CAST

Zangler	Fred Liewehr
Sonders	Heinz Ehrenfreund
Gertrude	Lilly Stepanek
Kraps	Edd Stavjanik
Melchior	Hugo Gottschlich
Hupfer	Fritz Lehmann
Weinberl	Josef Meinrad
Christopherl	Inge Konradi
Marie	Sylvia Lukan
Philippine	Trude Ackermann
Brunninger	Walter Gerhardt
Superintendent	Walter Stumvoll
Miss Knorr	Jane Tilden
Mrs. von Fischer	Lotte Ledl
First Waiter	Max Pfeiler
Coachman	Curth A. Tichy
Second Waiter	Hans Brand
Miss Blumenblatt	Adrienne Gessner
Lisette	Franziska Tilden
Watchman	Wolfgang Gasser
Rab	Michael Janisch

A Farce in 4 acts and 8 scenes presented in two parts. The action takes place in and near Vienna circa 1830.

Executive Director: Heinrich Kraus
Company Manager: George Zorn
Press: Nat and Irvin Dorfman
Stage Managers: Doris Einstein Siegel, Adalbert Jezel
Technical Director: Walter Hrnecek

° Presented in repertory for a limited engagement of 24 performances. Closed April 7, 1968.

NEW YORK CITY CENTER

Opened Thursday, April 25, 1968.°
City Center of Music and Drama Inc.
presents its Gilbert & Sullivan Company
(Felix Popper, General Director; John S.
White, Associate Director) in:

THE PIRATES OF PENZANCE

Music, Arthur Sullivan; Book, W. S. Gilbert;
Director, Allen Fletcher; Sets, Lloyd Evans;
Costumes, Patton Campbell; Lighting, Hans
Sondheimer; Conductor, Felix Popper.

CAST

Major-General Stanley	Douglas Watson
	or Emile Renan
Pirate King	William Chapman
Samuel	William Ledbetter
Frederic	Frank Porretta
	or John Harger Stewart
Sergeant of Police	Jack Bittner
Mabel	Patricia Wise
	or Margot Moser
Edith	Ellen Shade
Kate	Janet Winburn
Isabel	Diana Kehrig
Ruth	Muriel Greenspon

Opened Saturday, April 27, 1968.°

H. M. S. PINAFORE

Book, W. S. Gilbert; Music, Arthur Sullivan;
Conductor, Thomas P. Martin; Director, Allen
Fletcher; Sets and Costumes, Patton Campbell;
Lighting, Hans Sondheimer.

CAST

Sir Joseph Porter	Raymond Allen
	or Robert Trehy
Captain Corcoran	Richard Fredricks
Ralph Rackstraw	Enrico DiGiuseppe
	or Evan Thomas
Dick Deadeye	Paul Ukena
	or Don Yule
Bill Bobstay	Robert Hale
Bob Becket	Will Roy
Josephine	Joy Clements
	or Barbara Blanchard
Cousin Hebe	Janet Winburn
Little Buttercup	Joan Caplan

Opened Wednesday, May 1, 1968.°

THE MIKADO

Music, Arthur Sullivan; Book, W. S. Gil-
bert; Conductor, Byron Dean Ryan; Directors,
Jack and Virginia Frymire; Scenery, Donald
Oenslager; Costumes, Patton Campbell.

CAST

The Mikado of Japan	Paul Ukena
Nanki-Poo	Frank Porretta
Ko-Ko	John Lankston
Pooh-Bah	Richard Wentworth
Pish-Tush	William Ledbetter
Yum-Yum	Carol Bergey
Pitti-Sing	Mary Burgess
Peep-Bo	Janet Winburn
Katisha	Muriel Greenspon
Solo Dancer	Miyoko Watanabe

Top Right: Muriel Greenspon, Frank Porretta,
Margot Moser, Douglas Watson in "The Pirates
of Penzance. **Center:** Ray Allen (seated), Janet
Winburn, Richard Fredricks, Joy Clements,
Enrico DiGiuseppe in "H.M.S. Pinafore"

Paul Ukena, Muriel Greenspon in "The Mikado"

Opened Wednesday, May 8, 1968.°

THE YEOMAN OF THE GUARD

Music, Arthur Sullivan; Book, W. S. Gilbert;
Conductor, Felix Popper; Director, Allen Flet-
cher; Setting, Stephen O. Saxe; Costumes,
Alvin Colt; Lighting, Hans Sondheimer.

CAST

Sir Richard Cholmondeley	Robert Hale
Colonel Fairfax	Frank Porretta
Sergeant Meryll	Paul Ukena
Leonard Meryll	John Lankston
Jack Point	Robert Trehy
Wilfred Shadbolt	Jack Bittner
First Yeoman	Evan Thomas
Second Yeoman	David Hicks
First Citizen	Harris Davis
Second Citizen	Don Henderson
Elsie Maynard	Margot Moser
Phoebe Meryll	Mary Burgess
Dame Carruthers	Ellen Alexander
Kate	Fredreika Wisehart

Opened Wednesday, May 15, 1968.°

PATIENCE

Book, W. S. Gilbert; Music, Arthur Sullivan; Conductor, Felix Popper; Director, Leon
Major; Settings and Costumes, Motley; Lighting, Hans Sondheimer.

CAST

Colonel Calverley	William Chapman
Major Murgatroyd	Nico Castel
Lt., The Duke of Dunstable	John Lankston
Reginald Bunthorne	Emile Renan
Archibald Grosvenor	William Metcalf
Solicitor	John Henry Thomas
Lady Angela	Mary Burgess
Lady Saphir	Helen Guile
Lady Ella	Fredreika Wisehart
Lady Jane	Claramae Turner
Patience	Joy Clements

COMPANY: Ellen Alexander, Raymond Al-
len, Carol Bergey, Jack Bittner, Barbara Blan-
chard, Mary Burgess, Joan Caplan, Nico Castel,
William Chapman, Joy Clements, Enrico Di-
Giuseppe, Richard Fredricks, Muriel Greenspon,
Helen Guile, Robert Hale, David Hicks, John
Lankston, William Ledbetter, William Metcalf,
Margot Moser, Edward Pierson, Frank Por-
retta, Emile Renan, Will Roy, Ellen Shade,
Vern Shinall, John Harger Stewart, Evan
Thomas, Robert Trehy, Claramae Turner, Paul
Ukena, Miyoko Watanabe, Douglas Watson,
Richard Wentworth, Janet Winburn, Patricia
Wise, Fredreika Wisehart, Don Yule

ENSEMBLE: Arlene Adler, Ronald Bentley,
Don Carlo, Anthony Darius, Harris Davis, Jo-
seph Galiano, Nino Garcia, Pearle Goldsmith,
Marilyn Armstrong, Harriet Greene, Don Hen-
derson, Lila Herbert, Douglas Hunnikin, Suzy
Hunter, Diana Kehrig, Karl Patrick Krause,
Donna Owen, Hanna Owen, Raymond Papay,
Richard Park, Leo Postrel, Joaquin Roma-
guera, Stefanya Weicker, Maria West, Marie
Young

Artistic Cordinator: Ruth M. Hider
Music Administrator: Daniel R. Rule
Press: Nat and Irvin Dorfman
Company Managers: Catherine Parsons,
George Zorn
Technical Director: Hans Sondheimer
Stage Managers: Dan Butt, Bill Field,
David Sell

° Closed May 19, 1968 after a limited engagement of 31 performances.

Fred Fehl Photos

**Top Right: Jack Bittner, Mary Burgess
in "The Yeoman of The Guard"**

**William Metcalf, William Chapman, Emile Renan,
Joy Clements in "Patience"**

93

OFF-BROADWAY

SULLIVAN STREET PLAYHOUSE
Opened Tuesday, May 3, 1960.°
Lore Noto presents:

THE FANTASTICKS

Book and Lyrics, Tom Jones; Music, Harvey
Schmidt; Suggested by Edmond Rostand's play
"Les Romantiques"; Director, Word Baker;
Musical Direction and Arrangements, Julian
Stein; Designed by Ed Wittstein; Pianist, Rod
Derefinko; Harpist, Sally Foster; Associate Pro-
ducers, Sheldon Baron, Dorothy Olim, Robert
Alan Gold; Original cast album by MGM
Records.

CAST
The Narrator ------------------------------ John Boni†1
The Girl ------------------------------------ Carole Demas†2
The Boy ------------------------------------- Erik Howell†3
The Boy's Father ------------------ Richard Kinter†4
The Girl's Father -------------------- John J. Martin
The Actor ---------------------------- Jay Hampton†5
The Man Who Dies -------------------- Don Pomes†6
The Mute -------------------------------- Franc Geraci†7

UNDERSTUDIES: Narrator, David Cryer;
Boy, Richard Rothbard; Girl, Carole Demas

MUSICAL NUMBERS: "Try To Remember,"
"Much More," "Metaphor," "Never Say No,"
"It Depends On What You Pay," "Soon It's
Gonna Rain," "Rape Ballet," "Happy Ending,"
"This Plum Is Too Ripe," "I Can See It,"
"Plant A Radish," "Round and Round,"
"They Were You."

A Musical in two acts.

General Manager: Bob MacDonald
Press: Harvey B. Sabinson, David Powers
Stage Managers: Geoffrey Brown,
Jay Hampton, Ron Prather

° Still playing May 31, 1968. For original
production, see THEATRE WORLD, Vol.
16.

† Succeeded by: 1. Jack Crowder, Nils
Hendrick, Robert Goss, Joe Bellomo, 2. Leta
Anderson, Anne Kaye, 3. Gary Krawford,
Steve Skiles, 4. Ray Stewart, 5. F. Murray
Abraham, 6. Tom Lacy, 7. Ron Prather,
Franc Geraci.

Van Williams Photos

Top Right: (from front) Robert Goss, F. Murray
Abraham, Don Pomes, Franc Geraci,
Erik Howell, Carole Demas

Tom Lacy, Carole Demas, Joe Bellomo,
F. Murray Abraham

94

Clockwise from bottom: Ron Prather, F. Murray
Abraham, Ray Stewart, Steve Skiles, Joe Bellomo,
Carole Demas, John J. Martin, Tom Lacy

POCKET THEATER

Opened Sunday, November 6, 1966.°

Stephanie Sills Productions, Inc. presents:

AMERICA HURRAH

By Jean-Claude van Itallie; Incidental Music, Marianne du Pury, Fred Cantor; Lighting, Ken Glickfeld; Costumes, Tania Leontov; Slides and Poster Design, Francisca Duran-Reynals; Assistant to Producer, Lee Beltzer; Production Assistant, Richard Dunham.

CAST

"Interview"

Directed by Joseph Chaikin

First Interviewer ―――――― Cynthia Harris[†1]
First Applicant ―――――― Conard Fowkes[†2]
Second Interviewer ―――――― James Barbosa[†3]
Second Applicant ―――――― Ronnie Gilbert[†4]
Third Interviewer ―――――― Brenda Smiley[†5]
Third Applicant ―――――― Henry Calvert[†6]
Fourth Interviewer ―――――― Bill Macy[†7]
Fourth Applicant ―――――― Joyce Aaron[†8]

The action takes place at the present time in The City.

"TV"

Directed by Jacques Levy

Hal ―――――― Conard Fowkes[†2]
Susan ―――――― Brenda Smiley[†5]
George ―――――― Bill Macy[†7]
TV People ―――――― Jillian Lieder,
Roy London, Henry Calvert, Suzanne Gilbert, Alice Tweedie

The action takes place at the present time in the viewing room of a television rating company.

"Motel"

Directed by Jacques Levy

Dolls played by Conard Fowkes [†2], James Barbosa [†7], and Brenda Smiley [†5]. Motel Keeper's Voice: Ruth White.

General Manager: Krone-Olim Management Inc.
Press: Howard Atlee, William Cherry
Stage Manager: Kay Pollack

° Closed May 5, 1968 after 634 performances.
† Succeeded by: 1. Dorothy Lyman, Alice Tweedie, 2. Philip Harris, Keith Jochim, 3. Roy London, 4. Shami Chaikin, Suzanne Gilbert, 5. Peta Hargarther, 6. John Carpenter, Henry Calvert, 7. Ron Faber, Bill Macy, 8. Marcia Jean Kurtz, Jillian Lieder.

Bert Andrews Photos

Ron Faber, Marcia Jean Kurtz, Dorothy Lyman, Shami Chaikin, Roy London, Brank Bara, Peta Hargarther, Philip Harris. Above: Conard Fowkes, Bill Macy, Henry Calvert, James Barbosa, Cynthia Harris, Ronnie Gilbert, Brenda Smiley, Joyce Aaron

THEATRE 80 ST. MARKS

Opened Tuesday, March 7, 1967.°
Arthur Whitelaw and Gene Persson present:

YOU'RE A GOOD MAN, CHARLIE BROWN

Book, John Gordon; Based on Comic Strip "Peanuts" by Charles M. Schulz; Music and Lyrics, Clark Gesner; Director, Joseph Hardy; Sets and Costumes, Alan Kimmel; Lighting, Jules Fisher; Musical Supervision, Arrangements, and Additional Material, Joseph Raposo; Pianist, Ronald Clairmont; Percussions, Lou Nazarro; Associate Producer, Stanley Mann; Original cast album by MGM Records.

CAST

Linus	Bob Balaban†1
Charlie Brown	Gary Burghoff†2
Patty	Karen Johnson
Schroeder	Skip Hinnant
Snoopy	Bill Hinnant
Lucy	Reva Rose†3

MUSICAL NUMBERS: "You're A Good Man, Charlie Brown," "Schroeder," "Snoopy," "My Blanket and Me," "Kite," "Dr. Lucy," "Book Report," "The Red Baron," "T.E.A.M.," "Glee Club Rehearsal," "Little Known Facts," "Suppertime," "Happiness."

A Musical in two acts. The action takes place at the present time and is an average day in the life of Charlie Brown.

Company Manager: Larry Goossen
Press: Max Eisen, Carl Samrock,
Jeanne Gibson Merrick
Stage Managers: Ed Royce,
Chuck Brummitt

° Still playing May 31, 1968.

† Succeeded by: 1. Albert Sanders, 2. Sean Simpson, 3. Boni Enten.

Karen Johnson, Bill Hinnant. Top: Karen Johnson,
Bob Balaban, Skip Hinnant, Reva Rose,
Bill Hinnant, Gary Burghoff

PUERTO RICAN TRAVELING THEATER

Opened Monday, August 2, 1967.*
Mayor Lindsay's Summer Task Force
with August Heckscher present:

THE OX CART

By Rene Marques; Translated by Charles
Pilditch; Director, Lloyd Richards; Sets, Doug-
las Schmidt; Costumes, Joseph Aulisi; Sound,
George Jacobs; Production Supervisor, Jose
Ocasio; Project Director, Robert Buzzell; Tech-
nical Adviser, Richard Robbins; Production
Coordinator, Kathleen Scarlett.

CAST

Chaguito	Jose Perez
Dona Gabriela	Lucy Boscana
Juanita	Miriam Colon
Don Chago	Sol Serlin
Luis	Jaime Sanchez
Lito	Ruben Figueroa
Matilde	Carla Pinza
Dona Isa	Corina Magureanu
Paco	Jose Ocasio
Lidia	Mary Tahmin

A Drama in three acts. The action takes
place at the present time in San Juan, Puerto
Rico, and The Bronx, New York.

Business Manager: Gilberto Zaldivar
Press: David Lipsky, Marian Graham
Stage Manager: James Gore

* Closed Aug. 26, 1967 after 15 performances.

George Edgar Photo

Right: Miriam Colon, Jaime Sanchez

STAGE 73

Opened Thursday, June 1, 1967.*
David Hedges and William B. Allen in
association with Richard Herd present:

IN THE NICK OF TIME

Material by Barbara Fried, Charles Appel,
Herb Suffrin, Lenny Stern, Sue Lawless, Ted
Pugh; Director, Earl Durham; Lighting, Jene
Youtt; Technical Director, Donald Martin;
Production Assistant, Darice Schanfarber.

CAST

Sue Lawless   Ted Pugh
Andrew Orestes Lesko

An Intimate Revue in two acts.

General Manager: Show Management Inc.
Press: Betty Lee Hunt.
Fred Weterick, Henry Luhrman
Stage Manager: Charles Miller

* Closed June 18, 1967. (22 performances)

Sue Lawless, Ted Pugh

ROUNDABOUT THEATRE

Opened Friday, May 19, 1967.°
The Roundabout Theatre presents:

PINS AND NEEDLES

Music and Lyrics, Harold Rome; Sketches, Joseph Schrank; Director, Gene Feist; Musical Direction and Arrangements, Mary Chaffee; Dances and Musical Numbers Staged by Larry Life; Designed by I. Milton Duke; Costume Supervision, Rose Fedorin; Pianist, Tom Rehrig; Percussionist, Shelley Tominic; Coordinator, Gertrude Ketchel.

CAST

Zaida Coles	Joe Abramski
Loretta Long	Richard Allan
Ellen March	David Baker
Susan Stevens	John Byrd
Elaine Tishler	Roger Lawson

Larry Life

Standbys: Elizabeth Owens, Norman Lind

PROGRAM

ACT I: "Sing Me A Song of Social Significance," "Four Little Angels of Peace," "Chain Store Daisy," "Not Cricket To Picket," "I've Got The Nerve To Be In Love," "One Big Union For Two," "Bertha The Sewing Machine Girl," "What Good Is Love?," "Back To Work."

ACT II: "Sunday In The Park," "G-Man," "Status Quo," "I've Got The Nerve," "Cream of Mush," "Nobody Makes A Pass At Me," "Doing The Revolutionary," "Mene Mene Tekel."

A Musical Revue of the 1930's.

Press: Lawrence Rothman, Terese Kreuzer

Stage Managers: David Baker, Steve Toback

° Closed March 24, 1968 after 214 performances.

Ronald Berger Photos

Roger Lawson, Susan Stevens, Ellen March, John Byrd
Top: Wendy Lesniak, Larry Life

SHERIDAN SQUARE PLAYHOUSE

Opened Thursday, June 22, 1967.°
Edgar Lansbury, Stuart Duncan, Dina
and Alexander E. Racolin present:

ARMS AND THE MAN

By George Bernard Shaw; Director, Philip
Minor; Set and Costumes, Lloyd Burlingame;
Lighting, Fred Allison.

CAST

Catherine Petkoff	Jane Rose
Raina	Pamela Burrell
Louka	Jacqueline Coslow†
Captain Bluntschli	John Heffernan
Russian Officer	Theodore Sorel
Nicola	Karl Light
Major Petkoff	Daniel F. Keyes
Major Sergius Saranoff	Humbert Allen Astredo

A Comedy in three acts. The action takes
place in Bulgaria in 1885.

Company Manager: Jewel Howard
Press: Joseph Beruh, Max Eisen
Stage Manager: Don Judge

° Closed Dec. 3, 1967 after 190 performances.

† Succeeded by Gretchen Corbett, then Jenny
O'Hara.

Top: Pamela Burrell, Daniel F. Keyes, Jane Rose

Pamela Burrell, John Heffernan

THEATER DE LYS

Thursday, June 29, 1967.°
Theodore Mann and Paul Libin present
the Circle In The Square Production of:

A MIDSUMMER NIGHT'S DREAM

By William Shakespeare; Director, John
Hancock; Associate Director, Kenneth Kitch;
Designed by Robert LaVigne after drawings
by Jim Dine; Lighting, Al Jutzi; Presented
by special arrangement with Lucille Lortel
Productions, Inc.; Technical Director, William
Andrews; Production Manager, Charles Ham-
ilton; Prodution Associate, Connie Danielson.

CAST

Theseus	Alvin Epstein
Hippolyta	Gloria Foster†1
Philostrate	Barton Heyman
Ageus	Henry Oliver†2
Hermia	Susan Anspach
Demetrius	Stephen Wyman
Lysander	David Tress
Helena	Robert Benson
Peter Quince	Marshall Efron
Nick Bottom	Alan Manson†3
Francis Flute	Stephen Wyman
Robert Starveling	Mark Charlot
Snug	Henry Oliver†2
Tom Snout	Wayne Grace†4
Puck	Barton Heyman
First Fairy	Katie Heflin†5
Oberon	Alvin Epstein
Titania	Gloria Foster†1
Peaseblossom	Carol Anshein
Cobweb	Anna Stanovitch
Moth	Amy Vane
Mustardseed	Catherine Cleaves
Indian Girl	Nitza Sue

SOLDIERS, VESTALS, ZOMBIES: Carol Ans-
hein, Catherine Cleaves, Wayne Grace, Katie
Heflin, Tina Holmes, Dee Ann O'Keefe, Anna
Stanovitch, Amy Vane.

Presented in two acts.

General Manager: Paul Libin
Press: Merle Debuskey, Violet Welles,
Faith Geer
Stage Manager: Jan Moerel

° Closed Sunday, July 23, 1967. (28 performances)

† Succeeded by: 1. Mayo Loiseau, 2. David
Craven, 3. Sheldon Baron, 4. Jack Colombo,
5. Anna Stanovitch.

Friedman-Abeles Photos

Top Right: Gloria Foster, Alvin Epstein

Alvin Epstein, Gloria Foster

JONES BEACH THEATRE

Opened Sunday, July 2, 1967.°
Guy Lombardo presents:

ARABIAN NIGHTS

Book, George Marion, Jr.; Music and Lyrics, Carmen Lombardo, John Jacob Loeb; Musical Staging and Choreography, Yurek Lazowski; Scenery, Peter Dohanos; Costumes, Winn Morton; Lighting, Peggy Clark; Orchestrations, Joe Glover, John Jacob Loeb; Additional Ballet Arrangements, Vladimir Djury; Musical Direction, Oscar Kosarin; Choral Director, Robert Monteil; Entire Production under Supervision of Arnold Spector.

CAST

Genie	Norman Riggins
Captain of the Guard	Edmund Walenta
Grand Wazir, Lord High Executioner	Lee Cass
Na-eel-ah, Teeny Weeny Genie	Judy Knaiz
Ali, Court Magician, Medium Genie	Jack Adams
Scheherazade	Linda Bennett
Prince Ahmed, Sinbad, Aladdin	James Hurst
Sultan, Chinese Emperor	Norman Atkins
Court Dancer, Jewel Princess	Joy Holiday
Royal Dancer	Ron Holiday
Serpent and Charmer	Leslie and Simone
Kan-Shee	Sherry Lambert
Court Entertainers	Sahara Troupe
Royal Dancers	Ron & Joy Holiday, Leslie & Simone, Yurek Lazowski Ballet

SINGERS: Katherine Barnes, Doris Galiber, Genevieve George, Barbara Gregory, Sherry Lambert, Leonore Lanzillotti, Carol Marraccini, Joyce Olson, Mary Ann Rydzeski, Dixie Stewart, Marsha Tamaroff, Maggie Worth, Peter Clark, Peter Costanza, Daniel Entriken, Jack Fletcher, Nino Galanti, Leslie Meadow, Robert Monteil, Adam Petroski, Herbert Pordum, Edmund Walenta, David Wilder.

DANCERS: Harriet Ali, Sandra Brown, Joetta Cherry, Peggy Christiansen, Claude Duvernoy, Jean Ann Einwick, Mimi Funes, Sunny Hannum, Eugenia Hoeflin, Jane Jaffe, Virginia Karczewski, Eileen Lawlor, Melissa Martinez, Ruth Mills, Jannas Perlman, Virginia Putnam, Lucinda Ransom, Ellen Rievman, Francine Storey, Ellen Wollenhaupt, Fred Benjamin, John Giffin Bijan Kalantari, Alexis Kotimsky, George Lee, Stanley Levy, Robert Lupone, Stephen Reinhardt, Tony Salatino, Don Stromsvik.

MERMAIDS: Jean Adams, Amy Card, Barbara Fleming, Patti Lewis, Kathleen Shaughnessy.

UNDERSTUDIES: Scheherazade, Marsha Tamaroff; Ahmed, Norman Riggins; Sultan, Adam Petroski; Grand Wizer, Jack Fletcher.

MUSICAL NUMBERS: "What A Party," "It's Great To Be Alive," "The Grand Wazir's Lament," "A Thousand and One Nights," "Hail To The Sultan," "I Only Live For Today," "Royal Ritual," "Bring On The Bride To Be," "Hero Of All My Dreams," "A Whale of A Story," "Serpent Dance," "Ballet of Jewels," "Marry The One You Love," "Ladies' Maids In Waiting," "How Long Has It Been?," "Teeny Weeny Genie," "Chinese Wedding," "Royal Ballet," Finale.

A Musical Extravaganza in 2 acts and 7 scenes. The action takes place in Bagdad, at sea, and in China, in the past.

Company Manager: Leonard Soloway
Press: Saul Richman
Stage Managers: Mortimer Halpern, Norman Shelly, William Krot, Peter Lawrence

° Closed Sept. 3, 1967 after 63 performances.

Top Right: James Hurst, Norman Atkins, Linda Bennett

Lee Cass, Linda Bennett

NAVE THEATRE

Opened Wednesday, July 26, 1967.°
The Columbia University Summer Repertory Theatre (Isaiah Sheffer, Director) presents the American Premieres of:

CHRONICLES OF HELL

By Michel de Ghelderode; Director, Isaiah Sheffer; Settings, James F. Gohl; Costumes, Leigh Rand; Lighting, Lawrence Metzler.

CAST

Carnibos	Robert Silver
Krakenbus	Joseph Totaro
Dom Pikkedoncker	William Shorr
Real-Tremblor	Frank Groseclose
Duvelhond	Robert Weening
Simon Laquedeem	Clifton James
Veneranda	Elise Smith
Sodomati	Robert Walter Greenwood
Jan in Eremo	James Antonio
Guards	Gregory Kimmelman, Hale Hetherington
Master of Butchers	Art Callahan
Butchers	Antony Andrisano, Thomas Barto, Hale Hetherington, Edward Reese, Raymond Xifo

The action takes place in Medieval Flanders in an Episcopal Palace.

CHRISTOPHER COLUMBUS

By Michel de Ghelderode; Director, Isaiah Sheffer; Settings, James F. Gohl; Costumes, Leigh Rand; Lighting, Lawrence Metzler.

CAST

Christopher Columbus	Lou Gilbert
Reporter	Robert Silver
Photographer	Debby Locitzer
Businessman	Clifton James
Sleepwalker	Leah Laiman
Minister	Frank Groseclose
Scholar	Joseph Totaro
King	James Antonio
Folial	Antony Andrisano
Woman	Irene O'Brien
Crowd	William Shorr
Lookout	Robert Weening
Helmsman	Gregory Kimmelman
Sailors	Thomas Barto, Bill Compton, Raymond Xifo
Visquoisine	Flonnie Anderson
Azuret	Edward Reese
Montezuma	Robert Walter Greenwood
Indian Dancers	Beverly Daggett, Robert Walter Greenwood, Trelicia Gunawardana
Poet	Robert Weening
Admiral Death	Joseph Totaro
American	Robert Silver
Texas Couple	Art Callahan, Irene O'Brien
Drummer	Thomas Barto
Girl Scout	Lynn Folinus
Model	Kathleen Donohue
Lady with baby carriage	Jamie Randazzo
Teeny Bopper	Nikki Barteen
Knight of Columbus	Raymond Xifo

A Dramatic Fairy Tale in three scenes. The action takes place in the Old World and the New in 1492 and 1967.

Opened Tuesday, August 1, 1967.°

THE HAPPY HAVEN

By John Arden; Director, Isaiah Sheffer; Designed by Jim Rule; Music, Alan Miller.

CAST

Dr. Copperthwaite	James Antonio
Crape	Frank Groseclose
Hardrader	Lou Gilbert
Golightly	Robert Walter Greenwood
Letouzel	Kathryn Jones Rao

The action takes place in a hospital.

Production Coordinator: Ruth Gennrich
Technical Supervisor: Jim Rule
Stage Managers: Flonnie Anderson, Elise Smith

° Closed Aug. 13, 1967 after 19 performances in repertory.

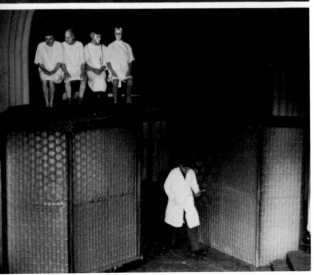

Frank Groseclose, Lou Gilbert, Robert Greenwood, Kathryn Jones Rao, James Antonio in "The Happy Haven". Above: Frank Groseclose. Top: Robert Silver, Joseph Totaro, William Shorr in "Chronicles of Hell"

THEATRE EAST

Opened Tuesday, September 12, 1967.°
Billy K Productions in association with
God presents:

KLENOSKY AGAINST THE SLINGS AND ARROWS OF OUTRAGEOUS FORTUNE

Music and Lyrics by William Klenosky;
Book, by Life; No Scenery by Klenosky;
Lighting, Con Edison; Assistants, James Eagan,
Charles Adler, Joe Kover.

CAST
William J. Klenosky

PART I: "The Hooligan's Hop," "Ye Shall
Know The Truth," "Which CAN See Further,
An Ant or An Eagle," "I See By The Pa-
pers," "The Making of President Fink," "The
Magillah," "How To Become The Lightest
Soldier In The History of The U.S. Army,"
"How To Get Rich Quick," "The Bald Eagle
and The Hairy Canaries," "The French Fink,"
"A Million Dollar Fiasco," "Guggenheim's
Bald Eagle," "The K-Bomb," "Krushchev,
Castro and Klenosky," "Independence Day,
July 4th, 1959."

PART II: "L'Audace, L'Audace et plus
L'Audace!," "A Little Moosic To Soothe The
Savage," "Malaguena," "Return To Utopia,"
"They That Buildeth A Wall Against Man,"
"The World's Greatest Loser?," "The Re-
publican Dilemma: Goldwater or Klenosky,"
"Lindsay Was Prettier and Taller Than Kle-
nosky and Who's Sorry Now?," "The Loser's
Dream Team," "Klenosky vs. Thaler," "No-
Holds Barred Press Conference," "An Ameri-
can Odyssey" in two parts.

Press: Richard H. Roffman

° Closed Sept. 24, 1967 after 12 performances.

William J. Klenosky

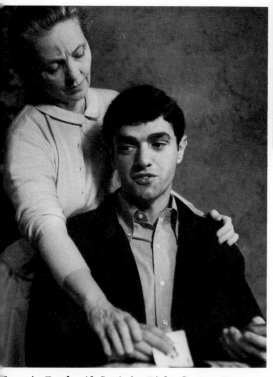

Eugenia Rawls, Al Settimio. Right Center: Ron
Liebman, Al Settimio

MARTINIQUE THEATRE

Opened Tuesday, September 19, 1967.°
Richard H. R. Smithies and Maura
Cavanagh present:

THE POKER SESSION

By Hugh Leonard; Director, Richard H. R.
Smithies; Designed by C. Murawski.

CAST

Billy Beavis	Al Settimio
Mrs. Beavis	Eugenia Rawls
Irene	Holland Taylor
Kevin	Tom Keena
Fran	Eileen Mitchell
Teddy	Ron Liebman

A Drama in three acts. The action takes
place on a summer evening of the present
time in the Beavis home.

General Manager: Krone-Olim Management
Press: David Rothenberg,
Larry Schneider
Stage Managers: Martha Knight,
Susan Kaslow

° Closed Oct. 1, 1967 after 16 performances.

Bert Andrews Photos

STAGE 73
Opened Thursday, September 21, 1967.°
Hal Thompson presents:

JONAH!

By T. J. Spencer; Director, Hal Thompson;
Costumes, Eileen MacHardy; Lighting, Peter
Russell; Music Composed by Morris Mamorsky;
Scenic Art, Ruth Dash; Assistant to Producer,
Dody Appl; Sound Effects, Filmsounds.

CAST
Bos'n	Colin Craig
Samuel	Lawrence Barrett
Nicholas	John Valentine †1
Zorgo	Arthur French
Seamen	John Shearer, Charles Murphy
Ezra	Jay Gerber †2
Captain	Russell Baker
Agent	W. P. Dremak
Jonah	Laurens Moore
Ulysses	Joseph Warren
Thersites	Bradley Bolke

A Comedy in two acts and four scenes. The
action takes place in B.C. aboard the Mary
Beth, inside a fish, and outside the gates of
Ninevah.

General Manager: Roan Management
Press: Nat Dorfman, Barbara Sergejev
Stage Manager: Phil Parker

† Succeeded by: 1. Jack Shearer, 2. John
Valentine.

Arthur French, Laurens Moore. Top: Laurens Moore,
Colin Craig, Jay Gerber

EAST 74th STREET THEATRE

Opened Sunday, September 24, 1967.°
Lyn Austin and Oliver Smith, Philip Mathias, by arrangement with Peter Bridge present:

STEPHEN D.

Adapted by Hugh Leonard from James Joyce's "A Portrait of The Artist As A Young Man," and "Stephen Hero;" Director, James D. Waring; Scenic Production and Lighting, Jack Brown; Music Consultant, Emerson Meyers; Choreography, Edward J. McPhillips; Songs Sung by Mrs. Mary Mulligan; Production Associate, Ann McIntosh; Production Assistant, Edith M. P. Wehle; Sound Technician, Will Richter; Production Aide, Kenneth Swiger.

CAST

Stephen Dedalus	Stephen Joyce
Mrs. Dedalus	Joan White
Dante	Betty Garde
Stephen (as a boy)	Chad Roche
Fleming	Jamie Roche
Wells	Geoffrey Martin
Athy	Sean Roche
Brother Michael	Drew Eliot
Mr. Dedalus	Brendan Fay
Mr. Casey	Neil Fitzgerald
Uncle Charles	Edward J. McPhillips
Father Arnall	William Prince
Father Dolan	Ian Edward
Stephen (as a youth)	John McGurran
Johnny Cashman	Drew Eliot
Woman	Jean Hickey
Preacher	William Prince
Confessor	Neil Fitzgerald
Director of College	Ian Edward
Maurice	Douglas Richardson
Cranly	Roy R. Scheider
Davin	Dermot McNamara
President of University	Edward J. McPhillips
McCann	Walker Daniels
Dixon	Thomas McCready
Temple	John Luce
Emma	Flora Elkins
Father Moran	Drew Eliot
Flower Seller	Patricia Fay
Isobel	Joan E. Spalding
Girl	Valerie Romig

UNDERSTUDIES: Cranley, Stephen D., John Luce; Mrs. Dedalus, Dante, Patricia Fay; Mr. Dedalus, Casey, Confessor, Director, Drew Eliot; Michael, Maurice, Temple, Walker Daniels; Cashman, Douglas Richardson; Arnall, Preacher, Edward J. McPhillips; McCann, Dakin, Thomas McCready; Emma, Jean Hickey; Uncle, Dermot McNamara.

A Drama in two acts. The action takes place in Dublin and other parts of Ireland between 1882 and 1902.

General Manager: Oscar Olesen
Press: Samuel Lurie,
Stanley F. Kaminsky
Stage Managers: Charles Atkin,
Drew Eliot

° Closed Nov. 12, 1967 after 56 performances.

Roy R. Scheider, Stephen Joyce

Stephen Joyce, Flora Elkins

THEATRE DE LYS

Opened Tuesday, September 26, 1967.°
David Cryer and Albert Poland present:

NOW IS THE TIME FOR ALL GOOD MEN

Book and Lyrics, Gretchen Cryer; Music, Nancy Ford; Director, Word Baker; Musical Direction, Stephen Lawrence; Musical Arrangements, Stephen Lawrence, Nancy Ford; Settings, Holly Haas; Costumes, Jeanne Button; Lighting, Carol Rubinstein; Photographic Effects, Henry Bigger; Presented by Special Arrangements with Lucille Lortel Productions; Technical Director, Jack Magnifico; Original Cast album by Columbia Records.

CAST

Sarah Larkin	Sally Niven
	(Gretchen Cryer)
Eugenie Seldin	Judy Frank
Mike Butler	David Cryer †1
Tooney	Donna Curtis
Albert McKinley	David Sabin
Betty Brown	Margot Hanson
Esther Mason	Regina Lynn
Herbert Heller	Art Wallace †2
Bill Miller	John Bennett Perry
Jasper Wilkins	Murray Olson †3
Ramona	Anne Kaye †4
Tommy	Steve Skiles

UNDERSTUDIES: Mike, John Bennett Perry; Sarah, Margot Hanson; Albert, Murray Olson; Tooney, Regina Lynn; Eugenie, Donna Curtis; Tommy, John Long; Ramona, Sharon Stuntz

MUSICAL NUMBERS: "We Shall Meet In The Great Hereafter," "Keep 'em Busy, Keep 'em Quiet," "What's In The Air," "Tea In The Rain," "What's A Guy Like You Doin' In A Place Like This?," "Halloween Hayride," "Campfire Songs," "See Everything New," "All Alone," "He Could Show Me," "Washed Away," "Stuck-Up," "My Holiday," "On My Own," "It Was Good Enough For Grandpa," "A Simple Life," "A Star On The Monument," "Rain Your Love On Me."

A Musical Play in two acts. The action takes place now in Bloomdale, Indiana.

General Manager: Paul B. Berkowsky
Press: Saul Richman
Stage Manager: David Shanstrom

° Closed Dec. 31, 1967 after 111 performances and 22 previews.

† Succeeded by: 1. John Bennett Perry, 2. Murray Olson, 3. John Long, 4. Judy Allen.

Barry Kramer Photos

Steve Skiles, Anne Kaye

Regina Lynn, David Sabin, Sally Niven
Top: Gretchen Cryer, David Sabin, David Crye

ORPHEUM THEATRE

Opened Sunday, October 1, 1967.°
Lyn Austin and Oliver Smith, Hale
Matthews present:

THE NIGGERLOVERS

By George Tabori; Director, Gene Frankel;
Scenery and Lighting, Jack Brown; Costumes,
Jeanne Button; Music, Richard Peaslee; Lyrics,
George Tabori; Production Associate, Ann Mc-
Intosh; Production Assistants, Jane Whitehill,
Edith M. P. Wehle; Technical Director, Wil-
liam Andrews.

CAST

"The Demonstration"

Creampuff	Morgan Freeman
Freckles	James Spruill
August	Stacy Keach
Angela	Viveca Lindfors

"Man and Dog"

The Dog	Viveca Lindfors
The Man	Stacy Keach
Freckles	James Spruill
Creampuff	Morgan Freeman

STANDBYS: Rosemary Tory, Gordon Watkins

Presented in two acts. The action takes
place today in New York City.

General Manager: Oscar Olesen
Press: Samuel Lurie, Stanley F. Kaminsky
Company Manager: James Walsh
Stage Managers: James Dwyer,
Gordon Watkins

° Closed Oct. 22, 1967 after 25 performances.

Viveca Lindfors, Stacy Keach,
James Spruill, Morgan Freeman

CHERRY LANE THEATER

Opened Monday, October 2, 1967.°
Edgar Lansbury and Marc Merson present:

FRAGMENTS

By Murray Schisgal; Director, Larry Arrick;
Scenery, Kert Lundell; Lighting, Roger Morgan; Costumes, Liz Dominick; Associate Producer, Charlotte Schiff; Production Assistant,
Emily Prager.

CAST

"Basement"

Zach	Gene Hackman
Minna	Sylvia Gassell
Leo	James Coco

The action takes place at the present time
in the basement of an old one-family house.

"Fragments"

Jax	Humbert Allen Astredo
Baxter	Gene Hackman
Max	James Coco
Ann	Tresa Hughes

The action takes place at the present time
in a furnished room.

General Manager: Joseph Beruh
Company Manager: Jewel Howard
Press: Max Eisen, Jeanne Gibson Merrick,
Carl Samrock
Stage Manager: Gigi Cascio

° Closed Oct. 22, 1967 after 24 performances.

Friedman-Abeles Photos

James Coco, Gene Hackman, Humbert Allen
Astredo in "Fragments". Above: James Coco, Gene
Hackman in "Basement"

Opened Tuesday, October 10, 1967.°
Ivor David Balding in association with
Alvin Ferleger and Gordon Crowe presents:

SCUBA DUBA

By Bruce Jay Friedman; Director, Jacques
Levy; Scenery, Peter Larkin; Costumes, Willa Kim; Lighting, Jules Fisher; Incidental
Music, Stanley Walden; Presented by Special
Arrangement with The Establishment Theatre
Co., Inc.; Production Coordinator, Richard
Scanga; Technical Adviser, Timothy F. Donovan.

CAST

Harold Wonder	Jerry Orbach
Miss Janus	Brenda Smiley
Tourist	Conrad Bain
Landlady	Rita Karin
Thief	Judd Hirsch
Gendarme	Bernard Poulain
Dr. Schoenfeld	Ken Olfson
Cheyenne	Christine Norden †
Jean Wonder	Jennifer Warren
Foxtrot	Cleavon Little
Reddington	Rudy Challenger
Voice of	
Harold's Mother	Stella Longo

UNDERSTUDIES: Harold, Judd Hirsch; Tourist, Doctor, Carl Low; Thief, Gendarme,
George Litter; Janus, Jean, Betti Seay; Foxtrot, Reddington, Roy Inman

A Comedy in two acts. The action takes
place in a chateau in the South of France at
the present time.

General Manager: Michael Brandman
Company Manager: Dean Delk
Press: Michael Alpert, Warren Pincus
Stage Managers: Richard Scanga,
Robert Anthony

° Still playing May 31, 1968.

† Succeeded by Phyllis Craig.

Bert Andrews Photos

Jennifer Warren, Rudy Challenger, Jerry Orbach, Cleavon Little
Top Left: Brenda Smiley, Jerry Orbach

THEATRE FOUR

Opened Tuesday, October 10, 1967.°
Jean Dalrymple presents:

BEYOND DESIRE

By Constance Loux; Adapted from novel by Pierre LaMure; Director, Jean Dalrymple; Sets and Lighting, Feder; Music Arranged by Max Marlin; Associate Producer, Homer Poupart; Production Assistant, Madge D. Graves; Hairstylist, Jene Chandler.

CAST

Karl Klingman	Franchot Tone
Leah Mendelssohn	Mary Bell
Abraham Mendelssohn	Jay Velie
Anna Bach	Ethel Smith
Herr Weinlick	Norman Budd
Herr Grumler	John Scanlan
Felix Mendelssohn	Richard Sterne
Frederic Chopin	Andre Plamondon
Amschel Rothschild	Ben Yaffee
Cecile Jeanrenaud	Betsy von Furstenberg
Nina	Jane Marla Robbins
Mayor Muller	Jay Barney
Herr Kruger	Richard Kuss
Pastor Hagen	John Scanlan
Herr Howlitz	Ben Yaffee
Gustave	John Scanlan
Herman Schmidt	Norman Budd
Otto Reinbach	Samuel Behar
Kristine Reinbach	Deirdre Sullivan
Tanzen	Michael Pederson
Magdalena Klupp	Jo Flores Chase

UNDERSTUDIES: Klingman, Jay Velie; Cecile, Jane Marla Robbins; Leah, Magdalena, Ethel Smith; Chopin, Felix, Kenneth Chertok; Anna, Jo Flores Chase.

A Play with music in two acts with prologue. The action takes place in Europe between 1750 and 1847.

Company Manager: Max Gendel
Press: Homer Poupart, John Clugstone
Stage Managers: Rachel Meltzer,
Wendy Ann Gardner

° Closed Oct. 15, 1967 after 8 performances and 7 previews.

Kurt Bergstroem Photo

Richard Sterne, Franchot Tone,
Betsy Von Furstenberg

BLACKFRIARS' THEATRE

Opened Tuesday, October 10, 1967.°
The Blackfriars' Guild presents:

GUIMPES AND SADDLES

By Rev. Edward A. Molloy; Director, Walter Cool; Settings and Lighting, Robert Charles; Costumes, Alice Merrigal.

CAST

Alec Konelli	Joe Anthony or John Davis
Ted Dugan	Ted Rado or William Houston
Dan Dugan	Christopher J. Keeley or Martin J. McHale
Cathy Wilson	Angela Kochera or Rebecca Young
Alice Dugan	Dorothy Ott or Evelyn Denon
Sister Monica	Josephine Harris or Nancy McHugh
Sister Clara	Joan A. Jahoda or Kathleen Phillips
Louise Gannon	Mary Ellen Flynn or Gwen Saska

A Comedy-Drama in 3 acts and 4 scenes. The action takes place at Christmas of 1967 in the living-room of the middle-class Dugan family in the Flatbush section of Brooklyn.

Press: Rev. Thomas F. Carey
Stage Managers: Robert Charles,
Thomas F. Stanton

° Closed Nov. 26, 1967 after 46 performances.

Josephine Harris, Christopher J. Keeley

Opened Tuesday, October 31, 1967.°

H.M.S. PINAFORE

Sir Joseph Porter .... John Carle
Captain Corcoran .... Richard Duncan
Tom Tucker .... Helene Andreu
Ralph Rackstraw .... James Wilson
Dick Deadeye .... William Fleck
Bill Bobstay .... William Tost
Josephine .... Sandra Darling
Bob Becket .... Bill Collins
Hebe .... Ruth Ray
Mrs. Cripps .... Marilyn Jewett
UNDERSTUDIES: Helene Andreu, Bruce
Campbell, Lana Caradimas, Dennis Carpenter,
Bill Collins, Brenda Gardner, Carol Grant,
Mina Jo King, Irma Rogers, Nick Titakis,
Robert Trombetta.
General Manager: Hedges-Allen, Inc.
Manager: Mark Durand
Press: Ben Kornzweig, Reginald Denenholz
Stage Manager: Bob Fahey
° Closed Dec. 31, 1967 after 88 performances
and 16 previews in repertory.

Van Williams Photos

John Carle, William Tost, Kate Hurney, Jim Wilson
in "Iolanthe"

110

JAN HUS PLAYHOUSE

Opened Thursday, October 12, 1967.°
American Gilbert & Sullivan Presentations
Inc. (Dorothy Raedler, Executive Direc-
tor) present The American Savoyards in:

PATIENCE

Libretto, W. S. Gilbert; Music, Arthur Sul-
livan; Staged by Dorothy Raedler; Musical
Direction, Lucille Burnham; Settings, Michael
Hotopp; Lighting, Kip Newland; Assistant
Musical Director, Margaret Singer; At the or-
gan, Margaret Singer; At the piano, Lucille
Burnham.

CAST

Colonel Calverley .... William Fleck
Major Murgatroyd .... Richard Duncan
Lt., The Duke
of Dunstable .... James Wilson
Reginald Bunthorne .... John Carle
Archibald Frosvenor .... William Tost
Solicitor .... Cliff Cunningham
Lady Angela .... Ruth Ray
Lady Saphir .... Carol Grant
Lady Ella .... Kate Hurney
Lady Jane .... Marilyn Jewett
Patience .... Sandra Darling

Opened Tuesday, October 17, 1967°

IOLANTHE

Lord Chancellor .... John Carle
Earl of Mountararat .... William Tost
Earl Tolloller .... James Wilson
Private Willis .... William Fleck
Strephon .... Richard Duncan
Queen of The Fairies .... Marilyn Jewett
Iolanthe .... Ruth Ray
Celia .... Sandra Darling
Leila .... Carol Grant
Fleta .... Helene Andreu
Phyllis .... Kate Hurney

Opened Thursday, October 19, 1967°

THE GONDOLIERS

Duke of Plaza-Toro .... John Carle
Luiz .... Robert Trombetta
Don Alhambra Del Bolero .... William Fleck
Marco Palmieri .... James Wilson
Giuseppe Palmieri .... Richard Duncan
Antonio .... William Tost
Francesco .... Don Derrow
Giorgio .... Bill Collins
Annibale .... Dennis Carpenter
Duchess of Plaza-Toro .... Marilyn Jewett
Casilda .... Kate Hurney
Gianetta .... Sandra Darling
Tessa .... Ruth Ray
Fiametta .... Irma Rogers
Vittoria .... Lana Caradimas
Giulia .... Brenda Gardner
Inez .... Mina Jo King
Solo Cachucha Dancers .... Helene Andreu
and Dennis Carpenter

Opened Tuesday, October 24, 1967.°

THE MIKADO

Mikado of Japan .... William Fleck
Nanki-Poo .... James Wilson
Ko-Ko .... John Carle
Pooh-Bah .... William Tost
Pish-Tush .... Richard Duncan
Yum-Yum .... Kate Hurney
Pitti-Sing .... Ruth Ray
Peep-Bo .... Helene Andreu
Katisha .... Marilyn Jewett

Top Right: James Wilson, Sandra Darling, Willia[m]
Fleck, Marilyn Jewett, John Carle, Carol Gran[t]
Ruth Ray in "Patience"

AMERICAN PLACE THEATRE

Opened Thursday, October 12, 1967.°
The American Place Theatre (Wynn Handman, Director) presents:

FATHER UXBRIDGE WANTS TO MARRY

By Frank Gagliano; Director, Melvin Bernhardt; Designed by Douglas Schmidt; Lighting, John Gleason; Special Sound and Music by James Reichert; Figure of Mother by Robert Steinberg; Bach arias sung by Sandra Gagliano; Words and Music for "Ballad of Great Fall Hill" and "Mother's Lullaby" by Frank Gagliano; Production Assistant, David Trainer; Technical Director, Owen McEvoy.

CAST

Mrs. Bethnal-Green, The Mother,
  Stepney Green, Debden .... Olympia Dukakis
Morden .... Gene Roche
Father Uxbridge .... John Coe
Angel .... Carol Carpenter
Father Ongar .... Ken Kercheval

A Drama presented without intermission. The action takes place at the present time.

Press: John Springer Associates,
  Robert Ganshaw, Louise Weiner
Stage Managers: Peter Galambos,
  Kate M. Pollock

° Closed Nov. 7, 1967 after 27 performances.

Martha Holmes Photo

Carol Carpenter, John Coe, Gene Roche

ANSPACHER THEATER

Opened Tuesday, October 17, 1967.°
New York Shakespeare Festival Public Theater (Joseph Papp, Producer) presents:

HAIR

Book and Lyrics, Gerome Ragni and James Rado; Music, Galt MacDermot; Director, Gerald Freedman; Scenery, Ming Cho Lee; Costumes, Theoni V. Aldredge; Lighting, Martin Aronstein; Musical Director, John Morris; Associate Producer, Bernard Gersten; Manager, David Black; Original cast album by RCA Victor.

CAST

Dionne .... Jonelle Allen
"Dad" .... Ed Crowley
Claude .... Walker Daniels
Woof .... Steve Dean
Jeannie .... Sally Eaton
"Mom" .... Marijane Maricle
Sheila .... Jill O'Hara
Crissy .... Shelley Plimpton
Berger .... Gerome Ragni
Hud .... Arnold Wilkerson
Susan .... Susan Batson
Linda .... Linda Compton
Suzannah .... Suzzanah Evans
Louise .... Jane Levin
Alma .... Alma Robinson
Charlie .... Warren Burton
Thommie .... Thommie Bush
Bill .... William Herter
Paul .... Paul Jabara
Bob .... Bob Johnson
Jim .... Edward Murphy, Jr.

MUSICAL NUMBERS: "Red, Blue and White," "Ain't Got No," "I Got Life," "Air," "Going Down," "Hair," "Dead End," "Frank Mills," "Where Do I Go," "Electric Blues," "Easy To Be Hard," "Manchester," "White Boys," "Black Boys," "Walking In Space," "Aquarius," "Good Morning Starshine," "Exanaplanetooch," "Climax!"

A Musical in two acts.

Production Manager: Andrew Mihok
Press: Merle Debuskey, Faith Geer,
  Lawrence Belling
Stage Managers: Russell McGrath,
  Michael Chambers

° Closed Dec. 10, 1967 after 15 previews and 50 performances, and opened at Cheetah Dec. 22, and closed there on Jan. 28, 1968. Re-opened with cast changes on Apr. 29, 1968 at the Biltmore. See page 59.

George E. Joseph Photos

Gerome Ragni (with flag). Above: (L) Walker Daniels, Gerome Ragni. (L) Ed Crowley, Marijane Maricle

EVERGREEN THEATER

Opened Tuesday, October 24, 1967.°
James Walsh and Queen of Spades Inc.
present:

THE BEARD

By Michael McClure; Director, Rip Torn;
Design and Media Mix Prologue by USCO;
Costumes, Ann Roth; Lighting, C. Murawski.

CAST

Harlow _____ Billie Dixon
Billy the Kid _____ Richard Bright
A Play presented without intermission.
Press: David Rothenberg
Stage Manager: Paul John Austin
° Closed Jan. 14, 1968. (100 performances)

Bert Andrews Photo

Billie Dixon, Richard Bright in "The Beard"

Janis Young, Dan Tyra in "Where People Gather"

BOUWERIE LANE THEATRE

Opened Monday, October 30, 1966.°
Gree-Moo Production Company presents:

THE LITTLE PRIVATE WORLD OF ARTHUR MORTON FENWICK

Written and Directed by John A. Topa;
Scenery and Lighting, Gregory Martin.

CAST

The Actor _____ John A. Topa
The Actress _____ Susan McMullen

and

NO EXIT

By Jean Paul Sartre; Adapted by Paul
Bowles; Director, Chester Moody; Scenery and
Lighting, Gregory Martin.

CAST

Cradeau _____ Raul Julia
Bellboy _____ Michael D. Moore
Inez _____ Carolyn Y. Cardwell
Estelle _____ Susan McMullen
The action takes place in a room at the
present time.
General Manager: Evelyn Moody
Press: David Lipsky, Marian Graham
Stage Manager: Ed Dougherty
° Closed Nov. 5, 1967 after 8 performances
and 15 previews.

Friedman-Abeles Photos

GRAMERCY ARTS THEATRE

Opened Wednesday, October 25, 1967.°
The W.P.G. Company presents:

WHERE PEOPLE GATHER

By Peter Copani; Directed and Designed by
James Nisbet Clark; Song "Hope Is A Beauti-
ful Thing" by Peter Copani and James Nisbet
Clark.

CAST

R. C. Cobb _____ Neighbor,
Masochist, several men
Elek Hartman _____ Joey's Father,
A Drunk, several men
Holly Hill _____ Neighbor,
Nun, several women
Michael Kapec _____ Joey,
Blind Boy, Teacher
June Miller _____ Joey's Mother,
several women
Andy Milligan _____ Mimir
Ruth Ann Norris _____ Lethe's Mother,
Prostitute, several women
Dan Tyra _____ Lethe's Father,
Old Man, several men
Janis Young _____ Lethe
A Drama in 2 acts and 10 scenes.
Business Manager: Lily Turner
Press: Bernard Simon
Stage Manager: Joan Lebowitz
° Closed Oct. 29, 1967 after 7 performances.

Jacques Simson Photo

Susan McMullen, Raul Julia, Carolyn Y. Cardwe
in "No Exit"

CHERRY LANE THEATER

Opened Sunday, November 5, 1967.°
Franklin de Boer presents The Judson
Poets Theater Production of a circular
play:

IN CIRCLES

By Gertrude Stein; Director, Lawrence
Kornfeld; Music, Al Carmines; Set, Roland
Turner and Johnnie Jones; Lighting, Eric
Gertner; Technical Director, Reathal Bean.
This Production is for Alice B. Toklas.

CAST

Cousins	Theo Barnes
Mildred	Jacque Lynn Colton
Mable	Lee Crespi
Jessie	Elaine Summers †1
George	George McGrath
Sylvia	Arlene Rothlein
Dole	Al Carmines †2
Ollie	David Vaughan
The Citizen	Arthur Williams
Lucy Armitage	Nancy Zala

A Free-Form Play in one act with music.

General Manager: Joseph Beruh
Company Manager: Jerry Arrow
Press: Samuel J. Friedman,
Jane Friedman
Stage Manager: Roland Turner

° Closed May 12, 1968 after 222 performances.

† Succeeded by: 1. Lee Guilliatt, 2. David
Tice.

Arlene Rothlein, Al Carmines

Micheál MacLiammóir

ORPHEUM THEATRE

Opened Thursday, November 16, 1967.°
St. John Terrell and Krone-Olim Productions present:

I MUST BE TALKING
TO MY FRIENDS

Designed and Directed by Hilton Edwards;
Manager and Stage Director, Brian Tobin;
Lighting, Kerry Pennington; Technical Coordi-
nators, Paul Holland, Fred Krimmelbein, Lon
Mitchell.

CAST

Micheál MacLiammóir

A Reading in two parts in which Mr.
MacLiammóir plays host to the dramatists,
poets, wits, and revolutionaries of Ireland.

General Manager: Krone-Olim Management
Company Manager: Dorothy Olim
Press: Max Eisen, Carl Samrock

° Closed Dec. 10, 1967 after a limited engagement of 27 performances.

GREENWICH MEWS THEATRE

Opened Thursday, November 9, 1967.°
Farris-Belgrave Productions in association
with Afolabi Ajayi presents:

THE TRIALS OF BROTHER JERO

By Wole Soyinka; Director, Cynthia Belgrave; Sets and Lighting, Jack Blackman; Music Composed and Arranged by Pat Patrick; Original costumes from Nigeria by Edward Wolrond; Technical Director, Allan Shevalow; Production Assistant, Norman Farris; Sound Technician, Ted Krysty; Production dedicated to the late Stella Holt.

CAST

Brother Jero	Harold Scott †1
Old Prophet	Dennis Tate †2
Chume	Afolabi Ajayi
Amope	Cynthia Belgrave
A Trader Woman	Peggy Kirkpatrick
Girl Who Passes By	Lauren Jones
Drummer Boy	Edward Luis Espinosa
Penitent	Yvonne Warden
Member of Parliament	Roger Robinson
Neighbors	Yvette Hawkins,
	G. Tito Shaw, Mary Alice,
	Vernon Washington, James Spruill,
	Aston Young, Elmira Espinosa

A Comedy in four scenes with prologue presented without intermission.

and

THE STRONG BREED

By Wole Soyinka; Director, Cynthia Belgrave; Sets and Lighting, Jack Blackman.

CAST

Eman	Harold Scott †2
Sunma	Mary Alice
Ifada	Edward Luis Espinosa
A Sick Girl	Yvette Hawkins
Jaguna	James Spruill
Orage	Dennis Tate
Villagers	Peggy Kirkpatrick,
	Afolabi Ajayi, Yvonne Warden,
	Tom Hawkins, Austin Briggs Hall, Jr.
Eman's Father	Robertearl Jones
Attendant	Willie Woods
Omae	Lauren Jones
Young Eman	G. Tito Shaw
Tutor	Vernon Washington †3
Priest	Roger Robinson

A Drama in one act and ten scenes.

General Manager: Kenneth B. Farris
Business Manager: Gilberto Zaldivar
Press: David Lipsky, Marian Graham
Stage Managers: Bernard Ward,
Vernon Washington

° Closed Feb. 18, 1968 after 115 performances.

† Succeeded by: 1. Chuck Gordone, 2. Vernon Washington, 3. Roger Robinson.

James E. Jackson Photos

114 Harold Scott, Lauren Jones, G. Tito Shaw
Above: Vernon Washington, G. Tito Shaw,
Lauren Jones in "The Strong Breed"

Harold Scott, Edward Luis Espinosa in "The
Strong Breed". Top Left: Afolabi Ajayi,
Cynthia Belgrave in "Trials Of Brother Jero"

CIRCLE IN THE SQUARE

Opened Tuesday, November 21, 1967.°
Circle in the Square Inc. (Theodore Mann, Artistic Director; Paul Libin, Managing Director; Gillian Walker, Associate Director) presents:

IPHIGENIA IN AULIS

By Euripides; English version by Minos Volanakis; Director, Michael Cacoyannis; Sets and Costumes, Michael Annals; Lighting, Jules Fisher; Music, Marvin David Levy; Associate Producer, Sheldon Soffer.

CAST

Agamemnon	Mitchell Ryan
Old Man	Tom Klunis
Menelaus	Alan Mixon
Messenger	Robert Stattell †1
Clytemnestra	Irene Papas †2
The Child	Frank Coleman IV or Paris Themmen
Iphigenia	Jenny Leigh †3
Achilles	Christopher Walken †4
Chorus Leader	Erin Martin
Soldiers	John Garber, Nick Cantrell

CHORUS: Kathleen Adams, Patricia Bower, Margaret Cathell, Karen Cross, Shirley Luban, Lynda Myles, Linda Simon, Valerie von Volz

UNDERSTUDIES: Clytemnestra, Lynda Myles; Iphigenia, Erin Martin; Agamemnon, Tom Klunis; Menelaus, Old Man, Robert Stattell; Achilles, Messenger, Nick Cantrell; Chorus Leader, Patricia Bower; Chorus, Carol Emshoff

A Drama presented without intermission. The action takes place in Aulis.

Production Manager: Charles Hamilton
Press: Merle Debuskey, Violet Welles, Faith Geer
Stage Manager: Jan Moerel

° Closed May 26, 1968 after 232 performances.

† Succeeded by: 1. David Little, 2. Jane White, 3. Gretchen Corbett, 4. Gastone Rossili.

Friedman-Abeles Photos

Tom Klunis, Jane White. Above: Irene Papas (C)
Top: Mitchell Ryan, Jenny Leigh, Irene Papas
Left: Irene Papas, Jenny Leigh

BERT WHEELER THEATRE

Opened Wednesday, November 22, 1967.°
The Curley Company presents:

CURLEY McDIMPLE

Book, Mary Boylan and Robert Dahdah; Music and Lyrics, Robert Dahdah; Entire Production Directed and Supervised by Robert Dahdah; Musical Numbers Staged by Lonnie Evans; Music Arranged by Keith McClelland and Robert Atwood; Settings, Richard Jackson; Costumes, John Hirsch; Lighting, Barry Arnold; Musical Direction, Robert Atwood; Percussion, Richard Cook; Curley's Clothes, Robert Newey; Hairstyles, Nino Raffaello; Production Coordinator, David Semenni; Technical Director, Jack Greverland.

CAST

Jimmy	Paul Cahill†1
Sarah	Helon Blount
Alice	Bernadette Peters†2
Curley McDimple	Bayn Johnson or Sunny Leigh
Bill	George Hillman
Miss Hamilton	Norma Bigtree†3
Mr. Gillingwater	Gene Galvin†4
Hattie	Butterfly McQueen†5

MUSICAL NUMBERS: "A Cup Of Coffee," "I Try," "Curley McDimple," "Love Is The Loveliest Love Song," "Are There Any More Rosie O'Gradys?," "Dancing In The Rain," "Be Grateful For What You've Got," "At The Playland Jamboree," "I've Got A Little Secret," "You Like Monkey, You," "Stars and Lovers," "The Meanest Man In Town," "Something Nice Is Going To Happen," "Swing-a-Ling," "Hi de hi de hi, Hi de hi de ho," "Dwarf's Song."

A Musical Comedy in two acts. The action takes place in Sarah's boarding house in New York City in 1934.

General Manager: Rea Hooker
Press: Max Eisen, Carl Samrock, Jeanne Gibson Merrick, Cheryl Sue Dolby
Stage Manager: Ken Costigan

° Still playing May 31, 1968.

† Succeeded by: 1. Ray Becker, Don Emmons, 2. Joyce Nolen, 3. Jane Stuart, 4. Hansford Rowe.

† 5. Character added to play May 9, 1968.

Bayn Johnson, Bernadette Peters, Paul Cahill

Bayn Johnson, Bernadette Peters

Gene Galvin, Joyce Nolen, Butterfly McQueen, Nell Evans, Bayn Johnson, Jane Stuart, George Hillman Above: Bayn Johnson, Don Emmons, Joyce Nolen, Hansford Rowe, Helon Blount

GRAMERCY ARTS THEATRE

Opened Wednesday, November 22, 1967.°
Duane Camp presents:

TAKE IT FROM THE TOP

Staged by Maurice Edwards; Piano Accompaniment by Rolf Barnes; Setting and Lighting, Duane Camp.

CAST

Ethel Colt

A solo presentation of numbers from American musicals from 1787 to the current Broadway hits.

Press: Bernard Simon

° Closed Dec. 3, 1967 after 11 performances.

Ethel Barrymore Colt

MARTINIQUE THEATRE

Opened Friday, December 8, 1967.°
Lily Turner presents:

THE PEDDLER AND THE DODO BIRD

By Emanuel Fried; Director, Sidney Walters; Scenery, Helen Pond, Herbert Senn; Lighting, James Nisbet Clark; Costume Supervision, Sonia Lowenstein; Music arranged by John Brancati; Stereo Sound, George Jacobs.

CAST

"The Peddler"

Pete Taylor .... Thomas Anderson
Art Sternmiller .... John Randolph†
Frank Nowak .... Philip Sterling

The action takes place at the present time on the second floor of Sternmiller's Repossessed Furniture Store.

"The Dodo Bird"

Bull Blatter .... Walter Flanagan
Nick .... Thomas Anderson
The Dodo Bird .... Leonardo Cimino
Russ Nowark .... John Randolph†

The action takes place at the present time in a bar across from a foundry in a western New York industrial town.

General Manager: Lily Turner
Press: Bernard Simon, Avivah Simon
Stage Manager: Leonard Ross

° Closed Dec. 31, 1967 after 29 performances.

† Played for one week by Emanuel Fried and Jack Dabdoub.

Bert Andrews Photos

hn Randolph, Thomas Anderson, Leonardo Cimino, Walter Flanagan. Above: Thomas Anderson, John Randolph, Philip Sterling

MASQUE THEATRE

Opened Wednesday, December 13, 1967.°
The Roundabout Repertory Company
(Gene Feist, Producing Director) presents:

WAITING FOR LEFTY

By Clifford Odets; Director, Gene Feist;
Sets, Bil Mikulewicz; Lighting, Richard Logethetis; Hairstyling, Shangri-La Salon; Costume Coordinators, Pat Long, Chrystal Winters.

CAST

Fatt	Robert A. Guinan
Henchmen	Ramon Ascencio, Peter Rome
Joe	Joe Abramski
Edna	Elizabeth Owens
Miller	John Alden Boyd
Fayette	Norman Lind
Irv	Jose Martinez
Florrie	Susan Stevens
Sid	Gil Pacheco
Clayton	Mace G. McCarthy
Man	Paul Scanno
Actor	John Byrd
Secretary	Ann D'Andrea
Producer	Walter Delano
Dr. Barnes	Robb McIntire
Dr. Benjamin	Mitchell McGuire
Agate Keller	Hector J. Troy
Cabbies	David Baker, Herschell Burton, Lewis Colca, Josephine Duffy, Kevin McSweeney, Sherman Miller, Peter Ruffett, Paul Walsky

A Play in one act. The action takes place
in a union meeting hall in New York City
in 1935.

and

THE BOND

By August Strindberg; Director, Gene Feist;
Set, Bil Mikulewicz; Lighting, Richard Logethetis.

CAST

Sheriff	Isaac Dostis
Constable	Peter Ruffett
Baron	Sterling Jensen
Baroness	Elizabeth Owens
Attorney	Herschell Burton
Alma Jonsson	Lynne Garmston
Dairy Maid	Josephine Duffy
Judge	Winston May
Pastor	William Jones
Alexandersson	David Baker
Court Clerk	Lewis Colca

A Play in one act. The action takes place
in a provincial court in Sweden in 1890.

Press: Lawrence Rothman
Stage Manager: Mel Moshlak
° Closed Feb. 4, 1968 after 41 performances.

Ronald Berger Photos

Peter Rome, Robert Guinan, Ramon Ascencio

Elizabeth Owens, Sterling Jensen in "The Bond"
Top: Joe Abramski, Hector Troy, John Byrd

AMERICAN PLACE THEATRE

Opened Thursday, December 14, 1967.°
The American Place Theatre (Wynn Handman, Director) presents:

THE CEREMONY OF INNOCENCE

By Ronald Ribman; Director, Arthur A. Seidelman; Scenery, Kert Lundell; Costumes, Willa Kim; Lighting. Roger Morgan; Production Assistant, Jeremy Lewis; Technical Director, Owen McEvoy; Musical Director, Robert Shattuck; Bridge Fight Staged by Ron Colbin.

CAST

First Monk	Robert Shattuck
Sussex	Dolph Sweet
Kent	William Devane
Bishop	Ralph Clanton
Abbot	Peter Bosche
Ethelred	Donald Madden
Alfreda	Nancy R. Pollock
Emma	Olive Deering
Thulja	Sandy Duncan
Sweyn	Ernest Graves
Edmund	David Birney
Thorkill	Howard Green

MONKS, SERVANTS: Oliver Lewis Bachelle, Lee J. Caldwell, Anthony T. Casco, Jr., Edward Gallardo, Davidson Lloyd, Lou Prudenti, Jeffrey A. Rasi, Ronn Ridgeley, James Robiscoe, Walter Skolnik

UNDERSTUDIES: Kent, Sweyn, Abbott, Lee Caldwell; Edmund, Sussex, Robert Shattuck; Emma, Thulja, Toni Becker; Thorkill, Davidson Lloyd

An Historical Drama in two acts. The action takes place in a monastery on the Isle of Wight, and in the castle of King Ethelred in 1013.

General Manager: Julia Miles
Press: John Springer Associates, Louise Weiner
Stage Managers: Peter Galambos, Kate M. Pollock

° Closed Jan. 13, 1968 after 36 performances.

Martha Holmes Photos

Olive Deering, Donald Madden, Nancy R. Pollock
Above: Olive Deering, David Birney. Top: Donald Madden, Sandy Duncan (R), Nancy R. Pollock (L)

119

ANSPACHER THEATER

Opened Tuesday, December 26, 1967.°
The New York Shakespeare Festival
Public Theater (Joseph Papp, Producer)
presents:

HAMLET

By William Shakespeare; Director, Joseph
Papp; Scenery, David Mitchell; Costumes,
Theoni V. Aldredge; Lighting, Martin Aronstein; Music, Galt MacDermot; Musical Director, John Morris; Choreography, George and
Ethel Martin; Manager, David Black; Production Assistant, Sally Lansing.

CAST

Hamlet	Martin Sheen
Horatio	Michael Heit
Claudius	Ralph Waite
Osric	Albert Quinton
Laertes	Jeff David
Polonius	John Call
Gertrude	Anita Dangler
Ghost	Fred Warriner
Ophelia	April Shawhan
Rossencraft	Merwin Goldsmith
Guilderstone	James J. Sloyan
Norwegian Captain	Jared Martin
Guards	Paul Benjamin,

Gerry Black, Paul M. Glaser,
Jared Martin, Tom McCready,
Paul Speyser, Lisle Wilson

UNDERSTUDIES: Ghost, Paul Benjamin;
Claudius, Gerry Black; Guilderstone, Paul M.
Glaser; Horatio, Tom McCready; Laertes,
Martin; Polonius, Albert Quinton; Rossencraft,
Osric, Paul Speyser; Hamlet, Lisle Wilson;
Ophelia, Gertrude, Lilyan Wilder

Production Manager: Andrew Mihok
Press: Merle Debuskey, Faith Geer
Stage Managers: Russell McGrath,
Gage Andretta

° Closed Feb. 11, 1968 after 56 performances
and 8 previews.

From top: Jeff David, Ralph Waite, Anita Dangler,
Martin Sheen, John Call. Top: James J. Sloyan,
Martin Sheen, Merwin Goldsmith

Friedman-Abeles Photos

STAGE 73

Opened Tuesday, December 26, 1967.°
Marjorie and Sherman Ewing in association with Oliver Smith present:

A CERTAIN YOUNG MAN

By Thomas deWitt Walsh; Director, Sherman Ewing; Settings, Robin Wagner; Lighting, Jene Youtt; Production Assistants, Joan E. Spalding, June Miller.

CAST

Irene Grenwood	Elizabeth Lawrence
Allan Grenwood	Richard Kronold
Margaret Grenwood	Constance Meng
Joe Carter	Roger Omar Serbagi
Tom Hunter	R. C. Cobb
Johnny Grenwood	Alan Howard
Charlie Danvers	Jay Barney
Cissy Haines	Jody Locker
Ed	Charles Hull

A Drama in 3 acts and 4 scenes. The action takes place in the living-room of the Grenwood home near Armonk, New York.

General Manager: Hedges-Allen Inc.
Press: Fred Weterick
Stage Manager: Will Richter

° Closed Dec. 31, 1967 after 8 performances.

Van Williams Photo

Right: Bernie Rachelle, Geraldine Teagarden in "Nighthawks". Top: Jody Locker, Alan Howard in "A Certain Young Man"

MERMAID THEATRE

Opened Friday, December 29, 1967.°
Bill Yellin in association with The New Playwrights Co., Inc. presents:

NIGHTHAWKS

By Alvin Aronson; Director, Mr. Aronson; Set, Jason Hayes; Props, Quinton Raines; Lighting, Bruce Bassman; Paintings, Dolph Attianese; Music, DiVenus Records, Inc.

CAST

Rose Feldman	Geraldine Teagarden
Morry Feldman	Ed Powers
Harold Schwartz	Bernie Rachelle
Jack Morrison	Robert Gray
Sadie Cohen	Pauline Marvel
Hy Shapiro	George Loros
Annie Shapiro	Ruth Brandeis
Mae Polaski	Holice Stander

A Comedy in two acts. The action takes place at the present time in The Third Street Deli, off Second Avenue in New York City.

Business Manager: Irving Yellin
Press: Reginald Denenholz, Ben Kornzweig
Stage Manager: Jason Hayes

° Closed Mar. 24, 1968 after 52 performances.

Werner J. Kuhn Photos

Carol Richards   Richard Blair   Janie Sell

Friedman-Abeles Photo

UPSTAIRS AT THE DOWNSTAIRS

Opened Saturday, December 30, 1967.°
The Upstairs at The Downstairs presents:

DARK HORSES

Produced and Directed by Rod Warren; Musical Direction, Edward Morris; Music arranged and performed by Edward Morris and Dale Phillips; Musical Staging and Choreography, Ed Kresley; Lighting, Derek Whittlesey; Sketches by Kenny Solms and Gayle Parent, Bob Lerner, Rod Warren, Drey Shepperd, Sidney Davis; Music and Lyrics by David Finkle and Bill Weeden, Gene Bissell, Drey Shepperd and Ed Kresley, Michael McWhinney and Rod Warren, Kenny Jerome and Ted Simons, Suzanne Buhrer, Don Tucker, Alan Foster Friedman, Tom Pasle, Michael McWhinney and Lance Mulcahy.

CAST

Richard Blair	Gary Crabbe
Diane Deckard	Larry Moss
Carol Richards	Janie Sell

PROGRAM

ACT I: "Dark Horses," "Dig We Must," "Singles On The Slopes," "Piggyback Partners," "Bloodshed and Brotherhood," "Little Brother," "Wednesday Matinee," "The Interview," "The Turn-On Song," "The Princess Lays A Golden Egg," "Charles," "Bedtime Story," "Nancy," "Whatever Happened To?"
ACT II: "The Tribute," "Token Gesture," "Won't Someone Give John Lindsay?," "Mr. Smith, Please Go Back To Washington," "Modern Communications," "Linguaphone," "I've Seen Shakespeare," "Ethel," "Requiem For The Queen," "High Finance," "Dark Horses."

A Musical Revue in two acts.
Press: Dorothy Ross
Stage Manager: Derek Whittlesey

° Still playing May 31, 1967.

SHERIDAN SQUARE PLAYHOUSE

Opened Wednesday, January 3, 1968.°
The L. & L. L. Company presents:

LOVE AND LET LOVE

Based on "Twelfth Night" by William
Shakespeare; Adapted and Directed by John
Lollos; Lyrics, John Lollos and Don Christopher; Music, Stanley Jay Gelber; Orchestrations and Musical Supervision, Arthur Rubinstein; Musical Direction, Daniel Paget; Musical Staging, Rhoda Levine; Settings, Barbara
Miller; Costumes, Ynés; Lighting, Fred Allison; Production Assistants, Neil and Donna
Peckett.

CAST

Viola	Marcia Rodd
Captain	Tom Lacy
Count Orsino	John Cunningham
Sir Toby Belch	Tony Hendra
Maria	Susan Willis
Sir Andrew Aguecheek	Nic Ullett
Feste	Joseph R. Sicari
Countess Olivia	Virginia Vestoff
Malvolio	Michael O'Sullivan
Antonio	Roy Clary
Sebastian	Michael Hawkins
Officer	Don Moran
Priest	Tom Lacy

UNDERSTUDIES: Don Moran, Tom Lacy

MUSICAL NUMBERS: "I've Got A Pain,"
"If She Could Only Feel The Same," "The
Dancing Rogue," "Will He Ever Know?," "I
Like It," "Man Is Made For Woman," "Epistle
of Love," "Love Lesson," "I'll Smile," "I
Will Have Him," "Write Him A Challenge," "She Called Me Fellow," "They'll Say
I've Been Dreaming," "How Do I Know You're
Not Mad, Sir?," "I Found My Twin," "Some
Are Born Great."

A Musical Comedy in two acts. The action
takes place in Illyria.

General Manager: Joseph Beruh
Company Manager: Jewel Howard
Press: Frank Goodman, Martin Shwartz
Stage Manager: George Callahan

° Closed Jan. 14, 1968 after 14 performances.

Friedman-Abeles Photo

Michael O'Sullivan, Marcia Rodd,
Tony Hendra, Nic Ullett
in "Love And Let Love"

THEATRE FOUR

Opened Sunday, January 7, 1968.°
Harlan P. Kleiman presents:

HAVE I GOT ONE FOR YOU

Book and Lyrics, Jerry Blatt, Lonnie Burstein; Music, Jerry Blatt; Director, Roberta
Sklar; Musical Supervision, George Taros; Musical Direction and Arrangements, Alan Marlowe; Scenery and Costumes, John Conklin;
Lighting, Peter Hunt; Special Orchestrations,
David Friedman; Original cast album on ABC-Paramount Records; Technical Director, Jack
Magnifico; Production Assistants, Dale Soules,
Enid Holloway, Susan Goldman, Howard Goldstein; Assistant to Producer, Judith Robin.

CAST

The Animals;	
Gertrude, Mother Toad	Gloria De Haven
Joshua, her son	Ted Pugh
Marcello, a Mole	Dick O'Neill
Moles,	Peter Roark,
	Fred Osin, Michael Schroeder
Butterflies	Ellen Shade,
	Alma Marshak, Mary Crawford
The People:	
Thumby	Anne Kaye
The Prince	John Michael King
Men and Women	
of the Court	Peter Roark,
	Fred Osin, Michael Schroeder, Ellen
	Shade, Alma/Marshak, Mary Crawford

MUSICAL NUMBERS: "The Toad's Lament,"
"Chapter One," "Fly Away," "It's Comin'
True," "Have I Got A Girl For You,"
"Imagine Me," "Ode To Marcello," "Livin'
In A Hole," "The Chicken Song," "I Should
Stay," "My Dream Is Through," "What A
Bore," "A Nice Girl Like You," "So It
Goes," "The Getaway Quintet," "¾ Drag,"
"The Presentation."

A Musical in two acts.

General Manager: Paul B. Berkowsky
Company Manager: Ronald Lee
Press: Saul Richman
Stage Manager: Martin Herzer

° Closed Jan. 7, 1968, after 1 performance.

Ted Pugh, Gloria De Haven
in "Have I Got One For You"

Barry Kramer Photo

ORPHEUM THEATRE

Opened Saturday, January 13, 1968.°
Zev Bufman and Dorothy Love present:

YOUR OWN THING

Book, Donald Driver; Music, and Lyrics by Hal Hester and Danny Apolinar; Suggested by Shakespeare's "Twelfth Night"; Staged by Donald Driver; Settings, Robert Guerra; Costumes, Albert Wolsky; Lighting, Tom Skelton; Visual Projection Effects, Des Pro Studios; Orchestrations, Hayward Morris; Musical Direction and Dance Arrangements, Charles Schneider; Technical Direction, Richard Thayer; Sound, Port-O-Vox; Associate Producer, Walter Gidaly; Wigs, Joe Domino; John Wayne's Voice, Ed Lauter; Original cast album by RCA-Victor.

CAST

Danny	Danny Apolinar
John	John Kuhner
Michael	Michael Valenti
Orson	Tom Ligon
Olivia	Marian Mercer †
Viola	Leland Palmer
Sebastian	Rusty Thacker
Purser	Igors Gavon
Nurse	Imogene Bliss
Stage Manager	Igors Gavon

STANDBYS: Susan Oakes, Horton Wills, Igors Gavon

MUSICAL NUMBERS: "No One's Perfect, Dear," "The Flowers," "I'm Me! I'm Not Afraid," "Baby! Baby!," "Come Away, Death," "I'm On My Way To The Top," "Let It Be," "She Never Told Her Love," "Be Gentle," "What Do I Know?," "The Now Generation," "The Middle Years," "When You're Young and In Love," "Hunca Munca," "Don't Leave Me," "Do Your Own Thing."

A Musical presented without intermissions.

General Manager: Norman Rothstein
Company Manager: Dorothy Olim
Press: Robert Ganshaw,
Michael F. Goldstein Inc.
Stage Managers: Richard Thayer,
Otto Pirchner

° Still playing May 31, 1968. Winner of New York Drama Critics Circle Award as best musical of the season.

† Succeeded by Marcia Rodd.

Imogene Bliss, Rusty Thacker, Michael Valenti, John Kuhner, Danny Apolinar

Marcia Rodd, Leland Palmer
Top: Leland Palmer, Rusty Thacker

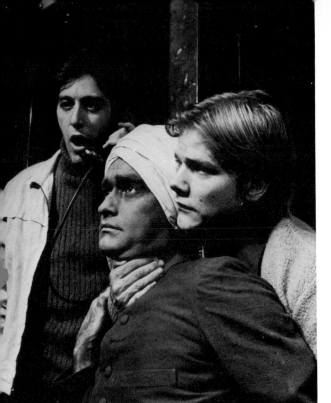

ASTOR PLACE THEATRE

Opened Wednesday, January 17, 1968.°
Ruth Newton Productions in association
with Diana Mathews presents:

THE INDIAN WANTS THE BRONX

By Israel Horovitz; Director, James Hammerstein; Designed by Fred Voelpel; Assistant to
the Producers, David Alton.

CAST

Gupta, and East Indian .... John Cazale
Murps .... Al Pacino
Joey .... Matthew Cowles

A One-Act Drama. The action takes place
at the present time on a chilly September
night at a bus stop on upper Fifth Avenue in
New York City.

and

IT'S CALLED THE SUGAR PLUM

CAST

Wallace Zuckerman .... John Pleshette †1
Joanna Dibble .... Marsha Mason †2

A Comedy in one act. The action takes place
at the present time in a cramped one-room
flat in Cambridge, Massachusetts.

General Manager: Jerry Livingood
Company Manager: Greg Hayes
Press: Howard Atlee, Margie Clay,
Bill Cherry
Stage Managers: Patrick Horrigan,
Merrily Mossman

° Still playing May 31, 1968.

† Succeeded by: 1. John Lefkowitz, 2. Jill
Clayburgh.

Bert Andrews Photos

**John Pleshette, Marsha Mason. Top: Al Pacino,
John Cazale, Matthew Cowles**

John Lefkowitz, Jill Clayburgh

Elly Stone
Above: Shawn Elliot

Alice Whitfield, Shawn Elliot, Elly Stone, Mort Shuman

VILLAGE GATE

Opened Monday, January 22, 1968.°
3W Productions Inc. presents:

JACQUES BREL IS ALIVE AND WELL AND LIVING IN PARIS

Production Conception, English Lyrics, Additional Material, Eric Blau and Mort Shuman; Based on Brel's Lyrics and Commentary; All Dialogue adapted from works of Jacques Brel; Music, Jacques Brel; Director, Moni Yakim; Musical Direction, Mort Shuman; Consultant, Nat Shapiro; Scenery, Henry E. Scott III; Costumes, Ilka Suarez; Lighting, James Nisbet Clark; Production Supervised by Eric Blau; Original cast album by Columbia Records.

CAST

Elly Stone†1   Shawn Elliot†3
Mort Shuman†2   Alice Whitfield†4

MUSICAL NUMBERS: "Marathon," "Alone," "Madeleine," "I Loved," "Mathilde," "Bachelor's Dance," "Timid Frieda," "My Death," "Girls and Dogs," "Jackie," "The Statue," "Desperate Ones," "Sons Of," "Amsterdam," "The Bulls," "Old Folks," "Marieke," "Brussels," "Fannette," "Funeral Tango," "The Middle Class," "You're Not Alone," "Next," "Carousel," "If We Only Have Love."

Presented in two acts.

General Manager: Lily Turner
Press: Ivan Black
Stage Manager: James Nisbet Clark

° Still playing May 31, 1968.

† Succeeded by: 1. Betty Rhodes, 2. Robert Guillaume, 3. Adam Stevens, 4. June Gable.

Betty Rhodes   Moni Yakim (Director)
Above: Robert Guillaume, June Gable

125

THEATRE DE LYS

Opened Sunday, January 28, 1968.°
Saint-Subber presents:

HOUSE OF FLOWERS

Book and Lyrics, Truman Capote; Music, Harold Arlen; Director, Joseph Hardy; Settings, Kert Lundell; Costumes, Richard Castler; Lighting, Tharon Musser; Choreography, Talley Beatty; Musical Direction and Arrangements, Joseph Raposo; Associate Producer, Charles Weiss; Production Assistant, Andi Ramsay; Presented by Special Arrangement with Lucille Lortel Productions; Original cast album on United Artists Records.

CAST

Drummer	Daniel Barrajanos
The Houngan	Charles Moore
Ottilie	Yolande Bavan
Mamselle Tulip	Hope Clarke
Mamselle Pansy	Thelma Oliver
Madame Fleur	Josephine Premice
Madame Tango	Novella Nelson
Senorita Maria	Carla Pinza
Lord Jamison	Tom Helmore
The Champion	Bob Broadway
Royal	Robert Jackson
Old Bonaparte	Josephine Premice
Woman	Trina Parks †
Man	Walter Raines

UNDERSTUDIES: Fleur, Bonaparte, Thelma Oliver; Royal, Bob Broadway; Tulip, Pansy, Trina Parks; Champion, Houngan, Walter Raines; Woman, Andi Ramsay; Man, Pernett Robinson

MUSICAL NUMBERS: "Two Ladies In De Shade," "A Sleepin' Bee," "Somethin' Cold To Drink," "Smellin' of Vanilla," "House of Flowers," "Don't Like Goodbyes," "Jump De Broom," "Waitin'," "I Never Has Seen Snow," "Walk To De Grave," "Woman Never Understan'," "Madame Tango's Particular Tango," "What Is A Friend For?."

A Musical in two acts. The action takes place on an island in the Caribbean.

General Manager: C. Edwin Knill
Company Manager: Paul B. Berkowsky
Press: Dorothy Ross, Ruth D. Smuckler
Stage Managers: Charles Kindl,
Pernett Robinson

° Closed Mar. 17, 1968 after 57 performances.
† Succeeded by Sandra Lein.

Bert Andrews

Josephine Premice, Novella Nelson, Carla Pinz in "House Of Flowers"

PLAYERS THEATRE

Opened Monday, January 29, 1968.°
Edmund J. Ferdinand and Charlotte Schiff by arrangement with George Wiener present:

WHO'S WHO, BABY?

Book, Gerald Frank; Music and Lyrics, Johnny Brandon; Settings and Costumes, Alan Kimmel; Lighting John Beaumont; Entire Production Directed and Choreographed by Marvin Gordon; Musical Direction and Dance Music, Leslie Harnley; Orchestrations and Dance Music, Clark McClellan; Production Associates, Robert E. Richardson, Marcel Perelmutter.

CAST

Carol Winslow	Jacqueline Mayro
Daisy	Marcia Lewis
Smitty	Danny Guerrero
Benny Hare	Frank André
Sabine	Glory Van Scott
Frankie	Gloria Kaye
Al	Tommy Breslin
Louis	Tom Eatman
Jean	Ural Wilson
Sir Peveril Ballantyne	Humphrey Davis
Toby	Erik Howell

Understudy: Michael J. Frank

MUSICAL NUMBERS: "Island of Happiness," "That'll Be The Day," "Come-Along-a-Me, Babe," "Nothin's Gonna Change," "There Aren't Many Ladies in the Mile End Road," "Syncopatin'," "Voodoo," "How Do You Stop Loving Someone?," "Drums," "Feminineinity," "That's What's Happening, Baby," "Me," "Nobody To Cry To," Finale.

A Musical in two acts with prologue. The action takes place here, there, and everywhere on the island of Manuella.

General Manager: Joseph Beruh
Company Manager: Al Isaac
Press: Bernard Simon, Avivah Simon
Stage Managers: Gail Bell, Michael J. Frank

° Closed Feb. 11, 1968 after 16 performances.

Jacqueline Mayro, Erik Howell, Frank André, Gloria Kaye

BARBIZON-PLAZA THEATRE

Opened Friday, February 2, 1968.°
Theatre of Latin America presents ITUCH
(Theatre Institute of the University of
Chile; Augustín Siré, Director) in:

LA REMOLIENDA
("The Bawdy Party")

By Alejandro Sieveking; Direction and Music, Victor Jara; Scenery and Costumes, Bruna
Contreras; Lighting, Sergio Zapata.

CAST

Dona Nicolasa	Belgica Castro
Nicolas	Mario Lorca
Graciano	Tomas Vidiella
Gilberto	Franklin Caicedo
Yola	Kerry Keller
Isaura	Claudia Paz
Chepa	Sonia Mena
Dona Rebeca	Carmen Bunster
Renato Sepulveda	Tennyson Ferrada
Mirta	Maria Canepa
Mauro	Sergio Aguirre
Telmo	Ruben Sotoconi
Baudilio	Jorge Boudon

A Play in 2 acts and 4 scenes. The action
takes place on a road and at an open air
restaurant.

Opened Sunday, February 4, 1968°

ITUCH ANTHOLOGY

Scenes from their repertoire, including "La
Celestina," "Who's Afraid of Virginia Woolf?,"
"El Perro Del Hortelano," "La Viuda de
Apablaza," "Coronacion," "Macbeth," "Death
of A Salesman," "Fuenteovejuna," "Chanarcillo," "Long Day's Journey Into Night,"
"Marat/Sade," "El Alcalde de Zalamea,"
"Threepenny Opera," "Joaquin Murieta,"
"Bernardo O'Higgins."

General Manager: David Hedges
Press: Sol Jacobson, Lewis Harmon

° Closed Feb. 9, 1968 after a limited engagement of 9 performances.

**Right: Tennyson Ferrada, Carmen Bunster in
"Death of A Salesman". Top: "La Remolienda"**

**Hermione Baddeley
in "I Only Want An Answer"**

STAGE 73

Opened Monday, February 5, 1968.°
Margaret Hewes and Rick Hobard present:

I ONLY WANT
AN ANSWER

By Fred Denger; English Translation, Basil
Ashmore; Director, Tony Tanner; Designed by
Stewart Chaney; Lighting, Roger Morgan; Music, Dolphe Martin; Technical Director, Jene
Youtt; Production Assistant, Joan E. Spalding;
Hair Stylist, John Quaglia.

CAST

Amy Turner .... Hermione Baddeley
A Drama in two acts. The action takes
place at the present time in the flat of Amy
Turner on the outskirts of London.

General Manager: Hedges Allen, Inc.
Press: Fred Weterick
Stage Manager: John Glennon

° Closed Feb. 11, 1968 after 8 performances.

Van Williams Photo

127

ACTORS PLAYHOUSE

Opened Thursday, February 8, 1968.°
Richard Lerner, Frances Drucker and
Gilberto Zaldivar present:

OH, SAY CAN YOU SEE L. A.

By John Allen; Music, Albert Hague; Designed by Boyd Dumrose; Choreography Vernon Lusby; Director John Allen; Pianists, Phyllis Grandy, Sande Campbell; This Production is dedicated to Stella Holt.

CAST

Sonny	George Welbes
Pop	George Voskovec
Uncle Charlie	Glenn Kezer
Harold	Alan Manson

A Play in two parts: "The Story," and "The Vaudeville." The action takes place here and now.

and

THE OTHER MAN

Dov	George Welbes
Teddy	George Voskovec
The Man	Glenn Kezer
The Other Man	Alan Manson

A Play in one act. The action takes place in 1952 in Buenos Aires.

Business Manager: Gilberto Zaldivar
Company Manager: Richard Lerner
Press: David Lipsky, Marian Graham,
M. J. Boyer
Stage Manager: Robert Buzzell

° Closed Feb. 18, 1968 after 14 performances.

Bert Andrews Photos

Right: George Voskovec, George Welbes in "The Other Man". Top: George Voskovec, Glenn Kezer, George Welbes, Alan Manson in "Oh, Say Can You See L. A."

Marilyn Tass, Joe Vaccarella, Maryellen Flynn, Dylan Stephen de Guzman, Kathleen Beal

BLACKFRIARS' THEATRE

Opened Tuesday, February 20, 1968.°
The Blackfriars' Guild presents:

BABES DON'T CRY ANYMORE

By Michael Kallesser; Director, Walter Cool; Settings and Lighting, Robert Charles; Costumes, Alice Merrigal.

CAST

Doris Conway	Marilyn Tass, Kathleen Madden, or Frances Panzella
Ronald Green	Vincent A. Greco or Reynaldo De Silva
Pinky Conway	Kathleen Beal, Dawn Eman, or Debbie Howard
George Conway	Dylan Stephen de Guzman, Thomas O'Callaghan, or James Gaughan
Andy Conway	Joe Vaccarella or Bob Atkinson
Marian Green	Maryellen Flynn or Mary Ann Strossner
Sheriff Smith	Norman M. Rosenbaum or Robert A. Kelly
Deputy Lookey	Carlo Grasso or Ross R. Rogers

A Domestic Farce-Comedy in 2 acts and 3 scenes. The action takes place at the present time in the living-dining room of the lower middle-class home of the Conways in a small lumber town in Pennsylvania.

Press: Rev. Thomas F. Carey
Stage Managers: Robert Charles,
Cheryl Chase

° Closed May 5, 1968 after 70 performances.

ST. CLEMENT'S EPISCOPAL CHURCH

Opened Wednesday, February 21, 1968.°
The American Place Theatre (Wynn
Handman, Director) presents:

THE ELECTRONIC NIGGER
AND OTHERS

Three short plays by Ed Bullins; Director,
Robert Macbeth; Scenery, John Jay Moore;
Lighting, Roger Morgan; Music, Gordon Wat-
kins; Production Assistants, Jeremy Lewis, Gor-
don Watkins; Technical Director, Owen
McEvoy.

"A Son, Come Home"
CAST
Mother ------------------------------------ Estelle Evans
Son -- Wayne Grice
Girl ----------------------------------- Kelly-Marie Berry
Boy -- Gary Bolling

The action takes place in the present and
past, in South Philadelphia and the Mind.

"The Electronic Nigger"
CAST
Mr. Jones ------------------------------------ Wayne Grice
Lenard --------------------------------------- Warren Pincus
Miss Moskowitz ------------------------ Jeanne Kaplan
Mr. Carpentier ----------------------------- L. Errol Jaye
Bill -- Roscoe Orman
Sue --- Hedy Sontag
Martha -------------------------------------- Helen Ellis
Students -------- Roland A. Hirsch, Maie Mottus

The action takes place at the present time
in a Southern California Community College.

"Clara's Ole Man"
CAST
Clara --------------------------------- Kelly-Marie Berry
Big Girl -------------------------- Carolyn Y. Cardwell
Jack -- Roscoe Orman
Baby Girl ----------------------------------- Helen Ellis
Miss Famie ------------------------------ Estelle Evans
Stoogie ------------------------------------- Kris Keiser
Bama -------------------------------------- George Miles
Hoss -- Gary Bolling
C. C. -- L. Errol Jaye

The action takes place in the mid-1950's in
South Philadelphia.

General Manager: Julia Miles
Press: John Springer Associates,
Louise Weiner
Stage Managers: Peter Galambos,
Kate M. Pollock

° Closed Mar. 16, 1968 after 26 performances.
Re-opened at the Martinique Theatre on
Thursday, March 28, 1968 with title changed
to "Three Plays By Ed Bullins," then to
"Ed Bullins' Plays." Closed May 26, 1968
after 70 additional performances.

Martha Holmes Photos

Top Right: Jeanne Kaplan, L. Errol Jaye, Warren
Pincus, Maie Mottus in "Electric Nigger". Below:
Kelly-Marie Berry, Roscoe Orman

Carolyn Y. Cardwell, Kelly-Marie Berry in
"Clara's Ole Man"

SHERIDAN SQUARE PLAYHOUSE
Opened Sunday, February 25, 1968.°
Dwubba Productions, Inc. presents:

SATURDAY NIGHT

By Jerome Kass; Director, Burt Brinckerhoff;
Sets, Jack H. Cornwell; Costumes, Joe Aulisi;
Lighting, Roger Morgan; Executive Producer,
Davis Weinstock.

CAST

Mr. Harris	Shimen Ruskin
Rochelle	Zina Jasper
Gabe	Lee Wallace †
Ellie	Gina Collens
Iggy	Marvin Lichterman
Policeman	Wendell Phillips, Jr.

A Comedy-Drama in two acts. The action
takes place at the present time in a Bronx
apartment on a Saturday night.

General Manager: Joseph Beruh
Company Managers: Jewel Howard,
Al J. Isaac
Press: Reuben Rabinovitch
Stage Manager: David Shanstrom

° Closed Apr. 21, 1968 after 66 performances.
† Succeeded by Marc Jordan.

Bert Andrews Photos

Left: Lee Wallace, Marvin Lichterman,
Zina Jasper, Gina Collens

Shimen Ruskin, Zina Jasper

Marvin Lichterman, Zina Jasper
Above: Gina Collens, Zina Jasper

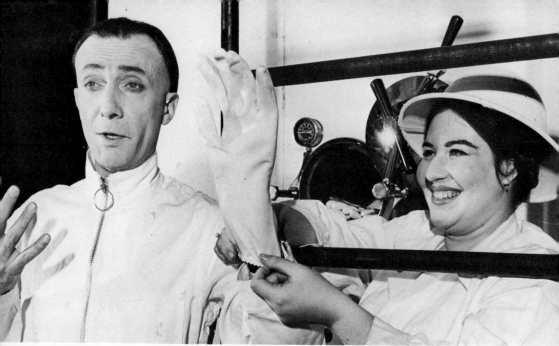

ANSPACHER THEATER

Opened Sunday, March 3, 1968.°
The New York Shakespeare Festival Public
Theater (Joseph Papp, Producer) presents:

ERGO

By Jakov Lind; Director, Gerald Freedman;
Scenery, Ming Cho Lee; Costumes, Theoni V.
Aldredge; Lighting, Martin Aronstein; Original Music and Sound Score, John Morris; Assistant Director, Amy Saltz; Assistant to Producer, Gail Merrifield.

CAST

Wondra	Tony Capodilupo
Bunzig	Frank Groseclose
Wacholder	Jack Hollander
Rita	Maxine Green
Wurz	Tom Aldredge
Arnulf	Cliff Gorman
Arnold	Irwin Pearl
Leo	Robert Stattel
Aslan	Sam Waterston
Commentator	Frank Groseclose
Dr. Gertrude Bockling	Miriam Lehmann-Haupt
Journalist	Steven Shaw
Citizens	Hope Arthur, Peter Burnell, Dutch Miller, C. Leonard Williams, Joel Wolfe

UNDERSTUDIES: Rita, Hope Arthur; Gertrude, Jean Bruno; Arnulf, Arnold, Peter
Burnell; Leo, Cliff Gorman; Wurz, Frank Groseclose; Journalist, Dutch Miller; Aslan, Bunzig,
Steven Shaw; Wacholder, Wondra, Joel Wolfe

A Comedy in 2 acts and 13 scenes. The
action takes place now in Vienna and everywhere else.

Production Manager: Andrew Mihok
Press: Merle Debuskey, Faith Geer
Stage Managers: Russell McGrath,
Michael Chambers

° Closed Apr. 14, 1968 after 49 performances
and 14 previews.

Friedman-Abeles Photos

...am Waterston, Robert Stattel, Jack Hollander
Above: Jack Hollander, Sam Waterston,
Maxine Greene, Tom Aldredge
Top: Tom Aldredge, Maxine Greene

MARTINIQUE THEATRE

Opened Thursday, February 22, 1968.°
Dhiandil Productions presents:

GOA

By Asif Currimbhoy; Director, Patricia Newhall; Setting and Lighting, C. Murawski; Costumes, Robert Pusilo; Sound, Terry Ross; Incidental Music, Ali Akbar Kahn.

CAST

Rose	Jody Locker
Administrator	Jay Barney
Goan Nationalist	Jose Perez
Chico	Elliot Paul
Old Woman	Mildred Chandler
Old Man	James Cook
Portugese Vicar	Elek Hartman
Goan Hindu	Tazewell Thompson
Smuggler	Dennis Tate
Senhora Miranda	Sylvia Gassell
Krishna	Cal Bellini
Alfonso	Erik Silju
Villagers	Hortensia Colorado,

Harriet Karr, Carrie Ann Kessler, Linda Taverna, Nancy Volkman

A Drama in two acts. The action takes place on a "patio" in Goa, in Portugese India, just before and after India invaded and annexed the tiny colony in 1961.

General Manager: Roy Franklyn
Press: David Rothenberg,
Lawrence Schneider
Stage Manager: Lewis Rosen

° Closed Mar. 17, 1968 after 28 performances.

Cal Bellini

KAUFMANN CONCERT HALL

Tuesday, March 5, 1968.°
The Japan Society, Inc. presents the New York debut of:

NOMURA KYOGEN COMPANY

In three traditional situation comedies: "Boshibari" (Tied To A Pole), "Tsurigitsune" (The Fox and The Trapper), and "Kusabira" (Mushrooms).

Press: Beate Gordon
Stage Managers: Gary Harris,
Dan Rosenfels

° Presented for one performance only.

(No photographs available)

GRAMERCY ARTS THEATRE

Opened Monday, March 4, 1968.°
LGB Productions and Esther Prince in association with David Morgan present:

THE BENCH

By N. R. Teitel; Director, Val Bisoglio; Scenery, Robert U. Taylor; Costumes, Jeanne Button; Lighting, Michael Davidson; Original Music, Teiji Ito; Technical Director, Geoffrey Leon.

CAST

Phillipi	Thayer David
Hortense	Fayne Blackburn
Count Alexei	Michael O'Sullivan
Ajax	Richard Hamilton
Earle	David Nillo
Sam Stein	Joseph Leon
Bettina	Carol Teitel
Jessie	Gretchen Corbett

A Drama in 2 acts and 4 scenes. The action takes place at the present time at a circle in the park.

General Manager: Krone-Olim
Management Inc.
Press: Howard Atlee, Margie Clay,
William Cherry
Stage Manager: Larry Catusi

° Closed Mar. 4, 1968 after 1 performance.

Michael O'Sullivan, Gretchen Corbett, David Nillo
Above: Thayer David, Richard Hamilton,
Carol Teitel, Michael O'Sullivan

132

Bert Andrews Photos

EAST 74th STREET THEATRE

Opened Tuesday, March 5, 1968.°
Yon Enterprises, Inc. presents:

THE VICTIMS

Three One-Act Plays; Artistic Director, Charles Fischer; Costumes, Cynthia Penn; Lighting, Jene Youtt; Sound Effects, Don Schaff; Production Assistant, Linda Shepard.

"On The Hazards of Smoking Tobacco"

By
Anton Chekhov; Translated by Charles Fischer

CAST

The Professor .... Charles Fischer

"Victims of Duty"

By
Eugene Ionesco; Translated by Donald Watson

CAST

Madeleine .... Kaye Kingston
Choubert .... Edward McPhillips
Detective .... Charles Lutz
Nicholas D'Eu .... Robert L. Ruth
The Lady .... Danis Regal

"Escurial"

By
Michel de Ghelderode
Translated by George Hauger

CAST

The King .... Charles Fischer
Folio .... Robert L. Ruth
The Monk .... Edward McPhillips
The Executioner .... Charles Lutz

Production Manager: Nicholas Shepis
Press: Fred Weterick
Stage Manager: Will Richter

° Closed Mar. 10, 1968 after 5 performances.

Kaye Kingston, Charles Lutz, Robert L. Ruth, Edward McPhillips in "Victims of Duty"

Lynne Carter as Phyllis Diller

JAN HUS PLAYHOUSE

Opened Wednesday, March 6, 1968.°
Jack Irving presents:

FUN CITY

Sketches Written and Staged by David Rogers; Musical Direction and Orchestrations, James Reed Lawlor; Lighting, David Anderson; Costumes, Frank Page, Michael Landi; Settings, Sal Tinnerello, Richard Burnside; Hair Styles, Mr. George of Derel; Special Material by Fred Silver, Nelson Garringer, Jay Jeffries, Franklin Underwood, Norman Martin.

CAST

Mr. Lynne Carter

Mel Edwards   Joan Porter[†1]
Dee Robinson   Ted Tingling[†1]

PROGRAM

ACT I: "Fun City," "A Voice That Will Ring Forever," "The Old Gray Mayor," "Have Piano and Hanky," "M Is For The Money Things," "A Tragic Queen," "Try Try," "Cover Girl," "Madison Avenue Jingle," "Where The Elite Meet," "Birth of A Nation," "Manners," "Louder!," "Goodness Had Nothing To Do With It."

ACT II: "Sudden Beauty," "Movies Are Your Best Entertainment," "Going Highbrow," "Fifth Avenue Movement," "A Bunny's Mother," "I Adore You," "Dear John—Help!," "Everybody Leaves Somebody Some Crime," "Make Me A Match," "Fun City."

A Musical Revue in two acts.

Production Manager: Walter S. Russell
Press: Dorothy Ross, Ruth D. Smuckler

° Closed Mar. 31, 1968 after 31 performances.
† Succeeded by Cari Stevens.

GREENWICH MEWS THEATRE

Opened Saturday, March 9, 1968.°
The Greenwich Mews Theatre presents a
Stella Holt production of:

JERICO-JIM CROW

By Langston Hughes; Directed by Alvin
Ailey and William Hairston; Musical Director,
Prof. Hugh Porter; Lighting, Ray McCutcheon;
Staged for this Production by Louis Johnson;
At the piano, Prof. Hugh Porter; At the
organ, Marion Franklin; Percussionist, James
W. Major.

CAST

Young Man	Dion Watts
Young Girl	Hilda Harris
Old Man	Joseph Attles
Old Woman	Rosalie King
Jim Crow	Barney Hodges
Woman	Dorothy Drake

GOSPEL SINGERS: Mary Brown, Roberta
Caldwell, Eleanor Howell, Marquette Miller,
Fletcher Rozier, Jon Harris, Herbert Slater,
Verma Moorehead, Brock Williams
MUSICAL NUMBERS: "A Meeting Here
Tonight," "I'm On My Way," "I Been 'Buked
and I Been Scorned," "Such A Little King,"
"Is Massa Gwine To Sell Us Tomorrow?,"
"How Much Do You Want Me To Bear?,"
"Where Will I Lie Down?," "Follow The
Drinking Gourd," "John Brown's Body,"
"Battle Hymn of The Republic," "Slavery
Chain Done Broke At Last," "Oh, Freedom,"
"Go Down, Moses," "Ezekiel Saw The Wheel,"
"Stay In The Field," "Freedom Land,"
"God's Gonna Cut You Down," "Better Leave
Segregation Alone," "My Mind On Freedom,"
"We Shall Overcome," "The Battle of Old
Jim Crow," "Come and Go With Me."

Press: David Lipsky, Marian Graham
Stage Manager: Brock Williams

° Closed May 5, 1968 after 5 performances
on weekends only.

Bert Andrews Photo

Rosalie King, Hilda Harris, Joseph Attles
in "Jerico-Jim Crow"

Aurelia De Felice, Kathleen Scarlett, Ann Rollins
in "Scarlet Lullaby"

MASQUE THEATRE

Opened Sunday, March 10, 1968.°
Myrnel Productions presents:

SCARLET LULLABY

By Elliott Taubenslag; Directed by Mr.
Taubenslag; Scenery, Donald Cotter; Costumes,
H. N. Hinkle; Lighting, Paul Inverso; Theme
Composed by Leo Stella; Production Assistant,
George Glagola.

CAST

Edna Mallory	Ann Rollins
Phoebe Albright	Dolly Vasta
Hedy Zarwadsky	Kathleen Scarlett
Seymour	Owen Hollander
Herby Sommers	Bob E. Lloyd
Alma Carson	Aurelia De Felice
Angie	Joseph Vasta
Kathy Louise	Lori Shelle
Mr. Arnold	Earl George
Policeman	Mel Boyd
Father Almonte	Richard Graham
Dr. Olsen	Earl George

A Dramatic Comedy in three acts. The
action takes place at the present time in
Mrs. Mallory's apartment in the East 80's in
New York City.

Company Manager: Myrna Barbara Schor
Press: David Lipsky, Marian Graham,
M. J. Boyer
Stage Manager: Leo Stella

° Closed Mar. 17, 1968 after 7 performances.

Richard V. Gray Photo

FELT FORUM

Opened Monday, March 11, 1968.°
The American League for Russian Jews
presents:

FINAL SOLUTIONS

By Jan Hartman; Director, Gene Lasko;
Original Music, Jacques Belasco; Choreography,
Valerie Bettis; Kinetic Light Art, Jackie Cassen
and Rudi Stern; Costume Coordinator, Claire
Ferraris; Pianist, Harry Fuchs; Associate Pro-
ducer, Amnon Kabatchnik.

CAST

The Woman	Marian Seldes
The Poet	Tony Lo Bianco
Chorus Leader	John Heffernan
Voice of Tyranny	Leonard Cimino
Voice of Tyranny II	Bruce Kimes

DANCERS: Ze'eva Cohen, Laura Glenn, Lorry
May, Edward DeSoto, Edward Effron, Phillip
Filiato, Louis Garcia, Jim May
CHORUS: Members of The Neighborhood
Playhouse School of Theatre.

A Musical Drama about the plight of Jews
in today's Soviet Russia.

Press: Max Eisen, Carl Samrock
Stage Manager: Ellen Wittman

° Presented for one performance only.

**Marian Seldes, Leonardo Cimino, John Heffernan,
Tony Lo Bianco**

GREENWICH MEWS THEATRE

Opened Tuesday, March 12, 1968.°
Herbert S. Alpert and Mitchell Nestor
present:

WINTER JOURNEY

By Clifford Odets; Originally "The Country
Girl"; Director, Mitchell Nestor; Sets and
Lighting, Richard Kerry; Costumes, Jan; Music
and Sound Effects, John Batiste.

CAST

Bernie Dodd	Robert Viharo
Phil Cook	Delos V. Smith, Jr.
Paul Unger	Patrick Baldauff
Larry	Walter Allen
Frank Elgin	Will Hare
Georgie Elgin	Barbara Loden
Nancy Stoddard	Jean Fowler
Ralph	John Batiste

A Drama in 2 acts and 8 scenes. The
action takes place at the present time in New
York and Boston.

General Manager: Anne Barr
Press: Max Eisen, Ben Rothman,
Cheryl Sue Dolby, Carl Samrock
Stage Manager: Carmine Pontilena

° Closed Mar. 23, 1968 after 13 performances.

Bert Andrews Photo

**Robert Viharo, Will Hare, Barbara Loden
in "Winter Journey"**

THEATRE FOUR

Opened Thursday, March 14, 1968.°
Bruce W. Stark in association with Savage-
Friedman presents:

THE FOUR SEASONS

By Arnold Wesker; Director, Arthur A.
Seidelman; Set and Lighting, C. Murawski;
Costumes, Jeanne Button; Music, Frangipane
and Dante; Production Manager, Vincent
Lynne.

CAST

Adam	Paul Roebling
Beatrice	Barbara Hayes

STANDBYS: Erin Fleming, Dino Narizzano

A Drama in two acts. The action takes place
at the present time in a deserted house.

General Manager: Bruce W. Stark
Press: David Rothenberg,
Lawrence Schneider
Stage Manager: Vincent Lynne

° Closed March 17, 1968 after 6 performances.

Henry Grossman Photo

**Paul Roebling, Barbara Hayes
in "The Four Seasons"**

Martha Swope Photo

Gretel Cummings, Eddie McCarty, Margaret Wright
in "The Last Triangle"

ACTORS PLAYHOUSE

Opened Monday, March 18, 1968.°
Barbara Wise Productions Inc. presents:

TWO CAMPS BY KOUTOUKAS

Written and Staged by H. M. Koutoukas;
Incidental Music, Robert Cosmos Savage; Costumes, Maria Irene Fornes; Lighting, Johnny
Dodd; Choreography, Eileen Passloff; Musical
Director and Pianist, Benji Heywood; Producer's Assistant, Helen Adam.

"The Last Triangle"
(An Embroidered Camp)

CAST

Noel Cowel	Eddie McCarty
Virginia Wolfgang	Margaret Wright
Lottie Lemming	Gretel Cummings
The Hawk	Aileen Passloff

The action takes place in the "No Longer"
in the ruins of Newswanstein.

"Only A Countess May Dance When She's Crazy"
(An Almost Historical Camp)

CAST

Countess Olie Sandowitch	Gretel Cummings

The action takes place in the tower of Dr.
Till's laboratory in the Mid-Atlantic.

General Manager: Krone-Olim
Management Inc.
Press: Howard Atlee, Margie Clay,
William Cherry
Stage Manager: Yon Koski

° Closed Apr. 2, 1968 after 17 performances.

PLAYERS THEATRE

Opened Monday, April 1, 1968.°
Monroe Productions presents:

RATE OF EXCHANGE

By Milo Thomas; Director, Dorothy Chernuck; Scenery and Costumes, Peter Wingate;
Lighting, Robert L. Benson; Production Assistant, Tony Canal; Sound Effects, Nick
Lewis.

CAST

Thelma Stewart	Esther Benson
Eve Stewart	Jill Harmon
Irene Hemple	Lydia Bruce
Adam Niger	George Renschler
Shamus	Strat Walling
Johnny Stewart	Jerry Strickler
George Washington Jones	Garrett Saunders
Kevin Piggott	Kevin Hanily
Sam	Nick Lewis
Bob Stewart	Donald Symington
Fred Hemple	Walter Flanagan

An Anti-War Drama in 2 acts and 5 scenes.
The action takes place at the present time in
the Stewart living room and in South Viet
Nam.

General Manager: Jerry Arrow
Press: Warren Pincus
Stage Managers: Frank S. Torok,
Kevin Hanily

° Closed Apr. 1, 1968 after 1 performance.

Bert Andrews Photo

Strat Walling, Jerry Strickler
in "Rate Of Exchange"

STAGE 73

Opened Monday, March 25, 1968.°
William Dorr in association with Michael White presents:

TOM PAINE

By Paul Foster; Direction and Music, Tom O'Horgan; Lighting, Johnny Dodd; Costumes, Michael Warren Powell; Conceived for the La Mama Troupe.

CAST

John Bakos ---------------- Tom Paine's Reputation, Dodger
Mari-Claire Charba -------------------- Deaf Woman, American Committee of Secret Correspondence, Greedy, Woman in Red, Marguerite Bonville
Peter Craig ------------------------ Major Domo, Roger
Jerry Cunliffe -------------------------------- Sergeant, Captain, General, Quartermaster, King George III, Sentry Edmund Burke
Michael Miller ------------------------------ Bishop, Caron de Beaumarchais, Bishop Horsely, Captain Lambes
Sally Kirkland ------------------------ Gin Seller, Deaf Woman, Greedy, Gouverneur Morris, Mary Wollstonecraft, Old Man, Registrar I
Kevin O'Connor ------------------------- Tom Paine
Victor Lipari ----------------------------------- Private, Mate Drummer, Silas Deane, Cromwell's Shadow, Private, Sentry, Lord Justice
Beth Porter ------------------------------------ Buleah, Count de Vergennes, Simonne, Registrar II, Greedy
Marilyn Roberts ------------------------------ Marie, John Jay, Greedy, Marie Antoinette, Marie, Greedy
Rob Thirkield ------------------------------ Governor, Black Dick, Altar Boy, Quaker, Old Man, Louis XVI, Blake

A Drama in 2 acts and 24 scenes. The action takes place in 1809 in a bear pit in Lower Manhattan.

General Manager: Krone-Olim Management Inc.
Press: David Rothenberg, Lawrence Schneider
Stage Manager: Steve Whitson

° Still playing May 31, 1968.

Friedman-Abeles Photos

Kevin O'Connor, John Bakos
Top: Kevin O'Connor, Marilyn Roberts

Kevin O'Connor

137

THEATRE FOUR

Opened Sunday, April 14, 1968.°
Richard Barr and Charles Woodward, Jr. present:

THE BOYS IN THE BAND

By Mart Crowley; Director, Robert Moore; Designed by Peter Harvey; Administrative Director, Barry Plaxen.

CAST

Michael	Kenneth Nelson
Donald	Frederick Combs
Emory	Cliff Gorman
Larry	Keith Prentice
Hank	Laurence Luckinbill
Bernard	Reuben Greene
Cowboy	Robert La Tourneaux
Alan	Peter White
Harold	Leonard Frey

A Comedy-Drama in two acts. The action takes place at the present time in Michael's apartment.

General Manager: Michael Kasdan
Press: David Rothenberg,
Lawrence Schneider
Stage Managers: Charles Kindl,
Richard Foltz

° Still playing May 31, 1968.

Friedman-Abeles Photos

Kenneth Nelson, Frederick Combs

Reuben Greene, Cliff Gorman, Kenneth Nels
Top: Laurence Luckinbill, Keith Prentice,
Reuben Greene, Cliff Gorman

ACTORS PLAYHOUSE

Opened Wednesday, April 17, 1968.°
James Walsh and Dina and Alexander E. Racolin present:

THE HAWK

By Murray Mednick and Tony Barsha; Director, Tony Barsha; Music, Eddie Hicks; Lighting, Barbara Nollman; Hairstyles, Salon St. Honore.

CAST

Prologue	Ching Yeh
The Hawk	Tony Serchio
The Double	Lee Kissman
First Victim	Sommer Sally
Second Victim	O-Lan Johnson
The Inspector	Walter Hadler
Third Victim	Scarlett Johnson
Fourth Victim	Barbara Eda-Young
The Dealer	Walter Hadler

A Play in two acts.

Press: David Rothenberg,
Lawrence Schneider
Stage Manager: Joel Walker

° Closed Apr. 28, 1968 after 15 performances.

Bert Andrews Photo

O-Lan Johnson, Tony Serchio
in "The Hawk"

BARBIZON-PLAZA THEATRE

Opened Thursday, April 18, 1968.°
Jacques Courtines and Seff Associates Ltd. present by special arrangement with Jean de Rigault Le Treteau de Paris in:

LE TARTUFFE

By Moliere; Staged by Yves Gasc; Scenery, Yves Gasc; Costumes, Jacques Mornas; Producer, Jean de Rigault; Special Production Coordinator, Carole S. Hofmann.

CAST

Madame Pernelle	Janine Souchon
Orgon	Gilles Leger
Elmire	Giselle Touret
Damis	Guy Michel
Mariane	Francine Walter
Valere	Pierre Cousteres
Cleante	Michel Favory
Tartuffe	Yves Gasc
Dorine	Marcelle Ranson
Monsieur Loyal	Philippe Laudenbach
Police Officer	Michel Herve

A Comedy in five acts presented in two parts.

Opened Monday, April 22, 1968.°

EN ATTENDANT GODOT
(Waiting For Godot)

By Samuel Beckett; Staged by Rene Lesage; Scenery, Bernard Floriet; Producer, Jean De Rigault.

CAST

Estragon	Jean Rodien
Vladimir	Rene Lesage
Pozzo	Raoul Marco
Lucky	Charles Schmitt
Un Garcon	Vincent Ridard

A Tragi-Comedy in two acts.

General Administrator: Yves Berthiau
Company Manager: Lawrence Witchel
Press: Arthur Cantor, Arthur Solomon
Stage Managers: Erwen Kerne,
Harry Abbott

° Closed May 14, 1968 after a limited engagement of 32 performances.

Ivan Farkas Photos

"Waiting For Godot"
bove: Gilles Leger, Marcelle Ranson in "Tartuffe"

139

ST. CLEMENT'S EPISCOPAL CHURCH

Opened Thursday, April 18, 1968.*
The American Place Theatre (Wynn Handman, Director) presents:

ENDECOTT AND THE RED CROSS

By Robert Lowell; Director, John Hancock; Scenery, John Wulp; Costumes, Robert La Vigne; Lighting, Roger Morgan; Music, Richard Peaslee, Robert Dennis; Technical Director, Owen McEvoy; Production Assistant, Donald Hawley; Production Assistants, Lee Rosenthal, Tom Lackey.

CAST

Assawamset	Gregory Sierra
Thomas Morton	John Harkins
Merry Mount Men	Jack Scalici, Jan Saint
Indians	James Brochu, Edward Zaloney, Dick Hobby
Daughter of Assawamset	Yolande Skeete
Mr. Blackstone	Nick Kepros
Man dressed as Witch	Marshall Efron
Merry Mount Woman	Felicia Quinn
Bear	Polly Harding
Indian Whore	Roberta Shubert
Edith	Frances Hession
Edward	Spalding Gray
Man with Wolf's Head	Jack Scalici
Man with Stag's Head	Jan Saint
Sargeant	Dan Morgan
Private	Stephen Wyman
Drummer	Donald Hawley
Standard Bearer	Luke Wymbs
Soldiers	Dick Hobby, Felicia Quinn, James Brochu
Governor Endecott	Kenneth Haigh
Palfrey	Ralph Clanton
Merry Mount Girl	Polly Harding
Musician	David Schoming
Executioner	William Catanese

A Drama in one act. The action takes place in the 1630's at Merry Mount, the settlement of Thomas Morton, near Wollaston, Massachusetts.

General Manager: Julia Miles
Press: John Springer Associates, Louise Weiner
Stage Managers: Peter Galambos, Anne Bliss

* Closed May 18, 1968 after 36 performances.

Martha Holmes Photos

Gregory Sierra, John Harkins

Nicholas Kepros, Kenneth Haigh. Above: Kenneth Haigh, Frances Hession. Top: Ralph Clanton, Kenneth Haigh

THE BITTER END

Opened Friday, April 19, 1968.°
Levendell Productions Inc. presents:

THE PROPOSITION

Written and Directed by Jeremy Leven;
Producer, C. W. Smith; Artistic Director,
Jeremy Leven; Musical Director and pianist,
John Forster; Bass, Joe Saah.

CAST

Lori Heineman   Fred Grandy
Karen Meyn   Paul Jones
Ken Tigar

PROGRAM: "Five Characters In Search of A
White House," "Kiesinger," "Little People's
Concert," "Ethnos In Song," "Felony," "Pro-
gressive Education," "Bleh," "Fenordin," "This
Week In The Arts," "Kennedy Cantata,"
"Prostretics," "Nuclear Chef," "Wedding
Night," "Angry Afro-American Artists' Insti-
tute," "Euclid's Elemental," "Bombs," "Trap
The Traitor," "Raleigh," "Repoz," "The
Death of God," "Milton Cross At The Met,"
"Nu?," "On The Scene," "Poetry."

A Satirical Musical Revue.

Business Manager: John Flym
Press: Hita Johnson

° Closed Apr. 20, 1968 after limited engagement of 2 performances.

(No photographs available)

Tony Capodilupo, Judy Allen
in "Carving A Statue"

Saylor Creswell, Fran Myers
Above: Larry Gates, Saylor Creswell
in "Carving A Statue"

GRAMERCY ARTS THEATRE

Opened Tuesday, April 30, 1968.°
Dina and Alexander E. Racoline and
Berenice Weiler present:

CARVING A STATUE

By Graham Greene; Director, Margaret
Webster; Designed by John Braden; Music,
John Duffy.

CAST

The Boy ---------------------------------- Saylor Creswell
His Father -------------------------------- Larry Gates
First Girl ---------------------------------- Fran Myers
Second Girl ------------------------------- Judy Allen
Dr. Parker -------------------------------- Tony Capodilupo

A Drama in 2 acts and 3 scenes. The action takes place at the present time in a
studio in South London.

Press: Samuel J. Friedman, Jane Friedman
Stage Manager: Martin Herzer

° Closed May 12, 1968 after 12 performances.

Bert Andrews Photos

141

ANSPACHER THEATER

Opened Tuesday, April 23, 1968.°
The New York Shakespeare Festival Public Theater (Joseph Papp, Producer; Gerald Freedman, Artistic Director; Bernard Gersten, Associate Producer) presents:

THE MEMORANDUM

By Vaclav Havel; Translated by Vera Blackwell; Director, Joseph Papp; Scenery, Douglas W. Schmidt; Costumes, Theoni V. Aldredge; Lighting, Martin Aronstein; Music, John Morris; Manager, David Black; Assistant to Producer, Gail Merrifield.

CAST

Josef Gross	Paul Stevens
Jan Ballas	John Heffernan
Hana	Sudie Bond
Mark Lear	Robert Ronan
Peter Thumb	William Duell
Otto Stroll	William Kiehl
Alex Savant	Fred Burrell
Helena	Olympia Dukakis
Maria	Mari Gorman
George	Brad Sullivan
Ferdinand Pillar	George Bartenieff
Ferdinand Column	George Bartenieff
Clerks	Raul Julia, Lisa Maria

UNDERSTUDIES: Lear, George Bartenieff; Pillar, William Duell; Gross, Thumb, Stroll, George, Raul Julia; Hana, Maria Helena, Lisa Maria; Ballas, Savant, Brad Sullivan

A Comedy in 2 acts and 12 scenes. The action takes place at the present time in Prague, Czechoslovakia.

Production Manager: Andrew Mihok
Press: Merle Debuskey, Faith Geer
Stage Managers: Gage Andretta,
Adam G. Perl

° Still playing May 31, 1968.

Friedman-Abeles Photos

Raul Julia, Lisa Maria, Brad Sullivan, William Duell, Robert Ronan, Paul Stevens
Above: John Heffernan, Olympia Dukakis. Top: Paul Stevens, Mari Gorman

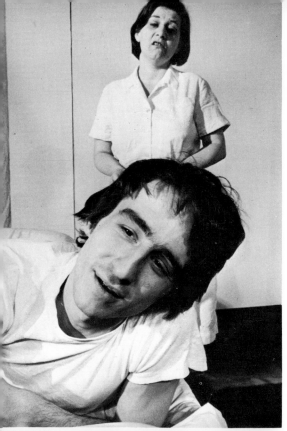

PROVINCETOWN PLAYHOUSE
Opened Sunday, April 28, 1968.*
Warren Lyons and Betty Ann Besch present:

RED CROSS

By Sam Shepard; Director, Jacques Levy; Designed by Peter Harvey; Lighting, Johnny Dodd; Sound, James Reichart; A Waterford Company Production; Production Assistant, Dennis Mitchell.

CAST

Carol	Marcia Jean Kurtz†1
Jim	Sam Waterston†2
The Maid	Florence Tarlow

The action takes place at the present time in a cabin in the forest.

and

MUZEEKA

By John Guare; Director, Melvin Bernhardt; Designed by Peter Harvey; Lighting, Johnny Dodd; Sound, James Reichart; Stage Movement, Ralf Harmer; A Waterford Company Production.

CAST

Jack Argue	Sam Waterston†3
Argue's Wife	Marcia Jean Kurtz†1
Evelyn Landis	Peggy Pope†4
Number Two	Sandy Baron†5
Stagehands	Kevin Bryan Conway, John Lawlor†6, Frank Prendergast†7

General Manager: Krone-Olim
Management Inc.
Press: David Rothenberg,
Lawrence Schneider, Warren Pincus
Stage Managers: Patrick Horrigan,
Frank Prendergast

* Still playing May 31, 1968.

† Succeeded by: 1. Karen Ludwig, 2. Jordan Charney, John Horn, 3. Joe Ponazecki, 4. Lynn Bernay, 5. Kevin Bryan Conway, 6. James Marmon, 7. Eric Concklin.

Bert Andrews, Friedman-Abeles Photos

James Marmon, Lynn Bernay, Eric Concklin in "Muzeeka". Top: Sam Waterston, Florence Tarlow in "Red Cross"

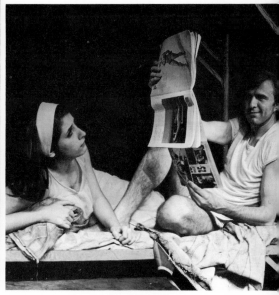

Karen Ludwig, Joe Ponazecki in "Muzeeka"

Judy Gibbs, Carolyn Bruce, James Castaldo
in "The Concept"

CAFE AU GO GO

Opened Wednesday, May 8, 1968.°
(Moved June 4, 1968 to Actors Playhouse)
Lyn Austin, Hale Matthews, Oliver Smith
present:

COLLISION COURSE

An Omnibus of 11 one-act plays; Director,
Edward Parone; Designed by Michael Davidson; Costumes, Diedre Cartier; Production Assistant, Edith M. P. Wehle; Assistant to Producers, Lisa Stamm; Technical Assistant,
Richard D'Arcy; Sound by Elizabeth Ives.

CAST

Susan Browning	Sam Groom
Leora Dana	Meg Myles
Scott Glenn	Tom Rosqui

Tom Scott

STANDBYS: Julia Curry, Mylo Quam

PROGRAM

PART I: "Wandering" by Lanford Wilson,
"Stars and Stripes" by Leonard Melfi, "Chuck"
by Jack Larson, "Skywriting" by Rosalyn
Drexler, "Jew!" by Harvey Perr, "Thoughts On
The Instant Of Greeting A Friend On The
Street" by Jean-Claude van Itallie and Sharon
Thie, "Tour" by Terrence McNally.
PART II: "Camera Obscura" by Robert
Patrick, "Metaphors" by Martin Duberman,
"The Unexpurgated Memoirs Of Bernard Mer-
gendeiler" by Jules Feiffer, "Rats" by Israel
Horovitz.

General Manager: Krone-Olim
Management Inc.
Press: Samuel Lurie, Stanley F. Kaminsky
Stage Manager: M. N. Streicher

° Still playing May 31, 1968.

Stanley Papich Photo

SHERIDAN SQUARE PLAYHOUSE

Opened Monday, May 6, 1968.°
Mortimer Levitt and Arthur Cantor present The Daytop Theatre Company in:

THE CONCEPT

Director, Lawrence Sacharow; Costumes,
Christofferson; Lighting, Gigi Cascio; The play
is the product of the director and actors working together.

CAST 1	CAST 2
Felix Arroyo	Dallas Sams
David Brabham	Frank Mojica
Judy Gibbs	Eileen Steiner
James Castaldo	Roger Pugliese
Roger Moore	George Withers
Carolyn Bruce	Pat Philbin
John Devlin	Torrido Marcial
Richard Rode	Bob DiSalvo

CAST 3
Cornelius Hines
Tony Ramirez
Julia McMillon
Gene Fox
David Beaudry
Linda Leone
John Galanaugh
Jimmy Halloran

An Improvisational Drama in two acts. The
action takes place in Daytop Village, a home
for drug addicts. The casts rotate weekly.
Press: Arthur Solomon

° Still playing May 31, 1968.

Ken Thompson Photo

Tom Rosqui, Leora Dana in "Skywriting"

GARRICK THEATRE

Opened Thursday, May 9, 1968.°
Jesse DeVore and Harold L. Oram in association with Gustav Henningburg present:

THE BELIEVERS
(The Black Experience In Song)

Written by Josephine Jackson and Joseph A. Walker; Music and Lyrics, Benjamin Carter, Dorothy Dinroe, Josephine Jackson, Anje Ray, Joseph A. Walker, Ron Steward; Musical Direction and Vocal Dimension, Brooks Alexander; Director, Barbara Ann Teer; Assistant Director, Louis Johnson; Sets, Joseph A. Walker; Costumes, Robert Pusilo; Lighting, R. Robert Lussier, J. D. Regan.

CAST
Voices, Inc.
Dorothy Dinroe, Josephine Jackson, Sylvia Jackson, Shirley McKie, Veronica Redd, Anje Ray, Jesse DeVore, Barry Hemphill, Don Oliver, Ron Steward, James Wright, Benjamin Carter, Joseph A. Walker.

A Musical in two acts. The action takes place in "The Gone Years," and "The Then and Now Years."

Press: David Rothenberg,
Lawrence Schneider
Stage Manager: J. Pat Regan

° Still playing May 31, 1968.

Friedman-Abeles Photos

Jesse DeVore, Veronica Redd
Top: "The Voices, Inc."

Howard Erskine, Elaine Stritch, Russell Nype
in "Private Lives"

THEATRE DE LYS

Opened Sunday, May 19, 1968.°
Haila Stoddard, Mark Wright, Duane Wilder present:

PRIVATE LIVES

By Noel Coward; Director, Richard Barr; Scenery, Herbert Senn and Helen Pond; Lighting, David F. Segal; Production Manager, Murray Gitlin; Mr. Coward"s Music Arranged and Performed by Don Elliott; Technical Director, Jack Magnifico; Production Assistant, John Toland; Presented by Special Arrangement with Lucille Lortel Productions Inc.

CAST
Sybil Chase	Betsy von Furstenberg
Elyot Chase	Russell Nype
Victor Prynne	Howard Erskine
Amanda Prynne	Elaine Stritch
Louise	Anita Palacine

A Comedy in three acts. The action takes place in France.

Manager: Paul B. Berkowsky
Press: David Rothenberg,
Warren Pincus, Lawrence Schneider

° Closed May 26, 1968 after 9 performances.

Friedman-Abeles Photo

THE NEGRO ENSEMBLE COMPANY

ST. MARKS PLAYHOUSE

Opened Tuesday, January 2, 1968.°
The Negro Ensemble Company (Douglas
Turner Ward, Artistic Director; Robert
Hooks, Executive Director; Gerald S.
Krone, Administrative Director) presents:

SONG OF THE LUSITANIAN BOGEY

By Peter Weiss; Translated by Lee Baxandall; Staged and Directed by Michael A. Schultz; Dance Direction, Louis Johnson; Sets, Edward Burbridge; Costumes, Bernard Johnson; Lighting, Marshall Williams; Music, Coleridge-Taylor Perkinson; Technical Coordinator, George Hayes.

CAST

Rosalind Cash	William Jay
David Downing	Judyann Jonsson
Arthur French	Denise Nicholas
Moses Gunn	Hattie Winston
Allie Woods	

A Drama in two acts.
Press: Howard Atlee, Margie Clay, William Cherry
Stage Manager: Edmund Cambridge
° Closed Feb. 4, 1968 after 40 performances.

Bert Andrews Photos

Rosalind Cash, Judyann Jonsson, David Downing, Arthur French, William Jay, Denise Nicholas, Hattie Winston, Allie Woods (on floor). Top: Moses Gunn

ST. MARKS PLAYHOUSE

Opened Tuesday, February 20, 1968.°

The Negro Ensemble Company (Douglas Turner Ward, Artistic Director; Robert Hooks, Executive Director; Gerald S. Krone, Administrative Director) presents:

SUMMER OF THE SEVENTEENTH DOLL

By Ray Lawler; Director, Edmund Cambridge; Sets, Edward Burbridge; Costumes, Gertha Brock; Lighting, Shirley Prendergast; Technical Coordinator, Tec Crans.

CAST

Pearl Cunningham	Esther Rolle
Bubba Ryan	Hattie Winston
Olive Leech	Frances Foster
Barney Ibbot	Norman Bush
Emma Leech	Clarice Taylor
Roo Webber	Moses Gunn
Johnnie Dowd	William Jay

STANDBYS: Rosalind Cash, David Downing, Arthur French, Judyann Jonsson, Denise Nicholas, Allie Woods

A Drama in three acts. The action takes place in a two-story house in New Orleans, and covers an unusually warm month from early December through the week after the New Year's Eve.

Press: Howard Atlee, Margie Clay, William Cherry
Stage Managers: .Dorothi Fox, Edmund Cambridge

° Closed March 24, 1968 after 40 performances.

Bert Andrews Photos

Norman Bush, Clarice Taylor, Moses Gunn, Esther Rolle, Frances Foster
Top: Frances Foster, Norman Bush, Moses Gunn, Esther Rolle

ST. MARKS PLAYHOUSE

Opened Sunday, April 14, 1968.°
The Negro Ensemble Company (Douglas Turner Ward, Artistic Director; Robert Hooks, Executive Director; Gerald S. Krone, Administrative Director) presents:

KONGI'S HARVEST

By Wole Soyinka; Director, Michael A. Schultz; Choreography, Louis Johnson; Sets, Edward Burbridge; Costumes, Jeanne Button; Lighting, Jules Fisher; Music, Pat Patrick; Technical Director, Donald Berry.

CAST

Oba Danlola	Douglas Turner
Sarumi	Clarice Taylor
Ogbo Aweri	Frances Foster †1
Wuraola	Roberta Raysor
Dende	Richard Mason
Superintendent	Judyann Jonsson
Praise Singers	Denise Nicholas, Hattie Winston
Members of the Reformed Aweri Fraternity	David Downing, Norman Bush, Allie Woods, Carl Gordon, William Jay, Tom Brimm III
Organizing Secretary	Arthur French
Daoudu	Robert Hooks
Segi	Rosalind Cash †2
Kongi	Moses Gunn
Right Ear of State	Charles Greene, Jr.
Left Ear of State	Ozzie Waite
Photographer	Bernard Marsh
Captain of Carpenter's Brigade	Afolabi Ajayi
Carpenter's Brigade	Ken Davis, Carl Gordon, Charles Greene, Jr., Bernard Marsh, Ozzie Waite
Night Club Habituees and Dancers	Maxine Griffith, Roberta Raysor, Gloria Schultz, Joyce Walker, Ken Davis, Ed Dougherty, Charles Greene, Jr., Bernard Marsh, Ozzie Waite
Segi's Entertainer	Afolabi Ajayi
Danlola's Ceremonial Corps	Youmi-Youmi, Sonny Morgan, Babafemi Akinlana, Richard Pablo Landrum

A Drama in two acts. The action takes place on the eve and day of the national celebration of Isma.

Press: Howard Atlee, Margie Clay, William Cherry
Stage Manager: Buddy Butler

° Closed May 12, 1968 after 40 performances.
† Succeeded by 1. Rosalind Cash, 2. Frances Foster.

Charles Stewart Photos

Carl Gordon, Norman Bush, William Jay, David Downing, Moses Gunn, Thomas Brimm, Allie Woods. Above: Clarice Taylor, Douglas Turner Ward, Frances Foster. Top: Maxine Griffith, Robert Hooks, Denise Nicholas

ST. MARK'S PLAYHOUSE

Opened Tuesday, June 4, 1968.°
The Negro Ensemble Company (Douglas Turner Ward, Artistic Director; Robert Hooks, Executive Director; Gerald S Krone, Administration Director) presents:

DADDY GOODNESS

By Richard Wright and Louis Sapin; Director, Douglas Turner Ward; Sets, Edward Burbridge; Costumes, Gertha Brock; Lighting, Michael A. Schultz; Technical Director, Donald Berry; Sound, Gary and Timmy Harris.

CAST

Sam	Bill Jay
Lena	Denise Nicholas
Thomas	Douglas Turner
Jeremiah	Arthur French
A Preacher	Allie Woods
Annie	Clarice Taylor
Fanny	Rosalind Cash
Sarah	Judyann Jonsson
David	David Downing
Daddy Goodness	Moses Gunn
Postman	Richard Mason
Milkman	Buddy Butler
Luke	Norman Bush
Chauffeur	Richard Mason
A Young Man	Theodore Wilson
An Old Woman	Clarice Taylor
The Mayor	Arthur French

STANDBYS: Frances Foster, Hattie Winston

A Play in 3 acts and 5 scenes. The action takes place in an unidentified American city during a hot sultry August in the recent past.

Press: Howard Atlee, Margie Clay, Bill Cherry
Stage Manager: Edmund Cambridge

° Still playing at press time.

Bert Andrews Photos

Left: Moses Gunn, Rosalind Cash, William Jay, David Downing, Denise Nicholas, Judyann Jonsson. Top: Denise Nicholas, William Jay, Judyann Jonsson, Rosalind Cash, David Downing

Moses Gunn, Judyann Jonsson, Theodore Wilson, William Jay, Denise Nicholas, Arthur French, Norman Bush, Rosalind Cash, David Downing

ANTA MATINEE SERIES
Twelfth Season
Lucille Lortel, Artistic Director.

THEATRE DE LYS
Monday, December 4, and Tuesday Matinee, December 5, 1967.

POSTCARDS

By James Prideaux; Director, Jean Dalrymple; Lighting, Timmy Harris; Production Assistant, Ken Richards; Administrative Assistant, Erika Roth.

CAST

Leonard ———————————— Hugh Marlowe
Margaret ———————————— Paula Trueman

with

THE CLUB BEDROOM

By Louis Auchincloss; Director, Robert Moss; Lighting, Timmy Harris.

CAST

Mrs. Ruggles ——————— Jessie Royce Landis
Mrs. Miles ————————————— Dorothy Sands
Elmina Ruggles ————————— Carolyn Coates

The action takes place mid-afternoon in October of 1965 in the sitting room of a fashionable ladies' club on Park Avenue, New York.

General Manager: Paul B. Berkowsky
Press: Saul Richman
Stage Manager: Yon Koski

Monday, December 11, and Tuesday Matinee, December 12, 1967.

LIMB OF SNOW

By Anna Marie Barlow; Director, Joel Friedman; Lighting, Timmy Harris; Production Coordinator, Ken Richards; Production Assistants, Minerva Farrell, Joan Hart.

CAST

Jim ——————————————————— Don Fellows
Hannah ————————————————— Mary Doyle

The action takes place in an isolated cabin in the High Sierras in the 1890's.

with

THE MEETING

CAST

Nancy —————————————————— Salome Jens
A Boy ———————————————— Robert Walden
Frank ——————————————— Leonard Hicks

The action takes place at a picnic in an open field.

General Manager: Paul B. Berkowsky
Press: Saul Richman
Stage Manager: Mitch Kessler

(No photographs available)

Monday, January 29, and Tuesday Matinee, January 30, 1968.

LET THEM DOWN, GENTLY

By Gert Hofmann; Director, Charles Maryan; Music Supervision, Sarah Sanders; Lighting, Timmy Harris; Costumes, Minerva Farrell; Production Coordinator, Ken Richards; Production Assistant, Joan Hart.

CAST

"Our Man In Madras"

Jim Seig ——————————————— Simm Landres
Jane ———————————————————— Sarah Sanders

"On Vacation"

Mr. Pendergast ————————— Patrick McVey
Mrs. Pendergast ———————— Courteen Landis
Hotel Manager (Karl) ——————— Stan Hart
Room Waiter ——————————— John Kendrick
Bellboy ———————————————— Jerry Hopkins
Chambermaid ——————————————— Irene Clark
Manicurist ————————————— Sarah Sanders
Jimmy ————————————————— Simm Landres
Masseur ————————————————— Bob Cessna
Funeral Director ————— Lamonte Richards
STANDBY: Celia Gittelson
General Manager: Paul B. Berkowsky
Press: Saul Richman
Stage Manager: Rilla Bergman

Monday, February 12, and Tuesday Matinee, February 13, 1968.

A MADRIGAL OF SHAKESPEARE

Director, Joan White; At the piano, John Ranck; Lighting, Timmy Harris; Production Coordinator, Ken Richards.

CAST

Peggy Wood   Ethel Barrymore Colt

Selections from Shakespeare's plays presented in three parts: "Women In Jeopardy," "Women In Authority," "Women In Love," with a prologue and epilogue.

General Manager: Paul B. Berkowsky
Press: Saul Richman
Stage Manager: Martin Herzer

Monday, March 4 and Tuesday Matinee, March 5, 1968.

MR. AND MRS. LYMAN

By Joel Friedman; Director, Alfred Christie; Lighting, Timmy Harris; Production Coordinator, Ken Richards.

CAST

Dodie ————————————————— Sylvia Gassells
Neil ———————————————————————— Alan Mixon

A Play in 2 acts and 5 scenes. The action takes place at the present time in a Greenwich Village apartment.

General Manager: Paul B. Berkowsky
Press: Saul Richman
Stage Manager: Martin Herzer

OFF-BROADWAY PRODUCTIONS FROM OTHER SEASONS THAT CLOSED DURING THIS SEASON

Title	Opened	Closed	Performances
The Mad Show	Jan. 9, 1966	Sept. 10, 1967	871
The Pocket Watch	Jan. 5, 1966	June 18, 1967	624
Fortune and Men's Eyes	Feb. 23, 1967	Jan. 21, 1968	382
MacBird!	Feb. 22, 1967	Jan. 14, 1968	379
Man With A Load Of Mischief	Nov. 6, 1966	June 4, 1967	240
Absolutely Freeee	May 24, 1967	Sept. 4, 1967	206
Hamp	Mar. 9, 1967	June 4, 1967	101
Drums In The Night, in repertory with Eh?	May 17, 1967	July 16, 1967	69
Gorilla Queen	Apr. 24, 1967	June 18, 1967	63
The Coach With The Six Insides	May 11, 1967	June 25, 1967	53
A Time For The Gentle People	May 25, 1967	June 3, 1967	12

Leonard Kuras, Clement Fowler, Peter Carew, Peter Blaxsill in "He Who Gets Slapped"

Renata Mannhardt, Reuben Shafer, Ed Owens, Chris Manor, Parke Godwin, Jack Somack in "The Visit"

Patrick McCullough, Jan Owen, George Harris II, Stori Reed, Donald Bishop in "An Enemy of The People"

Don Blakely, Freda Payne, Verdelle Smith, Woodie King, Ed Smith in "Lost In The Stars"

Jacquie Ullendorf, John Kuhner, Sally Stark, Jamie Donnelly, Erik Howell in "Babes In Arms"

Bayne Ellis, Bob Berger, James Heath in "Next Time I'll Sing To You"

EQUITY THEATRE PRODUCTIONS

NEW YORK SHAKESPEARE FESTIVAL
Delacorte Theater, Central Park
June 7 through August 26, 1967
Joseph Papp, Producer

DELACORTE THEATER

Opened Wednesday, June 7, 1967.°
New York Shakespeare Festival in co-
operation with the City of New York
presents:

THE COMEDY OF ERRORS

By William Shakespeare; Director, Gerald
Freedman; Setting, Ming Cho Lee; Lighting, Martin Aronstein; Costumes, Theoni V.
Aldredge; Music, John Morris; Associate Producer, Bernard Gersten; Technical Director,
Donald Koehler; Production Coordinator, Andrew Mihok.

CAST

Egeon	Ralph Drischell
Solinus	Jonathan Reynolds
Gaoler	James A. Preston
First Merchant	Joseph R. Sicari
Antipholus of Syracuse	David Birney
Antipholus of Ephesus	Joseph Bova
Dromio of Syracuse	John Call
Dromio of Ephesus	Charles Durning
Adriana	Julienne Marie
Luciana	Elizabeth Eis
Angelo	Robert Ronan
Balthazar	Jack Hollander
Luce (Nell)	Zoe Kamitses
Second Merchant	Albert Quinton
Officer	Charles Seals
Courtesan	Shellie Feldman
Dr. Pinch	Joseph R. Sicari
Emilia	Eve Collyer
Clockworks	Steven Shaw, Donald K. Warfield

ATTENDANTS, LORDS, OFFICERS: Mik
Cribben, Lydia Fisher, Robert Gold, Phillip
Johnson, George McGrath, James A. Preston,
Charles Seals, William Shephard, Donald K.
Warfield, Gene Whittington

Press: Merle Debuskey, Faith Geer
Stage Managers: Russell McGrath,
Timothy Ward, Amy Saltz

° Closed July 1, 1967 after 23 performances.

Friedman-Abeles Photos

David Birney, Elizabeth Eis. Top Right: Charles
Durning, Joseph Bova, John Call

Julienne Marie, Joseph Bova. Above: Charles
Durning, Joseph Bova, Julienne Marie

DELACORTE THEATER

Opened Wednesday, July 5, 1967.°
New York Shakespeare Festival in cooperation with the City of New York presents:

KING JOHN

By William Shakespeare; Director, Joseph Papp; Setting, Douglas Schmidt; Costumes, Theoni V. Aldredge; Lighting, Martin Aronstein; Music, David Amram; Fights, James J. Sloyan; Associate Producer, Bernard Gersten; Artistic Director, Gerald Freedman; Technical Director, Donald Koehler.

CAST

King John	Harris Yulin
Chatillon	Ralph Drischell
Queen Elinor	Cavada Humphrey
Lord Bigot	Stephen Van Benschoten
Philip The Bastard	Robert Burr
Robert Faulconbridge	David Clennon
Lady Faulconbridge	Winifred Mann
James Gurney	Charles Durning
Philip, King of France	David O'Brien
Arthur, Duke of Britain	Mark Jenkins
Duke of Austria	Gregory Sierra
Constance	Marian Winters
Citizen of Angiers	Albert Quinton
French Herald	James A. Preston
English Herald	Donald K. Warfield
Blanche of Spain	Elizabeth Eis
Lewis, the Dauphin	David Birney
Earl of Salisbury	Michael McGuire
Cardinal Pandulph	Staats Cotsworth
Hubert De Burgh	Clarence Williams III
Earl of Pembroke	Stan Dworkin
Executioner	James Daniel
Messengers to King John	David Clennon, Donald K. Warfield
Peter of Pomfret	James A. Preston
Melun	Albert Quinton
Messenger to Lewis	Stephen Coleman
Prince Henry	Matthew Cowles

SOLDIERS AND MONKS: William Beckwith, Stephen Coleman, James Daniel, Lydia Fisher, Phillip Johnson, Zoe Kamitses, George McGrath, Anthony Lang, James A. Preston, Maro Riofrancos, Harold Schwartz, Charles Seals, William Shephard, Stephen Van Benschoten, Donald K. Warfield, Gene Whittington, Paul Zimet.

Manager: David Black
Press: Merle Debuskey, Faith Geer
Stage Managers: Russell McGrath, Timothy Ward, Amy Saltz

° Closed July 29, 1967 after 22 performances.

Friedman-Abeles Photos

Harris Yulin, Cavada Humphrey
Top Right: Harris Yulin, Robert Burr

Robert Burr, Cavada Humphrey
Above: Miriam Winters, Mark Jenkins

DELACORTE THEATER

Opened Wednesday, August 2, 1967.°
New York Shakespeare Festival in co-operation with the City of New York presents:

TITUS ANDRONICUS

By William Shakespeare; Director, Gerald Freedman; Setting, Ming Cho Lee; Lighting, Martin Aronstein; Costumes and Masks, Theoni V. Aldredge; Music and Sound Score, John Morris; Choreographic Movement, Joyce Trisler; Associate Producer, Bernard Gersten; Technical Director, Donald Koehler; Assistant to Directors, Wendy Shepard; Assistant to Producer, Gail Merrifield.

CAST

The Narrator .... Charles Durning
Saturninus .... Robert Stattel
Bassianus .... John LaGioia
Marcus Andronicus .... Clayton Corbin
Titus Andronicus .... Jack Hollander
Lucius .... Jonathan Reynolds
Tamora .... Olympia Dukakis
Chiron .... David Birney
Demetrius .... Raul Julia
Alarbus .... George McGrath
Lavinia .... Erin Martin
Mutius .... William Shephard
Quintus .... Donald K. Warfield
Martius .... David Clennon
Aaron .... Moses Gunn
Young Lucius .... Alan Howard
Nurse .... Zoe Kamitses

ENSEMBLE: William Beckwith, David Glennon, Steven Coleman, James Daniel, Taro Ichinose, Philip Johnson, George McGrath, Ralph Nelson, Harold Schwartz, Charles Seals, William Shephard, Carlos Sille, Terje Thoresen, Steven Van Benschoten, Donald K. Warfield, Lydia Fisher, Zoe Kamitses.

Manager: David Black
Press: Merle Debuskey, Faith Geer
Stage Managers: Russell McGrath, Timothy Ward, Amy Saltz

° Closed Aug. 26, 1967 after 22 performances.

Friedman-Abeles Photos

Olympia Dukakis, Jack Hollander, Erin Martin
Above: Jack Hollander, Moses Gunn, Erin Martin, Olympia Dukakis

Jack Hollander, Erin Martin
in "Titus Andronicus"

MOBILE THEATRE

Opened Friday, June 23, 1967.°
New York Shakespeare Festival in association with the City of New York presents:

VOLPONE

By Ben Johnson; Director, George Sherman; Set, David Mitchell; Costumes, Jose Varona; Lighting. Lawrence Metzler; Music, David Amram.

CAST

Volpone .... Alexander Panas
Mosca .... Roscoe Lee Browne
Nano .... Roger Hendricks Simon
Castrone .... John McCurry
Androgyno .... C. Leonard Williams
Voltore .... Paul Hecht
Corbaccio .... Fred Warriner
Corvino .... Alfred Leberfeld
Celia .... Marlene Warfield
Bonario .... Saul Fredericks
Lady Wouldbe .... Susan Peters
Drunk .... Robert Einenkel
Beggar .... Catherine Ryan
Streetwalker .... Laura Bendersky
Ultra Fop .... Darryl Croxton
Fop Boy .... Lawrence Cook
Servant .... Peter Jacob
Pickpocket .... Joseph Mydell
Old Man .... Joseph Cazalet
Gentlemen .... Lisle Wilson,
        William Gearhart, Lawrence Cook,
        Samual Blue, Jr.
Ladies .... Mallory Hoover, Sally Lansing
Chief Advocate .... Herb Davis
Second Judge .... Peter Jacob
Third Judge .... Joseph Cazalet
Commandatore .... Joseph Capone
Court Clerk .... Darryl Croxton
Officers .... Samual Blue, Jr., Joseph Mydell

Press: Merle Debuskey, Faith Geer
Stage Manager: Hal DeWindt

° Closed Aug. 19, 1967.

(No photographs available)

AMERICAN SHAKESPEARE FESTIVAL
Stratford, Connecticut
June 17 through September 10, 1967
Joseph Verner Reed, Sr., Producer

AMERICAN SHAKESPEARE FESTIVAL
THEATRE

Opened Saturday, June 17, 1967.
(Joseph Verner Reed, Sr., Joseph Verner
Reed, Jr., Producers) The American
Shakespeare Festival presents in repertory:

A MIDSUMMER NIGHT'S DREAM

By William Shakespeare; Director, Cyril
Ritchard; Assisted by Myles Eason; Scenery,
William and Jean Eckart; Costumes, Robert
Fletcher; Lighting, Tharon Musser; Chore-
ography, Robert Tucker; Music and Songs,
Conrad Susa; Musical Director, John Duffy;
Associate Producer, Berenice Weiler; Produc-
tion Assistants, Thomas Rosica, Norman King-
off, Joan Lebowitz.

CAST

Theseus	Myles Eason
Hippolyta	Marilyn McKenna
Philostrate and Egeus	James Valentine
Hermia	Diana Davila
Lysander	Ted Graeber
Demetrius	John Cunningham
Helena	Dorothy Tristan
Quince	Tom Aldredge
Snug	Carl Don
Bottom	Cyril Ritchard
Flute	Mylo Quam
Snout	Tom Lacy
Starveling	Robert Frink
First Fairy	Linda Caputi
Puck	Jerry Dodge
Oberon	Cyril Ritchard
Titania	Jane Farnol
Peaseblossom	Ian Tucker
Cobweb	Laura Michaels
Mustardseed	Rusty Thacker
Moth	Michael Scotlin
Titania's Fairies	Janyce Wagner, Peff Modelski, Jan LaPrade, Denise Winston
Oberon's Fairies	Tony Bassell, William MacAdam, William Herter, Fred Jackson
Wall	Robert Frink
Moon	Tom Lacy
Lion	Carl Don
Pyramus	Cyril Ritchard
Thisby	Mylo Quam
Major Domo	William Pritz
Indian Prince	Ricky West

GUARDS: Peter Norden, Charles Turner, Elliot Paul, Ronald DiMartile, Brandwell Teuscher, Alan Causey

Friedman-Abeles Photos

Jane Farnol, Jerry Dodge. Above: Cyril Ritchard
Top: Mylo Quam, Cyril Ritchard

Carl Don, Tom Lacy, Mylo Quam

AMERICAN SHAKESPEARE FESTIVAL THEATRE

Opened Sunday, June 18, 1967.
The American Shakespeare Festival presents in repertory:

ANTIGONE

By Jean Anouilh; Translated by Lewis Galantiere; Director, Jerome Kilty; Scenery, Donald Oenslager; Costumes, Gordon Micunis; Lighting, Tharon Musser; Music and Musical Director, John Duffy; Lyrics, John Devlin.

CAST

Chorus	Tom Aldredge
Antigone	Maria Tucci
Haemon	Anthony Mainionis
Ismene	Marian Hailey
Creon	Morris Carnovsky
Page	Billy Partello
Eurydice	Jane Farnol
Nurse	Doris Rich
Messenger	John Devlin
First Guard	Richard Castellano
Second Guard	Garry Mitchell
Third Guard	Edward Rudney
Secret Service	Peter Norden, Elliot Paul
Singers	Bill MacAdam, Peff Modelski, Michael Scotlin, Ian Tucker

Friedman-Abeles Photos

Right: Maria Tucci, Morris Carnovsky. Top: Garry Mitchell, Maria Tucci, Edward Rudney, Richard Castellano

Tom Aldredge, Peter Norden, Elliot Paul, Morris Carnovsky

Marian Hailey, Morris Carnovsky, Maria Tucci

156

AMERICAN SHAKESPEARE FESTIVAL THEATRE

Opened Sunday, June 20, 1967.
The American Shakespeare Festival presents in repertory:

THE MERCHANT OF VENICE

By William Shakespeare; Director, Michael Kahn; Scenery, Ed Wittstein; Costumes, Jose Varona; Music, Richard Peaslee; Choreography, Robert Tucker; Musical Director, John Duffy.

CAST

Antonio	John Devlin
Salarino	Ted Graeber
Salerio	Richard Mathews
Salanio	Mylo Quam
Bassanio	John Cunningham
Gratiano	Tom Aldredge
Lorenzo	Jack Ryland
Portia	Barbara Baxley
Nerissa	Marian Hailey
Neapolitan Prince	Charles Stallman
County Palatine	Fred Jackson
M. LeBon	Anthony Mainionis
Falconbridge	Ronald DiMartile
Saxony	Ian Crosby
Guests	Jane Farnol, Frank Caltabiano, Jan LaPrade, Bill MacAdam, Peff Modelski, Anthony Bassett
Balthazar	Robert Frink
Stephano	Rusty Thacker
Lucentio	Ian Tucker
Shylock	Morris Carnovsky
Prince of Morocco	Robert Kya-Hill
Attendant to Morocco	Charles Turner
Lancelot Gobbo	Jerry Dodge
Old Gobbo	Tom Lacy
Leonardo	Elliot Paul
Francesco	Luiz Lopez-Cepero
Jessica	Maria Tucci
Prince of Arragon	James Valentine
Mother of Arragon	Peff Modelski
Tubal	William Myers
Guards	Anthony Mainionis, Alan Causey, Charles Turner
Duke of Venice	Richard Mathews

Friedman-Abeles Photos

Morris Carnovsky, Richard Mathews, Tom Aldredge, Barbara Baxley, John Cunningham, Marian Hailey, Jack Ryland. Above: Robert Kya-Hill (L) Barbara Baxley, Marian Hailey. Top: John Cunningham, John Devlin, Morris Carnovsky

AMERICAN SHAKESPEARE FESTIVAL THEATRE

Opened Tuesday, July 25, 1967.
The American Shakespeare Festival presents in repertory:

MACBETH

By William Shakespeare; Director, John Houseman; Scenery and Costumes, Rouben Ter-Arutunian; Lighting, Jennifer Tipton; Music and Musical Director, John Duffy; Fights Choreographed by Rod Colbin.

CAST

Witches	Peff Modelski, William MacAdam, Frederick C. Jackson
Duncan	Ernest Graves
Malcolm	John Cunningham
Donalbain	Richard Novello
Captain	Jack Ryland
Ross	Richard Mathews
Lennox	Ted Graeber
Macbeth	John Colicos
Banquo	John Devlin
Lady Macbeth	Carrie Nye
Seton	Anthony Mainionis
Fleance	Ian Tucker
Porter	Jerry Dodge
Macduff	Tom Aldredge
Angus	Jack Ryland
First Murderer	Richard Castellano
Second Murderer	Mylo Quam
Lady Macduff	Dorothy Tristan
Young Macduff	Michael Liquigli
Doctor	William Myers
Gentlewoman	Peff Modelski
Old Siward	Alan Causey
Messengers	Brandwell Teuscher, Garry Mitchell

SCOTTISH LORDS: Frank Caltabiano, Ian Crosby, Peter Norden, Elliot Paul, Edward Rudney, Charles Stallman

SCOTTISH SOLDIERS: Tony Bassett, Ronald DiMartile, Norman Kingoff, Luis Lopez-Cepero, Garry Mitchell, Michael Scotlin, Brandwell Teuscher, Rusty Thacker

ENGLISH SOLDIERS: Frank Caltabiano, Ian Crosby, Robert Frink, William Herter, Peter Norden, Elliot Paul, William Pritz, Edward Rudney, Charles Stallman, Charles Turner

Manager: Donald Bundock
Press: Shirley Herz, Bob Beard, Sandra Manley
Stage Managers: David Clive, Lo Hardin, Robert Herrman

Shirley Herz Photos

John Colicos. Top Right: John Devlin, Carrie Nye, John Colicos

John Devlin, Carrie Nye, John Colicos. Above Carrie Nye, Richard Mathews, John Colicos

158

SAN DIEGO NATIONAL SHAKESPEARE FESTIVAL
Old Globe Theatre, Balboa Park
June 13 through September 10, 1967
Craig Noel, Producing Director

OLD GLOBE THEATRE

Opened Tuesday, June 13, 1967.
The Eighteenth San Diego National Shakespeare Festival presents in repertory:

TWELFTH NIGHT

By William Shakespeare; Staged by Edward Payson Call; Scenery, Peggy Kellner; Costumes, John T. Naccarato; Music and Songs composed by Conrad Susa; Lighting, Joseph Anthony Rubino; William Roesch, Associate Director; Technical Directors William C. Roberts; Bernard deSelm; Production Assistant, William Gonzalez.

CAST

Feste	Donald West
Pages	Dennis Manuel, John David Peters
Orsino	George Backman
Curio	Robert Lawson
Gentlemen	Tom Corcoran, Jim Eggleston
Valentine	Joseph Lambie
Viola	Katherine Henryk
Sea Captain	John Oldham
Sailors	Fred Coleman, Edward Horton
Malvolio	Josef Sommer
Olivia	Dixie Marquis
Attendants	Annette Cammer, Madelon Lambie, Elizabeth Lowry
Sir Toby Belch	James B. Douglas
Maria	Jacqueline Brookes
Sir Andrew Aguecheek	Joseph Maher
Sebastian	Richard Kavanaugh
Antonio	Charles Napier
Officers	Al Wallen, Robert Andersen, Biff Manard
Priest	Joseph Lambie

James B. Douglas, Joseph Maher, Jacqueline Brookes, Donald West
Top: Katherine Henryk, George Backman

OLD GLOBE THEATRE

Opened Thursday, June 15, 1967.
The San Diego National Shakespeare Festival presents in repertory:

OTHELLO

By William Shakespeare; Director, Milton Katselas; Setting and Costumes, Peggy Kellner; Music composed by Conrad Susa; Lighting, Joseph Anthony Rubino.

CAST

Othello	Douglas Watson
Brabantio	John Holland
Cassio	Joseph Lambie
Iago	Anthony Zerbe
Roderigo	Joseph Maher
Duke of Venice	Donald West
Senators	John Oldham, Al Wallen
Gratiano	Al Wallen
Desdemona	Dixie Marquis
Emilia	Jacqueline Brookes
Bianca	Katherine Henryk

CITIZENS, SERVANTS, GUARDS: Robert Andersen, Janice Fuller, Madelon Lambie, Robert Lawson, Elizabeth Lowry, Charles Napier, Annette Cammer, Fred Coleman, Tom Corcoran, Jim Eggleston, Edward Horton, Biff Manard, Dennis Manuel, John David Peters, J. Michael Ross

Press: William B. Eaton, Patti Parsons
Stage Managers: Bruce A. Hoover, Michol Pawlowski, Jean Holloway

Douglas Watson, Dixie Marquis in "Othello"

OLD GLOBE THEATRE

Opened Friday, June 16, 1967.
The San Diego National Shakespeare Festival presents in repertory:

ALL'S WELL THAT ENDS WELL

By William Shakespeare; Staged by Malcolm Black; Scenery and Costumes, Peggy Kellner; Music Composed by Conrad Susa; Lighting, Joseph Anthony Rubino.

CAST

Countess of Roussillion	Susan French
Bertram	James B. Douglas
Lafeau	Donald West
Helena	Jacqueline Brookes
Rinaldo	Al Wallen
Lavache	Anthony Zerbe
Parolles	Douglas Watson
Servant to Bertram	Joseph Lambie
King of France	John Holland
Captain G. Dumain	George Blackman
Captain E. Dumain	Josef Sommer
Young French Lord	Richard Kavanaugh
King's Physician	Jim Eggleston
Gentleman	John Oldham
Duke of Florence	Charles Napier
Widow	Halcyon Oldham
Diana	Katherine Henryk
Mariana	Janice Fuller
Interpreter	Joseph Maher

LORDS, LADIES, SOLDIERS: Robert Anderson, Annette Cammer, Fred Coleman, Tom Corcoran, Edward Horton, Robert Lawson, Madelon Lambie, Elizabeth Lowry, Dennis Manuel, John David Peters, J. Michael Ross

160

Donald West, John Holland, James B. Douglas, Jacqueline Brookes, Susan French Above: Douglas Watson, James B. Douglas in "All's Well That Ends Well"

OREGON SHAKESPEAREAN FESTIVAL
Lithia Park, Ashland, Oregon
July 22 through September 10, 1967
Twenty-seventh Season
~us L. Bowmer, Founder and Producing Director

Tom Donaldson, Hal Poe, Shirley Patton
in "Pericles"

SHAKESPEAREAN FESTIVAL THEATER

Opened Saturday, July 22, 1967.
The Oregon Shakespearean Festival Association presents in repertory:

PERICLES, PRINCE OF TYRE

By William Shakespeare; Director, Nagle Jackson; Stage Designer, Clayton Karkosh; Costumes, Jack A. Byers; Music Director, W. Bernard Windt; Choreographer, Shirlee Dodge; Lighting, Robert Brand; Technical Director, Peter B. Young.

CAST

Gower as Chorus	Philip Davidson
Antiochus	Glenn Mazen
Pericles	Tom Donaldson
Helicanus	Roald B. Wulff
Escanes	Patrick Omeirs
Simonides	Hal Poe
Cleon	Tom Martin
Lysimachus	Scott Porter
Cerimon	Arnold Hummasti
Thaliard	Milton Tarver
Philemon	Joseph G. Medalis
Leonine	Richard Lincoln
A Pandar	Ken DeGusta
Boult	Vincent Landro
Fishermen	George Brown, Jonathan Hardy, Timothy Shelton
Gentlemen of Mytilene	Robert Black, Tom Oleniacz
Daughter of Antiochus	Mary Ed Peters
Dionyza	Cindy Kay Veazey
Thaisa	Shirley Patton
Marina	Joanne Bayless
Lychorida	Valerie Zellerhoff
A Bawd	Claudia Wilkens
Diana	Rosemary Shevlin
Whores	Evelyn C. Davenport, Sandy Logan

MIMES: Randall Craig, Jay Theodore Sterling, Karen Sue Boettcher, Betsy Sacks Hamilton

LORDS, LADIES; ETC.: Ken DeGusta, Sherman Dorsey, Dick Hooser, Richard Lincoln, Tom Oleniacz, Mary Ed Peters, Dennis Sparks, Vernon Statler, Robert Black, Evelyn C. Davenport, Larry Alan Haynes, Bob Horn, Sandy Logan, Cathy Christy, David Kent Nale

Ann Kinsolving, Glenn Mazen in
"Antony and Cleopatra"

SHAKESPEAREAN FESTIVAL THEATER

Opened Sunday, July 23, 1967.
The Oregon Shakespearean Festival Association presents in repertory:

ANTONY AND CLEOPATRA

By William Shakespeare; Director, Jerry Turner; Stage Designer, Clayton Karkosh; Costumes, Jack A. Byers; Music Director, W. Bernard Windt; Choreographer, Shirlee Dodge; Lighting, Robert Brand.

CAST

Philo	Tom Donaldson
Demetrius	Tom Oleniacz
Iras	Karen Sue Boettcher
Charmian	Rosemary Shevlin
Cleopatra	Ann Kinsolving
Antony	Glenn Mazen
Alexas	Rick Hamilton
Soothsayer	Ken DeGusta
Enobarbus	Philip Davidson
Mardian	Arnold Hummasti
Octavius Caesar	Nagle Jackson
Lepidus	Joseph G. Medalis
Pompey	Vincent Landro
Menas	William Roberts
Menecrates	Sherman Dorsey
Varrius	Hal Poe
Maecenas	Thomas Martin
Agrippa	Tom Donaldson
Proculeius	William Roberts
Messenger from Rome	Timothy Shelton
Octavia	Cindy Kay Veazey
Octavia's Lady	Mary Ed Peters
Scarus	Hal Poe
Canidius	Patrick Omeirs
Thidias	Roald B. Wulff
Dollabella	Tom Oleniacz
Decretas	Dennis Sparks
Diomedes	Patrick Omeirs
Seleucus	Ken DeGusta
Clown	Joseph G. Medalis

SOLDIERS, ATTENDANTS, ETC: George Brown, Randall Craig, Jonathan Hardy, Dan Hays, Dick Hooser, Richard Lincoln, Hank McCormick, David Owen, Dennis Sparks, Vernon Statler, Jay Theodore Sterling, Milton Tarver, David Kent Nale, Randall Eugene Stothers, Craig Williams

Whitland Locke Photos

161

SHAKESPEAREAN FESTIVAL THEATER

Opened Monday, July 24, 1967.
The Oregon Shakespearean Festival Association presents in repertory:

THE TAMING OF THE SHREW

By William Shakespeare; Director, Richard D. Risso; Stage Designer, Clayton Karkosh; Costumes, Jack A. Byers; Music Director, W. Bernard Windt; Choreographer, Shirlee Dodge; Lighting, Robert Brand.

CAST

A Lord	William Roberts
Christopher Sly	Philip Davidson
Hostess	Valerie Zellerhoff
Page	Dick Hooser
Tapster	Roald B. Wulff
Huntsmen and Servants	Randall Craig, Tom Oleniacz
Baptista	Hal Poe
Vincentio	Joseph G. Medalis
Lucentio	Scott Porter
Petruchio	Tom Donaldson
Gremio	Arnold Hummasti
Hortensio	Nagle Jackson
Tranio	Vincent Landro
Biondello	Tom Martin
Grumio	Rick Hamilton
Curtis	Timothy Shelton
A Pedant	Ken DeGusta
Katharina	Ann Kinsolving
Bianca	Karen Sue Boettcher
Widow	Claudia Wilkens
Tailor	Sidney McLain
Haberdasher	Jay Theodore Sterling
Petruchio's Servants	Tom Oleniacz, David Owen, Dan Hays, Sherman Dorsey, Jay Theodore Sterling

Whitland Locke Photos

**Top Right: Ann Kinsolving, Tom Donaldson
in "Taming Of The Shrew"**

**Ann Kinsolving, Richard D. Risso in
"Richard III"**

SHAKESPEAREAN FESTIVAL THEATER

Opened Tuesday, July 25, 1967.
The Oregon Shakespearean Festival Association presents in repertory:

RICHARD THE THIRD

By William Shakespeare; Director, Hugh C. Evans; Stage Designer, Clayton Karkosh; Costumes, Jack A. Byers; Music Director, W. Bernard Windt; Choreographer, Shirlee Dodge; Lighting, Robert Brand.

CAST

King Edward IV	Philip Davidson
Edward, Prince of Wales	Sidney McLain
Richard, Duke of York	Michael Poe
George, Duke of Clarence	William Roberts
Richard, Duke of Gloucester	Richard D. Risso
Henry, Earl of Richmond	Tom Donaldson
Archbishop of Canterbury	Dennis Sparks
Archbishop of York	Patrick Omeirs
Bishop of Ely	Sherman Dorsey
Duke of Buckingham	Vincent Landro
Duke of Norfolk	Tom Oleniacz
Earl of Surrey	Scott Porter
Earl Rivers	Hal Poe
Marquess of Dorset	George Brown
Lord Grey	Robert Black
Lord Hastings	Glenn Mazen
Lord Stanley	Joseph G. Medalis
Lord Lovel	Scott Porter
Sir Richard Ratcliff	Milton Tarver
Sir William Catesby	Thomas Martin
Sir Thomas Vaughan	Roald B. Wulff
Sir James Tyrrel	Patrick Omeirs
Sir James Blunt	Ken DeGusta
Sir Walter Herbert	Rick Hamilton
Earl of Oxford	Randall Craig
Sir William Brandon	Philip Davidson
Sir Robert Brakenbury	Arnold Hummasti
Lord Mayor of London	Dan Hays
Christopher Urswick	Jay Theodore Sterling
Tressel	Rick Hamilton
Berkeley	Sherman Dorsey
Keeper in the Tower	Vernon Statler
Scrivener	Richard Lincoln
Pursuivant	David Owen
First Murderer	Rick Hamilton
Second Murderer	Ken DeGusta
Queen Elizabeth	Molly Risso
Margaret	Claudia Wilkens
Duchess of York	Cindy Kay Veazey
Lady Anne	Ann Kinsolving
Daughter to Clarence	Karen Sue Boettcher
Ladies	Mary Ed Peters, Rosemary Shevlin, Valerie Zellerhoff
Pages	Randall Craig, Jonathan Hardy, Dick Hooser, Richard Lincoln, Hank McCormick, Timothy Shelton

General Manager: William W. Patton
Press: Carl Ritchie, Gary Aldridge
Stage Managers: Pat Patton, David Ostwald, E. St. John Villard

STRATFORD FESTIVAL OF CANADA
Stratford, Ontario
June 12 through October 14, 1967
Fifteenth Season
Michael Langham, Artistic Director

FESTIVAL THEATRE

Opened Monday, June 12, 1967.
The Stratford Shakespearean Festival presents in repertory:

RICHARD III

By William Shakespeare; Director, John Hirsch; Designed by Desmond Heeley; Music, Stanley Silverman; Artistic Director, Michael Langham; Associate Directors, Jean Gascon, John Hirsch; Administrative Director, Victor Polley; Director of Music, Oscar Shumsky; Production Director, John Hayes.

CAST

King Edward IV	Brian Petchey
Queen Elizabeth	Ann Firbank
Edward	Leatham Carroll
Richard, Duke of York	John Livingston
Richard, Duke of Gloucester, afterwards Richard III	Alan Bates
George	William Hutt
Clarence's Son	Jimmy McGorman
Clarence's Daughter	Judy Murray
Lady Anne	Zoe Caldwell
Duchess of York	Barbara Bryne
Queen Margaret	Frances Hyland
Earl Rivers	Kenneth Pogue
Marquess of Dorset	Colin Fox
Lord Grey	Leon Pownall
Sir Thomas Vaughan	Blaine Parker
Archbishop of Canterbury	Dominic Hogan
Archbishop of York	John Gardiner
Bishop of Ely	Eric Donkin
Duke of Buckingham	Leo Ciceri
Sir William Catesby	Christopher Newton
Sir Richard Ratcliff	James Blendick
Lord Lovel	Joel Kenyon
Sir Robert Brakenbury	Max Helpmann
Sir James Tyrell	Bernard Behrens
Duke of Norfolk	Jonathan White
Earl of Surrey	August Schellenberg
Lord Hastings	Kenneth Welsh
Lord Stanley	Mervyn Blake
Henry, Earl of Richmond	Barry MacGregor
Sir James Blunt	Max Helpmann
Sir Walter Herbert	Dominic Hogan
Christopher Urswick	Eric Donkin
Lord Mayor of London	Eric Christmas
Berkeley	John Gardiner
Tressel	Tim Henry
Sheriff	Blaine Parker
Prison Keeper	August Schellenberg
Scrivener	Neil Dainard
First Murderer	Eric Christmas
Second Murderer	Neil Dainard
Pursuivant	Cedric Smith
Priest	Peter Jobin
Messengers	Patrick Crean, Neil Dainard, John Gardiner, Richard Monette, Jonathan White

MONKS, CITIZENS, AND OTHERS: David Bolt, Jane Casson. Laurence Cherniak, Peter Cheyne, Richard Davidson, Ronald East, Kathleen Flaherty, David Foster, Terry Judd, Marilyn Lightstone, Jack Messinger, William Mockridge, Dermot Nolan, Paul Robertson, Patricia Steenberg, John Turner, Anna Wing, Jean Yundt

Douglas Spillane Photos

Top Right: Bernard Behrens, Alan Bates

Barbara Bryne, Ann Firbank, Frances Hyland, Zoe Caldwell

163

FESTIVAL THEATRE

Opened Tuesday, June 13, 1967.
The Stratford Shakespearean Festival presents in repertory:

THE GOVERNMENT INSPECTOR

By Nikolai Gogol; Adapted by Peter Raby; Director, Michael Langham; Designed by Leslie Hurry; Music, Raymond Pannell.

CAST

Anton Antonovich	Tony van Bridge
Ammos Fyodorovich Lyapkin-Tyapkin	Leo Ciceri
Artemy Filippovich Zemlyanika	Mervyn Blake
Luka Lukich Khlopov	Christopher Newton
Kristian Ivanovich	Joel Kenyon
Ivan Kuzmich Shpekin	Colin Fox
Peter Ivanovich Dobchinsky	Barry MacGregor
Peter Ivanovich Bobchinsky	Eric Donkin
Mishka	Al Kozlik
Derzhimorda	Jonathan White
Stepan Ilich	John Gardiner
Anna Andreyevna	Amelia Hall
Marya Antonovna	Roberta Maxwell
Avdotya	Jane Casson
Osip	Bernard Behrens
Ivan Alexandrovich Khlestakov	William Hutt
A Waiter	Neil Dainard
Abdulin	Leon Pownall
Two other merchants	James Blendick, Neil Dainard
Locksmith's Wife	Barbara Bryne
Corporal's Widow	Ann Firbank
Lyapkin-Tyapkin's Wife	Marilyn Lightstone
Korobkin	Joseph Shaw
Rastakovsky	Joel Kenyon
Korobkin's Wife	Barbara Bryne
Juka Lukich's Wife	Ann Firbank
Gendarme	Patrick Crean

GUESTS, TOWNSPEOPLE: Peter Cheyne, Richard Davidson, Kathleen Flaherty, David Foster, Tim Henry, Dominic Hogan, Peter Jobin, Terry Judd, Marilyn Lightstone, William Mockridge, Blaine Parker, August Schellenberg, Cedric Smith, John Turner, Jean Yundt.

Peter Smith, Douglas Spillane Photos

Mervyn Blake, William Hutt in
"The Government Inspector"

FESTIVAL THEATRE

Opened Wednesday, June 14, 1967.
The Stratford Shakespearean Festival presents in repertory:

THE MERRY WIVES OF WINDSOR

By William Shakespeare; Director, David William; Designed by Brian Jackson; Music, Louis Applebaum.

CAST

Justice Shallow	Eric Christmas
Abraham Slender	Colin Fox
Sir Hugh Evans	Bernard Behrens
George Page	Kenneth Pogue
Sir John Falstaff	Tony van Bridge
Pistol	Max Helpmann
Nym	Al Kozlik
Bardolph	Leon Pownall
Mrs. Page	Zoe Caldwell
Anne Page	Roberta Maxwell
Mrs. Ford	Frances Hyland
Simple	Richard Monette
Host of Garter Inn	Mervyn Blake
Robin	John Livingston
Mistress Quickly	Anna Wing
Rugby	Joseph Shaw
Dr. Caius	Jean Gascon
Fenton	Kenneth Welsh
Frank Ford	Alan Bates
John	August Schellenberg
Robert	Dominic Hogan
William Page	Leatham Carroll

MAIDS, TAPSTERS, LORDS, ETC.: David Bolt, Barbara Bryne, James Blendick, Jane Casson, Peter Cheyne, Richard Davidson, Kathleen Flaherty, David Foster, Elliot Hayes, Peter Jobin, Terry Judd, Joel Kenyon, Marilyn Lightstone, Jack Messinger, William Mockridge, Edward Neigh, Dermot Nolan, Blaine Parker, Paul Robertson, John Smythe, Patricia Steenberg, John Turner, Jean Yundt.

Eric Christmas, Tony van Bridge. Right Center:
Frances Hyland, Zoe Caldwell in
"Merry Wives of Windsor"

FESTIVAL THEATRE

Opened Monday, July 31, 1967.
The Stratford Shakespearean Festival presents in repertory:

ANTONY AND CLEOPATRA

By William Shakespeare; Director, Michael Langham; Designed by Tanya Moiseiwitsch; Music, Louis Applebaum.

CAST

Ventidius	Kenneth Pogue
Proculeius	John Gardiner
Gallus	Eric Donkin
Ambassador	August Schellenberg
Mark Antony	Christopher Plummer
Cleopatra	Zoe Caldwell
Mardian	James Blendick
Seleucus	David Bolt
Diomed	Neil Dainard
Eros	Richard Monette
Decretas	Al Kozlik
Charmian	Dawn Greenhalgh
Iras	Marilyn Lightstone
Alexas	Brian Petchey
Soothsayer	Eric Christmas
Domitius Enobarbus	William Hutt
Octavius Caesar	Kenneth Welsh
Thidias	Jonathan White
Aemilius Lepidus	Bernard Behrens
Sextus Pompeius	Christopher Newton
Menas	Max Helpmann
Varrius	Peter Jobin
Agrippa	Leo Ciceri
Maecenas	Joel Kenyon
Octavia	Ann Firbank
Scarus	Leon Pownall
Dolabella	Barry MacGregor
A Peasant	Eric Christmas

ANTONY'S SOLDIERS: Patrick Crean, Richard Davidson, Ronald East, Jack Messinger, Dermot Nolan, Cedric Smith, John Turner

CAESAR'S SOLDIERS: Peter Cheyne, Jack Cunningham, David Foster, Roger Gaskell, Dominic Hogan, Terry Judd, Blaine Parker

LADIES-IN-WAITING AND SLAVES: Jane Casson, Kathleen Flaherty, Lewis Gordon, William Mockridge, Patricia Steenberg, Jean Yundt

Production Manager: Jack Hutt
Company Manager: Bruce Swerdfager
Press: John Paterson, Tom Patterson
Stage Managers: Thomas Bohdanetzky,
Bill Kearns, Graham Spicer,
William Webster, Katherina Allan

Douglas Spillane Photos

William Hutt, Leo Ciceri, Christopher Plummer. Top: Christopher Plummer, Zoe Caldwell

HELLO, DOLLY!

Book, Michael Stewart; Based on play by
Thornton Wilder; Music and Lyrics, Jerry
Herman; Original Production Directed and
Choreographed by Gower Champion; Re-
staged by Lucia Victor; Settings, Oliver Smith;
Costumes, Freddy Wittop; Lighting, Jean Ro-
senthal; Musical Direction, Gil Bowers; Or-
chestrations, Philip J. Lang; Dance and Inci-
dental Music Arrangements, Peter Howard;
Hairstylist, Robert Murphy; Associate Produ-
cer, Samuel Liff; Staff Associate, Sylvia
Schwartz; A David Merrick and Champion-
Five Inc. Production. Opened Tuesday, November 14, 1967 in Indiana University
Auditorium, Bloomington, and still touring May
31, 1968.

CAST

Mrs. Dolly Gallagher Levi	Dorothy Lamour[1]
Ernestina	Judith Drake
Ambrose Kemper	William Sissov
Horse	Heather Hendricks, Nancy Lewis
Horace Vandergelder	Eric Brotherson
Ermengarde	Judy Jenson
Cornelius Hackl	Dick Leppig
Barnaby Tucker	Jess Richards
Irene Molloy	Leslie Daniel
Minnie Fay	Andrea Bell
Mrs. Rose	Joan Shea
Rudolph	Charles Scott
Judge	Eddie Hanley
Court Clerk	Wayne Clark

TOWNSPEOPLE, WAITERS: Lisa Ackerman,
Donna Barry, Cindi Bulak, Roberta Country-
man, Dorothy Hanning, Heather Hendricks,
Melodie Jarvis, Nancy Lewis, Sally Riggs, Roy
Barry, Jerry Bell, James Bovaird, Norman
Cancelose, Wayne Clark, Stephan de Ghelder,
Karl Dixson, Don George, William Harrod,
Cary La Spina, Don Lawrence, Arnott Mader,
Frank Newell, Tony Stevens, Ron Sukiennik

UNDERSTUDIES: Dolly, Joan Shea; Horace,
Eddie Hanley; Irene, Dorothy Hanning; Hackl,
Don George; Barnaby, Jerry Bell; Minnie,
Judy Jenson; Ernestina, Cindi Bulak; Rudolph,
Roy Barry; Ambrose, Don Lawrence; Ermen-
garde, Donna Barry; Mrs. Rose, Sally Riggs.

A Musical in 2 acts and 15 scenes.

General Manager: Jack Schlissel
Company Manager: Boris Bernardi
Press: Lee Solters, Harvey B. Sabinson,
Zac Freedman, Alan Eichler
Stage Managers: Lee Murray,
Dorothy Hanning

† 1. Miss Lamour performed with the Las
Vegas company for 8 weeks beginning Aug.
23, 1967 before beginning tour with this
company produced for her. For original NY
production, see THEATRE WORLD, Vol. 20.
In Vol. 23, it was erroneously noted that
Carol Channing succeeded Eve Arden in the
Chicago company. A new company was
formed for her tour beginning in October
1966 in Houston, Tex., where she closed with
the company on June 11, 1967 after breaking
all previous records for a "Dolly" tour.

Friedman-Abeles Photos

Top Right: Dorothy Lamour, Eric Brotherson
Below: Leslie Daniel, Dick Leppig,
Andrea Bell, Jess Richards

Bill Sissov, Judy Jenson, Dick Leppig,
Dorothy Lamour, Jess Richards

FIDDLER ON THE ROOF

Book, Joseph Stein; Based on Sholom Aleichem's stories; Music, Jerry Bock; Lyrics, Sheldon Harnick; Directed and Choreographed by Jerome Robbins; Settings, Boris Aronson; Costumes, Patricia Zipprodt; Lighting, Jean Rosenthal; Orchestrations, Don Walker; Musical Director, Joseph D. Lewis; Dance Music Arranged by Betty Walberg; Vocal Arrangements, Milton Greene; Presented by Harold Prince; Original cast album by RCA Victor Records. Opened Tuesday, April 19, 1966 at the Music Center, Los Angeles, and still touring May 31, 1968.

CAST

Fiddler	Al DeSio†1
Tevye	Luther Adler†2
Golde	Dolores Wilson
Tzeitel	Felice Camargo†3
Hodel	Royce Lenelle
Chava	Kelly Wood†4
Shprintze	Renee Tetro
Bielke	Maureen Polye†5
Yente	Lois Zetter†6
Motel	Stanley Soble
Perchik	Joseph Masiell
Lazar Wolf	Paul Lipson†7
Mordcha	Fyv Finkel
Rabbi	Baruch Lumet
Mendel	Lewis J. Stadlen
Avram	Maurice Brenner
Nachum	Herb Corben
Russian Dancer	Michael Maurer†8
Grandma Tzeitel	Enid Hart
Fruma-Sarah	Maralyn Nell
Constable	Clarence Hoffman
Fyedka	Keith Caporal
Shandel	Glenna Evans†9

VILLAGERS: Bagel Man, Michael Gray; Streetsweeper, Pascual Vaquer; Fishmonger, Del Lewis; Seltzer Man, Michael Aubrey; Surcha, Violet Lane; Woodsman, Myron Curtis; Potseller, Steve Bohm; Grocer, Ralph Vucci; Fredel, Barbara Coggin; Knifeseller, John Spina; Bluma, Enid Hart; Berille, Patricia Lens; Mirala, Barbara Logan; Sima, Cherie Cannon; Rivka, Leona Evans; Moishe, Michael Burke; Anya, Emily Byrne; Hatmaker, Lee Delmer; Vladimir, Martin Gavin; Singer, James Hobson; Ivan, Myron Meljie.

UNDERSTUDIES: Tevye, Joseph Cusanelli; Golde, Lois Zetter; Tzeitel, Fruma, Carol Fox; Hodel, Grandma, Barbara Coggin; Chava, Patricia Lens; Motel, Lewis Stadlen; Lazar, Maurice Brenner; Yente, Shandel, Violet Lane; Fyedka, Perchik, James Hobson; Shprintze, Enid Hart; Bielke, Cherie Cannon; Mordcha, Michael Burke; Rabbi, Avram, Ralph Vucci; Mendel, Pascual Vaquer; Fiddler, Michael Aubrey; Constable, Del Lewis; Beggar, Steve Bohm.

A Musical in two acts.

General Manager: Carl Fisher
Company Manager: James Miller
Press: Sol Jacobson, Lewis Harmon, Joe Shea, Bev Kelly
Stage Managers: Ruth Mitchell, Ben Strobach, Ed Lynch, Jay Jacobson

† Succeeded by: 1. Ross DiVito, 2. Paul Lipson, Theodore Bikel, Paul Lipson, 3. Kathleen Noser, 4. Marsha Meyers, 5. Ilene Karnow, 6. Lois Zetter, Ruth Jaroslow, 7. Joseph Cusanelli, 8. Myron Meljie, 9. Martha Webster.

For original NY production, see THEATRE WORLD, Vol. 21.

Friedman-Abeles Photos

Top Right: Theodore Bikel, Dolores Wilson
Below: Paul Lipson, Dolores Wilson (L)

Theodore Bikel, Lewis J. Stadlen, Kathleen Noser, Baruch Lumet, Dolores Wilson

MAN OF LA MANCHA

By Dale Wasserman; Music, Mitch Leigh; Lyrics, Joe Darion; Book and Musical Staging, Albert Marre; Choreography, Jack Cole; Settings and Lighting, Howard Bay; Costumes, Howard Bay, Patton Campbell; Dance Arrangements, Neil Warner; Musical Arrangements, Music Makers, Inc.; Musical Director, Joseph Klein; Technical Adviser, John Higgins; An ANTA-Goodspeed Presentation; Original cast album on Kapp Records; Presented by Albert W. Selden and Hal James. Opened Saturday, Sept. 24, 1966 in New Haven's Shubert Theatre, and still touring May 31, 1968.

CAST

Don Quixote (Cervantes)	Richard Kiley†1
Sancho	Harvey Lembeck†2
Aldonza	Joan Diener†3
Innkeeper	Wilbur Evans†4
Padre	Dale Malone
Dr. Carrasco	David Atkinson†5
Antonia	Dianne Barton†6
Barber	Taylor Reed†7
Pedro, Head Muleteer	Kirby Smith
Anselmo	Wilson Robey
Housekeeper	Lu Leonard
Jose	Carlos Macri†8
Juan, Muleteer, Mule	Grant Lashley†9
Paco	Jack Murray†10
Tenorio, Muleteer, Horse	Fernando Grahal†11
Maria	Patti Winston†12
Fermina	Natalie Costa
Moorish Dancer	Marilyn Sokol†13
Captain of Inquisition	William C. Wendt†14
Guitarists	David Serva, Robert Roberts
Guards and Men of Inquisition	Alan Coleridge, Richard Frock, John Roberson

UNDERSTUDIES: Don Quixote, Sandy Kenyon; Aldonza, Natalie Costa; Sancho, Barber, Louis Criscuola; Innkeeper, Kirby Smith; Padre, Anselmo, John Roberson; Carrasco, Ian Sullivan; Antonia, Fermina, Maria, Harriet Slaughter; Housekeeper, Judith Davies; Captain, Pedro, Richard Frock; Tenorio, Juan, Jose, John Grigas; Fermina, Maria, Moorish Dancer, Heather Golambo.

A Musical Play suggested by the life and works of Miguel de Cervantes, and presented without intermission.

General Manager: Walter Fried
Company Manager: Joseph M. Grossman
Press: Merle Debuskey, Harry Davies
Stage Managers: Sammy Lambert, Bob Burland, Alan Coleridge

† Succeeded by: 1. Keith Andes, 2. Tony Martinez, 3. Marian Marlowe, Carolyn Maye, Natalie Costa at matinees, 4. Earle MacVeigh, 5. Sandy Kenyon, 6. Kari Howard, 7. Robert Gibbons, 8. Nick Andrews, 9. Kenneth Novarro, 10. Mark Ross, 11, Ben Vargas, 12. Judith Davies, 13. Harriet Slaughter who plays Fermina for matinees, 14. Ian Sullivan.

For original NY production, see THEATRE WORLD, Vol. 22.

Top Right: Keith Andes, Carolyn Maye in "Man of La Mancha" **Below:** Dana Andrews, Don McArt, Bob Basso, Robert Q. Lewis, Bill Browder, Page Johnson in "The Odd Couple"

THE ODD COUPLE

By Neil Simon; Director, Richard Vath; Scenic Design, Oliver Smith; Lighting, Jean Rosenthal; Wardrobe, Marge Mann; Production Associate, Louis Maurer; Presented by Stan Seiden and Norman Dolin. Opened Monday, Oct. 16, 1967 in Boston's Shubert Theatre, and closed June 1, 1968 at the Mechanic in Baltimore.

CAST

Speed	Bill Browder
Murray	Bob Basso†1
Roy	Page Johnson
Vinnie	Don McArt
Oscar Madison	Dana Andrews†2
Felix Unger	Robert Q. Lewis
Gwendolyn Pigeon	Carol Lawson
Cecily Pigeon	Gita Breslin†3

UNDERSTUDIES: Tom Winston, Bill Browder, Inger Wegge

A Comedy in 3 acts and 4 scenes. The action takes place at the present time in an apartment on Riverside Drive in New York.

Company Managers: Robert Rapport, Don Haley, Gerald O'Connell
Press: Richard Falk
Stage Managers: Tony Di Milo, L. doran-Maurer, Richard Vath

† Succeeded by: 1. Tom Winston, 2. Lyle Talbot, Don Ameche, 3. Kerry Slattery.

For original NY production, see THEATRE WORLD, Vol. 21.

SWEET CHARITY

Book, Neil Simon; Music, Cy Coleman; Lyrics, Dorothy Fields; Based on original screenplay "Nights of Cabiria" by Federico Fellini, Tullio Finelli, Ernio Flaiano; Scenery and Lighting, Robert Randolph; Costumes, Irene Sharaff; Staging Re-created from Bob Fosse's original by Robert Linden and Paul Glover; Musical Direction, Jack Lee; Orchestrations, Ralph Burns; Dance Music Arranged by Fred Werner; Production Supervisor, Robert Linden; Associate Producer, John Bowab; Original cast album on Columbia Records; Hairstylist, Ronald DeMann; Presented by Fryer, Carr and Harris. Opened Sept. 11, 1967 at the Shubert in Boston, and closed Jan. 20, 1968 at the O'Keefe in Toronto.

CAST

Charity	Chita Rivera
Dark Glasses	Lathan Sanford
Bystander	John Stratton
Married Couple	Patrick Spohn, Renata Powers
Woman with hat	Jeanne Lucas
Ice Cream Vendor	Terry Nicholson
Football Player	Dick Corrigan
Ballplayer	Dan Tylor
Shopper	Mary Roche
Young Spanish Man	Phillip Filiato
Man with dog	Earl Lamartiniere
Dirty Old Man	Clifton Steere
First Cop	Tom Batten
Second Cop	James O'Sullivan
Helene	Thelma Oliver†
Nickie	Helen Gallagher
Herman	Tom Batten
Doorman	James O'Sullivan
Ursala	Marybeth Lahr
Vittorio Vidal	James Luisi
Waiter	John Stratton
Manfred	Patrick Spohn
Receptionist	Jeanne Lucas
Old Maid	Mary Roche
Poetry Lover	Sally Cooke
Oscar	Lee Goodman
Daddy Johann Sebastian Brubeck	Ben Vereen
Brother Paul	Paul Glover
Brother Lathan	Lathan Sanford
Policeman	Ben Vereen
Rosie	Renata Powers
Barney	Lathan Sanford
Mike	Richard Corrigan
Good Fairy	Jeanne Lucas

SINGERS AND DANCERS: Juanita Boyle, Susanne Carroll, Ciya Challis, Sally Cooke, Jean Even, Joan Jaffe, Marybeth Lahr, Linda Lees, Jeanne Lucas, Renata Powers, Mary Roche, Ellen Wollenhapt, Dick Corrigan, Phillip Filiato, Paul Glover, Earl Lamartiniere, Terry Nicholson, James O'Sullivan, Lathan Sanford, Patrick Spohn, Clifton Steere, Dan Taylor, Ben Vereen.

UNDERSTUDIES: Charity, Helen Gallagher; Oscar, John Stratton; Ursala, Mary Roche; Nickie, Jean Even; Helene, Joan Jaffee; Vidal, James O'Sullivan; Herman, Clifton Steere; Daddy, Patrick Spohn; Frug, Ellen Wollenhapt

MUSICAL NUMBERS: "You Should See Yourself," "The Rescue," "Big Spender," "Rich Man's Frug," "If My Friends Could See Me Now," "Too Many Tomorrows," "There's Gotta Be Something Better Than This," "I'm The Bravest Individual," "Rhythm Of Life," "Baby Dream Your Dream," "Sweet Charity," "Where Am I Going?," "I'm A Brass Band," "I Love To Cry At Weddings."

A Musical in 2 acts and 19 scenes, with prologue. The action takes place at the present time in and around New York City.

General Manager: Joseph P. Harris
Company Manager: Al Jones
Press: Betty Lee Hunt, Mae S. Hong
Stage Managers: Edward Strum, John D. Molthen, Paul Glover, Dick Corrigan

† Succeeded by Elaine Cancilla.

For original NY production, see THEATRE WORLD, Vol. 22.

Friedman-Abeles Photos

Center: Helen Gallagher, Chita Rivera, Thelma Oliver in "Sweet Charity"

WAIT A MINIM

Devised and Directed by Leon Gluckman; Musical Direction and Arrangements, Andrew Tracey; Decor and Lighting, Frank Rembach, Leon Gluckman; Costumes, Heather MacDonald-Rouse; Choreography, Frank Staff, Kendrew Lascelles; Lighting and Design Supervision, Klaus Holm; Costume Supervision, Patton Campbell; A Management Three Productions Tour; Original cast album on London Records; Presented by Frank Productions. Opened at the Mechanic Theatre, Baltimore, on July 10, 1967 and closed May 25, 1968 at the Colonial in Boston.

CAST

Andrew Tracey	Kendrew Lascelles
Nigel Pegram	Helene Ireland
Paul Tracey	Michel Martel
April Olrich	Barbara Quaney Tracey

A Musical Entertainment in two parts.

General Manager: Ira Bernstein
Company Manager: Abe Cohen
Press: Willard Keefe
Stage Manager: Elizabeth Caldwell

For original NY production, see THEATRE WORLD, Vol. 22.

Nigel Pegram, Barbara Quaney Tracey, Kendrew Lascelles, Michel Martel, Andrew Tracey, April Olrich, Helene Ireland, Paul Tracey

169

ON A CLEAR DAY YOU CAN SEE FOREVER

Book and Lyrics, Alan Jay Lerner; Music, Burton Lane; Scenery, Peter Wexler; Choreography, Eddie Roll; Director, Milton Katselas; Musical Director, Richard Parrinello; Lighting, James Riley; Costumes, Brooks-Van Horn; Orchestrations, Robert Russell Bennett; Music Continuity and Vocals by Trude Rittman; Dance Music, Betty Walberg; Special Coordinator, Diana Krasny; Presented by Zev Bufman in association with Nederlander-Steinbrenner Productions. Opened May 22, 1967 at the O'Keefe Center, Toronto, and closed Oct. 7, 1967 at the Shubert, Chicago.

CAST

Dr. Mark Brucker	Howard Keel
James Preston	William J. Coppola
Mrs. Hatch	Francine Beers
Muriel Bunson	Jodi Perselle
Daisy Gamble	Barbara Lang
Edward Moncrief	Lester James
Samuel Welles	Leon Benedict
Mrs. Welles	Nancy Wiench
Sir Hubert Insdale	William J. Coppola
Sir Hubert's Son	Joseph Pichette
Solicitor	George Comtois
Warren Smith	Cy Young
Patty	Harriet Lynn
Sally	Cindy Roberts
Flora	Marjory Edson
Dr. Conrad Fuller	Rowan Tudor
B.C.A. Official	Leon Benedict
Melinda (perhaps)	Barbara Lang

STUDENTS, FRIENDS, PASSENGERS: Patty Anne, Diana Broderick, Lynn Carlysle, George Comtois, William J. Coppola, Edgar Coronado, Marjory Edson, Haruki Fujimoto, Renee Herman, Mark Holliday, Leona Louise, Harriet Lynn, Lawrence Marshall, Glen E. McClaskey, Don Miller, Jodi Perselle, Joseph Pichette, Cindy Roberts, Steven Ross, Joan Tannen, Nancy Wiench

UNDERSTUDIES: Mark, Lester James; Daisy, Lynn Carlysle; Moncrief, Joseph Pichette; Mrs. Hatch, Marjory Edson; Fuller, Leon Benedict; Warren, William J. Coppola; Preston, Lawrence Marshall; Muriel, Harriet Lynn; Welles, Glen E. McClaskey; Mrs. Welles, Joan Tannen; Hubert, Solicitor, Mark Holliday; Patty, Leona Louise; Sally, Patty Anne; Flora, Renee Herman

A Musical in 2 acts and 10 scenes. The action takes place in the present and past.

General Manager: Irving Cone
Press: John L. Toohey
Stage Managers: George Quick, William Hammond, Joseph Pichette

For original NY production, see THEATRE WORLD, Vol. 22.

Linda Michele (C), Howard Keel (R) in "On A Clear Day You Can See Forever"

THE IMPOSSIBLE YEARS

By Bob Fisher and Arthur Marx; Director, Charles Forsythe; Scenery and Lighting, Leo B. Meyer; Presented by The Producing Managers Company (James B. McKenzie, Spofford J. Beadle, Ralph Roseman). Opened at Memorial Auditorium in Greensboro, N.C., Oct. 2, 1967. Suspended from Dec. 16, 1967 to Feb. 14, 1968 when it reopened in Red Bank, N.J., and closed March 30, 1968 in Ashtabula, Ohio.

CAST

Dr. Jack Kingsley	Tom Ewell
Linda Kingsley	Lynn Bilek
Abbey Kingsley	Jan Rhodes†1
Alice Kingsley	Michaele Myers
Ricky Fleisher	Tom Yourk
Richard Merrick	Eric James
Miss Hammer	Jeanne Bolan
Francine	Nanci Addison
Wally	Michael Patton†2
Dennis	Schorling Schneider
Andy	Kevin Dobson
Bartholomew Smuts	William Tynan
Dr. Harold Fleisher	Maxton Latham
Arnold Brecher	Carl Bensen

UNDERSTUDIES: Kingsley, Fleisher, Carl Bensen; Alice, Jeanne Bolan; Linda, Abbey, Hammer, Nanci Addison; Richard, Tom Yourk; Brecher, Maxton Latham; Ricky, Dennis, Andy, Michael Patton; Smuts, Kevin Dobson, Francine, Jan Rhodes

A Comedy in 2 acts and 7 scenes. The action takes place at the present time in the den and living room of the Kingsley home in Old Westbury, Long Island.

Company Manager: Robert Hulter
Press: Margie Clay, Bernard Simon
Stage Managers: Heinz Hohenwald, Schorling Schneider

† Succeeded by: 1. Connie Otto, 2. Roger Garrett

For original NY production, see THEATRE WORLD, Vol. 22.

Michael Patton, Tom Yourk, Nancy Addison, Tom Ewell, Schorling Schneider, Kevin Dobson, Lynn Bilek, William Tynan

ON A CLEAR DAY YOU CAN SEE FOREVER

Book and Lyrics, Alan Jay Lerner; Music, Burton Lane; Director, Ross Bowman; Choreography and Musical Numbers Staged by Luis de Yberrando; Scenery, Herbert Senn and Helen Pond; Lighting, Robert L. Steele; Costumes, Brooks-Van Horn; Coordinated by Edward Meyers; Musical Director, Gordon Munford; Presented by Robert Cherin Productions in association with Joseph Weill and Arthur C. Kellman. Opened Sunday, Dec. 31, 1967 in Sacramento, Calif., Civic Auditorium, and closed May 26, 1968 at the Music Hall, Seattle.

CAST

Dr. Mark Bruckner	Howard Keel, John Raitt, Bill Hayes or John Ericson
Mrs. Hatch	Ruth Warshawsky
Daisy Gamble	Linda Michele or Carla Alberghetti
Muriel Bunson	Sandra Nitz
James Preston	Walter Willison
Samuel Welles	Bert Conway
Mrs. Welles	Ruth Warshawsky
Sir Hubert Insdale	Robert Hatton
Hubert Insdale	John Rubinstein
Solicitor	Craig Yates
Edward Moncrief	Brian Avery
Warren Smith	John Rubinstein
Flora	Carole Carle
Dr. Conrad Fuller	Bert Conway
B.C.A. Official	R. G. Denison

STUDENTS, FRIENDS, PASSENGERS: Marcia Callis, Carole Carle, Dan Cartagena, R. G. Denison, Robert Hatton, Barbara Heuman, John Houy, Linda King, Merle Duane King, Marsha Kramer, Mara Margolis, Steve Michaels, Sandra Nitz, Richard Stack, Susan Stewart, Dyan Vincent, Walter Willison, Craig Yates, Meredith-Anne Borden, Lee Clark, John Ellis

UNDERSTUDIES: Mark, R. G. Denison; Daisy, Barbara Heuman; Edward, Robert Hatton; Fuller, Merle Duane King; Warren, Walter Willison; Mrs. Hatch, Susan Stewart

MUSICAL NUMBERS: "Hurry! It's Lovely Up Here," "Solicitor's Song," "The Gout," "On A Clear Day You Can See Forever," "S.S. Bernard Cohn," "She Wasn't You," "Melinda," "Trelawney No. 1," "When I Come Around Again," "What Did I Have That I Don't Have," "Wait 'Til We're 65," "Come Back To Me."

A Musical in 2 acts and 10 scenes. The action takes place in the present and past.

Press: Howard Atlee, Margie Clay, Herb Cherin
Stage Managers; John L. Moorehead, Jack Welles

For original NY production, see THEATRE WORLD, Vol. 22.

Carla Alberghetti (C) Top: (L) Linda Michele, John Raitt (R) Bill Hayes, Carla Alberghetti in "On A Clear Day . . ."

THE IMPOSSIBLE YEARS

By Bob Fisher and Arthur Marx; Director, Sam Levene; Scenery, William Pitkin; Costumes, Ann Roth; Lighting, Martin Aronstein; Production Supervisor, Jose Vega; Presented by Nederlander-Steinbrenner Productions and Bob Fisher. Opened Oct. 23, 1967 at the Playhouse, Wilmington, and closed at the National in Washington, D.C. on Feb. 24, 1968.

CAST

Dr. Jack Kingsley	Sam Levene
Linda Kingsley	Madeleine Fisher
Abbey Kingsley	Trudy Van
Alice Kingsley	Elizabeth Fleming
Ricky Fleisher	Kipp Osborne
Richard Merrick	David Selly
Miss Hammer	Judith Tillman
Francine	Alexandra Murphy
Wally	Terry McKerrs
Dennis	Horton Willis
Andy	Philip Bonnell
Bartholomew Smuts	Alexander Cort
Dr. Harold Fleisher	Abe Vigoda
Arnold Brecher	Donald Boore

A Comedy in 2 acts and 7 scenes. The action takes place at the present time in the den and living room of the Kingsley home in Old Westbury, Long Island.

General Manager: Allentuck, Azenberg & Wolsk
Company Manager: Sam Handelsman
Press: Bill Doll & Co.
Stage Managers: Leon Gersten, Roger Franklin

For original NY production, see THEATRE WORLD, Vol. 22.

Alexander Cort, Sam Levene in "The Impossible Years"

Friedman-Abeles Photo

MAME

Book, Jerome Lawrence and Robert E. Lee; Based on novel "Auntie Mame" by Patrick Dennis, and play by Lawrence and Lee; Music and Lyrics, Jerry Herman; Director, Gene Saks; Settings, William and Jean Eckart; Costumes, Robert Mackintosh; Lighting, Tharon Musser; Musical Direction and Vocal Arrangements, Donald Pippin; Orchestrations, Philip J. Lang; Dance Music Arranged by Roger Adams; Conductor, Myron Roman; Original Dances and Musical Numbers staged by Onna White; Re-created by Pat Cummings; Associate Producer, John Bowab; Original cast album by Columbia Records; Presented by Fryer, Carr and Harris. Opened Tuesday, Aug. 29, 1967 at the Mechanic Theatre in Baltimore, and still touring May 31, 1968.

CAST

Patrick Dennis, age 10	Shawn McGill
Agnes Gooch	Loretta Swit
Vera Charles	Vicki Cummings
Mame Dennis	Celeste Holm
Ralph Devine	Michael Amber
Bishop	Jim Connor
M. Lindsay Woolsey	William Gibberson
Ito	Arsenio Trinidad
Doorman	Alan Sanderson
Messenger	Don Prieur
Dwight Babcock	Wesley Addy
Art Model	Stacey Jones
Dance Teacher	Louise Kirtland
Leading Man	George Tregre
Stage Manager	Alan Sanderson
Madame Branislowski	Ruth Gillette
Gregor	Jim Connor
Beauregard Jackson Pickett Burnside	Robert Kaye
Uncle Jeff	Austin Colyer
Cousin Fan	Sheila Coleman
Sally Cato	Betty McGuire
Mother Burnside	Ruth Gillette
Patrick Dennis (19 to 29)	John Stewart
Junior Babcock	Gerry Dalton
Mrs. Upson	Louise Kirtland
Mr. Upson	David Huddleston
Gloria Upson	Stacey Jones
Pegeen Ryan	Kathryn Malone
Peter Dennis	Lee Franklin

MAME'S FRIENDS: Michael Amber, Bette Jane Bent, Carol Bostick, Ronald Bostick, Susan Cartt, Austin Colyer, Jim Connor, Sheila Coleman, John Gorrin, Rosemary Harvey, Spence Jackson, Michele Karaty, Donald Mark, James L. Piersall, Don Prieur, Dorothy Poiselle, Eric Paynter, Roger Rathbun, Alan John Sanderson, Lana Sloninger, Claire Theiss, George Tregre, Nancy Wilmarth.

UNDERSTUDIES: Mame, Vera, Betty McGuire; Babcock, Upson, Austin Colyer; Agnes, Mrs. Upson, Sheila Coleman; Beauregard, Woolsey, Michael Amber; Patrick at 10, Lee Franklin; Older Patrick, Roger Rathbun; Madame, Mother Burnside, Louise Kirtland; Sally, Claire Theiss; Gregor, Ito, Eric Paynter; Model, Susan Cartt; Fan, Rosemary Harvey; Junior, Stage Manager, Spence Jackson; Devine, Don Prieur.

A Musical in 2 acts and 16 scenes. The action takes place between 1928 and 1946 in Mame's Beekman Place apartment in New York, and various locales in which she becomes involved.

General Manager: Joseph P. Harris
Company Manager: Milton M. Pollack
Press: David Lipsky, Gertrude Bromberg
Stage Managers: Henri Caubisens, Hal Halvorsen, Austin Colyer

For original NY production, see THEATRE WORLD, Vol. 22.

Friedman-Abeles Photo

Top Right: Jane Connell, Anne Francine, Angela Lansbury in "Mame." Below: Phyllis Kirk, William Traylor, Joseph Mascolo, James Tolkan in "Wait Until Dark"

WAIT UNTIL DARK

By Frederick Knott; Director, Windsor Lewis; Scenery, Fred Voelpel; American Theatre Productions tour; Presented by Producing Managers' Company (James B. McKenzie, Spofford J. Beadle, Ralph Roseman). Opened Sept. 22, 1967 at the Music Hall, Kansas City, Mo., and closed Nov. 30, 1967 in Fort Wayne, Ind.

Cast

Mike Talman	William Traylor
Sergeant Carlino	Joseph Mascolo
Harry Roat, Jr.	James Tolkan
Susy Hendrix	Phyllis Kirk
Sam Hendrix	Richard Branda
Gloria	Gemma Dennis
Policemen	Barry Hoffman, Hubert Englund

UNDERSTUDIES: Susy, Alice Mulvihill; Gloria, Maura Mulvihill; Mike, Harry, Carlino, Richard Branda; Sam, Barry Hoffman

A Drama in 2 acts and 6 scenes. The action takes place at the present time in the Hendrix basement apartment in Greenwich Village, New York.

Company Manager: Barry Hoffman
Press: Lee Solters, Harvey B. Sabinson, Ralph Roseman, Bernard Simon
Stage Managers: Sean S. Cunningham, Richard Branda

For original NY production, see THEATRE WORLD, Vol. 22.

MAME

Book, Jerome Lawrence and Robert E. Lee; Based on novel "Auntie Mame" and play by Lawrence and Lee; Music and Lyrics, Jerry Herman; Director, Gene Saks; Dances and Musical Numbers Staged by Onna White; Settings, William and Jean Eckart; Costumes, Robert Mackintosh; Lighting, Tharon Musser; Musical Direction and Vocal Arrangements, Donald Pippin; Musical Conductor, David Saidenberg; Orchestrations, Philip J. Lang; Dance Music Arrangements, Roger Adams; Hairstylist, Ronald DeMann; Associate Producer, John Bowab; Original cast album on Columbia Records; Presented by Fryer, Carr and Harris. Opened Tuesday, April 30, 1968 at San Francisco's Curran Theatre, and still touring May 31, 1968.

CAST

Patrick Dennis at 10	Stuart Getz
Agnes Gooch	Jane Connell
Vera Charles	Anne Francine
Mame Dennis	Angela Lansbury
Ralph Devine	Ron Stratton
Bishop	Jack Davison
M. Lindsay Woolsey	Robert Goss
Ito	Sab Shimono
Doorman	Gerard Brentte
Elevator Boy	Edward Becker
Messenger	Dom Angelo
Dwight Babcock	Willard Waterman
Art Model	Ann Willis
Dance Teacher	Lorraine MacMartin
Leading Man	Jack Davison
Stage Manager	Dom Angelo
Madame Branislowski	Tally Brown
Gregor	Edward Becker
Beauregard Jackson Pickett Burnside	Charles Braswell
Uncle Jeff	David Lile
Cousin Fan	Ruth Ramsey
Sally Cato	Cathryn Damon
Mother Burnside	Tally Brown
Patrick Dennis (19-29)	Jerry Lanning
Junior Babcock	Roy Smith
Mrs. Upson	Lorraine MacMartin
Mr. Upson	Gordon Connell
Gloria Upson	Ann Willis
Pegeen Ryan	Suellen Estey
Peter Dennis	Michael Maitland

MAME'S FRIENDS: Nancy Lynch, Mary Zahn, Cindy Roberts, Penelope Guerard, Cynthia Grabinski, Dean Taliaferro, Suellen Estey, Ann Willis, Florence Merce, Lynn Dovel, Ruth Ramsey, Bill Richards, Dom Angelo, Danny Joel, Gary Wales, Roy Smith, David Lile, Larry Burton, Mark East, Jerry Grant, Ben Laney, Edward Becker, Jack Davidson, Gerard Brentte

UNDERSTUDIES: Agnes, Mrs. Upson, Ruth Ramsey; Mame, Vera, Cathryn Damon; Woolsey, Gregor, Jeff, Jack Davison; Beauregard, Dwight, Robert Goss; Older Patrick, Jerry Grant; Mr. Upson, Stage Manager, Edward Becker; Pegeen, Mary Zahn; Young Patrick, Michael Maitland; Madame, Mother Burnside, Lorraine MacMartin; Sally, Dean Taliaferro

A Musical in 2 acts and 16 scenes. The action takes place in Mame's Beekman Place apartment and various locales in which she becomes involved during a period from 1928 to 1946.

General Manager: Joseph Harris
Company Manager: Milton Pollock
Press: David Lipsky
Stage Managers: Terence Little,
Edward Strum, Edward Becker,
Nancy Lynch

For original NY production, see THEATRE WORLD, Vol. 22.

Friedman-Abeles Photo

Celeste Holm, Vicki Cummings, Stacey Jones, Louise Kirtland (seated), John Stewart, Kathryn Malone, David Huddleston, Wesley Addy in "Mame"

THE IMPOSSIBLE YEARS

By Bob Fisher and Arthur Marx; Director, David Tihmar; Scenery, William Pitkin; Presented by Stan Seiden and Harry Zevin. Opened April 8, 1968 at the Hartman Theatre, Columbus, Ohio, and closed May 4, 1968 at the Studebaker in Chicago.

CAST

Dr. Jack Kingsley	George Gobel
Linda Kingsley	Judith Sherven
Abby Kingsley	Leslie Gobel
Alice Kingsley	Eve Brent
Ricky Fleisher	David Galligan
Richard Merrick	Michael Brooks
Miss Hammer	Renie Riano
Francine	B. Allen
Wally	James Walker
Dennis	Dick Taylor
Andy	Lloyd Beardsley
Bartholomew Smuts	Paul Nesbitt
Dr. Harold Fleisher	Adam Scott
Arnold Brecher	Michael Hinn

A Comedy in 2 acts and 6 scenes. The action takes place at the present time in the den and living room of the Kingsley home in Old Westbury, Long Island.

Company Manager: Robert Hulter
Press: Maurice Turet
Stage Managers: Joseph De Pauw,
Chuck Linker

For original NY production, see THEATRE WORLD, Vol. 22.

Friedman-Abeles Photos

Right Center: Judith Sherven, George Gobel, Eve Brent in "The Impossible Years"

CABARET

Book, Joe Masteroff; Based on play by John van Druten and stories of Christopher Isherwood; Music, John Kander; Lyrics, Fred Ebb; Dances and Cabaret Numbers, Ronald Field; Director, Harold Prince; Scenery, Boris Aronson; Costumes, Patricia Zipprodt; Lighting, Jean Rosenthal; Musical Direction, Joseph Lewis; Orchestrations, Don Walker; Dance Arrangements, David Baker; Hair Dresser, Charles Kurtz; Production Supervisor, Ruth Mitchell; Presented by Harold Prince in association with Ruth Mitchell. Opened Satuday, Dec. 23, 1967 at New Haven's Shubert Theatre, and still touring May 31, 1968.

CAST

Master of Ceremonies	Robert Salvio
Clifford Bradshaw	Gene Rupert
Ernst Ludwig	David Rounds
Custom Official	Kenneth Garner
Fraulein Schneider	Signe Hasso
Herr Schultz	Leo Fuchs
Fraulein Kost	Catherine Gaffigan
Telephone Girl	Darlene Parks
Kit Kat Band	Jessie Cary, Jean Packard, Marianne O'Malley, Carol Smith
Maitre D'	John Hamilton III
Max	David Haine
Sally Bowles	Melissa Hart
Two Ladies	Mary Ann Bruning, Patricia Haine
German Sailors	Ralph Nelson, Carlos Gorbea, Raymond Bussey, Philip Arsenault
Frau Wendel	Rhoda Gemignani
Herr Wendel	George Axler
Frau Kruger	Carole Griffith
Herr Kruger	Moose Peting
Maria	Carol Petri
Lulu	Janet Sumner
Rosie	Marilyn Joseph
Fritzie	Michon Peacock
Texas	Linda Berry
Frenchie	Pichie Vives
Patsy	Rita Abrams
Bobby	Michael Toles
Victor	Charles Abbott
Greta	Holly Smith
Felix	Brown Bradley
Oscar	Allin Leslie

UNDERSTUDIES: Sally, Holly Smith; Fraulein Schneider, Carole Griffith; Herr Schultz, George Axler; Cliff, David Rounds; Master of Ceremonies, Charles Abbott; Fraulein Kost, Rhoda Gemignani; Ernst, John Hamilton III.

A Musical in two acts. The action takes place in Berlin, Germany, before the start of the Third Reich in 1929-30.

General Manager: Carl Fisher
Company Manager: James Preston
Press: Mary Bryant, Bev Kelly
Stage Managers: Kathleen A. Sullivan, Fritz Holt, Moose Peting

Friedman-Abeles Photos

Leo Fuchs, Signe Hasso
Above: (C) Robert Salvio in "Cabaret"

THE FANTASTICKS

Book and Lyrics, Tom Jones; Music, Harvey Schmidt; Director, Tom Jones; Designed by Ed Wittstein; Musical Direction, Rod Derefinko; Musical Arrangements, Julian Stein; Associate Producer, Elissa Lane; Presented by David Cryer and Albert Poland. Opened Oct. 2, 1967 at Royal Alexandra, Toronto, and closed Jan. 6, 1968 at the Mechanic in Baltimore.

CAST

The Narrator	John Cunningham†
The Girl	Constance Moffit
The Boy	Ty McConnell
The Boy's Father	Donald Babcock
The Girl's Father	Wayne E. Martens
The Actor	Hugh Alexander
The Man Who Dies	Justin Morley
The Mute	James Cook

MUSICIANS: Rod Derefinko, piano; Henry Clay Fanelli, harp; John Kaye, drums; Isabel Edmonds, bass.

A Musical in two acts.

Company Manager: Jay Kingwill
Press: Arthur M. Brilant
Stage Managers: Elissa Lane, Justin Morley, James Cook

† Succeeded by Keith Charles, David Cryer.

For original NY production, see THEATRE WORLD, Vol. 16.

Wayne E. Martens, Constance Moffit,
Ty McConnell, James Cook

YOU KNOW I CAN'T HEAR YOU WHEN THE WATER'S RUNNING

By Robert Anderson; Director, Alan Schneider; Scenery, Ed Wittstein; Costumes, Theoni V. Aldredge; Lighting, Jules Fisher; Presented by Jack Farren and Gilbert Gates. Opened Monday, Oct. 16, 1967 at the Hanna Theatre in Cleveland, Ohio, and still touring May 31, 1968.

CAST

"The Shock Of Recognition"
Jack Barnstable .... Robert Elston
Herb Miller .... Jack Murdock
Dorothy .... Susan Bracken
Richard Pawling .... Eddie Bracken

"The Footsteps Of Doves"
Salesman .... Robert Elston
Harriet .... Ruth Manning
George .... Eddie Bracken
Jill .... Susan Bracken

"I'll Be Home For Christmas"
Chuck .... Eddie Bracken
Edith .... Ruth Manning
Clarice .... Susan Bracken

"I'm Herbert"
Herbert .... Robert Elston
Muriel .... Ruth Manning
UNDERSTUDIES: Mr. Bracken, Jack Murdock; Miss Manning, Connie Bracken; Miss Bracken, Barbara Sands; Mr. Elston, Rand Mitchell

General Manager: Robert Kamlot
Company Manager: William Orton
Press: Lee Solters, Harvey B. Sabinson, John L. Toohey
Stage Managers: Jack Leigh, Rand Mitchell

For original NY production, see THEATRE WORLD, Vol. 23.

Friedman-Abeles Photos

Top Right: Susan Bracken, Robert Elston, Jack Murdock. Below: Ruth Manning, Eddie Bracken

Justin Morley, Donna Curtis, John Long

THE FANTASTICKS

Book and Lyrics, Tom Jones; Music, Harvey Schmidt; Staged by Elissa Lane; Designed by Ed Wittstein; Musical Direction. Rod Derefinko; Musical Arrangements, Julian Stein; Presented by David Cryer and Albert Poland. Opened Monday, Jan. 29, 1968 in Ovens Auditorium, Charlotte, N.C., and closed Mar. 2, 1968 in Jacksonville, Fla.

CAST

The Narrator .... David Cryer
The Girl .... Donna Curtis
The Boy .... Don Pinson
The Boy's Father .... Tom Lacy
The Girl's Father .... Art Wallace
The Actor .... John Long
The Man Who Dies .... Justin Morley
The Mute .... Robert Gerlach
At the piano .... Rod Derefinko
At the harp .... Nanette Norton
At the drums .... John Kaye

A Musical in two acts.

Company Manager: Jay Kingwill
Press: Albert Poland
Stage Managers: Elissa Lane, Justin Morley

For original NY production, see THEATRE WORLD, Vol. 16.

Steve Sbarge Photo

HELLO, DOLLY!

Book, Michael Stewart; Music and Lyrics, Jerry Herman; Director-Choreographer, Gower Champion; Settings, Oliver Smith; Costumes, Freddy Wittop; Lighting, Jean Rosenthal; Dance and Incidental Music Arrangements, Peter Howard; Musical Direction, Jay Blackton; Orchestrations, Philip J. Lang; Vocal Arrangements, Shepard Coleman; A David Merrick and Champion-Five Inc. Production. Opened at the Tivoli Theatre, Chattanooga, Tenn., Nov. 3, 1965 and closed at the Shubert in Boston, March 23, 1968.

CAST

Mrs. Dolly Gallagher Levi .... Ginger Rogers
Ernestina .... Mary Jo Catlett
Ambrose Kemper .... Robert Lenn
Horse .... Cathy Haas, Bobbie Freeman
Horace Vandergelder .... David Burns
Ermengarde .... Beverlee Weir
Cornelius Hackl .... Bill Mullikin
Barnaby Tucker .... Danny Lockin
Irene Molloy .... Patte Finley
Minnie Fay .... Sondra Lee
Mrs. Rose .... Polly Dawson
Rudolph .... Robert Hocknell
Judge .... Skedge Miller
Court Clerk .... Robert L. Hultman

TOWNSPEOPLE, WAITERS, ETC.: Vicki, Ally, Monica Carter, Mary Jane Caveny, Polly Dawson, Bobbie Freeman, Cathy Haas, Leslie Kimble, Naomi Kimura, Irma Kingsley, Lois LaBonte, Trish Mahoney, Janyce Nyman, Jacqueline Payne, Eileen Sarafis, Fay Webb, Janice Winkelman, Reese Burns, Jack Craig, Dieter Curt, Richard Dodd, Norman Fredericks, Edward Goldsmid, Mickey Hinton, Robert L. Hultman, Jeff King, Clyde Laurents, Alex Mackay, Tom Mavison, Richard Maxon, George Mazer, Sean Nolan, Greg Rodgers, Bill Sisson, Paul Solen, Kent Thomas

UNDERSTUDIES: Dolly, Anne Russell; Horace, Skedge Miller; Cornelius, Robert Hocknell; Irene, Lois LaBonte; Minnie, Leslie Kimble; Barnaby, Edward Goldsmid; Ermengarde, Bobbie Freeman; Rudolph, Robert L. Hultman; Ernestina, Mary Jane Caveny; Mrs. Rose, Irma Kingsley, Judge, Norman Fredericks

A Musical in 2 acts and 15 scenes.

General Manager: Jack Schlissel
Company Manager: Fred Cuneo
Press: Lee Solters,
Harvey B. Sabinson, David Powers,
Eleanor Pinkham
Stage Managers: Alan Hall, Mary Porter,
Moose Peting, Skedge Miller

For original NY production, see THEATRE WORLD, Vol. 20.

Victor Arnold, Robert Christian in
"Fortune and Men's Eyes"

FORTUNE AND MEN'S EYES

By John Herbert; Director, Mitchell Nestor; Designed by C. Murawski; Costumes, Jan; Music and Sound Effects, Terry Ross; Presented by David Rothenberg and Mitchell Nestor in association with The Little Room. Opened Oct. 19. 1967 in Toronto, and closed May 18, 1968 in San Francisco.

CAST

Rocky .... Victor Arnold
Mona .... Robert Christian
Queenie .... Bill Moor
Guard .... Edward Kovens
Smitty .... Peter Beiger

A Drama in 2 acts and 3 scenes. The action takes place at the present time in a dormitory cell inside a Canadian penal institution.

General Management: Krone-Olim
Press: David Rothenberg, Larry Schneider
Stage Manager: Jimmy Foster

David Burns, Ginger Rogers (also top right)
in "Hello, Dolly!"

GOLDEN BOY

Book, Clifford Odets and William Gibson; Based on Mr. Odet's play; Music, Charles Strouse; Lyrics, Lee Adams; Director, Michael Thoma; Designed by Tony Walton; Costume Coordinator, Florence Klotz; Lighting, Tharon Musser; Musical Direction, Shepard Coleman; Orchestrations, Ralph Burns, Danny Hurd; Additional Orchestrations, George Rhodes; Dances and Musical Numbers Staged by Jaime Rogers and Lester Wilson; Based on Choreography by Donald McKayle; Musical Coordinator, George Rhodes; Production Associate, Jay Campbell; Associate Producers, George Platt, Donald Flamm; Original cast album on Capitol Records; An Epic Production; Presented by Hillard Elkins. Opened April 23, 1968 at the Auditorium Theatre in Chicago, and closed there on May 25, 1968 to open in London.

CAST

Tom Moody	Mark Dawson
Roxy Gottlieb	Louis Basile
Tokio	Frank Nastasi
Lorna Moon	Gloria DeHaven
Joe Wellington	Sammy Davis
Ronnie	John Bassette
Ma Wellington	Hilda Haynes
Anna	Altovise Gore
Frank Wellington	Al Kirk
Eddie Satin	Lon Satton
Lola	Lola Falana
Les	Lester Wilson
Lopez	Tony Catanzaro
Reporter	Dan Frazer
Baayork	Baayork Lee
Flight Announcer	Ben Vereen
Driscoll	John Gorrin

ENSEMBLE: Jabie Abercrombie, Michele Barry, Nancy Bruner, Marguerite DeLain, Lorraine Fields, Loli Hinton, Marlene Johnson, Baayork Lee, Urylee Leonardos, Michele Simmons, Marcelo Gamboa, John Gorrin, Alfred Perryman, Harold Pierson, Albert Popwell, Samuel Smalls, Dan Strayhorn, Ben Vereen, Lester Wilson

UNDERSTUDIES: Joe, Lon Satton; Eddie, Frank, Ben Vereen; Ronnie, Albert Popwell; Tom, Roxy, Tokio, Dan Frazer; Ma, Urylee Leonardos; Anna, Jabie Abercrombie; Lola, Marguerite DeLain; Lorna, Marilyne Mason

MUSICAL NUMBERS: "Workout," "Night Song," "Everything's Great," "Lorna's Here," "Here's A Party Going On," "Don't Forget 127th Street," "Tour," "This Is The Life," "Yes, I Can!," "Trio," "I Want To Be With You," "No More," "You're No Brother Of Mine," "The Fight," "What Became Of Me?"

A Dramatic Musical in 2 acts and 18 scenes. The action takes place in New York City from 1964 to 1968.

Company Manager: G. Warren McClane
Press: Bill Liberman, Morton Wax, Paul Gallis, Howard Mendelsohn
Stage Managers: Tom Porter, Walter Mason, George Rondo

For original NY production, see THEATRE WORLD, Vol. 21.

Tony Romano Photos

Sheilah Wells, Anthony Perkins, Remak Ramsay in "The Star-Spangled Girl"

Gloria DeHaven, Sammy Davis, Jr.
Top Right: Sammy Davis, John Bassette, Hilda Haynes, Altovise Gore, Al Kirk in "Golden Boy"

THE STAR-SPANGLED GIRL

By Neil Simon; Director, Anthony Perkins; Associate Producer, Morry Efron; Production Associate, Norman Rothstein; Presented by Zev Bufman. Opened Monday, Feb. 26, 1968 at the Huntington Hartford Theatre in Los Angeles, and still touring May 31, 1968.

CAST

Andy Hobart	Anthony Perkins†1
Norman Cornell	Remak Ramsay†2
Sophie Rauschmeyer	Sheilah Wells†3

STANDBY: Tom Sawyer

A Comedy in 3 acts and 5 scenes. The action takes place at the present time in a duplex studio apartment in San Francisco.

Manager: Irving Cone
Press: Horace Greeley McNab
Stage Managers: Ed Dimond, Tom Sawyer

† Succeeded by: 1. George Hamilton, 2. Jimmy Boyd, 3. Dina Martin.

For original NY production, see THEATRE WORLD, Vol. 23.

BLACK COMEDY

By Peter Shaffer; Director, Randall Brooks; Scenery and Costumes, Alan Tagg; Lighting, Jules Fisher; Production Associate, Hildy Parks; Associate Producer, Sidney Lanier; Production Supervisor, Jerry Adler; Production Assistants, Jan Monkhouse, Gloria Banta, Davina Crawford; Staff Assistant, Ted Landry; Presented by Alexander H. Cohen. Opened Dec. 4, 1967 at the Hanna Theatre in Cleveland, Ohio, and closed May 25, 1968 at the Playhouse in Wilmington, Del.

CAST

"White Lies"

Sophie, Baroness Lemberg _____ Angela Wood
Frank _____ Barry Boys†
Tom _____ Jeremy Clyde

"Black Comedy"

Brindsley Miller _____ Jeremy Clyde
Carol Melkett _____ Jennifer Tilston
Miss Furnival _____ Angela Wood
Colonel Melkett _____ Byron Webster
Harold Gorringe _____ Barry Boys†
Clea _____ Monica Evans
Schuppanzigh _____ Charles Mayer
George Bamberger _____ Richard Lederer
UNDERSTUDIES: Frank, Tom, Miller, Harold, Sean MacDuff; Sophie, Furnival, Constance Dix; Carol, Clea, Rosemary Shevlin; Colonel, Schuppanzigh, Richard Lederer.

General Manager: Roy A. Somlyo
Company Manager: James O'Neill
Press: James D. Proctor, Max Gendel
Stage Managers: Don Christy,
Richard Lederer

† Succeeded by John Tillinger.

For original NY production, see THEATRE WORLD, Vol. 23.

Friedman-Abeles Photos

Top Right: Angela Wood, Barry Boys, Jeremy Clyde in "White Lies." Below: Barry Boys, Monica Evans, Jeremy Clyde, Jennifer Tilston, Byron Webster in "Black Comedy"

David C. Jones, Edward Earle in "The Roar Of The Greasepaint, The Smell Of The Crowd"

THE ROAR OF THE GREASEPAINT, THE SMELL OF THE CROWD

Book, Music and Lyrics, Leslie Bricusse and Anthony Newley; Staged and Choreographed by Edward Earle; Designed and Lighted by Barry C. Tuttle; Musical Director, Suzanne Wigg; American Theatre Productions tour; Presented by Barry C. Tuttle and William A. Carrozo. Opened Thursday, Sept. 21, 1967 at the Rajah Theatre, Reading, Pa., and closed April 6, 1968 at Hershey Community Theatre, Pa.

CAST

Cocky _____ Edward Earle
Sir _____ David C. Jones
The Kid _____ Sherry Lynn Diamant†1
The Girl _____ Lisa Damont†2
The Negro _____ Henry Baker
The Bully _____ Harold Norbut
URCHINS: Susan Campbell, Leigh Carole, Kathy Conry, Carol Ehmann, Judy Gibson, Pat Guadalupe, Helenann, Susan McCollom, Meredith Pogue, Vickie Ruane
UNDERSTUDIES: Cocky, James Carrozo; Sir, Harold Norbut; Kid, Helenann; Girl, Kathy Conry

A Musical in two acts. The action takes place in a rocky place.

General and Company Manager:
Donald Antonelli
Press: Cindy Goessman
Stage Managers: Barry C. Tuttle,
William A. Carrozo, James Carrozo

† Succeeded by: 1. Edie Andrews, 2. Louise White.

For original NY production, see THEATRE WORLD, Vol. 21.

NATIONAL REPERTORY THEATRE

Producers, Michael Dewell, Frances Ann Dougherty; Associate Producer, Gina Shield; Assistant to Producers, Carey King; Administrative Coordinator, Brooke Lappin; Technical Director, Ervin G. Reid, Jr.; Production Assistants, Mimi Carr, Joan Stoner, John Wilson. Opened Oct. 16, 1967 in Aycock Auditorium, University of North Carolina, Greensboro, and closed Dec. 16, 1967 at the Civic Theatre in Chicago to become the resident company at Ford's Theatre in Washington, D.C. where it opened Feb. 12, 1968 and closed May 18, 1968.

THE COMEDY OF ERRORS

By William Shakespeare; Director, G. Wood; Settings, William Pitkin; Costumes, Jane Greenwood; Lighting, Tharon Musser; Music, Liza Redfield.

CAST

Vendor	Samual Blue, Jr.
Fisherman	Ralston Hill
Beggar	Jerry Dodge
Luce	Paula Bauersmith
Emilia	Ann Mitchell
Nun	Katherine McGrath
Balthasar	Paul Milikin
Gypsy Palmist	Ellen Holly
Egeon	Wyman Pendleton
Gaoler	Arthur Berwick
Young Merchant	Louis Thompson
Antipholus of Ephesus	Terence Scammell
Adriana	Patricia Guinan
Officer	Herb Davis
Solinus, Duke of Ephesus	G. Wood
Angelo	Todd Drexel
Antipholus of Syracuse	Paul Massie
Dromio of Syracuse	Geoff Garland
Dromio of Ephesus	Geoff Garland
Luciana	Anne Draper
Merchant of Persia	Ralston Hill
Servant	Louis Thompson
Dr. Pinch	Jerry Dodge
Courtesan	Ellen Holly

JOHN BROWN'S BODY

By Stephen Vincent Benet; Devised and Directed by Jack Sydow; Settings, William Pitkin; Costumes, Alvin Colt; Lighting, Tharon Musser; Music, Liza Redfield.

CAST

Narrator for the North	Ralston Hill
Captain Ball	Wyman Pendleton
Mate	Geoff Garland
Spiritual Singer	Ann Mitchell
Narrator for Ellyat	Terence Scammell
Jack Ellyat	Jerry Dodge
Narrator for Wingate and the South	Todd Drexel
Clay Wingate	Paul Massie
Narrator for Brown	Wyman Pendleton
John Brown	G. Wood
Narrator for Washington Slaves and Shepherd Heyward	Samual Blue, Jr.
Mr. Brua	Paul Milikin
Fontaine Beckham	Arthur Berwick
Narrator for Cudjo	Samual Blue, Jr.
Cudjo	Herb Davis
Sally Dupre	Ellen Holly
Ellyat's Mother	Paula Bauersmith
Ellyat's Father	Ralston Hill
Union General	Geoff Garland
Narrator for Lincoln	Herb Davis
Abraham Lincoln	G. Wood
Narrator for Melora	Patricia Guinan
Melora Vilas	Anne Draper
Bailey	Paul Milikin
Melora's Father	Wyman Pendleton
Confederate Soldier	Arthur Berwick
Narrator for Aunt Bess	Ellen Holly
Narrator for Mary Lou Wingate	Paula Bauersmith
Mary Lou Wingate	Ann Mitchell
Lucy Weatherby	Katherine McGrath
Robert E. Lee	G. Wood
Seward	Wyman Pendleton
Narrator for Sally Dupre	Paula Bauersmith
Ulysses S. Grant	Geoff Garland
Narrator for Gettysburg	Ann Mitchell
Clark	Louis Thompson
Ellis	Arthur Berwick

The Company in "John Brown's Body"

Geoff Garland, Sylvia Sidney, G. Wood, Susan Sullivan in "She Stoops To Conquer"

SHE STOOPS TO CONQUER

By Oliver Goldsmith; Director, James D. Waring; Settings, William Pitkin; Costumes, Alvin Colt; Lighting, Tharon Musser; Music, Dean Fuller. Added to repertoire at Ford's Theatre, Washington.

CAST

Diggory	Arthur Berwick
Roger	Timothy Taylor
Thomas	Ralston Hill
Pimple	Katherine McGrath
Mrs. Hardcastle	Sylvia Sidney
Mr. Hardcastle	G. Wood
Tony Lumpkin	Geoff Garland
Miss Hardcastle	Susan Sullivan
Miss Neville	Patricia Guinan
Tavern Guests	Samual Blue, Jr., Todd Drexel, Tony Thomas, Paul Collins
Landlord	Paul Milikin
Mr. Marlow	Terence Scammell
Mr. Hastings	Paul Massie
Jeremy	Paul Collins
Sir Charles Marlow	Wyman Pendleton

Company Manager: James Preston
Press: Dorathi Bock Pierre, John Springer, Louise Weiner, Robert W. Jennings
Stage Managers: James Frasher, James Haire, William Armitage

Carolyn Jones, William Roerick, Denis Holmes,
Jerry Mickey, John Church
in "The Homecoming"

THE HOMECOMING

By Harold Pinter; Staged by Peter Hall;
Designed by John Bury; Produced in associa-
tion with Gerry Geraldo; Production Super-
visor, Jerry Adler; Production Associate, Hildy
Parks; Production Assistants, Jan Monkhouse,
Gloria Banta; Presented by Alexander H. Cohen
by arrangement with The Royal Shakespeare
Theatre and Theatre Guild Productions. Opened
Monday, Oct. 16, 1967 in Philadelphia at the
Forrest Theatre and closed March 30, 1968
at the Playhouse in Wilmington, Del.

CAST

Max	William Roerick
Lenny	John Church
Sam	Denis Holmes
Joey	Danny Sewell
Teddy	Jerry Mickey
Ruth	Carolyn Jones

UNDERSTUDIES: Max, Denis Holmes; Lenny, Teddy, Joey, Philip Cusak; Sam, Donald
Keyes; Ruth, Joan Jeffri

A Drama in two acts. The action takes
place at the present time in an old house in
North London.

General Managers: Roy A. Somlyo,
Victor Samrock
Company Manager: Leonard A. Mulhern
Press: James D. Proctor, Maurice Turet
Stage Manager: Donald Keyes

For original NY production, see THEATRE
WORLD, Vol. 23.

CACTUS FLOWER

Written and Directed by Abe Burrows;
Based on play by Pierre Barillet and Jean
Pierre Gredy; Scenic Production, Oliver Smith;
Costumes, Theoni V. Aldredge; Lighting,
Martin Aronstein; Associate Producer, Samuel
Liff; Staff Associates, Sylvia Schwartz, Robert
Greenwald, Linda Paton; Dance Adviser, Ver-
non Lusby; Produced in association with
Beresford Productions Ltd.; Presented by
David Merrick. Opened at the Blackstone
Theatre, Chicago, Oct. 17, 1967, and still
touring May 31, 1968.

CAST

Toni	Ethelyne Dunfee
Igor	Gene Lindsey
Stephanie	Elizabeth Allen
Mrs. Durant	Barbara Louis
Julian	Hugh O'Brian
Harvey	Kenneth Kimmins
Senor Sanchez	Arthur Anderson†
Music Lover	David Logan
Botticelli's Springtime	Gay Edmond
Waiter	David Logan

UNDERSTUDIES: Julian, Kenneth Kimmins;
Stephanie, Barbara Louis; Toni, Gay Edmond;
Igor, David Logan; Mrs. Durant, Springtime,
Laura Wallace; Harvey, Sanchez, Music Lover,
Bill Joyce

A Comedy in 2 acts and 15 scenes. The
action takes place at the present time in uptown and downtown Manhattan.

General Manager: Jack Schlissel
Company Manager: Al Rosen
Press: Harvey B. Sabinson, Lee Solters,
Alan Edelson
Stage Managers: James Burrows,
Bill Joyce, David Logan, Laura Wallace
·† Succeeded by Woody Romoff

For original NY production, see THEATRE
WORLD, Vol. 22.

Hugh O'Brian, Arthur Anderson, Elizabeth Allen
Above: Hugh O'Brian, Ethelyne Dunfee,
Elizabeth Allen, Kenneth Kimmins

THE KILLING OF SISTER GEORGE

By Frank Marcus; Director, Warren Crane; Costume Supervisor, Jack Edwards; Presented by Helen Bonfils and Morton Gottlieb by arrangement with Michael Codron in association with Bernard Delfont. Opened Dec. 29, 1967 at the Playhouse in Wilmington, Del., and closed June 11, 1968 at the Walnut Theatre in Philadelphia.

CAST

June Buckridge (Sister George)	Claire Trevor†1
Alice "Childie" McNaught	Patricia Sinnott
Mrs. Mercy Croft	Natalie Schafer†2
Madame Xenia	Polly Rowles

STANDBYS: Mary Riddle, Diana Eden

A Comedy in three acts. The action takes place at the present time in the living room of June Buckridge's flat on Devonshire Street, London.

General Manager: Richard Seader
Company Manager: Clayton Coots
Press: Dorothy Ross, George Deber
Stage Managers: Jack Woods, Mary Riddle

† Succeeded by: 1. Hermione Baddeley, 2. Sylvia O'Brien.

For original NY production, see THEATRE WORLD, Vol. 23.

Bert Andrews Photos

Left: Patricia Sinnott, Claire Trevor
Above: Polly Rowles, Claire Trevor, Patricia Sinnott, Natalie Schafer
in "The Killing Of Sister George"

NATIONAL THEATRE OF THE DEAF

General Director, David Hays; Directors, Alvin Epstein, Yoshio Aoyama, John Hirsch, Gene Lasko, Joe Layton; Settings and Costumes, Fred Voelpel, David Hays, Patricia Zipprodt; Lighting, John Gleason; Music, Edward Fearon; Dance. Alwin Nikolais, Susan Buirge. Opened Sept. 21, 1967 in Waterford, Conn., and closed Apr. 15, 1968 in Los Angeles. New York performances were Oct. 17 and 18, 1967 at Hunter College Playhouse, and Mar. 4, 1968 at the Forum, Lincoln Center.

CAST

Violet Armstrong	Audree Norton
Bernard Bragg	Howard Palmer
Charles Corey	June Russi
Gilbert Eastman	Tim Scanlon
Phyllis Frelich	Andrew Vasnick
Lou Fant	Joe Velez
Mary Beth Miller	Ralph White

Narrators: Joyce Flynn, William Rhys

PROGRAM: "The Tale of Kasane," "Tyger! Tyger! And Other Burnings," "Gianni Schicchi," "On The Harmfulness of Tobacco."

Press: Ben Kornzweig, Reginald Denenholz, Tom Trenkle, Marian Graham
Stage Managers: Rilla Bergman, Charles Corey, Robert Steinberg

Audree Norton, Joyce Flynn

YOU'RE A GOOD MAN, CHARLIE BROWN

Book, John Gordon; Based on Comic Strip "Peanuts" by Charles M. Schulz; Music and Lyrics, Clark Gesner; Director, Joseph Hardy; Set, Gary Newton; Assistant to Director, Patricia Birch; Musical Supervision, Arrangements, and Additional Material, Joe Raposo; Original cast album on MGM Records; Presented by Arthur Whitelaw and Gene Persson. Opened at the Little Fox Theatre in San Francisco, and still playing May 31, 1968.

CAST

Linus	Al Perez
Charlie Brown	Wendell Burton
Patty	Sydney Daniels
Schroeder	Roy Casstevens
Snoopy	Austin O'Toole
Lucy	Janell Pulis

Opened Oct. 18, 1967 at the Playhouse in Toronto, and still playing May 31, 1968.

Linus	Derek McGrath
Charlie Brown	Alan Lofft
Patty	Marylu Moyer
Schroeder	Blaine Parker
Snoopy	Grant Cowan
Lucy	Minnie Gaster

Opened Dec. 19, 1967 in Boston, and still playing May 31, 1968.

Linus	Joel Kimmel
Charlie Brown	Jim Ricketts
Patty	Rena Fredrics
Schroeder	Barry Pearl
Snoopy	Bob Becker
Lucy	Ann Gibbs

Opened March 12, 1968 at the Ivar Theatre in Los Angeles, and still playing May 31, 1968.

Linus	Russ Caldwell
Charlie Brown	Gary Burghoff
Patty	Nicole Jaffe
Schroeder	Hal-James Pederson
Snoopy	Robert Towers
Lucy	Judy Kaye

Manager: Larry Goossen
Press: Max Eisen, Carl Samrock

Marylu Moyer, Blaine Parker

Rena Fredrics, Joel Kimmel, Barry Pearl,
Ann Gibbs, Bob Becker, Jim Ricketts

Shirley Cox, Robert Blackburn, John MacAllan
in "Phaedra"

PHAEDRA

By Jean Racine; New translation by Robert Lowell; Director, Joseph Gistirak; Scenic Design and Lighting, Barry C. Tuttle; Costumes, Jack Edwards; Background Music, George Gaber; Presented by American Theatre Productions. Opened Monday, Feb. 5, 1968 at C. W. Post College, Brookville, L.I., and closed at University of North Carolina, Chapel Hill, N.C., April 6, 1968.

CAST

Hippolytus	John MacAllan
Theramenes	Ralph Nilson
Oenone	Audrey Ward
Phaedra	Shirley Cox
Panopes	David Metcalf
Aricia	Nancy Donohue
Ismene	Paula Shaw
Theseus	Robert Blackburn

UNDERSTUDIES: Phaedra, Paula Shaw; Hippolytus, Theramenes, George Vaughn Lowther; Theseus, David Metcalf; Ismene, Oenone, Vivian Brown.

A Drama in two acts. The action takes place in Troezen, a city about forty miles from Athens.

Press: Cindy Goessman,
Arthur G. Hadley
Stage Manager: Owen Ryan

THE LION IN WINTER

By James Goldman; Director, Milton Katselas; Scenery and Lighting, Clarke Dunham; Costumes, Will Steven Armstrong, Sara Brook; Assistant to Mr. Katselas, Michael Montel; Presented by The Overland Stage Co. Opened Jan. 17, 1968 in the Cochran Auditorium, Johnstown, Pa., and still touring May 31, 1968.

CAST

Henry II, King of England	Walter Slezak
Alais	Elizabeth Farley
John	Peter Howard
Geoffrey	Michael Goodwin
Richard	Alexander Courtney
Queen Eleanor	Margaret Phillips
Philip, King of France	James Storm

UNDERSTUDIES: Celia Howard, Daniel Landis

A Drama in 2 acts and 9 scenes. The action takes place at Christmas of 1183 in Henry's castle at Chinon, France.

Company Manager: Barry Hoffman
Press: Wally Beach
Stage Manager: Dale Parkinson

For original NY production, see THEATRE WORLD, Vol. 22.

Michael Goodwin, Peter Howard, Margaret Phillips, Walter Slezak, Elizabeth Farley, James Storm, Alexander Courtney in "The Lion In Winter"

Mary Martin, Robert Preston in "I Do! I Do!"

I DO! I DO!

Book and Lyrics, Tom Jones; Music, Harvey Schmidt; Based on play by Jan de Hartog; Director, Gower Champion; Scenic Production, Oliver Smith; Costumes, Freddy Wittop; Lighting, Jean Rosenthal; Musical Direction, Mitchell Ayres; Orchestrations, Philip J. Lang; Associate Producer, Samuel Liff; Staff Associates, Sylvia Schwartz, Lynn Middleton, Juliet Taylor; Hair Dresser, Richard Sabre; A David Merrick and Champion-Six Inc. Production; Presented by David Merrick. Opened April 8, 1968 in Rochester, N.Y., Auditorium, and still touring May 31, 1968.

CAST

She (Agnes)	Mary Martin
He (Michael)	Robert Preston

A Musical in two acts. The action takes place in a bedroom and covers fifty years of marriage, beginning just before the turn of the century.

General Manager: Jack Schlissel
Company Manager: Fred Cuneo
Press: Harvey B. Sabinson,
Lee Solters, Richard Ullman
Press: Harvey B. Sabinson, Lee Solters,
Richard Ullman
Stage Managers: Alan Hall, Mary Porter,
Patricia Drylie

For original NY production, see THEATRE WORLD, Vol. 23.

THE FREAKING OUT OF STEPHANIE BLAKE

By Richard Chandler; Director, Michael Kahn; Sets and Lighting, Ben Edwards and Jean Rosenthal; Costumes, Jeanne Button; Music and Lyrics, Jeff Barry; Projection Photographs, Bruce W. Stark; Light Paintings, Jason B. Fishbein; Hairstylist, Nino Raffaello; Production Assistant, Anita Shapiro; Presented by Cheryl Crawford and Carl Schaeffer. Opened Monday, Oct. 30, 1967 at the Eugene O'Neill Theatre and closed because of Miss Arthur's illness after Wednesday's matinee, Nov. 1, 1967.

CAST

Nancy Reed	Jan Miner
Hamilton Reed	Franklin Cover
Stephanie Blake	Jean Arthur

The Band:

Bumpy	Steve Curry
Randy	Ronald Dante
Tom	Frank Thumhart
Ron	Ronald Frangipane
Day Glo	John Bassette
Joy	Joy Bang
Mary	Marilyn Webb
Butterscotch	Andrea Martin
Timmy	James Fouratt
Motherball	William Devane
Man	Barton Heyman
Blake Reed	Mariclare Costello
Bonnie	Ellen O'Mara
Chuck	Michael McClanathan
Mildred	Dena Dietrich
Noah Crocker	Sidney Lanier
Passerby at Protest Show	Dena Dietrich
Policeman	Joseph Hardy
Lieutenant	Robert Hacha
Photographers	Dena Dietrich, Barton Heyman

UNDERSTUDIES: Stephanie, Jan Miner; Blake, Joy Bang; Hamilton, Noah, Robert Hacha; Motherball, Barton Heyman; Bumpy, Michael McClanathan; Dayglo, Michael Schultz.

A Comedy in 2 acts and 15 scenes. The action takes place at the present time in New York.

General Manager: Arthur Waxman
Press: Betty Lee Hunt, Henry Luhrman
Stage Managers: Richard Blofson, Charles Likar, Jr., Michael Schultz

Jean Arthur

LEDA HAD A LITTLE SWAN

By Bamber Gascoigne; Director, Andre Gregory; Scenic Production, Wolfgang Roth; Lighting, Jean Rosenthal; Costumes, Carrie Fishbein; Visual Projection Effects, DesPro Studios; Music, Teiji Ito; Companions, Bil Baird; Production Manager, Charles Maryan; Hair Designs, Paul Mitchell; Presented by Claire Nichtern. Opened Friday, March 29, 1968 in New York at the Cort Theatre, and closed there after 14 previews on Apr. 10, 1968.

CAST

Harry	Severn Darden
Virginia	Joan Darling
Sir George	Fred Stewart
Harry as a Boy	John Pleshette
Lady Fitch	Cavada Humphrey
Headmaster	Michael J. Pollard
Doctor	Cavada Humphrey
Herbert	Paul Benedict
Matron	Maxine Greene
Aunt Mildred	Cavada Humphrey
Noah	John Pleshette
Rebecca	Margaret Ladd
Granger	Merwin Goldsmith
Hodgkinson	Michael J. Pollard
Beggar	Seth Allen
Matt	Paul Benedict
Mary Wollen	Maxine Greene
Robinson Minor	Seth Allen

UNDERSTUDIES: Harry, Allan Arbus; Headmaster, Seth Allen; Virginia, Cis Corman; Sir George, Merwin Goldsmith; Lady Fitch, Elizabeth Thurman; Noah, Matt, David Spielberg; Granger, Herbert, Robert Cessna; Rebecca, Mary, Ann Freeman.

A Comedy in two acts. The action takes place in London from Saturday, June 1968 to Saturday, October 1985.

General Manager: Robert Kamlot
Press: Reginald Denenholz, Ben Kornzweig
Stage Managers: Richard Nelson, Robert Cessna

Joan Darling, Michael J. Pollard,
Severn Dardern, Fred Stewart (front)

Friedman-Abeles Photos

MATA HARI

Book, Jerome Coopersmith; Lyrics, Martin Charnin; Music, Edward Thomas; Director, Vincente Minnelli; Dances and Musical Numbers Staged by Jack Cole; Scenery and Lighting, Jo Mielziner; Costumes, Irene Sharaff; Orchestrations, Robert Russell Bennett; Musical Direction and Vocal Arrangements, Colin Romoff; Dance Music Arranged by Roger Adams; Associate Producer, Samuel Liff; Staff Associates, Sylvia Schwartz, Lynn Middleton, Linda Patton; Hairstylist, Ronald DeMann; Presented by David Merrick. Opened Saturday, Nov. 18, 1967 in Washington, D.C. at the National Theatre, and closed there on Dec. 9, 1967.

CAST

Young Soldier	Jake Holmes
Lt. Boulet	Mark Dempsey
Capt. Henry LaFarge	Pernell Roberts
Lt. Devries	Joseph Corby
Christiana	Kuniko Narai
Carlotta	Reiko Sato
Midge	Myrna White
Mata Hari	Marisa Mell
Vaudeville Man	George Marcy
Vaudeville Woman	Sandy Ellen
Vaudeville Child	Ellen Kravitz
Paulette LaFarge	Martha Schlamme
Flower Vendor	Paul Glaser
Philipe	Seymour Penzner
Claudine	Nadine Lewis
Pierre	Ryan Harrison
Michele	Blythe Danner
Mrs. Dupre	Helen G. Ross
Mr. Dupre	Paul Glaser
Maurice	Dominic Chianese
Innkeeper	Lewis Pierce
First German	Robert Kelly
Second German	Gordon Voorhees
Lt. Grant	Bill Reilly
Stage Manager	Gordon Voorhees
Major Bonnard	W. B. Brydon
Landlady	Jacque Dean

OFFICERS, MUSICIANS, PARISIANS, ETC.: Bobbi Baird, Baruch Blum, Eileen Casey, Joseph Corby, Peter Costanza, Jacque Dean, Anthony Devecchi, Judith Dunford, Carolyn Dyer, Sandy Ellen, Jack Fletcher, Garold Gardiner, Luigi Gasperinetti, Joanne Geahry, Altovise Gore, Peggy Hagen, Robert Kelly, Betty Kent, Ellen Kravitz, Tracy Moore, Ray Morgan, Lewis Pierce, Jeff Philips, Bill Reilly, Skiles Ricketts, Don StomsVik, Francine Storey, Caryl Tenney, Marshall Thomas, Nina Trasoff, Martha Velez, Gordon Voorhees, Masha Wolfson

MUSICAL NUMBERS: "Is This Fact?," "Everyone Has Something To Hide," "How Young You Were Tonight," "I'm Saving Myself For A Soldier," "Maman," "The Choice Is Yours," "Sextet," "Not Now, Not Here," "Hello, Yank!," "In Madrid," "I Don't See Him Very Much Anymore," "You Have No Idea," "The Arrest," "Interrogation and Ballet," "There Is No You," "There Will Be Love Again."

A Musical in 2 acts and 20 scenes. The action takes place during World War I in Paris, Madrid, and Switzerland.

General Manager: Jack Schlissel
Company Manager: Oscar Berlin
Press: Harvey B. Sabinson, Lee Solters, Richard Robert Ullman, Muffy Newman
Stage Managers: Pat Tolson, George Rondo, Henry Sutton

Friedman-Abeles Photos
(Rehearsal shots)

Top Right: Director Vincente Minnelli, Pernell Roberts, Marisa Mell. Below: Choreographer Jack Cole, Marisa Mell, Bill Reilly

Pernell Roberts, Martha Schlamme, Marisa Mell

185

PROFESSIONAL RESIDENT COMPANIES
throughout the United States
(Failure to meet deadline unfortunately necessitated omission of several important companies)

AMERICAN CONSERVATORY THEATRE
San Francisco, California
October 29, 1967 through August 18, 1968
William Ball, General Director

Managing Director, William Bushnell; Executive Director, Edward Hastings; Production, Director, John Seig; Director in Residence, Jerome Kilty; Training Director, Robert W. Goldsby; Guest Directors, Allen Fletcher, Byron Ringland; Design and Production Staff, Robert Bonaventura, Lewis Brown, Dorothy Fowler, John McLain, Walter Watson, Stuart Wurtzel; Associate Directors, Eugene Barcone, Nagle Jackson, Richard Nesbitt, Robert Six; Training Staff, Frank Ottiwell, Julius Palffy-Alpar, Marco Pogacar, Robert Weede, Nancy White; Administrators, Vern Armstrong, William R. Baer, David Blakeslee, John Kuntz, Dennis Powers.

COMPANY

Lynne Arden, Rene Auberjonois, Ramon Bieri, Dion Chesse, Barbara Colby, Peter Donat, Jay Doyle, George Ede, Patricia Falkenhain, Harry Frazier, Ellen Geer, Robert Gerringer, David Grimm, Scott Hylands, Ruth Kobart, DeAnn Mears, Judith Mihalyi, Josephine Nichols, William Paterson, Angela Paton, Charlene Polite, Marguerite Ray, Ray Reinhardt, Ken Ruta, John Schuck, Paul Shenar, Deborah Sussel, Patrick Tovatt, Ann Weldon, Mark Bramhall, David Dukes, Robert Feero, Larry Ferguson, Kate Hawley, Karen Ingenthron, Carol Mayo Jenkins, Enid Kent, Barry Kraft, Ray Laine, Dana Larson, Michael Lerner, Terry Mace, Glenn Mazen, Kimo Perry, Herman Poppe, James Ragan, Mary Ellen Ray, Mark Schell, Izetta Smith, Gil Turner, Don Watson, Kitty Winn.

PRODUCTIONS

"Twelfth Night," "Dear Liar," "The Zoo Story," "The American Dream," "Two For The Seesaw," "Under Milk Wood," "Long Day's Journey Into Night," "Endgame," "Tartuffe," "Thieves' Carnival," "Charley's Aunt," "In White America," "Tiny Alice," "Our Town," "Don't Shoot, Mable, It's Your Husband," "The Crucible," "An Evening's Frost," "A Delicate Balance," "The Misanthrope," "Long Live Life," "Hamlet," "Caught In The Act," "A Streetcar Named Desire," "Deedle, Deedle Dumpling," "My Son God," "Your Own Thing."

Hank Kranzler Photos

Peter Donat, DeAnn Mears in "An Evening's Frost"

Robert Gerringer, Ellen Geer in
"A Delicate Balance"

Paul Shenar, Ludi Claire in "Tiny Alice"

Scott Hylands, Jay Doyle in
"The American Dream"

ARENA STAGE
Washington, D. C.
Sept. 14, 1967 through June 2, 1968
Zelda Fichandler, Producing Director

Executive Director, Thomas C. Fichandler; Associate Producing Director, Edwin Sherin; Scenic Designer, Robin Wagner; Lighting, William Eggleston; Costumes, Leigh Rand, Marjorie Slaiman; Directors, Edwin Sherin, Harold Stone, Donald Moreland, Gladys Vaughan, Robert Alexander; Production Manager, Albert L. Gibson; Technical Directors, Richard Montford Cary, Henry R. Gorfein; Stage Managers, Patricia Christian, Gage Andretta, John A. M. dePianelli, Assistant Executive Director, Kenneth K. Kitch; General Manager, Catherine A. Knockey; Assistant, JoAnn Magill; Press, Susanne Roschwalb, Peggi Drum; Staff Assistant, Sandra Shankewitz.

COMPANY

Jane Alexander, Richard Bauer, David Congdon, George Ebeling, Robert Foxworth, Grayce Grant, Tana Hicken, James Kenny, Landra Lee, Richard McKenzie, Robert Prosky, Mimi Norton Salamanca, Anna Shaler, Richard Venture, Eugene R. Wood, Max Wright, Verona Barnes, Gisela Caldwell, David Connell, Ronny Cox, Ronald Duncan, Mara Lane, Harold Miller, Donegan Smith, Dolores St. Amand Ned Beatty, Don Blakely, Norma Donaldson, Hector Elizondo, Antonio Fargas, Hilda Haynes, L. Errol Jaye, James Earl Jones, Al Kirk, George Mathews, Jimmy Pelham, Gil Rogers, Bill Terry, John E. Rudder, Benjamin Sands, Mary Esther Sands, Frank Sarles, Don Scimonelli, Lee Shlosberg, Carole Singleton, Danette Small, Nicholai G. Speransky, Marcellus G. Stewart, Lou Teitel, Jay Williams Patricia Hawkins, Richard G. Holmes, Robert Koch, John Edward Malarkey, Marian L. Matthews, Kirk Morris, Marian Myles, Barbara Neill, Eugene M. Oliver, Jr., Dolores Porter, Gerald Ragland, Jr., John Bell, Roger Brown, Mitchell Bryant, St. Clair Christmas, William G. Clark, Ralph G. Cooper, Glenn Davis, Brian E. Donohue, George Dupor, Calvin Gibson, Stanley Handleman, Rita Hargrave.

PRODUCTIONS

"Major Barbara," "Poor Bitos," "The Great White Hope" (World Premiere), "The Tenth Man," "Room Service," "The Iceman Cometh," "The Blood Knot," "Wind In The Willows."

Joe Cameron Photos

Right: "The Iceman Cometh." Top: James Kenny, Jane Alexander in "Major Barbara"

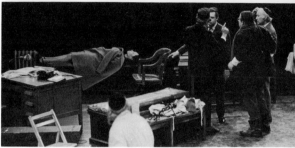

Anna Shaler (L), Lou Gilbert (R)
in "The Tenth Man"

obert Prosky, David Congdon, Eugene R. Wood, Anna Carparelli, Max Wright, Richard Venture
in "Poor Bitos"

Gerry Ragland, Richard Bauer, Jane Alexander, Lou Gilbert, James Earl Jones in
"The Great White Hope"

187

Anthony Heald, Robert Britton, Polly Holliday,
Charlotte Moore in "Look Back In Anger"

ASOLO THEATER FESTIVAL
Sarasota, Florida
Feb. 16 through May 11, 1968
Richard G. Fallon, General Director

The State Theater of Florida; Resident Artistic Directors, Robert Strane, Eberle Thomas; Guest Director, Paul Weidner; Scenic Designer and Technical Director, Ray Perry; Costumes, Joy Breckenridge; Lighting, Richard C. Evans; Musical Composer, Stephen Smith; Stage Managers, Sandy Moffett, Fred Breckenridge, Arthur Bayol; Press, Annette Grubbs; Business Manager, Jeannine Hale; Production Coordinator, Elizabeth Kaler; Sound Technican, Greg Congleton.

COMPANY

Robert Britton, C. David Colson, Anthony Heald, Donald C. Hoepner, Polly Holliday, Margaret Kaler, Linda Kampley, Michael P. Keenan, Charlotte Moore, David O. Petersen, Michael Reynolds, Walter Rhodes, Albert L. Smelko, Isa Thomas, Bradford Wallace.

PRODUCTIONS

"Henry IV, Part I," "Servant Of Two Masters," "Tartuffe," "J. B.," "Look Back In Anger."

Wayne Manley Photos

"Tartuffe"

Anthony Heald, Albert L. Smelko, Robert
Britton in "J. B."

Donald C. Hoepner, C. David Colson, Bradford
Wallace, Michael P. Keenan, Arthur Bayol,
Michael Reynolds in "Henry IV, Part I"

David O. Petersen, Polly Holliday
in "Servant Of Two Masters"

Fritz Weaver, Albert Dekker in
"The Sorrows of Frederick"

Edward Andrews, Nan Martin in
"The Marriage of Mr. Mississippi"

CENTER THEATRE GROUP
Mark Taper Forum
Los Angeles, Calif.
Gordon Davidson, Artistic Director

General Manager, Mitchell Brower; Administrative Coordinator, Ditta Oliker; Administrative Assistant, Lillian Proctor; Directors, Gordon Davidson, Albert Marre, Malcolm Black, Douglas Campbell, Milton Katselas; Designers, Peter Wexler, Ralph Alswang, Robert Fletcher, Archie Sharp, Dorothy Jeakins, Michael Devine, Lewis Brown; Music, Conrad Susa, Pia Gilbert, Dion McGregor, Michael Barr, Paul Fetler; Press; Peggy Phillips, Allen Burry, Barry Hyams; Production Manager, Robert Calhoun; Stage Managers, Tom A. Larson, Helen Page Camp, John L. Weisman; Design Coordinator, William Cruse.

COMPANY

Jayne Abby, Alan Abelew, Jack Albertson, Edward Andrews, Malcolm Atterbury, Philip Austin, Jacques Aubuchon, Rene Auberjonois, Al Alu, Anna-Lee Austin, Lucian Baker, Harry Basch, Warren Berlinger, Robert Bock, Jim Boles, James Burleson, Ronald Boulden, Helen Page Camp, Robert Casper, Paul Carr, Sid Conrad, George Coulouris, Margaret Cowles, Oren Curtis, Jeff Corey, Wallace Chappel, Hume Cronyn, Adolph Caesar, Thayer David, Albert Dekker, Frederic Downs, Eugene Dynarski, Joyce Ebert, Ed Flanders, Robert Fletcher, Ivor Francis, Eduard Franz, Bert Freed, G. Alan Freeman, Liam Gannon, Betty Garrett, Bill Glover, Bruce Glover, Harold Gould, Jerome Guardino, Robert Guidi, Gwynne Gilford, Katherine Henryk, William Hickey, David Hurst, John Hancock, Patrick Horgan, Mariette Hartley, Nancy Jeris, Dennis Jones, Jonathan Kidd, Frank Langella, Jama Laurent, Mark Lenard, Richard Levin, Reveta Lynn, William Lucking, Raymond Lynch, Lawrence Linville, John Mackay, Nancy Marchand, Nan Martin, Billy McMickle, Caroline McWilliams, Laurie Mock, Dale Morse, Nigel McKeand, Oliver McGowan, Diana Maddox, Philip Mishkin, Warren Oates, David Opatoshu, Alan Oppenheimer, Peggy Pope, Philip Proctor, Eldon Quick, Dolores Quinton, John Ragin, Ann Raymond, John Rose, Joseph Reale, Edmon Ryan, John Randolph, Joseph Ruskin, Helen Seamon, Frank Schofield, Paul Stevens, Karl Swenson, Abraham Sofaer, Stephen Strimpell, Gillian Tomlin, Frederic Tozere, Jessica Tandy, Harry Townes, Michael Vlastas, Herbert Voland, James Walker, Fritz Weaver, William Wintersole, Ian Wolfe, Iggie Wolfington, Joseph Wiseman, Anthony Zerbe, Ed Zimmermann.

PRODUCTIONS

"The Devils," "The Sorrows Of Frederick" (World Premiere), "The Marriage of Mr. Mississippi," "Who's Happy Now?" (World Premiere), "The Miser," "In The Matter of J. Robert Oppenheimer" (American Premiere).

Hume Cronyn, Jessica Tandy
in "The Miser"

Warren Berlinger, Betty Garrett in
"Who's Happy Now?"

189

CLEVELAND PLAY HOUSE
Cleveland, Ohio
Sept. 29, 1967 through May 12, 1968
Fifty-second Season
K. Elmo Lowe, Director

Manager, Leonore Klewer; Coordinating Director, Richard Oberlin; Press, Ruth Fischer; Scenic Director, Paul Rodgers; Costume Designer, Carol Margolis; Directors, Jonathan Bolt, Tom Brennan, Henry Butler, John Marley, Richard Oberlin, Mario Siletti, Robert Snook, Stuart Vaughn; Stage Managers, Larry Tarrant, Ben Letter.

COMPANY

Robert Allman, Peter Bartlett, Jonathan Bolt, L. Bramer Carlson, Don Cooper, Maury Cooper, David Frazier, June Gibbons, Gigi Gibson, Richard Halverson, Anne Heil, Catherine Heiser, Addie Johnson, Myrna Kaye, Allen Leatherman, Stuart Levin, Myriam Lipari, Elizabeth Lowry, Keith Mackey, Vaughn McBride, Joan McConocha, Evie McElroy, Bob Moak, Jean Morris, Beccy Myers, Richard Oberlin, Edith Owen, Ronald Parady, Dorothy Paxton, Fran Precario, Terry Quartin, Mario Siletti, David Snell, Robert Snook, Nancy Stewart, Vivienne Stotter, Larry Tarrant, Robert Thorson.

PRODUCTIONS

"The Government Inspector," "Luv," "The Strong Are Lonely," "Morning's At Seven," "The Odd Couple," "Charley's Aunt," "The Dumbwaiter," "The Collection," "Generation," "The Rose Tattoo," "Dear Liar," "The Glass Menagerie," "The Merry Wives of Windsor," "Halfway Up The Tree," "Waiting For Godot."

Ben Bliss Photos

Michael Ebert, Marsha Frank, Vincent Gardeni in "A View From The Bridge"

Will Lee, Eda Reiss Merin in "Awake And Sing"

THE CHARLES PLAYHOUSE
Boston, Mass.
June 1, 1967 through May 25, 1968
Eleventh Season
Michael Murray, Artistic Director

Managing Director, Frank Sugrue; Associate Director, Terrence Currier, General Manager, Hugh Lester; Press, Alice Webb, Pat Webb, Hita Johnson; Assistant to Producers, Mary Deininger; Technical Directors, Philip Watts, Stephen Linn; Costumiere, Cecelia Eller; Stage Managers, Peter Golden, Frederick Orner, Sandy Underwood, Barbara Bachman; Designers, Hugh Lester, William Schroeder, Richard W. Kerry, Bruce Owen, Jan, Jeanne Button; Directors, Michael Murray, Thomas Bissinger, Ted Kazanoff, Mitchell Nestor, Arthur Storch.

COMPANY

Jake Dengel, Jill Clayburgh, Roger Robinson, John Seitz, William Lafe, Roger Davis, Kevin O'Neal, Philip Hanson, Jack Gianino, Jennifer Salt, Nancie Phillips, Gwyllum Evans, Philip J. Mantos, Richard Spiegel, Zoe Kamitses, Bernard Wurger, Al Pacino, Eda Reiss Merin, Dennis Helfend, Annette Oliver, Don Lochner, Lynn Milgrim, Will Lee, Michael Elliot Keen, Bob McDonald, Gerald McGonagill, Michael Smith, Jay Fletcher, Paul Harrington, Robert Gaus, Peter MacLean, Judy McMurdo, Ronald DiMartile, Walter Kidder, Edward Finnegan, Gary Gage, Christopher Groden, Tom Noel, Lee Dupree, Ben Hammer, Vincent Gardenia, Marsha Frank, Jo Flores Chase, Constantine Katsanos, Michael Ebert, William Joliff, Jill Cagan, Teri Owen, Linda Lyman, Will Hare, Danny Meehan, Edward Morehouse, James Tolkan, Jonathan Currier.

PRODUCTIONS

"MacBird!," "America Hurrah," "Awake and Sing," "The Nine O'Clock Mail," "The Madness of Lady Bright," "Dutchman," "Room Service," "A View From The Bridge," "Waiting For Godot."

Jonathan Bolt, Richard Oberlin, Elizabeth Lowry in "Luv"

Robert Thorson, Peter Bartlett, Myriam Lipari, Bob Moak, Gigi Gibson in "Charley's Aunt"

Larry Tarrant (seated), Mario Siletti in "The Collection"

Addie Johnson, Jonathan Bolt in "The Glass Menagerie"

Jose Ferrer, Maureen O'Sullivan in "You Know I
Can't Hear You When The Water's Running"

Fritzi Burr, Hans Conried, Nancy Pinkerton
in "Don't Drink The Water"

COCONUT GROVE PLAYHOUSE
Miami, Florida
June 27, 1967 through June 2, 1968

Producer, Zev Bufman in association with
James Riley; Directors, Hal Halvorsen, Billy
Matthews, Danny Simon, Joey Faye, Robert
Linden, Anthony Perkins, Malcolm Black,
Robert Moore, Richard Altman; Choreographers,
Ron Bostick, Larry Fuller, Phil Black, Ray
Chabean, George Tapps; Designers, James
Riley, Richard Seger; Musical Director, Pem-
broke Davenport; Technical Director, Harry
Schmale, Jr.; Production Associate, Mark Hiers;
Production Assistants, Shawn McAllister, Ken-
neth Calender; Press, Charles Cinnamon, Nomi
Zank; Stage Managers, Frank Martin, William
Shrewsbury, Shawn McAllister.

PRODUCTIONS
"Half A Sixpence" with Kenneth Nelson
and Linda Rae Hager, "The Unsinkable
Molly Brown" with Harve Presnell and Rita
Gardner, "Camelot" with Michael Allinson,
Lola Fisher and Bob Holiday, "The Apple
Tree" with Sue Ane Langdon, Darryl Hick-
man and George S. Irving, "Anatomy Of
Burlesque" with Sally Rand, "Sweet Charity"
with Gretchen Wyler and Dick Patterson,
"Don't Drink The Water" with Hans Conried,
Fritzi Burr, Dick Van Patten and John Fink,
"The Star-Spangled Girl" with Anthony
Perkins, Lynn Benish and Remak Ramsay,
"You Know I Can't Hear You When The
Water's Running" with Jose Ferrer, Maureen
O'Sullivan and Ben Piazza, "Lock Up Your
Daughters" with Cyril Ritchard, Holly Harris
and Carleton Carpenter, "There's A Girl In
My Soup" with Van Johnson and Joan Ander-
son, "Is The Real You Really You?" with
Richard Schaal and Louise Lasser, "Call Me
Madam" with Ethel Merman, Richard East-
ham and Russell Nype, "Cactus Flower" with
Eve Arden, "Blue Hour."

Ray Fisher Photos

Kenneth Nelson, Linda Rae Hager in
"Half A Sixpence"

Van Johnson in "There's A Girl In My Soup"

American Premiere of "Vasco"

Mary Sue Jones, Jane Tracy in
"A Streetcar Named Desire"

DALLAS THEATER CENTER
Dallas, Texas
June 6, 1967 through June 8, 1968
Paul Baker, Managing Director

Assistant Director, Mary Sue Fridge Jones; Executive Coordinators, Judith Davis, Barbara Gilstrap; Technical Director, Bob Baca; Press, Lynn Trammel; Designers, Nancy Levinson, Charlote Cole, Tina Navarro, Bob Baca, Pat Baca, Kathleen Latimer, Yoichi Aoki, Anne Butler, Arthur Jensen Rogers, Reta LaForce, Virgil Beavers, David Pursley, Kathleen Benke, Ella-Mae Brainard, Carleton Tanner; Directors, Ryland Merkey, Preston Jones, David Pursley, Norman Ayrton, Mike Dendy, James Nelson Harrell, George Webby, Louise Mosley, Kosta Spaic, Burgess Meredith, Anna Paul Marsh-Neame, Paul Baker, Anna Paul Rogers, John Logan, Ken Latimer, Bob Baca; Stage Managers Matt Tracy, Johnny McBee, Kaki Dowling, Leonard T. Wagner, Edward Kirk Herrmann, Fritz Lennon, Frank Jarrett, Harry Porter, John Figlmiller, John Fish, Dale Blair, Roberta Rude, Maurice Harrell, Deanna Dunagan.

RESIDENT COMPANY
Bob Baca, Ella-Mae Brainard, Charlote Cole, Mike Dendy, Kaki Dowling, John Figlmiller, Claudette Gardner, Anna Gonyaw, James Nelson Harrell, Betty June Lary, Fritz Lennon, Sally Netzel, Richard Slocum, Buddy Smith, Randolph Tallman, Leonard T. Wagner.

RESIDENT ARTISTS
Robyn Baker Flatt, Preston Jones, Ken Latimer, Ryland Merkey, Randy Moore, Louise Mosley, David Pursley, Mona Pursley, Lynn Trammell, Patti O'Donnell Wilcox, Ronald Wilcox.

PRODUCTIONS
KALITA HUMPHREYS THEATER: "Luv," "Barefoot In The Park," "Ben Bagley's The Decline and Fall of the Entire World As Seen Through The Eyes of Cole Porter," "Twelfth Night," "Spoon River Anthology," "The Odd Couple," "A Delicate Balance," "Pinocchio," "A Streetcar Named Desire," "Vasco" (American Premiere), "The Latent Heterosexual" (World Premiere with guest star Zero Mostel), "Charley's Aunt."
DOWN CENTER STAGE: "R. U. Hungry," "Look Back In Anger," "A Delicate Balance," "The Private Ear," "The Public Eye," "The Knack," "Chamber Music," "The Day It Rained Forever," "The Finger Tomb" (World Premiere).

Andy Hanson Photos

Zero Mostel (L) in "The Latent Heterosexual"

"Twelfth Night"

HARTFORD STAGE COMPANY
Hartford, Conn.
Oct. 20, 1967 through June 23, 1968
Jacques Cartier, Producing Director

Business Manager, Thomas E. Vachon; Press, Anne V. Goodrich, Norma Plumley, Frances J. Ford; Stage Managers, Fred Hoskins, Frank Prendergast; Scenery, John Conklin, Santo Loquasto, Holmes Easley; Costumes, John Conklin, Kate Vachon, Holmes Easley; Lighting, Peter Hunt; Technical Director, William A. Meinecke; Directors, Jacques Cartier, Peter Hunt, Michael Murray, Louis Beachner, Melvin Bernhardt; Musical Direction, Arthur Rubinstein; Pianist-Conductor, Lenny LaCroix; Choreography, Rudy D'Angona.

COMPANY

Don Barshay, John Bottoms, Kent Broadhurst, Saylor Creswell, Virginia Downing, Peter DeMaio, Elizabeth Farley, Mary Fogarty, Robert Jennings, John Jiler, Marion Killinger, John Leighton, Karen Ludwig, Macon McCalman, Rue McClanahan, Marilyn Murphy, Annette Oliver, Ken Parker, Don Plumley, Jennifer Salt, Frank Savino, Henry Thomas, Sherry Alden, Louis Beachner, Michael Bradshaw, Laurie Crews, John Dignan, Katherine Helmond, Dana Ivey, Sue Kelly, John Long, Judith McCauley, Joan Pape, Tom Urich, Bernard Wurger, Richard Ward, Andrew Winner, Michael Henderson, Barbara Hollis, Fred Hoskins, Barbara Cason, Julia Curry, Swoosie Kurtz, Linda Segal.

PRODUCTIONS

"The Miser," "A View From The Bridge," "Hay Fever," "The Hostage," "Antigone," "The Firebugs," "The Threepenny Opera."

Barbara Cason, Marion Killinger in "Hay Fever"
Above: Rue McClanahan, John Leighton in "The Hostage"

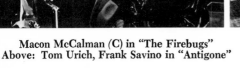

Macon McCalman (C) in "The Firebugs"
Above: Tom Urich, Frank Savino in "Antigone"

Karen Ludwig, Don Barshay, Peter DeMaio, Frank Savino in "A View From The Bridge"
Above: Tom Urich, Katherine Helmond (C) in "Threepenny Opera"

194

LONG ISLAND FESTIVAL REPERTORY
Mineola, L. I., N. Y.
April 30 through June 23, 1968
Dr. Frank A. Calderone, Producer

Presented by the Theatre Society of Long Island in association with Harlan P. Kleiman; General Manager, Robert S. Fishko; Assistants, Steve M. Goldberg, Helen M. Neuschaefer; Press, Ruth Whiting, Julia Ann Liantonio, Carolyn Wessel; Robert S. Fishko in charge of Production; Directors, Howard DaSilva, Edwin Sherin, Harold Stone, Arvin Brown; Scenery and Lighting. C. Murawski; Costumes, Sydney Smith, Robert Pusilo; Stage Managers, David Eliscu, Martha Knight; Hairstyles, Steve Atha; Music, Gordon Emerson; Production Assistant, Charles Fischl; Casting Director, Jessica Levy.

COMPANY

Barbara Bel Geddes, Bibi Besch, Tom Brannum, Don Briscol, Stan Dworkin, James Broderick, Alvin Epstein, Ed Flanders, Arthur Hill, Jane Hoffman, Kim Hunter, Earle Hyman, Frank Langella, James Luisi, Arlan Dean Snyder, Art Wallace, Alan Yorke, Haig Chobanian, Patricia Elliot, Paul Jenkins, Nancy Pinkerton, Mary Savidge, Carol Teitel, David Ackroyd, Carol Fox, Colin Fox, William Hansen, Howard Honig, Ken Jenkins, David Marsh, Eda Reiss Marin, Joseph Shaw, Beatrice Straight.

PRODUCTIONS

"Come Back, Little Sheba," "Eccentricities Of A Nightingale," "Light Up The Sky," "The Three Sisters."

(No production photographs available)

Kim Hunter

Arthur Hill. Above: Barbara Bel Geddes

195

Eric Berry, Jenny Laird, Leora Dana
in "John Gabriel Borkman"

JOHN FERNALD COMPANY
Meadow Brook Theatre
Rochester, Mich.
Oct. 6, 1967 through June 2, 1968

Artistic Director, John Fernald; Managing Director, David Bishop; Press, Merle Debuskey, Ted Rancont, Jr., Faith Geer; Technical Director, Shan Covey; Directors, Eric Berry, John Fernald, Johan Fillinger, John Broome, George Guidall, Milo Sperber; Scenery and Lighting, Frank Masi; Costumes, Elizabeth Penn; Stage Managers, Peter Stephens, William Carpenter, Richard Allen, Bruce Blakemore Leon Leake.

COMPANY
Richard Allen, Eric Berry, Bruce Lyman Blakemore, Otho Burr, Barbara Caruso, Leora Dana, Curt Dawson, Herbert Foster, Roy Frady, George Guidall, Amy Gundlach, Bonnie Hurren, Betty Sinclair, Jenny Laird, Lorna Lewis, Victor Holchak, Neil Hunt, Colin Pinney, Jill Tanner, Lans Traverse, Beverly Atkinson, Booker T. Bradshaw, Jr., Joshua Bryant, Pat Carson, Pam Guest, Henry Thomas, Frank Wilson, Phillip Piro, Christopher Ross-Smith.

PRODUCTIONS
"The Importance Of Being Earnest," "John Gabriel Borkman," "Charley's Aunt," "And People All Around," "King Lear," "No Exit," "The Firebugs," "The Sea Gull."

Leslie Howey Photos

Eric Berry, Betty Sinclair in "The Sea Gull"

Lorna Lewis, Curt Dawson, Colin Pinney,
Neil Hunt in "Charley's Aunt"

Curt Dawson, Lorna Lewis, Eric Berry, Otho Burr,
Colin Pinney in "King Lear"

Booker Bradshaw, Josh Bryant, Pam Guest
Lorna Lewis in "People All Around"

Joyce Ebert, Denise Ferguson
in "The Rehearsal"

LONG WHARF THEATRE
New Haven, Conn.
Oct. 20, 1967 through May 25, 1968
Arvin Brown, Artistic Director

General Manager, Douglas Buck; Executive Assistant, Claire Wolf; Press, Sally Douds, Paula Grossman, Eva Rubenstein; Technical Director, Therald Todd; Resident Composer, Gordon Emerson; Sets and Lighting, Will Steven Armstrong, Arthur Barrow, John Conklin, Virginia Doncy, Betsy Clinton, James Gohl, Peter Hunt, Richard Klein, Therald Todd, Elmon Webb, Santo Loquasto; Costumes, Rosemary Ingham, Alec Sutherland, Margaret Mahoney; Stage Managers, James Way, Charles J. Likar, Jean Weigel; Directors, Arvin Brown, Jon Jory, Siobhan McKenna, James Way, Jeff Bleckner, Joseph Cazalet, Michael Youngfellow; Sound Technician, Michael O'Malley.

COMPANY

Tom Atkins, Michael Bradshaw, Leo Ciceri, Charles Cioffi, Kevin Conway, Mildred Dunnock, Joyce Ebert, Denise Ferguson, Roland Hewgill, Joseph Hindy, Ken Jenkins, Laurie Kennedy, Dermot McNamara, Michael McGuire, Garry Mitchell, Robert Moberly, Don Plumley, Roger Omar Serbagi, Richard B. Shull, William Swetland, Ray deMatteis, Larry Blauvelt, Richard Eno, William Hayes, Barrie Rivchun, Ingrid Sonnichsen, Steven Trinwith.

PRODUCTIONS

"The Glass Menagerie," "The Rehearsal," "The Playboy Of The Western World," "Room Service," "A Whistle In The Dark," "A Doctor In Spite Of Himself," "Tiny Alice," "Don Juan In Hell.'"

Sean Kernan, Joseph Cazalet Photos

Michael Bradshaw, Dermot McNamara
in "Room Service"

Joseph Hindy, Joyce Ebert
in "The Glass Menagerie"

Charles Cioffi, Leo Ciceri. Above: Don Plumley, William Swetland, Garry Mitchell
in "A Whistle In The Dark"

197

McCARTER REPERTORY COMPANY
Princeton University
October 6, 1967 through April 3, 1968
Arthur W. Lithgow, Executive Director

General Manager, Nancy Shannon; Production Director, Clyde Blakeley; Press, Michael T. Leech; Costumes, Marney Welmers, Charles Blackburn; Designers, Walter K. Sloan, Clyde Blakeley; Lighting; Clyde Blakeley, John C. Schenk; Directors, Basil Langton, Robert Moss, Ken Costigan, Jon Jory, Arthur W. Lithgow; Stage Managers, Hamilton Williams, Daniel Hamilton.

COMPANY

Susan Babel, Anne Gee Byrd, David Byrd Yusef Bulos, Rudy Caringi, Grady Clarkson, Ken Costigan, Jake Dengel, Mary Doyle, John Grimaldi, Daniel Hamilton, George Hearn, Pamela Hawthorn, Will Hicks, Bryan Hull, Timothy Jerome, Susan Kaslow, K. Lype O'Dell, Phillip Piro, Ronald Steelman, James Tripp, Mimmi-Garth, Norman Kingoff, Judith Lane, Elizabeth Pergerson, Dionis Spitzer.

PRODUCTIONS

"The Devil's Disciple," "Twelfth Night," "Enrico IV," "The Words Upon The Window Pane," "It Should Happen To A Dog," "The Second Shepherd's Pageant," "The Crucible," "The Beggars' Opera," "Doctor Faustus," "The Marriage Of Figaro."

Anne Gee Byrd, Bryan Hull
in "The Devil's Disciple"

Susan Kaslow, George Hearn, Judith Lane
in "The Beggar's Opera"

MILWAUKEE REPERTORY THEATER
Milwaukee, Wisc.
Oct. 12, 1967 through May 19, 1968
Tunc Yalman, Artistic Director

Managing Director, Charles R. McCallum; Press, Mary McDonald Welles.

COMPANY

Clayton Corbin, Michael Fairman, Erika Slezak, Charles Kimbrough, Penelope Reed, Rhoda B. Carrol, Diana Kirkwood, Michael Tucker, Jeff Chandler, Marc Alaimo, Harry Zummach, Frank Borgman, Mary Jane Kimbrough.

PRODUCTIONS

"Othello," "A Streetcar Named Desire," "Amphitryon '38," "Mary Stuart," "Waiting For Godot," "The Big Knife," "The Importance Of Being Earnest," World Premieres of "The Head Of Hair" and "Oh, Pioneers."

Gene of Aida Photos

Right: Mary Jane Kimbrough, Erika Slezak, Frank Borgman in "Oh, Pioneers." Above: Erika Slezak, Michael Tucker in "The Head of Hair"

Michael Fairman, Erika Slezak, Clayton Corbin in "Othello"

Penelope Reed, Marc Alaimo in "Mary Stuart"

Michael Fairman, Diana Kirkwood, Erika Slezak, Michael Rucker, Charles Kimbrough, Jeff Chandler in "Amphitryon '38"

Mary Jane Kimbrough, Charles Kimbrough, Erika Slezak, Jeff Chandler in "The Importance of Being Earnest"

U. S. Premiere of "The Cavern"

PLAYHOUSE IN THE PARK
Cincinnati, Ohio
May 11 through Sept. 23, 1967
Brooks Jones, Producer

Managing Director, William Stewart; Associate Director, David Hooks; Business Manager, Jane Krause; Press, William Casstevens; Scenery, Douglas W. Schmidt; Stage Manager, Robert Stevenson; Technical Director, Joe Pacitti; Costumer, Martha Braun; Assistant to Producer, Peggy Marks; Assistant to Manager, Jean Trounstine.

COMPANY

Ronald Bishop, David Hooks, Brooks Jones, Michael Lipton, Bernard McInerney, Lynn Milgrim, Joe Pacitti, Robert Rovin, Douglas W. Schmidt, Robert Stevenson, William Stewart, Caleb Summers, Joan White, Susan Willis, Edward Zang, Roger Abrams, Katie Allen, Stephanie Block, Lisa Bouldin, Clinton Bramkamp, Jill Diefenbach, John Fowler, Randie Garfield, Pat Golder, Susan Goodman, Judi Gregory, Skip Harris, Gloria House, Susan Ann Juvelier, Lorin Kaufman, Barbara Moran, Cynthia Schatz, Linda Tritsch, Nicholas Valle, Rex Weil, Mike De Francesco, Bill Shorr, Linda Franklin.

PRODUCTIONS

"The Birthday Party," "The Cavern" (U.S. Premiere), "Escurial," "The Lesson," "Uncle Vanya," "Anatol."

"The Importance of Being Earnest"

Paul Benedict in "The Birthday Party"

Lynn Milgrim, Al Corbin in "The Lesson"

Michael Lipton, Diane Danzi in "Anatol"

PURDUE UNIVERSITY THEATRE
Lafayette, Indiana
Sept. 12, 1967 through Mar. 31, 1968
First Season
Joseph Stockdale, Artistic Director

Executive Director, Ross D. Smith; General Manager, Alan Light; Director-Choreographer, Wayne Lamb; Designer, Jerry Williams; Lighting, Randy Earle; Musical Director, Dick Jaeger; Press, Susan J. Weiss; Stage Managers, Wayne Lamb, Jim Fox, K. L. Coughenour, Richard Lake.

COMPANY

Anne Revere, Robert Donley, James Earl Jones, Robertearl Jones, Ed Setrakian, Michael Walsh, Robert Browning, Susan Murray, Leon Benedict, Joseph Boley, Cathryn Damon, Will Gregory, Dorothy Harlan, Dale Helward, Stuart Howard, Tom Jennings, Beecher Ketchum, Roy Kirkpatrick, Susan Lehman, James McDonald, John Morrow, Jr., Philip Polito, Jeanne Repp, Peter Shawn, Reid Shelton, Brian McMaster, Michael Yelton.

PRODUCTIONS

"Of Mice and Men," "Irma La Douce," "Long Day's Journey Into Night," "Incident At Vichy," "A Funny Thing Happened On The Way To The Forum," "Uncle Vanya."

Robert Donley, Michael Walsh in
"Long Day's Journey Into Night"

Will Gregory, Cathryn Damon
in "Uncle Vanya"

Robertearl Jones, James Earl Jones in
"Of Mice And Men"

Reid Shelton in "A Funny Thing Happened
On The Way To The Forum"

THE REPERTORY THEATRE
at Loretto-Hilton Center
St. Louis, Mo.
July 7, 1967 through Mar. 31, 1968
Second Season
Michael Flanagan, Artistic Director

Associate Artistic Director, James Bernardi; Guest Directors, Louis Criss, J. Robert Dietz; Philip Minor; Administrative Coordinator, Kevin J. Manning; Administrative Assistants, Robert Olin, Connie Gantry; Designers, John Wright Stevens, Raymond Jens Klausen, Grady Larkins, Vita and Peter Sargent; Stage Manager, Frank Schmitt, Michael Judson, Sara Garrity.

COMPANY

Bruce Brown, Madelyn Cain, J. Robert Dietz, Jane Dreyer, Lillian Evans, Elizabeth Farley, Joan Hanson, Glenn Johnson, Thomas Kampman, Dermot McNamara, Marian Mercer, Robert Moberly, Robert Murch, Anthony Ponzini, Gerald Simon, Stephanie Stoyanoff, John Arlington, Louis Basile, James Carruthers, Doris Diener, James Duncan, Patricia Egglinger, Donald Gantry, George Gitto, Les Gruner, Dale Helward, Michael Hill, Alex Iorio, Susan Loughran, Jane Lowry, Patrick Manion, Joy Mills, Timothy Neller, Bernie Passeltiner, Seth Richards, James Scott, James Simmons, Elizabeth Simon, Frank Warninsky, Judith Willis, George Addis, Marian Clarke, David Huffman, Pamela Mathews, Philip Minor, Virginia Payne, Thomas Spalding.

PRODUCTIONS

"The Hostage," "Rashomon," "A Streetcar Named Desire," "The Caucasian Chalk Circle," "The Time Of Your Life," "The Miser," "The Merchant Of Venice," "Six Characters In Search Of An Author," "Misalliance."

George Tichacek Photos

Marian Mercer, Lillian Evans,
Dermot McNamara, in "The Hostage"

Robert Murch, Anthony Ponzini,
Elizabeth Farley in "Rashomon"

Marian Mercer, Robert Murch in
"A Streetcar Named Desire"

Marian Clarke, Philip Minor, Chet London,
Carol Keefe in "The Merchant of Venice"

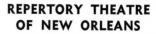

General Manager, Walter Paddy Ryan; Assistant, Warren Logan; Assistant Director, David Scanlan; Scenery and Costumes, Gordon Micunis, Matthew Ryan; Technical Director, R. Patrick Mitchell; Lighting, R. Patrick Mitchell, Louise Guthman; Business Manager, Alex Fedoroff; Press, Jack Gallier; Stage Managers, Ted Sheraton, Jason Reed, Richard Voinche.

COMPANY

Robert Benson, Rand Bridges, Thomas Coley, John Creamer. Dillon Evans, Joanna Featherstone, Suzanne Grossmann, Kristine Hatch, Evelyn Hendrickson, Margaret Kennedy, Nicholas R. Krieger, Barbara McMahon, Herbert Nelson, Don Perkins, Steve Perry, Nina Polan, Ed Preble, Jane Rose, David Scanlan, Peter Stuart, Tom Tammi, Anne Thompson, Jenneth Webster, Rudolph Willrich.

PRODUCTIONS

"The Crucible," "A Midsummer Night's Dream," "Saint Joan," "Tartuffe."

Frank Methe Photos

Left: Suzanne Grossmann, Herbert Nelson, Joanna Featherstone, Don Perkins in "The Crucible." **Above:** Suzanne Grossmann, Don Perkins in "Saint Joan"

Barbara McMahon, Dillon Evans in "Tartuffe"

Steve Perry, Stuart Vaughan, Nina Polan, Dillon Evans in "A Midsummer Night's Dream"

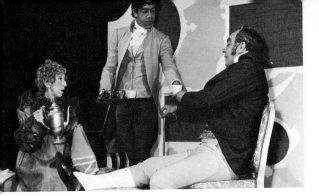

Margaret Hamilton, Glenn Johnson, George Vogel in "The Rivals"

SEATTLE REPERTORY THEATRE
Seattle, Wash.
Nov. 1, 1967 through Apr. 14, 1968
Fifth Season
Allen Fletcher, Artistic Director

Executive Director, Donald Foster; General Manager, Peter Donnelly; Assistant General Manager, William Parsons; Press, Shirley Dennis, Jean Findlay; Scenic Designers, Robert E. Darling, S. Todd Muffatti, John Conklin; Costumes, Allan Granstrom, Sandee Strand Kerr, Jack E. Smith; Lighting, David F. Segal, Phil Schermer, Roger Morgan; Technical Director, Floyd E. Hart; Stage Managers, Meribeth Meacham, Mark S. Krause, Clarence Morley, James Bertholf; Production Assistants, Susan Berg, Jan Haag; Music, Conrad Susa, Stan Keen, Kenneth W. Benshoof; Directors, Byron Ringland, Pirie MacDonald, George Vogel, Hal Todd, James Bertholf, Patrick Hines, Archie Smith, Robert Loper.

COMPANY
Margaret Hamilton, Patricia Hamilton, Myrna Walker, Jason Bernard, Olivia Cole, Jacqueline Coslow, Kay Doubleday, Jonathan Farwell, Pauline Flanagan, Bernard Frawley, John Gilbert, Patrick Gorman, Patrick Hines, Richard Kavanaugh, Maureen Quinn, Eve Roberts, Archie Smith, Josef Sommer, Theodore Sorel, Vern Taylor, Stanley Anderson, Pearl Castle, Jeffery Craggs, Glenn Johnson, John Odegard, Kent Bishop, Ellen Caster, Chris Ditmars, John M. Gavigan, Jana Hellmuth, Mel Kleb II, Vincent Landro.

PRODUCTIONS
CENTER PLAYHOUSE: "Henry IV, Part I," "The Rehearsal," "You Can't Take It With You," "The Rivals," "The Father," "Threepenny Opera."

OFF CENTER THEATRE: "The Death of Bessie Smith," "The American Dream," "U.S.A.," "Little Murders," "Christopher" (World Premiere), "Krapp's Last Tape," "Infancy," "Childhood," "Brecht On Brecht."

Camera West Photos

John Gilbert, Jeffery Craggs, Patricia Hamilton in "Little Murders"

Archie Smith, Maureen Quinn, Theodore Sorel, Jacqueline Coslow, Patrick Hines in "You Can't Take It With You"

Josef Sommer, Pauline Flanagan in "The Fath—

Nancy Black, Joseph Medalis, Sirin Devrim
in "The Inspector General"

STANFORD REPERTORY THEATER
Stanford University, Calif.
Nov. 29, 1967 through May 11, 1968
Gerald Hiken, Artistic Director

Directors, Sirin Devrim, Douglas Johnson, Charles Olsen, William Sharp; Manager, Judith Burgess; Technical Director, Derek Hunt; Designers, Larry Davidson, Richard L. Hay, James Lyons, Jerome Marcel, Steven A. Maze, Carol Rountree, Douglas A. Russell, Nancy TenBroeck, Warren Travis; Stage Manager, Katherine Robertson; Costume Supervisor, Robin Coon; Press, Maggie McComas, Thomas Stockfisch.

COMPANY

Glenn Cannon, Sirin Devrim, Sheldon Feldner, Anne Gerety, Gerald Hiken, Elizabeth Huddle, Ruth Hunt, Stephen D. Newman, Paul E. Richards.

PRODUCTIONS

"The Cavern," "Candaules, Commissioner," "Cock-A-Doodle Dandy," "The Inspector General."

Hank Kranzler Photos

Sirin Devrim, Mary Staton in "The Cavern"

Sirin Devrim (L), William Clebsch (R)
in "The Cavern"

Gerald Hiken, Paul E. Richards, Joseph Medalis
in "Cock-A-Doodle Dandy"

Elizabeth Huddle, Sheldon Feldner,
N. R. Davidson in "Candaules, Commissioner"

205

STUDIO ARENA THEATRE
Buffalo, N. Y.
Sept. 28, 1967 through June 8, 1968
Neal Du Brock, Executive Producer

Associate Director, Allan Leicht; General Manager, Norman Leger; Assistant Director, Kathryn Kingdon; Press, Blossom Cohan; Director Emeritus, Jane Keeler; Stage Managers, Stephen H. Foreman, Peter J. Hajduk, Louis Pulvino; Technical Directors, Ed Cox, Harold Head; Production Assistant, Terry Baum; Scenery and Lighting, William Ritman, David Zierk, Eugene Lee; Costumes, Jean M. Blanchette; Judith Haugan; Original Music, T. V. Figenshu; Musical Director, Stuart Hamilton, Philip Saltz; Directors, Tom Gruenewald, Donald Davis, Allan Leicht, Stephen Porter, Warren Enters, Alan Schneider, Maurice Breslow.

COMPANY
Vincent Baggetta, Milton Bailey, Ann Bailey, Alice Beardsley, Sally Birckhead, Montgomery Davis, Donald Ewer, Frank Georgianna, Jean Hebborn, Patricia Lebby, Betty Leighton, Betty Lutes, Kenneth McMillan, Joe Servello, Laura Stuart, David Rae Smith, Dennis Thatcher, Kenneth Wickes, Vincent Milana, Philip Polito, Stefan Gierasch, John Devlin, Dean Santoro, Jean Paul Lanvin, Henderson Forsythe, Carolyn Coates, Sada Thompson, Barbette Tweed, Georgia Hester, Douglas Easley, Ruth White, Lucille Patton, Jenny Egan, Conrad Yama, William Needles, Bruce Gray, Leslie Carlson, Paxton Whitehead, Melody Greer, Margaret Gathright, Kristine Hatch, John Glover, Laurie Kennedy, Paul Vincent.

PRODUCTIONS
"The Threepenny Opera," "The Imaginary Invalid," "H.M.S. Pinafore," "The Emperor," "A Delicate Balance," World Premier of "Box" and "Quotations From Chairman Mao Tse-Tung," "Charley's Aunt," "The Knack."

Sherwin Greenberg, McGranahan and May Photos

Right Top: John Devlin, Betty Leighton in "The Emperor." **Below:** Bruce Gray, John Glover, Laurie Kennedy, Paul Vincent in "The Knack"

William Needles, Conrad Yama, Lucille Patton, Jenny Egan in "Quotations From Chairman Mao Tse-Tung"

Sada Thompson, Henderson Forsythe, Carolyn Coates in "A Delicate Balance"

THEATRE ATLANTA
Atlanta, Ga.
Oct. 11, 1967 through May 26, 1968
Jay Broad, Managing Director

Administrative Director, Leonard Edelstein; Press, Bolton Lunceford, Marianna Lines, Carolyn Oettinger; Executive Design, David Chapman; Technical Director, Ted Harris; Costumer, David Charles; Scenic Artist, James Othuse; Stage Manager, Peter J. Perry; Sound Technician, Gary Heyden; Lighting, Carolyn Saunders.

COMPANY

Georgia Allen, Sam Andrews, Terrell Bennett, Lee Blackwell, Mildred Brown, Arthur Burghardt, Ronald Bush, Fred Chappell, Stuart Culpepper, Raymond Edmonds, Karl Emery, Clarence Felder, Jim Garner, Gordon Greene, Anne Haney, Ted D. Harris, Sandy McCallum, Dick Montagne, Kelly McEvoy, Linda Moore, Muriel Moore, Margo McElroy, Charles Munro, Arlene Nadel, George Riddle, Cathy Rives, Judy Schoen, Susan Shalhoub, Dino Shorte, Patricia Walsh.

PRODUCTIONS

"Who Was That Lady I Saw You With?," "The Andersonville Trial," "Who's Afraid Of Virginia Woolf?," "MacBird!," "The Mad Show," "The Marriage-Go-Round," "J. B.," "The Member Of The Wedding," "Lysistrata," "The Investigation," "Lee Harvey Oswald,' "The Unknown Soldier and His Wife."

Charles Rafshoon Photos

Top Right: Clarence Felder, Jim Garner in
"The Unknown Soldier and His Wife"
Below: "Lee Harvey Oswald"

"The Member of The Wedding"
Above: "The Investigation"

"Lysistrata." Above: Jim Garner (L)
in "MacBird!"

Paul Benedict, Jon Voight, Jeremiah Sullivan
in "The Dwarfs"

THEATRE COMPANY OF BOSTON
Boston, Mass.
Nov. 30, 1967 through Apr. 28, 1968
David Wheeler, Director

Producer, Frank Cassidy; Associate Producer, Sara O'Connor; Assistant to Producer, Timothy Affleck; Scenery, Charles Norton, Robert Allen; Costumes, Cynthia Pallian, Catherine King; Lighting, Lance Crocker; Associate Director, Paul Benedict; Music, Ervin Henning, Michael Tschudin, Willie Alexander; Press, Marsha Hanlon; Sound Consultant, Peter Judd; Guest Director, Theodore Mann; Production Coordinator, William King; Stage Manager, Lance Crocker.

COMPANY

Paul Benedict, Susan Channing, Laurie Gould, Richard Hughes, Arthur Merrow, Jeremiah Sullivan, Jon Voight, Larry Bryggman, Carolyn Coates, Roberta Collinge, William Cottrell, Theodore Kazanoff, Josephine Lane, Lisa Richards, Robert Rockman, Harriet Rogers, James Spruill, William Young, Rodger W. Loomis, Joan Abrahams, John Parriott, Dana Nelson, Jeanette K. Caurant, Carolyn Michel, Charles Siebert, Felicia Soper, Linda DeCoff, Jack Lipner, Raymond Singer, Steven Ryan, George Ross Bickell, Jr., Michael St. George, W. G. McMillan, Paul Crafin, Dan Goldman, Gustave Johnson, Naomi Thornton, Joan Potter, Patricia O'Connell, Joan Croydon, Guy Spaull, Michael Currie, Christopher Clark, Ellen Olivier, John Hanley, Ralph Waite, Eve Whyte.

PRODUCTIONS

American Premiere of "The Dwarfs," "The Local Stigmatic," and "Left-Handed Liberty," "Who's Afraid Of Virginia Woolf?," "Stop, You're Killing Me!," "The End Of The World," "The Fun War," "The Innocent Party," "Hogan's Goat," "Phaedra," "The Great Fugue."

B. F. Herzog Photos

Larry Bryggman, Paul Benedict in "The Fun War"
Above: Roberta Collinge, Larry Bryggman in
"Stop, You're Killing Me!"

Michael Currie, Patricia O'Connell
in "Hogan's Goat"

Clinton Anderson, William Cain,
Ed Hall in "Julius Caesar"

TRINITY SQUARE REPERTORY COMPANY
Providence, R. I.
Oct. 5, 1967 through May 18, 1968
Fifth Season
Adrian Hall, Artistic Director

Managing Director, David H. Harper; Music, Richard Cumming; Settings, Eugene Lee; Lighting, Roger Morgan; Costumes, John Lehmeyer; Stage Managers, Franklin Keysar, Robert Applegarth; Press, Nance Movsesian; Technical Director, Steve Crowley; Technical Coordinator, Bree Cavazos; Directors, Adrian Hall, Henry Butler.

COMPANY

Andra Akers, Clinton Anderson, Leta Anderson, William Cain, Robert J. Colonna, June Emery, James Eichelberger, Ronald C. Frazier, James Gallery, Peter Gerety, Ed Hall, Katherine Helmond, Dorrie Kavanaugh, Richard Kneeland, Stephen Knox, Marguerite H. Lenert, Marius F. Mazmanian, Barbara Orson, Anthony Palmer, Robert Patterson, Donald Somers, Terence Turner, Robert Van Hooton, Joan White.

PRODUCTIONS

"The Threepenny Opera," "Julius Caesar," "The Importance Of Being Earnest," World Premiere of "Years Of The Locust," "An Enemy Of The People," "Phaedra."

This company was invited to present its World Premiere production of "Years Of The Locust" at the Edinburgh International Festival in August of 1968.

Left: Marguerite Lenert, Clinton Anderson, Katherine Helmond, Richard Kneeland, June Emery, William Cain, James Gallery in "The Importance of Being Earnest"

Katherine Helmond, Marguerite Oenone
in "Phaedra"

James Gallery, Katherine Helmond, Richard
Kneeland in "Years of The Locust"

209

YALE REPERTORY THEATRE COMPANY
New Haven, Conn.
Oct. 16, 1967 through May 18, 1968
Larry Arrick, Artistic Director

Dean of Drama School, Robert Brustein; Administrative Dean, Howard Stein; Managing Director, Thomas Burrows; Assistant, Jan Geidt; Press, David Freeman; Technical Director, William Taylor; Stage Managers, Mark Daniel Healy, Roger Hendricks Simon; Costumer, Lucie Palmer; Administrative Assistant, Charles Dillingham; Lighting, Steven Waxler; Sound, Jeffrey Milet; Directors, Larry Arrick, Kenneth Haigh, Carl Weber.

COMPANY
Rose Arrick, Kenneth Haigh, Jeanne Hepple, Anthony Holland, Richard Jordan, John Karlen, Stacy Keach, Ron Leibman, Michael Lombard, Paul Mann, John McCurry, Barry Morse, Estelle Parsons, Tom Rosqui, Roger Hendricks Simon, Nancy Wickwire, Kathleen Widdoes, Harris Yulen.

PRODUCTIONS
" 'Tis Pity She's A Whore," "We Bombed In New Haven" (Premiere), "Henry IV," "The Three Sisters," "Coriolanus."

Henry Grossman, Sedat Pakay, Joseph Cazalet Photos

Kathleen Widdoes, Paul Mann, Ron Leibman in "The Three Sisters"

Ron Leibman in "We Bombed New Haven"

John Karlen, Kathleen Widdoes in
" 'Tis Pity She's A Whore" Above:
Kenneth Haigh, Jeanne Hepple in "Henry IV"

PROMISING PERSONALITIES OF 1967-68

David Birney of "Summertree"

Pamela Burrell of "Arms and The Man"

Sandy Duncan of "Ceremony of Innocence"

Jordan Christopher of "Black Comedy"

Julie Gregg of "The Happy Time"

Jack Crowder of "Hello, Dolly!"

Stephen Joyce of "Stephen D."

Bernadette Peters of "George M!"

Alice Playten of "Henry, Sweet Henry"

Mike Rupert of "The Happy Time"

Rusty Thacker of "Your Own Thing"

Brenda Smiley of "Scuba Duba"

1944-45: Betty Comden, Richard Davis, Richard Hart, Judy Holliday, Charles Lang, Bambi Linn, John Lund, Donald Murphy, Nancy Noland, Margaret Phillips, John Raitt

1945-46: Barbara Bel Geddes, Marlon Brando, Bill Callahan, Wendell Corey, Paul Douglas, Mary James, Burt Lancaster, Patricia Marshall, Beatrice Pearson

1946-47: Keith Andes, Marion Bell, Peter Cookson, Ann Crowley, Ellen Hanley, John Jordan, George Keane, Dorothea MacFarland, James Mitchell, Patricia Neal, David Wayne

1947-48: Valerie Bettis, Edward Bryce, Whitfield Connor, Mark Dawson, June Lockhart, Estelle Loring, Peggy Maley, Ralph Meeker, Meg Mundy, Douglas Watson, James Whitmore, Patrice Wymore

1948-49: Tod Andrews, Doe Avedon, Jean Carson, Carol Channing, Richard Derr, Julie Harris, Mary McCarty, Allyn Ann McLerie, Cameron Mitchell, Gene Nelson, Byron Palmer, Bob Scheerer

1949-50: Nancy Andrews, Phil Arthur, Barbara Brady, Lydia Clarke, Priscilla Gillette, Don Hanmer, Marcia Henderson, Charlton Heston, Rick Jason, Grace Kelly, Charles Nolte, Roger Price

1950-51: Barbara Ashley, Isabel Bigley, Martin Brooks, Richard Burton, James Daly, Cloris Leachman, Russell Nype, Jack Palance, William Smithers, Maureen Stapleton, Marcia Van Dyke, Eli Wallach

1951-52: Tony Bavaar, Patricia Benoit, Peter Conlow, Virginia de Luce, Ronny Graham, Audrey Hepburn, Diana Herbert, Conrad Janis, Dick Kallman, Charles Proctor, Eric Sinclair, Kim Stanley, Marian Winters, Helen Wood

1952-53: Edie Adams, Rosemary Harris, Eileen Heckart, Peter Kelley, John Kerr, Richard Kiley, Gloria Marlowe, Penelope Munday, Paul Newman, Sheree North, Geraldine Page, John Stewart, Ray Stricklyn, Gwen Verdon

1953-54: Orson Bean, Harry Belafonte, James Dean, Joan Diener, Ben Gazzara, Carol Haney, Jonathan Lucas, Kay Medford, Scott Merrill, Elizabeth Montgomery, Leo Penn, Eva Maria Saint

1954-55: Julie Andrews, Jacqueline Brookes, Shirl Conway, Barbara Cook, David Daniels, Mary Fickett, Page Johnson, Loretta Leversee, Jack Lord, Dennis Patrick, Anthony Perkins, Christopher Plummer

1955-56: Diane Cilento, Dick Davalos, Anthony Franciosa, Andy Griffith, Laurence Harvey, David Hedison, Earle Hyman, Susan Johnson, John Michael King, Jayne Mansfield, Sarah Marshall, Gaby Rodgers, Susan Strasberg, Fritz Weaver

1956-57: Peggy Cass, Sydney Chaplin, Sylvia Daneel, Bradford Dillman, Peter Donat, George Grizzard, Carol Lynley, Peter Palmer, Jason Robards, Cliff Robertson, Pippa Scott, Inga Swenson

1957-58: Anne Bancroft, Warren Berlinger, Colleen Dewhurst, Richard Easton, Timmy Everett, Eddie Hodges, Joan Hovis, Carol Lawrence, Jacqueline McKeever, Wynne Miller, Robert Morse, George C. Scott

1958-59: Lou Antonio, Ina Balin, Richard Cross, Tammy Grimes, Larry Hagman, Dolores Hart, Roger Mollien, France Nuyen, Susan Oliver, Ben Piazza, Paul Roebling, William Shatner, Pat Suzuki, Rip Torn

1959-60: Warren Beatty, Eileen Brennan, Carol Burnett, Patty Duke, Jane Fonda, Anita Gillette, Elisa Loti, Donald Madden, George Maharis, John McMartin, Lauri Peters, Dick Van Dyke

1960-61: Joyce Bulifant, Dennis Cooney, Nancy Dussault, Robert Goulet, Joan Hackett, June Harding, Ron Husmann, James MacArthur, Bruce Yarnell

1961-62: Elizabeth Ashley, Keith Baxter, Peter Fonda, Don Galloway, Sean Garrison, Barbara Harris, James Earl Jones, Janet Margolin, Karen Morrow, Robert Redford, John Stride, Brenda Vaccaro

1962-63: Alan Arkin, Stuart Damon, Melinda Dillon, Robert Drivas, Bob Gentry, Dorothy Loudon, Brandon Maggart, Julienne Marie, Liza Minnelli, Estelle Parsons, Diana Sands, Swen Swenson

1963-64: Alan Alda, Gloria Bleezarde, Imelda De Martin, Claude Giraud, Ketty Lester, Barbara Loden, Lawrence Pressman, Gilbert Price, Philip Proctor, John Tracy, Jennifer West

1964-65: Carolyn Coates, Joyce Jillson, Linda Lavin, Luba Lisa, Michael O'Sullivan, Joanna Pettet, Beah Richards, Jaime Sanchez, Victor Spinetti, Nicholas Surovy, Robert Walker, Clarence Williams III

1965-66: Zoe Caldwell, David Carradine, John Cullum, John Davidson, Faye Dunaway, Gloria Foster, Robert Hooks, Jerry Lanning, Richard Mulligan, April Shawhan, Sandra Smith, Lesley Ann Warren

1966-67: Bonnie Bedelia, Richard Benjamin, Dustin Hoffman, Terry Kiser, Reva Rose, Sheila Smith, Connie Stevens, Pamela Tiffin, Leslie Uggams, Jon Voight, Christopher Walken

| Carol Channing | George Grizzard | Rosemary Harris | Paul Newman |

Murray Abraham

George Addis

Joe Alfasa

Mary Alice

Osceola Archer

BIOGRAPHIES
OF THIS SEASON'S CASTS

ABEL, WALTER. Born in St. Paul, Minn., June 6, 1898. Studied at American Academy of Dramatic Arts. Made NY bow in 1918 and has appeared in such plays as "Forbidden," "Back To Methuselah", "A Square Peg," "As You Like It," "The Enemy," "Taming of The Shrew," "Hangman's House," "Beyond The Horizon," "Skidding," "The Seagull," "Mourning Becomes Electra," "When Ladies Meet," "Invitation To A Murder," "Merrily We Roll Along," "Wingless Victory," "Mermaids Singing," "Parlor Story," "Biggest Thief In Town," "Wisteria Trees," "The Long Watch," "The Pleasure of His Company," "Night Life," "90 Day Mistress."

ABRAHAM, F. MURRAY. Born Oct. 24, 1939 in Pittsburgh. Attended U.Tex. Made Off-Bdwy bow in 1967 in "The Fantasticks," followed by "An Opening In The Trees," "The Fourteenth Dictator," and "Young Abe Lincoln."

ADDIS, GEORGE. Born in NYC. Has appeared Off-Bdwy in "Dr. Faustus," and made Bdwy bow this season with the APA-Phoenix production of "Pantagleize."

ADLER, LUTHER. Born in New York City, May 4, 1903. Attended Lewis Inst. Made first appearance in 1908 in "Schmendrick." Other performances include "Night Over Taos," "Success Story," "Alien Corn," "Men In White," "Gold Eagle Guy," "Awake And Sing," "Paradise Lost," "Johnny Johnson," "Golden Boy," "Rocket To The Moon," "The Russian People," "Two On An Island," "Common Ground," "Beggars Are Coming To Town," "Dunnigan's Daughter," "A Flag Is Born," "The Merchant of Venice," "A Month In The Country," "A Very Special Baby," "The Passion of Josef D," "The Three Sisters," "Fiddler On The Roof."

ADRIAN, MAX. Born in Ireland, Nov. 1, 1903. Attended Portora Royal School. Appeared with Old Vic, in London musicals, and in NY in "College Sinners," "Candide," "Mary Stuart," "The Lesson," "The Deadly Game," and "By George."

ALDA, ALAN. Born in New York City, Jan. 28, 1936. Attended Fordham Univ. and Cleveland Playhouse. Broadway credits include "Only In America," "Purlie Victorious," "Fair Game For Lovers" for which he won a THEATRE WORLD Award, and "Cafe Crown." Off-Broadway credits: "Darwin's Theories," "A Whisper In God's Ear," and "Second City" (1963 edition), "The Owl and the Pussycat," "The Apple Tree."

ALDREDGE, TOM. Born in Dayton, Ohio, Feb. 28, 1928. Attended U. of Dayton, and Goodman Theatre. Made Broadway bow in 1959 in "The Nervous Set." Has appeared Off-Bdwy in "The Tempest," "Between Two Thieves," "Henry V," "The Premise," "Love's Labour's Lost," "Troilus and Cressida," and in "UTBU," "Slapstick Tragedy," "The Butter and Egg Man," "Everything In The Garden," "Ergo" (OB).

ALFASA, JOE. Born in NYC. Dec. 13, 1914. Attended American Theatre Wing, Columbia. Made Broadway debut in 1938 in "Pins and Needles," followed by many productions including "And The Wind Blows," "Capacity For Wings," "Out Of This World," "Look After Lulu," "Once Upon A Mattress," "The Wall," "Illya, Darling."

ALICE, MARY. Born in Indianola, Miss., Dec. 3, 1941. Has appeared Off-Bdwy in "Happy Ending," "Day of Absence," "Trials of Brother Jero," "Strong Breed."

ALLEN, JUDY. Born Aug. 14, 1945 in NYC. Graduate of Brandeis U. Made Debut Off-Bdwy in 1967 in "Now Is The Time For All Good Men," followed by "Carving A Statue" (OB).

ALLEN, MICHAEL K. Born in NYC Jan. 23, 1940. Graduate of Boston U. Made NY debut in "New Faces of 1968."

ALPERN, SUSAN. Born in Forest Hills, N.Y., July 23, 1955. Appeared Off-Bdwy in "Heidi" before making Bdwy debut Feb. 1, 1968 in "Joe Egg."

ALVAREZ, CARMEN. Born July 2 in Hollywood, Calif. Made Bdwy debut in 1954 in "Pajama Game," followed by "Li'l Abner," "West Side Story," "Bye Bye Birdie," "That Hat" (OB), "Cole Porter Revisited" (OB), "The Apple Tree."

AMECHE, DON. Born May 31, 1908 in Kenosha, Wis. Made NY debut in 1929 in "Jerry-For-Short," followed by "Silk Stockings," "Holiday For Lovers," "Goldilocks," "13 Daughters," "Henry, Sweet Henry," and "The Odd Couple" on tour.

AMES, LEON. Born Jan. 20, 1903 in Portland, Ind. Attended Ind. U. Appeared in stock and touring companies before his Bdwy debut in 1936 in "Bright Honor," followed by "A House In The Country," "Thirsty Soil," "The Male Animal," "The Land Is Bright," "Guest In The House," "Little Darling," "The Russian People," "Slightly Married," "Paradise Question," "Winesberg, Ohio," "Howie," "Life With Father" (CC).

AMIC-ANGELO, ANDREW. Born Feb. 27, 1943 in Boston. Attended Leland Powers School of Theatre. Appeared Off-Bdwy in "A View From The Bridge" before making Bdwy debut in "The Unknown Soldier and His Wife."

ANDRE, FRANK. Born Dec. 30, 1942 in Philadelphia. Attended Stella Adler School. Made Bdwy bow in 1964 in "Ben Franklin In Paris," followed by "As I Lay Dying," "Brigadoon" (CC1967), "Who's Who, Baby?" and "Now" (OB).

ANGEL, LOU. Born in Chicago, Aug. 18, 1940. Made Bdwy debut in 1967 in "Hallelujah, Baby!"

ARCHER, OSCEOLA. Born in Albany, Ga. Degrees from Howard U. and NYU. Made Bdwy debut in 1934 in "Between Two Worlds," followed by "Panic," "The Cat Screams," "Hippolytus," "Romeo and Juliet" (CP), with Natl. Rep. Theatre in "Ring Round The Moon," "The Crucible," and "The Sea Gull," "The Guide."

ARMUS, SIDNEY. Born in the Bronx, Dec. 19, 1924. Attended Bklyn College. Has appeared in "South Pacific," "Wish You Were Here," "Flowering Peach," "A Hole In The Head," "The Cold Wind and The Warm," "Harold," "A Thousand Clowns," "Never Live Over A Pretzel Factory," "The Odd Couple."

ARNOLD, VICTOR. Born July 1, 1936 in Herkimer, N.Y. Graduate of NYU. Made Broadway bow in 1964 in "The Deputy." Has appeared Off-Bdwy in "Shadow Of Heroes," "Merchant Of Venice," "3 X 3," and "Lovey," and in "Malcolm," "Fortune and Men's Eyes."

ARTHUR, BEATRICE. Born in NYC, May 13. Attended The New School. Has appeared in "Seventh Heaven" (1954), "Nature's Way," "The Threepenny Opera," "Shoestring Revue," "Ulysses in Nighttown," "The Gay Divorce," "Fiddler On The Roof," "Mame."

| Hope Arthur | John C. Attle | Charles Austin | Patrick Baldauff | Leslie Barret |

ARTHUR, HOPE. Born in Chicago. Graduate of Northwestern U. Attended Royal Academy, London. Made Bdwy debut in "The Best House In Naples," and appeared Off-Bdwy in "Murder In The Cathedral," "The Learned Ladies," "Othello," "Golden Boy," "Blood Wedding," "Queen After Death," "The Cenci," "Lady From The Sea," "Hey, You, Light Man," and "Ergo."

ASTREDO, HUMBERT ALLEN. Born in San Francisco where he attended its Univ. Made NY debut Off-Bdwy in "Arms and The Man" (1967) followed by "Fragments."

ATHAS, NICK. Born in Paterson, N.J., Apr. 22, 1937. Attended Fairleigh Dickinson U. Appeared Off-Bdwy in "Carousel" (LC), and "The Secret Life of Walter Mitty" before making Bdwy bow in 1967 in "Illya Darling."

ATKINS, EILEEN. Born in London, June 16, 1934. Attended Guildhall School. Appeared on London stage before making Bdwy debut in 1966 in "The Killing of Sister George," followed by "The Promise."

ATKINS, TOM. Born in Pittsburgh, Pa. Graduate of Duquesne U. and American Academy of Dramatic Art. Has appeared on Bdwy in "Keep It In The Family," and with LC Rep. Co. in "The Unknown Soldier and His Wife" and "Cyrano de Bergerac."

ATKINSON, DAVID. Born in Montreal, Can., Oct. 20, 1921. Attended McGill U. and Pasadena Playhouse. Has appeared in "Inside U.S.A.," "Girl In Pink Tights," "The Vamp," City Center revivals of "Carousel," "Kiss Me, Kate," "Brigadoon," and "Annie Get Your Gun," "Man of La Mancha."

ATTLE, JOHN C. Graduate of U. Wash. Toured in "Bye Bye Birdie" before making Bdwy debut in "Fiddler On The Roof."

AUSTIN, CHARLES. Appeared in stock and with American Shakespeare Festival before making Bdwy bow in 1967 "Halfway Up The Tree."

BACALL, LAUREN. Born in NYC, Sept. 16, 1924. Attended AADA, and made Bdwy debut in 1942 in "Johnny 2 x 4," followed by "Goodbye Charlie," "The Cactus Flower."

BADDELEY, HERMIONE. Born in Broseley, Eng. on Nov. 13. Established London star before making Bdwy debut in 1961 in "A Taste of Honey," followed by "The Milk Train Doesn't Stop Here Anymore," and Off-Bdwy in "I Only Want An Answer."

BAILEY, PEARL. Born in Newport News, Va., Mar. 29, 1918. Appeared in vaudeville and nightclubs before making Bdwy debut in 1946 in "St. Louis Woman," followed by "Arms and The Girl," "House of Flowers," "Hello, Dolly!"

BAIN, CONRAD. Born in Lethbridge, Can. Feb. 4, 1923. Attended AADA. Has appeared in "Sixth Finger In A Five Finger Glove," "Candide," "The Makropoulos Secret," "Hot Spot," "Advise and Consent," "The Queen and The Rebels," "Hogan's Goat," "The Kitchen," "Scuba Duba."

BALABAN, ROBERT. Born in Chicago, Aug. 16, 1945. Attended Colgate U. and NYU. Made NY debut Off-Bdwy in 1967 in "You're A Good Man, Charlie Brown," and Bdwy debut in 1968 in "Plaza Suite."

BALDAUFF, PATRICK. Born Feb. 18, 1938 in Butler, Pa. Attended Columbia. Appeared Off-Bdwy in "Barroom," "Like I'm Talking To You Now," "A Dream of Love," "Winter Journey," and made Bdwy bow in 1967 in "The Natural Look."

BALSAM, MARTIN. Born in NYC, Nov. 4, 1919. Trained at Actors Studio. Has appeared in "Ghost For Sale," "The Closing Door," "Sundown Beach," "Macbeth," "The Rose Tattoo," "Camino Real," "Middle of The Night," "The Porcelain Year," "You Know I Can't Hear You When The Water's Running."

BANCROFT, ANNE. Born in NYC Sept. 17, 1931. Attended AADA. Made Bdwy debut in 1958 in "Two For The Seesaw" for which she received a THEATRE WORLD Award, followed by "The Miracle Worker," "Mother Courage and Her Children," "The Devils," "The Little Foxes." (1967).

BARBOUR, THOMAS. Born in NYC July 25, 1921. Graduate of Princeton and Harvard. Has appeared Off-Bdwy in "Twelfth Night," "Merchant of Venice," "The Admirable Bashville," "River Line," "The Lady's Not For Burning," "The Enchanted," "Antony and Cleopatra," "The Saintliness of Margery Kemp," "Dr. Willy Nilly," "Under The Sycamore Tree," "Epitaph For George Dillon," "Thracian Horse," "The Old Glory," "Serjeant Musgrave's Dance," and on Bdwy in "Portrait of A Queen."

BARNEY, JAY. Born in Chicago, Mar. 14, 1918. Attended U. of Chicago, Am. Theatre Wing, Actors Studio. Has appeared in "The Respectful Prostitute," "Hope's The Thing With Feathers," "Detective Story," "The Number," "The Grass Harp," "Richard III," "Stockade," "The Immoralist," "The Trial," "The Young and Beautiful," "Eugenia," and Off-Bdwy in "A Certain Young Man," "Beyond Desire," and "Goa."

BARON, SANDY. Born in Brooklyn in 1938. Graduate of Bklyn College. Has appeared in "Second City," "The Premise," "Tchin-Tchin," "One Flew Over The Cuckoo's Nest," "Arturo Ui," "Generation," and "Muzeeka" (OB).

BARRETT, LAURINDA. Born in NYC in 1931. Attended Wellesley College and Royal Academy. Has appeared Off-Bdwy with the Shakespearewrights, in "The Misanthrope," and "Palm Tree In A Rose Garden," and on Bdwy in "Too Late The Phalarope," "The Girls In 509," "The Milk Train Doesn't Stop Here Anymore," "UTBU," "I Never Sang For My Father."

BARRETT, LESLIE. Born in NYC, Oct. 30, 1919. Made Bdwy bow in 1936 in "But For The Grace of God," followed by "An Enemy of The People," "Dead End," "Sunup To Sundown," "There's Always A Breeze," "Primrose Path," "Stroke of Eight," "Horse Fever," "Good Neighbor," "All In Favor," "Counsellor At Law," "Deadfall," "Rhinocerous," "The Investigation," "Hamp" (OB).

BARRS, NORMAN. Born in London, Nov. 6, 1917. Appeared in NY with Dublin Gate Co. in "The Old Lady Says No!" and "Where Stars Walk," and in "Now I Lay Me Down To Sleep," "The Little Glass Clock," "The Apple Cart," "The Little Moon of Alban," "Kwamina," "Poor Bitos," "The Zulu and The Zayda," "Hostile Witness," "Loot."

BARTENIEFF, GEORGE. Born in Berlin, Jan. 24, 1933. Made Bdwy bow in 1947 in "The Whole World Over," followed by "Venus Is," "All's Well That Ends Well," and Off-Bdwy in "Walking To Waldheim" and "The Memorandum."

BARTON, GARY. Born in Boston, Sept. 1, 1947. Attended NYU. Made Bdwy debut in 1966 in "The Loves of Cass McGuire," followed by LC Repertory productions of "The Unknown Soldier and His Wife," and "Cyrano de Bergerac."

hard Basehart   Yolande Bavan   Edward Becker   Bob Berger   Stephen Bernstein

BASEHART, RICHARD. Born in Zanesville, Ohio. Has appeared in "Counterattack," "Othello," "Take it As It Comes," "Ramshackle Inn," "Hickory Stick," "The Hasty Heart," "The Day The Money Stopped," 1962 Stratford Shakespeare productions, and in name role of LC Rep. Co. previews of "Cyrano de Bergerac" which he had to leave because of illness.

BATTLES, MARJORIE. Born in Philadelphia, June 5, 1939. Attended Brandeis U. Appeared in stock before making Bdwy debut in 1965 in "The Cactus Flower."

BAUERSMITH, PAULA. Born in Pittsburgh, July 26, 1909. Attended Carnegie Tech. Has appeared in "Lean Harvest," "East of Broadway," "The Warrior's Husband," "The Anatomist," "Three-Cornered Moon," "All Good American," "Mahogany Hall," "Let Freedom Ring," "Bury The Dead," "200 Were Chosen," "20th Century," "The Lesson," "Sail Away," and with Natl. Rep. Theatre.

BAVAN, YOLANDE. Born in Ceylon, June 1, 1942. Attended Univ. of Colombo, Ceylon. Appeared in London before making NY debut in 1964's CP production of "A Midsummer Night's Dream," followed by Off-Bdwy performances in "Jonah" and "House of Flowers."

BAXTER, CHARLES. Born in Paterson, N.J., Apr. 17, 1924. Attended Washington and Lee U., and Yale Drama School. Has appeared in "Oklahoma!," "Texas Li'l Darlin'," "Stalag 17," "Hook 'n' Ladder," "The Advocate," "Everything In The Garden."

BAXTER, KEITH. Born in Newport, Wales, Apr. 29, 1935. Graduate of Royal Academy of Dramatic Art. Made Bdwy debut in 1961 in "A Man For All Seasons" for which he received a THEATRE WORLD Award, followed by "The Affair," "Avanti!"

BEAN, ORSON. Born in Burlington, Vt., July 22, 1928. Made Bdwy bow in 1953 in "Men of Distinction," followed by "John Murray Anderson's Almanac" for which he received a THEATRE WORLD Award, "Will Success Spoil Rock Hunter?," "Nature's Way," CC revivals of "Mister Roberts" and "Say, Darling," "Subways Are For Sleeping," "Never Too Late," "Home Movies" (OB), "I Was Dancing," "Illya, Darling."

BECKER, EDWARD. Born in Astoria, N.Y. Studied at American Theatre Wing. Made Bdwy bow in 1951 in "Paint Your Wagon," followed by "Silk Stockings," "Happy Hunting," "Body Beautiful," "Whoop-Up," "Bye Bye Birdie," "Family Affair," "Camelot," "Here's Love," "Illya Darling," "Brigadoon" (CC1967).

BEDFORD, BRIAN. Born in Morley, Eng., Feb. 16, 1935. Attended RADA. Made NY bow in 1960 in "Five Finger Exercise," followed by "Lord Pengo," "The Private Ear" and "The Public Eye," "The Knack" (OB), "The Astrakhan Coat," "The Unknown Soldier and His Wife," "The Seven Descents of Myrtle."

BEL GEDDES, BARBARA. Born in NYC, Oct. 31, 1923. Has appeared in "Out of The Frying Pan," "Little Darling," "Nine Girls," "Mrs. January and Mr. X," "Deep Are The Roots" for which she received a THEATRE WORLD Award, "Burning Bright," "The Moon Is Blue," "The Sleeping Prince," "Silent Night, Lonely Night," "Mary, Mary," "The Porcelain Year," "Luv," "Everything In The Garden."

BELL, MARY. Born in Austin, Tex., Nov. 17, 1904. Attended U. of Texas. Among her many plays are "The Shrike," "Cat On A Hot Tin Roof," "Cloud 7," "The Miracle Worker," "Beyond Desire" (OB).

BELLINI, CAL. Born in San Francisco. Attended Princeton. Made Bdwy bow in 1959 in "Cut of The Axe," followed by "Ross," and "The Royal Hunt of The Sun," and Off-Bdwy in "Shakuntala," "Two by Saroyan," "The Immoralist," and "Goa."

BEN-AMI, JACOB. Born in 1890 in Minsk, Russia. Prominent on both English and Yiddish stages. Has appeared in "Samson and Delilah," "Johannes Kreisler," "The Idle Inn," "The Failures," "The Race With The Shadow," "Man and The Masses," "Schweiger," "Diplomacy," Civic Rep. Theatre productions, "Evensong," "A Ship Comes In," "Who Is Who," "The Tenth Man," and Off-Bdwy in "The Seagull," "The Infernal Machine," "The World of Sholom Aleichem," "Walking To Waldheim" and "Happiness."

BENJAMIN, RICHARD. Born in NYC, May 22, 1938. Attended Northwestern U. After touring in "The Odd Couple," made Bdwy bow in 1966 in "The Star Spangled Girl" for which he received a THEATRE WORLD Award.

BENNETT, LINDA. Born in Salt Lake City, June 19, 1942. Has appeared in City Center revivals of "Brigadoon" (1964), and "Wonderful Town" (1967).

BERGER, BOB. Born July 25, 1922 in Davenport Iowa. Attended St. Ambrose College, AADA, and American Theatre Wing. Made Bdwy bow in 1946 "G.I. Hamlet," followed by "Trouble In July," "Our Town," Off-Bdwy in "Macbeth," "Many Loves," "Master Builder," "A Doll's House," and "Climate of Eden," and in "Dr. Cook's Garden."

BERGMAN, INGRID. Born Aug. 29, 1917, in Stockholm where she studied at Royal Dramatic Theatre. Appeared on stage and screen before making Bdwy debut in 1940 revival of "Liliom," followed by "Joan of Lorraine" and "More Stately Mansions."

BERLIN, ALEXANDRA. Born in NYC. Studied at Royal Academy, London. Has appeared Off-Bdwy in "La Ronde," "The Establishment Review," with NY and American Shakespeare Festivals, "The Knack," and "Eh?," and on Bdwy in "All In Good Time," "The Birthday Party," "Happiness Is Just A Little Thing Called A Rolls Royce."

BERNSTEIN, STEPHEN. Born in NYC, Mar. 27, 1944. Attended Carnegie Tech. and Goodman Theatre. Made Bdwy debut Oct. 16, 1967 in "Rosencrantz and Guildenstern Are Dead."

BIRD, JOSEPH. Born in Pittsburgh, Sept. 22, 1926. Graduate of Penn. State. Appeared Off-Bdwy in "Moon In The Yellow River," "Electra," "Go Show Me A Dragon," and made Bdwy debut with APA, with whom he appeared in "You Can't Take It With You," "Wild Duck," "School For Scandal," "Right You Are," "The Show-off" and "Pantagleize."

BIRNEY, DAVID. Born in Washington, D.C., Apr. 23, 1939. Graduate of Dartmouth and UCLA. Has appeared Off-Bdwy with NY Shakespeare Festival in "Comedy of Errors," "Titus Andronicus," and "King John," and in "MacBird," "Ceremony of Innocence," and "Summertree" for which he won a THEATRE WORLD Award.

BISHOP, RONALD. Born in New Haven, Conn., Mar. 28, 1923. Graduate of Ithaca College. Made Bdwy bow in 1943 in "Othello," followed by "Julius Caesar," "The Visit," and at Lincoln Center in "Galileo" and "St. Joan."

BLAKELY, GENE. Born in Osceola, Iowa, June 8, 1922. Attended U. of Wisc. Has appeared in "Brighten The Corner," "John Loves Mary," "Red Gloves," "The Traitor," "Mr. Barry's Etchings," "The Desperate Hours," "Teahouse of The August Moon," "A Mighty Man Is He," "Calculated Risk," "Weekend."

| Stephen Bolster | Ruth Brandeis | John Branon | Sherri Brewer | Oceana Briggs |

BLEEZARDE, GLORIA. Born in Albany, NY, Oct. 12, 1940. Attend Southern Seminary Jr. College. Appeared Off'Bdwy in "Just For Fun" and "New York Coloring Book" before Bdwy debut in 1964 in "Never Live Over A Pretzel Factory" for which she received a THEATRE WORLD Award, followed by "New Faces of 1968."

BLISS, IMOGENE. Born in Cleveland, O., Feb. 24, 1928. Attended Conn. College, Cleveland Playhouse and Max Reinhardt Workshop. Made Bdwy debut in 1967 in "Marat/DeSade," followed by "Your Own Thing" (OB).

BLOCK, CHAD. Born in Twin Falls, Idaho, May 1, 1938. Made Bdwy bow in 1954 in "The Vamp," followed by "Li'l Abner," "Destry Rides Again," "Take Me Along," "Do Re Mi," "Come On Strong," "Hello, Dolly!," "Walking Happy," "Hallelujah, Baby!"

BLYDEN, LARRY. Born in Houston, Tex., June 23, 1925. Made Bdwy bow in 1949 in "Mister Roberts," followed by "Wish You Were Here," "Oh, Men! Oh, Women!," "Italian Straw Hat" (OB), "Who Was That Lady I Saw You With?," "Flower Drum Song," "Foxy," "Blues For Mr. Charlie," "Luv," "The Apple Tree."

BOGERT, WILLIAM. Born in NYC, Jan. 25, 1936. Graduate of Yale. Has appeared Off-Bdwy in "The Country Wife," and with NY Shakespeare Festival in "The Taming of The Shrew," "Henry V," and "Love's Labour's Lost," and on Bdwy in "A Man For All Seasons," "Hamlet" (1964), "Star Spangled Girl," "The Cactus Flower."

BOLSTER, STEPHEN. Born in Cambridge, Mass., Apr. 7, 1933. Graduate of Harvard. Has appeared in "An Enemy of The People" (OB), "One More River," "Big Fish, Little Fish," "Here's Where I Belong," "The Education of Hyman Kaplan."

BOND, RUDY. Born in Philadelphia, Oct. 1, 1915. Attended U. Pa. Has appeared in "O'Daniel," "A Streetcar Named Desire," "Bird Cage," "Two Blind Mice," "Romeo and Juliet," "Glad Tidings," "Golden Boy," "Fiorello!," Off-Bdwy in "After The Fall," "Incident At Vichy," "Big Man" and "Match-Play," "Illya, Darling."

BOND, SUDIE. Born in Louisville, Ky., July 13, 1928. Attended Va. Intermont and Rollins Colleges, NYU. Has appeared Off-Bdwy in "Summer and Smoke," "Tovarich," "The American Dream," "The Sandbox," "Endgame," "Theatre of The Absurd," "Home Movies," "Softly and Consider The Nearness," and "The Memorandum," and on Bdwy in "Waltz of The Toreadors," "Auntie Mame," "The Egg," "Harold," "My Mother, My Father and Me," "The Impossible Years," "Keep It In The Family."

BOSCO, PHILIP. Born in Jersey City, N.J., Sept. 26, 1930. Graduate of Catholic U. Has appeared in "Auntie Mame," "Rape of The Belt," "Ticket of Leave Man" (OB), "Donnybrook," "Man For All Seasons," in American Shakespeare Festival productions, and with LC Rep. in "The Alchemist," "East Wind," "Galileo," "St. Joan," "Tiger At The Gates" and "Cyrano de Bergerac."

BOSLEY, TOM. Born in Chicago, Oct. 1, 1927. Attended DePaul U. Made Bdwy bow in 1959 in "Fiorello!," followed by "Nowhere To Go But Up," "Natural Affection," "A Murderer Among Us," "Catch Me If You Can," "Luv," "Education of Hyman Kaplan."

BOVA, JOSEPH. Born in Cleveland, O., May 25. Graduate of Northwestern U. Made NY debut Off-Bdwy in "On The Town" (1959), followed by "Once Upon A Mattress," "The Rape of The Belt," "Irma La Duce," "Hotspot," and with NY Shakespeare Festival in "Taming of The Shrew," "King Richard III," and "Comedy of Errors."

BRACKEN, EDDIE. Born in Astoria, N.Y., Feb. 7, 1920. Made Bdwy bow in 1931 in "The Man On Stilts," followed by "The Lady Refuses," "Life's Too Short," "The Iron Men," "Brother Rat," "What A Life," "Too Many Girls," "The Seven Year Itch," "Teahouse of The August Moon," "Shinbone Alley," "Beg, Borrow or Steal," "The Odd Couple."

BRANDEIS, RUTH. Born in NYC, May 31, 1942. Attended San Francisco State College. Has appeared Off-Bdwy in "Theatre of The Absurd," "Leave From Quintessence," "The Killers," and "Nighthawks."

BRANDON, BILL. Born in Newark, N.J., June 14, 1944. Attended college in Little Rock, Ark. Made Bdwy debut in 1965 in "Oliver," followed by "Funny Girl," "George M!"

BRANON, JOHN. Born in Chicago, Oct. 7, 1939. Attended Chicago City College. Made NY debut Off-Bdwy in 1967 in "Scuba Duba," and Bdwy bow in 1968 in "The Guide."

BRASWELL, CHARLES. Born in McKinney, Tex., Sept. 7. Attended Arlington State College. Made Bdwy bow in 1960 in "A Thurber Carnival," followed by "Wildcat," "Sail Away," "Hot Spot," "Here's Love," "I Had A Ball," "Me and Thee," "Mame."

BRESLIN, TOMMY. Born in Norwich, Conn., Mar. 24, 1946. Attended Iona College. Has appeared Off-Bdwy in "For Love Or Money," "Freedom Is A Two-edged Sword," and "Who's Who, Baby?"

BREWER, SHERRI "PEACHES". Born in Chicago, May 29. Studied at Goodman Theatre. Made Bdwy debut in 1967 in "Hello, Dolly!"

BRIDGES, LLOYD. Born in San Leandro, Calif., Jan. 15, 1913. Graduate of UCLA. Made Bdwy debut in 1953 in "Dead Pigion," followed by "Oh, Men! Oh, Women!," "Man of La Mancha," "The Cactus Flower."

BRIGGS, OCEANA. Born aboard the S.S. Arabia at sea in the Atlantic on Mar. 20, 1928. Appeared in vaudeville and circuses before making Bdwy debut in 1965 in "A Man For All Seasons," followed by "Spofford."

BRIGHT, RICHARD. Born in Brooklyn, June 28, 1937. Has appeared Off-Bdwy in "The Balcony," "Does A Tiger Wear A Necktie?," and "The Beard."

BRINCKERHOFF, BURT. Born in Pittsburgh, Oct. 25, 1936. Made Bdwy debut in 1958 in "Blue Denim," followed by "The Cactus Flower," "Keep It In The Family."

BRITTON, GARY. Born in East Cleveland, O., Dec. 19, 1943. Attended Hruby Conservatory of Music. Has appeared Off-Bdwy in "Awakening of Spring," "No Exit" and "Hamp."

BRODERICK, JAMES. Born in Charlestown, N.H., Mar. 7, 1928. Attended U. of N.H., and Neighborhood Playhouse. Made Bdwy bow in 1953 in Maggie," followed by Off-Bdwy roles in "A View From The Bridge," "A Touch Of The Poet," "Two By Saroyan," "The Firebugs," and "Rooms," and in "Johnny No Trump."

| Kermit Brown | Susan Browning | Norman Budd | Catherine Burns | Susan Camber |

BROWN, GRAHAM. Born in NYC, Oct. 24, 1924. Graduate of Howard U. Appeared Off-Bdwy in "Widower's Houses," "The Emperor's Clothes," "Time of Storm," "Major Barbara," "A Land Beyond The River," "The Blacks," "The Firebugs," before Bdwy debut in 1968 in "Weekend."

BROWN, KERMIT. Born in Asheville, N.C., Feb. 3, 1937. Graduate of Duke U. Has appeared with APA in "War and Peace," "Judith," "Man and Superman," "The Show-Off," "Pantagleize," "The Cherry Orchard."

BROWN, WALTER P. Born in Newark, N.J., Apr. 18, 1926. Attended Bklyn Conservatory of Music. Made Bdwy bow in "Porgy and Bess," followed by "Fiorello!," "The Advocate," City Center revivals of "Guys and Dolls," and "South Pacific," "Kelly," "Hello, Dolly!"

BROWNING, SUSAN. Born Feb. 25, 1941 in Baldwin, L.I., N.Y. Graduate Penn. State U. Made Bdwy debut in 1963 in "Love and Kisses," followed by Off-Bdwy roles in "Jo," "Dime A Dozen," "The Night Little Girl Blue Made Her Social Debut," "Seventeen," "Boys From Syracuse," and "Collision Course."

BRUCE, CAROL. Born in Great Neck, L.I., N.Y., Nov. 15, 1919. Made Bdwy debut in "George White's Scandals of 1939," followed by "Nice Goin'," "Louisiana Purchase," "Show Boat" (1946), "Along Fifth Avenue," "A Family Affair," "Pal Joey" (CC), "Do I Hear A Waltz?," "Henry, Sweet Henry."

BRYDON, W. W. Born in Newcastle, Eng., Sept. 20, 1933. Studied at Ray Lawlor Studio, Canada. Made NY bow Off-Bdwy in 1960 in "The Long, The Short, and The Tall," followed by "Live Like Pigs," "Sgt. Musgrave's Dance," "The Kitchen," "Come Slowly Eden," "The Unknown Soldier and His Wife."

BUBBLES, JOHN. Born in Louisville, Ky., Feb. 19, 1902. Appeared in minstrels, carnivals, circuses, and nightclubs, and on Bdwy in "Ziegfeld Follies," "Porgy and Bess," "Carmen Jones," "George White's Varieties," "Show Time," "Laugh Time," "Curtain Time," "At Home At The Palace."

BUDD, NORMAN. Born in Liverpool, Eng., Jan. 27, 1914. Attended DePaul U., Chicago U. Made Bdwy bow in 1937 in "The Eternal Road," followed by "As You Like It," "Candida," "Julius Caesar," "Tobacco Road," "The Merry Widow," "La Serva Padrona," "Hold It," and Off-Bdwy in "Winkleberg," "Mandragola," and "Beyond Desire."

BULL, PETER. Born in London, Mar. 21, 1912. Attended Winchester College, and Tours U. Has appeared on Bdwy in "Escape Me Never," "The Lady's Not For Burning," "Luther," "Pickwick," "Black Comedy."

BURGHOFF, GARY. Born in Bristol, Conn., May 24, 1943. Appeared in stock and nightclubs before making NY bow Off-Bdwy in 1967 in "You're A Good Man, Charlie Brown."

BURKS, DONNIE. Born in Martinsville, Va. Graduate of St. John's U. Appeared Off-Bdwy in 1964 in "Dutchman," and made Bdwy debut in 1968 in "Hair."

BURNS, CATHERINE. Born in NYC, Sept. 25, 1945. Attended Hunter College High School and AADA. Made Broadway debut in 1968 in "The Prime of Miss Jean Brodie."

BURNS, DAVID. Born in NYC, June 22, 1902. Has appeared in "Polly Preferred," "Wonder Boy," "Face The Music," "The Man Who Came To Dinner," "Pal Joey," "My Dear Public," "Billion Dollar Baby," "Make Mine Manhattan," "Out of This World," "Two's Company," "Men of Distinction," "A Hole In The Head," "Music Man," "A Funny Thing Happened On The Way To The Forum," "Hello, Dolly!"

BURR, ROBERT. Born in Jersey City, N.J. Attended Colgate U. Has appeared in "The Cradle Will Rock," "Mister Roberts," "Romeo and Juliet," "Picnic," "The Lovers," "Anniversary Waltz," "Top Man," "Remains To Be Seen," "The Wall," "Andersonville Trial," "A Shot In The Dark," "A Man For All Seasons," "Luther," "Hamlet" (1964), "Bajour," "The White Devil," "The Royal Hunt of The Sun," "Dinner At Eight," "King John" (CP).

BURRELL, FRED. Born in Cedar Rapids, Iowa, Sept. 18, 1936. Graduate of UNC and RADA, London. Made Bdwy bow in 1964 in "Never Too Late," followed by "Illya, Darling," "The Memorandum" (OB).

BURRELL, PAMELA. Born in Tacoma, Wash., Aug. 4, 1945. Made Broadway debut in 1966 in "Funny Girl," followed by an Off-Bdwy revival of "Arms and The Man" for which she received a THEATRE WORLD Award.

BURTON, WARREN. Born in Chicago, Oct. 23, 1944. Attended Wright College. Made NY bow in 1967 in "Hair."

BUZZI, RUTH. Born in Westerly, R.I., July 24, 1936. Studied at Pasadena Playhouse. Appeared Off-Bdwy in "Mis-Guided Tour," "A Man's A Man," "Babes In The Wood," "Baker's Dozen," and "The Game Is Up," before making Bdwy debut in 1966 in "Sweet Charity."

CALBES, ELEANOR. Born Feb. 20, 1940 in Aparri, Philippines. Graduate of U. Phil. and Royal Conservatory of Music, Toronto. Appeared in City Center revivals of "South Pacific" (1964 and 1967) and "The King and I" (1968).

CALDWELL, ZOE. Born in Melbourne, Aust., Sept. 14, 1933. Attended Methodist Ladies College. Made Bdwy debut in 1965 in "The Devils," followed by "Slapstick Tragedy" for which she received a THEATRE WORLD Award, "The Prime of Miss Jean Brodie."

CALL, JOHN. Born in Philadelphia, Nov. 3, 1915. Attended U. Pa. Has appeared in "Father Malachy's Miracle," "Merchant of Yonkers," "As You Like It," "Be So Kindly," "But For The Grace of God," "The Flying Gerardos," "So Proudly We Hail," "Bet Your Life," "Bloomer Girl," "Pipe Dream," "A Touch of The Poet," "Oliver!," "Pickwick," "A Time For Singing," NY Shakespeare Festival's "Comedy of Errors," and "Hamlet."

CAMBER, SUSAN. Born in Seattle, Jan. 1, 1947. Studied ballet before making Bdwy debut in 1968 in "The Education of Hyman Kaplan."

CAPODILUPO, TONY. Born in Boston, Oct. 30, 1940. Attended Boston U. and Yale. Made Bdwy bow in 1965 in "The Royal Hunt of The Sun," followed by Off-Bdwy roles in "MacBird," "To Clothe The Naked," "Ergo," and "Carving A Statue."

CARDWELL, CAROLYN Y. Born in Chicago, Nov. 17, 1938. Graduate of Marquette U. Has appeared in "Marat/Sade," and Off-Bdwy in "No Exit" and "Clara's Ole Man."

CARPENTER, CAROL. Born in Staten Island, Feb. 9, 1957. Made stage debut Off-Bdwy in 1967 in "Father Uxbridge Wants To Marry."

Dorothy Chace	Jo Flores Chase	Haig Chobanian	Oliver Clark	Richard Clark

CARR, KENNETH. Born May 3, 1943 in the Bronx, NY. Studied at Max Slater Academy. Made Bdwy debut in 1965 in "The Impossible Years."

CARROLL, DANNY. Born May 30, 1940 in Maspeth, L.I., N.Y. Made Bdwy bow in 1957 in "Music Man," followed by "The Boys From Syracuse" and "Babes In The Wood" Off-Bdwy, "Flora The Red Menace," "Funny Girl," "George M!"

CARROLL, HELENA. Born in Glasgow, Scot. Attended Weber-Douglas School of Drama in London. Came to US with Dublin Players. Founded, produced, directed, and acted with the Irish Players Off-Bdwy. Made Bdwy debut in 1956 in "Separate Tables," followed by "A Touch Of The Poet," "Happy As Larry," "Little Moon of Alban," "The Hostage," "Oliver!," "Pickwick," "Three Hand Reel" (OB), "Something Different."

CARSON, JOHN. Born in Colombo, Ceylon, Feb. 28, 1927. Attended Oxford U. Made Bdwy debut in 1968 in "A Day In The Death of Joe Egg."

CASE, ALLEN. Born in Dallas, Tex. Attended SMU. Has appeared in "Damn Yankees," "South Pacific" (CC), "Once Upon A Mattress," Off-Bdwy in "Pleasure Dome" and "The Carefree Heart," "Hallelujah, Baby!"

CASH, ROSALIND. Born in Atlantic City, Dec. 31, 1938. Attended CCNY. Made Bdwy debut in 1966 in "The Wayward Stork," followed by Off Bdwy roles in "Junebug Graduates Tonight," "Fiorello!" (CC), "To Bury A Cousin," "Song of The Lusitanian Bogey," "Kongi's Harvest."

CASS, PEGGY. Born in Boston, May 21, 1926. Attended Wyndham. Has appeared in "Touch and Go," "The Live Wire," "Bernardine," "Phoenix '55," "Othello," "Henry V," "Auntie Mame" for which she received a THEATRE WORLD Award, "A Thurber Carnival," "Children From Their Games," "Don't Drink The Water."

CASTELLANO, RICHARD. Born in Jackson Heights, N.Y., Sept. 4, 1933. Attended Columbia. Has appeared in "A View From The Bridge" (OB), "The Investigation," "That Summer—That Fall," "Mike Downstairs."

CATLETT, MARY JO. Born in Denver, Colo., Sept. 2, 1938. Graduate of Loretto Heights College. Has appeared in "Along Came A Spider," "New Girl In Town," "Fiorello!," "Pajama Game," "Hello, Dolly!"

CAVENS, ALBERT. Born in Brussels, Belgium, Oct. 7, 1921. After working in numerous films as fencing instructor, made NY debut in Lincoln Center's "Cyrano de Bergerac."

CHACE, DOROTHY. Born in North Bergen, N.J. Attended San Diego and San Francisco State Colleges, Stanford, and Yale. Has appeared with Lincoln Center Rep. Co. in "The Caucasian Chalk Circle" and "Cyrano de Bergerac."

CHALLENGER, RUDY. Born in NYC, Oct. 2, 1928. Has appeared in "Along Came A Spider" (OB), "Shakespeare In Harlem" (OB), "Tiger, Tiger, Burning Bright," "Tambourines To Glory," "Golden Boy," "Do I Hear A Waltz?," "On A Clear Day You Can See Forever," "My Sweet Charlie," "Scuba Duba" (OB).

CHANDLER, MILDRED. Born in 1902 in Florida. After dancing with Met. Opera Ballet, made Bdwy debut in "The World We Live In," followed by "International Revue," "Roman Candle," Mrs. McThing," and Off-Bdwy in "Six Characters in Search of An Author," "Anything Goes," and "Goa."

CHANNING, CAROL. Born in Seattle, Jan. 31, 1921. Attended Bennington College. Made Bdwy debut in 1941 in "No For An Answer," followed by "Let's Face It," "Proof Through The Night," "Lend An Ear" for which she received a THEATRE WORLD Award, "Gentlemen Prefer Blondes," "Wonderful Town," "The Vamp," "Show Girl," "Hello, Dolly!"

CHAPLIN, GERALDINE. Born July 31, 1944 in Santa Monica, Calif. Studied at Royal Ballet School, London. Made Bdwy debut Dec. 19, 1967 in "The Little Foxes."

CHARNEY, JORDAN. Born in NYC. Graduate of Bklyn College. Appeared Off-Bdwy in "Harry, Noon and Night," "A Place For Chance," "Hang Down Your Head and Die," "The Pinter Plays," "Telemachus Clay," "The Zoo Story," "Viet Rock," "MacBird," and "Red Cross," on Bdwy in "Slapstick Tragedy," "The Birthday Party."

CHASE, JO FLORES. Born in Pittsburgh. Graduate of Carnegie Tech. Has appeared Off-Bdwy in "Ivanov," in 1966 revival of "The Rose Tattoo," "Beyond Desire" (OB).

CHILD, MARILYN. Born in Santa Monica, Calif. Graduate of U. Cal. Made Bdwy debut in 1960 in "Do Re Mi," followed by "Hot Spot," "Upstairs At The Downstairs", and "The Mad Show" (OB), "New Faces of 1968."

CHOBANIAN, HAIG. Born in Racine, Wisc., Oct. 26, 1937. Attended U. Wisc. Has appeared Off-Bdwy in "The Shoemaker and The Peddler," "Banquet For The Moon," "MacBird," and 1967 City Center revival of "The Tenth Man."

CHOW, CARYN ANN. Born Dec. 13, 1957 in NYC. Made stage debut May 23, 1968 in "The King and I" (CC).

CHRISTOPHER, JORDAN. Born in Youngstown, O., Oct. 23, 1940. Attended Kent State U., and Akron Art Inst. Made Bdwy debut June 26, 1967 in "Black Comedy" for which he received a THEATRE WORLD Award.

CHURCH, TONY. Born in London, May 11, 1930. Attended Clare College, Eng. Has appeared in NYC with Royal Shakespeare Co. in 1964 in "King Lear," and in "Soldiers."

CLANTON, RALPH. Born in Fresno, Calif., Sept. 11, 1914. Studied at Pasadena Playhouse. Has appeared in "Victory Belles," "Macbeth," "Richard III," "Othello," "Lute Song," "Cyrano de Bergerac" (1953), "Antony and Cleopatra," "Design For A Stained Glass Window," "The Taming of The Shrew" (1951), "The Burning Glass," and Off-Bdwy in "Ceremony of Innocence" and "Endecott and The Red Cross."

CLARK, ALEXANDER. Born in NYC, May 2, 1904. Has appeared in "Merton of The Movies," "Excess Baggage," "Biography," "Too True To Be Good," "Victoria Regina," "Abe Lincoln In Illinois," "Margin For Error," "In Time To Come," "Sheppy," "Legend of Lovers," "The Captains and The Kings," "Calculated Risk," City Center revivals of "Brigadoon," "Carousel," and "Life With Father."

CLARK, OLIVER. Born in Buffalo, N.Y., Jan. 4, 1939. Graduate of Buffalo U. Made Bdwy bow in 1963 in "Arturo Ui," followed by "Ben Franklin In Paris," "Caucasian Chalk Circle" (LC Rep), "Don't Drink The Water."

CLARKE, RICHARD. Born in England, Jan. 31, 1933. Graduate of Univ. of Reading, Eng. Has appeared with Lincoln Center Rep. Co. in "St. Joan," "Tiger At The Gates," and "Cyrano de Bergerac."

| Roy Clary | Zaida Coles | James Cook | Roy Cooper | Al Corbin |

CLARY, ROY. Born in Winnepeg, Can., Aug. 20, 1939. Graduate of Ohio State U. and Goodman School of Drama. Made NY debut Off-Bdwy in 1968 in "Love and Let Love."

COATES, CAROLYN. Born Apr. 29, 1930 in Oklahoma City. Attended UCLA. Appeared Off-Bdwy in "The Innocents," "The Balcony," "Electra," "The Trojan Women" for which she won a THEATRE WORLD AWARD, "A Whitman Portrait," "Party On Greenwich Avenue," and "The Club Bedroom," with LCRep. Co. in "The Country Wife," "The Condemned of Altona" and "The Caucasian Chalk Circle."

COCO, JAMES. Born in NYC, Mar. 21, 1930. Has appeared Off-Bdwy in "The Moon In The Yellow River," "That 5 A.M. Jazz," "Lovey," "Squat Betty and The Sponge Room," "Salome" and "Fragments," and on Bdwy in "Hotel Paradiso," "Everybody Loves Opal," "A Passage To India," "Arturo Ui," "The Devils," "The Astrakhan Coat," "Here's Where I Belong."

COE, JOHN. Born in Hartford, Conn., Oct. 19, 1925. Graduate of Tufts U. and Boston U. Made Bdwy bow in 1964 in "The Passion of Josef D," and has appeared Off-Bdwy in "The Marrying Maiden," "Thistle In My Bed," "Johan," "The Wicked Cooks," "June Bug Graduates Tonight," "Drums In The Night," "America Hurrah," "Father Uxbridge Wants To Marry."

COLES, ZAIDA. Born Sept. 10, 1933 in Lynchburg, Va. Appeared Off-Bdwy in "The Father" and "Pins and Needles" before making Bdwy debut in 1968 in "Weekend."

COLICOS, JOHN. Born Dec. 10, 1928 in Toronto, Can. Made Bdwy bow in 1966 in "The Devils" followed by "Soldiers," and has appeared Off-Bdwy in "King Lear" (CC) and "Sergeant Musgrave's Dance."

COLLINS, PAUL. Born in London, July 25, 1937. Attended City and State College in Los Angeles, Actors Studio. Appeared Off-Bdwy in "Say Nothing" and "Cambridge Circus," and on Bdwy in "The Royal Hunt of The Sun," "A Minor Adjustment."

COLYER, AUSTIN. Born in Brooklyn, Oct. 29, 1935. Attended SMU. Has appeared in "Darwin's Theories," "Let It Ride," and City Center revivals of "Brigadoon," "Music Man," "How To Succeed In Business," "Where's Charley?," "Elizabeth The Queen," "Carousel," "Finian's Rainbow," and "Wonderful Town."

CONFORTI, GINO. Born in Chicago, Jan. 30, 1932. Attended Catholic U. Appeared Off-Bdwy in "The Fantasticks," and "Smiling The Boy Fell Dead," and on Bdwy in "A Family Affair," "She Loves Me," "Fiddler On The Roof," "Poor Bitos," "Never Live Over A Pretzel Factory," "Man of La Mancha."

CONNELL, GORDON. Born Mar. 19, 1923 in Berkeley, Calif. Graduate of U. Cal and NYU. Appeared Off-Bdwy before making Bdwy bow in 1961 in "Subways Are For Sleeping," followed by "Hello, Dolly!"

CONNELL, JANE. Born Oct. 27, 1925 in Berkeley, Calif. Attended U. Calif. Appeared Off-Bdwy in "Shoestring Revue," "Threepenny Opera," "Pieces of Eight," "Demi-Dozen," and on Bdwy in "New Faces of 1956," "Drat! The Cat!," "Mame."

CONNOR, WHITFIELD. Born in Ireland, Dec. 3, 1916. Attended Wayne U. and U. Mich. Has appeared in "Hamlet," Redgrave's "Macbeth" for which he received a THEATRE WORLD Award, "The Winner," "Lunatics and Lovers", Off-Bdwy in "Six Characters In Search of An Author," "The Makropoulos Secret" and "The Disenchanted," and in "There Was A Little Girl," "Everything In The Garden."

CONOLLY, PATRICIA. Born Aug. 29, 1933 in Tabora, Tanganyika, East Africa. Attended U. of Sydney, Aust. Has appeared with the APA in "You Can't Take It With You," "War and Peace," "School For Scandal," "The Wild Duck," "Right You Are," "We Comrades Three," "Pantagleize," "Exit The King," and "The Cherry Orchard."

CONVY, BERT. Born July 23, 1935 in St. Louis. Graduate of UCLA. Made NY bow in "Billy Barnes Revue," followed by "Nowhere To Go But Up," "Morning Sun," "Love and Kisses," "Fiddler On The Roof," "The Impossible Years," "Cabaret."

CONWAY, DIANE. Born June 10, 1944 in NYC. Attended Teachers College. Made Bdwy debut in 1967 in "Hello, Dolly!"

COOK, JAMES. Born in NYC, Mar. 7, 1937. Attended Fairfield U., AADA. Has appeared Off-Bdwy in "The Fantasticks," and "Goa," and with LCRep. Co. in "Cyrano de Bergerac."

COONEY, DENNIS. Born in NYC, Sept. 19, 1938. Attended Fordham U. Appeared Off-Bdwy in "Whisper To Me," "Every Other Girl" for which he received a THEATRE WORLD Award, and "In A Summer House," on Bdwy in "Ross," "Love and Kisses," Lion In Winter," and with LCRep. Co. in "Tiger At The Gates" and "Cyrano de Bergerac."

COOPER, MARILYN. Born in NYC, Dec. 14, 1936. Attended NYU. Has appeared in "Mr. Wonderful," "West Side Story," "Brigadoon" (1957CC), "Gypsy," "I Can Get It For You Wholesale," "The Mad Show" (OB), "Hallelujah, Baby!," "Golden Rainbow."

COOPER, ROY. Born Jan. 22, 1930 in London. Made Bdwy debut in 1968 in "The Prime of Miss Jean Brodie."

CORBIN, AL. Born Apr. 13, 1926 in New Britain, Conn. Graduate of Syracuse U. Made Bdwy bow in 1955 in "The Wayward Saint," followed by Off-Bdwy roles in "The White Devil," "Henry IV" (CC), "Our Town," "Fashion," "The Crucible," "Colombe," and with LCRep. Co. in "Tiger At The Gates," and "Cyrano de Bergerac."

CORT, ALEX. Born in the Bronx, Nov. 13, 1939. Principal dancer with Bertram Ross and Mary Anthony companies. Has appeared Off-Bdwy in "Much Ado About Nothing," "Hamlet," "The Owl Answers," "The Baccantes," "To Clothe The Naked," and on tour in "The Impossible Years."

CORZATTE, CLAYTON. Born in Fairhope, Ala., Mar. 4, 1927. Graduate of U. Ala. Has appeared with the APA since 1961 in "The Wild Duck," "The Lower Depths," "School For Scandal," "A Midsummer Night's Dream," "Ghosts," "The Seagull," "War and Peace," "You Can't Take It With You," "The Show-Off," "Exit The King," "Pantagleize," "The Cherry Orchard."

COSTER, NICOLAS. Born in London, Dec. 3, 1934. Studied at Neighborhood Playhouse. Made Bdwy bow in "Becket," followed by "90 Day Mistress." Off-Bdwy credits: "Epitaph For George Dillon," "Shadow and Substance," "The Thracian Horses," and "O Say Can You See."

COTSWORTH, STAATS. Born in Oak Park, Ill, Feb. 17, 1908. Trained with Eva LeGallienne's Civic Rep. Theatre. Among his many plays are "Romeo and Juliet," "Alice In Wonderland," "Rain From Heaven," "Murder At The Vanities," "Madame Capet," "Macbeth," "She Stoops To Conquer," "Richard III," "Advise and Consent," "Hamlet," "I Knock At The Door" and "Pictures In A Hallway" (OB), "Right Honourable Gentleman," NY Shakespeare Festival productions, "Weekend."

Phyllis Craig   Mary Crawford   Ed Crowley   Kathleen Dabney   Angela D'Ambi

COUPE, DIANE. Born in Widnes, Eng., Nov. 19, 1939. Made Bdwy debut in 1962 in "Nowhere To Go But Up," followed by "Hot Spot," "Jenny," "Funny Girl," "La Grosse Valise," "Mame."

COURTNEY, ALEXANDER. Born in NYC, Mar. 21, 1940. Has appeared at NY Shakespeare Festival in "Hamlet," and "Othello," with APA in "The Wild Duck" and "War and Peace," and in "Rosencrantz and Guildenstern Are Dead."

COWLES, MATTHEW. Born in NYC, Sept. 28, 1944. Studied at Neighborhood Playhouse. Made Bdwy debut in 1966, followed by Off-Bdwy roles in "King John" (CP), and "The Indian Wants The Bronx."

CRAIG, HELEN. Born in San Antonio, Tex., May 13, 1914. Made Bdwy debut in 1936 in "Russet Mantle," followed by "New Faces," "Julius Caesar," "Soliloquy," "Family Portrait," "The Unconquered," "Johnny Belinda," "As You Like It," "Lute Song," "Land's End," "The House of Bernarda Alba," "Maya," "Diamond Orchid," "Medea" and "To Clothe The Naked" (OB), "More Stately Mansions."

CRAIG, PHYLLIS. Born Aug. 5, 1936 in London. Made NY debut Off-Bdwy in 1968 in "Scuba Duba."

CRAWFORD, MARY. Born Sept. 21, 1940 in Ashland, Miss. Graduate of Yale Drama School. Made NY debut Off-Bdwy in "Have I Got One For You" in 1968.

CRESWELL, SAYLOR. Born Nov. 18, 1939 in Pottstown, Pa. Graduate of Brown U. Made NY bow Off-Bdwy in 1968 in "Carving A Statue."

CROWDER, JACK. Born Nov. 15, 1939 in Miami, Fla. Attended U. Redlands. Appeared Off-Bdwy in "Fly Blackbird" (1962) and "The Fantasticks" (1967) before Bdwy debut Nov. 12, 1967 in "Hello, Dolly!" for which he won a THEATRE WORLD Award.

CROWLEY, EDWARD. Born Sept. 5, 1926 in Lewiston, Me. Attended AADA. Has appeared Off-Bdwy in "The Admirable Bashville," "An Evening With G.B.S.," "Once Around The Block," "I Want You," "Lion In Love," "Telemachus Clay," and "Hair," and on Bdwy in "Make A Million," "The Family Way."

CRYER, DAVID. Born Mar. 8, 1936 in Evanston, Ill. Attended DePauw U. Has appeared Off-Bdwy in "The Fantasticks," "The Streets of New York," and "Now Is The Time For All Good Men," and on Bdwy in "110 In The Shade."

CRYER, GRETCHEN (Sally Niven). Born Oct. 17, 1935 in Indianapolis, Ind. Graduate of DePauw U. and Radcliffe. Has appeared on Bdwy in "Little Me" and "110 In The Shade," and Off-Bdwy in "Now Is The Time For All Good Men."

CULLUM, JOHN. Born Mar. 2, 1930 in Knoxville, Tenn. Graduate of U. Tenn. Made Bdwy bow in 1960 in "Camelot," followed by "Infidel Caesar," "The Rehearsal," "Hamlet," "On A Clear Day You Can See Forever" for which he received a THEATRE WORLD Award, "Three Hand Reel" (OB), "Man of La Mancha."

CUMMINGS, VICKI. Born in Northampton, Mass. Made Bdwy debut in 1931 in "Here Goes The Bride," followed by "The Time, The Place, The Girl," "The Man Who Came To Dinner," "Dinner At Eight," "Skylark," "The Voice of The Turtle," "For Love or Money," "Oh, Mr. Meadowbrook," "Buy Me Blue Ribbons," "I've Got Sixpence," "Midsummer," "Lunatics and Lovers," "The Hot Corner," "Palm Tree In A Rose Garden" (OB), "How To Make A Man," "Who's Afraid of Virginia Woolf?," "The Butter and Egg Man" (OB), "Mame."

CUNNINGHAM, JOHN. Born in Auburn, NY, June 22, 1932. Graduate of Dartmouth and Yale. Has appeared on Bdwy in "Hot Spot," and Off-Bdwy in "Love Me Little," "Pimpernel," "The Fantasticks," Am. Shakespeare Festival, "Love and Let Love."

CURTIS, DONNA. Born Jan. 12, 1938 in Ft. Dodge, Iowa. Graduate of Northern State College, Aberdeen, S.D. Has appeared Off-Bdwy with the American Savoyards, and in "Now Is The Time For All Good Men."

CURTIS, KEENE. Born Feb. 15, 1923 in Salt Lake City. Graduate of U. Utah. Made Bdwy bow in 1949 in "Shop At Sly Corner," and after stage managing many productions, joined APA in 1960 and has appeared in "The School For Scandal," "The Tavern," "Anatole," "Scapin," "Right You Are," "The Importance of Being Earnest," "Twelfth Night," "King Lear," "The Seagull," "Lower Depths," "Man and Superman," "Judith," "War and Peace," "You Can't Take It With You," "Pantagleize," "The Cherry Orchard."

DABNEY, KATHLEEN. Born Nov. 10, 1942 in Brownwood, Tex. Graduate of Stephens College and U. Miss. Appeared Off-Bdwy in "Sara B. Devine" and "The Unknown Soldier and His Wife," before making Bdwy debut in 1967 in "You Know I Can't Hear You When The Water's Running."

DAILEY, IRENE. Born in NYC, Sept. 12, 1920. Made Bdwy debut in 1943 in "Nine Girls," followed by "Truckline Cafe," "Idiot's Delight," (CC1951), "The Good Woman of Setzuan" (OB), "Miss Lonelyhearts," "Andorra," "The Subject Was Roses," "Rooms" (OB), "You Know I Can't Hear You When The Water's Running."

D'AMBROSIA, ANGELA. Born in Beaver Falls, Pa. Graduate of Carnegie Tech. Made Bdwy debut in 1961 in "The Wall," followed by "The Guide."

DANA, LEORA. Born Apr. 1, 1923 in NYC. Attended Barnard College, and RADA, London. Made Bdwy debut in 1947 in "The Madwoman of Chaillot," followed by "The Happy Time," "Point of No Return," "Sabrina Fair," "The Best Man," "In The Summer House" (OB), "Beekman Place," Natl. Rep. Theatre productions, and Off-Bdwy in "Wilder's Triple Bill" and "Collision Course."

DANGLER, ANITA. Born in NYC, Sept. 26. Attended NYU. Made Bdwy debut in 1956 in "Affair of Honor," followed by "The Hostage," APA's "Right You Are," "You Can't Take It With You," and "War and Peace," "Hamlet" (OB).

DANIELS, EDGAR. Born June 3, 1932 in Raleigh, N.C. Attended UNC. Has appeared in "New Girl In Town," "La Plume de Ma Tante," "Caligula," "The Affair," "A Man For All Seasons," "Hostile Witness," "The Butter and Egg Man" (OB), and with LCRep. in "Galileo," "Tiger At The Gates," and "Cyrano de Bergerac."

DANIELS, WALKER. Born June 4, 1943 in Hartford, Conn. Attended AADA. Has appeared in "Stephen D" (OB), and "Hair."

DANIELS, WILLIAM. Born Mar. 31, 1927 in Brooklyn. Graduate of Northwestern U. Made Bdwy bow in 1943 in "Life With Father," followed by "Richard II," "Seagulls Over Sorrento, Legend of Lizzie," "Cat On A Hot Tin Roof," "A Thousand Clowns," Off-Bdwy in "The Zoo Story," "The Iceman Cometh," and "Look Back In Anger," "Dear Me, The Sky Is Falling," "One Flew Over The Cuckoo's Nest," "On A Clear Day You Can See Forever," "Daphne In Cottage D."

rma Dardin   Jeff David   Frank DeSal   B. J. DeSimone   Jamie Donnelly

DARDIN, NORMA. Born Nov. 4 in Newark, N.J. Graduate of Sarah Lawrence College. Made Bdwy debut in 1968 in "Weekend."

DARLING, JOAN. Born Apr. 14, 1940 in Boston. Attended Carnegie Tech., U. Tex. Appeared Off-Bdwy in "Country Wife," "The Crucible," "Ivanov," "The Premise," and "Squat Betty and The Sponge Room" before making Bdwy debut in 1967 in "A Minor Adjustment."

DARVAS, LILI. Born in Budapest, Hungary. Discovered by and appeared in many Max Reinhardt productions. Made Bdwy debut in 1944 in "Soldier's Wife," followed by "Hamlet," "Bravo," "Cry of The Peacock," "Horses In Midstream," "Hidden River," "Waltz of The Toreadors," "Cheri," "The Far Country," "First Love," "My Mother, My Father and Me," "Happiness" (OB).

DAVID, JEFF. Born Sept. 16, 1940 in Philadelphia. Graduate of Carnegie Tech. Has appeared Off-Bdwy in "Arms and The Man," "Phaedra," "Country Wife," "Caucasian Chalk Circle," "The Butter and Egg Man," "Francesca da Remini," and "Hamlet."

DAVID, THAYER. Born Mar. 4, 1927 in Medford, Mass. Graduate of Harvard. Has appeared in "The Relapse," "King Lear" (CC), "Mister Johnson," "Protective Custody," "A Man For All Seasons," "Andorra," NRT's "The Seagull" and "The Crucible," "The Royal Hunt of The Sun," "Those That Play The Clowns," and Off-Bdwy in "Carefree Tree," "White Devil," "Oscar Wilde," and "The Bench."

DAVILA, DIANA. Born Nov. 5, 1947 in NYC. Made Bdwy debut in 1967 in "Song Of The Grasshopper," followed by "The Prime of Miss Jean Brodie."

DeANDA, PETER. Born in Pittsburgh, Mar. 10, 1940. Attended Actors Workshop and Pittsburgh Playhouse. Appeared Off-Bdwy in "The Blacks," "Dutchman," "Sound of Silence," and "The Kitchen," and on Bdwy in "The Zulu and The Zayda," "The Guide."

DeBEER, GERRIT. Born in Amsterdam, Holland, June 17, 1935. Made Bdwy bow in 1965 in "Pickwick," followed by "Illya, Darling."

DEERING, OLIVE. Made Bdwy debut in 1932 in "Girls In Uniform," followed by "Growing Pains," "Picnic," "Daughters of Atreus," "The Eternal Road," "Winged Victory," "Skydrift," "The Front Page," "Marathon '33," "Ceremony of Innocence" (OB).

DeHAVEN, GLORIA. Born July 23, 1925 in Los Angeles. Made Bdwy debut in 1955 in "Seventh Heaven," followed by "Have I Got One For You" (OB).

DeKOVEN, ROGER. Born Oct. 22, 1907 in Chicago. Attended U. Chicago, Northwestern and Columbia. Made Bdwy bow in 1926 in "Juarez and Maximilian," followed by "The Mystery Man," "Once In A Lifetime," "Counsellor-at-Law," "Murder In The Cathedral," "The Eternal Road," "Brooklyn, USA," "The Assassins," "Joan of Lorraine," "Abie's Irish Rose" (1954), "The Lark," "Hidden River," "Compulsion," "Miracle Worker," "Fighting Cock," "Tovarich (1963)," "Arturo Ui," "Funny Girl," and Off-Bdwy in "The Deadly Game," and with LCRep. in "St. Joan," "Tiger At The Gates," "Walking To Waldheim," "Cyrano de Bergerac."

DELL, GABRIEL. Born Oct. 7, 1930 in Barbados, B.W.I. Has appeared in "Dead End," "Tickets, Please!," "Ankles Aweigh," "Fortuna," City Center revivals of "Can-Can," "Wonderful Town," and "Oklahoma!," "Marathon '33," "Anyone Can Whistle," "The Sign In Sidney Brustein's Window," "Luv," "Chocolates" (OB), "Something Different."

DEMAS, CAROLE. Born May 26, 1940 in Brooklyn. Attended U. Vermont, and NYU. Appeared with NY Shakespeare Festival, and Off-Bdwy in "Morning Sun," and "The Fantasticks."

DENNIS, SANDY. Born Apr. 27, 1937 in Hastings, Neb. Has appeared in "The Dark at The Top Of The Stairs," "Burning Bright" (OB), "Face of A Hero," "The Complaisant Lover," "A Thousand Clowns," "Any Wednesday," "Daphne In Cottage D."

DeSAL, FRANK. Born Apr. 14, 1943 in White Plains, N.Y. Studied at American Theatre Wing, and Am. School of Ballet. Has appeared in "Anything Goes" (OB), "110 In The Shade," "Marco Millions" (LCRep.), "Sherry," "Sweet Charity," "How Now, Dow Jones?"

DeSIMONE, B. J. Born Dec. 7, 1939 in Boston. Graduate of Tufts U. Made NY bow in "West Side Story" (CC), followed by "The Royal Hunt of The Sun," "The Unknown Soldier and His Wife," "Rosencrantz and Guildenstern Are Dead."

DEWHURST, COLLEEN. Born Montreal, Can. Attended Downer College, and AADA. Has appeared in "Desire Under The Elms" (1952), "Tamburlaine The Great," "The Country Wife," "Caligula," Off-Bdwy in "The Taming of The Shrew," "The Eagle Has Two Heads," "Camille," "Macbeth," "Children of Darkness" for which she received a THEATRE WORLD Award, and "Antony and Cleopatra" (CP), "All The Way Home," "Great Day In The Morning," "Ballad of The Sad Cafe," "More Stately Mansions."

DIENER, JOAN. Born Feb. 24, 1934 in Cleveland, O. Attended Sarah Lawrence College. Made Bdwy debut in 1948 in "Small Wonder," followed by "Season In The Sun," "Kismet" for which she received a THEATRE WORLD Award, "Man of La Mancha."

DIETRICH, DENA. Born in Pittsburgh, Dec. 4, 1928. Attended AADA. Made NY debut in 1962 Off-Bdwy in "Out Of This World," followed by "Cindy," "The Rimers of Eldritch," and on Bdwy in "Funny Girl," "Here's Where I Belong."

DIETRICH, MARLENE. Born Dec. 27, 1904 in Berlin where she attended Musical Academy, and Max Reinhardt School. Appeared on Berlin stage, and in many films and nightclubs before making Bdwy debut in a one-woman show on Oct. 9, 1967.

DILLON, MELINDA. Born Oct. 13, 1939 in Hope Ark. Attended Goodman Theatre School. Made Bdwy debut in 1962 in "Who's Afraid of Virginia Woolf?" for which she received a THEATRE WORLD Award, followed by "You Know I Can't Hear You When The Water's Running."

DODGE, JERRY. Born Feb. 1, 1937 in New Orleans. Graduate of Notre Dame U. Made Bdwy bow in 1961 in "Bye Bye Birdie," followed by "Sap of Life" (OB), "110 In The Shade," Am. Shakespeare Festival productions of "A Midsummer Night's Dram," "Merchant of Venice," and "Macbeth," "Hello, Dolly!," "George M!"

DOLIVE, WILLIAM. Born Oct. 17, 1943 in Mobile, Ala. Graduate of U. Tex. Made NY debut in 1967 in "The Unknown Soldier and His Wife."

DONNELLY, DONAL. Born July 6, 1931 in Bradford, Eng. Appeared with Dublin Gate Theatre and in London before Bdwy debut in 1966 in "Philadelphia, Here I Come!," followed by "A Day In The Death of Joe Egg."

DONNELLY, JAMIE. Made Bdwy debut in 1965 in "Flora The Red Menace," followed by "You're A Good Man, Charlie Brown" (OB), "George M!"

| Vincent Dowling | Anne Draper | Ralph Drischell | Ethelyne Dunfee | Michael Dur... |

DORRIN, JOHN. Born July 17, 1920 in Omaha, Neb. Attended LA City College. Made Bdwy bow in 1944 in "Song of Norway," followed by "Kismet," "Silk Stockings," "Most Happy Fella," "Best Man" "My Fair Lady," "What Makes Sammy Run?," "Fade Out—Fade In," revivals of "Carousel," "Annie Get Your Gun," "Finian's Rainbow," and "St. Joan," "I'm Solomon."

DOTRICE, ROY. Born May 26, 1925 in Guernsey, Channel Islands. Appeared with Royal Shakespeare Co. before making Bdwy debut in 1967 in "Brief Lives."

DOUGLAS, JOHANNA. Born July 23, 1917 in Minneapolis. Graduate of U. Minn. Toured in several productions before making Bdwy debut in 1965 in "Never Too Late," followed by "Mame."

DOUGLAS, MELVYN. Born Apr. 5, 1901 in Macon, Ga. Has appeared in "A Free Soul," "Back Here," "Recaptured," "Tonight Or Never," "No More Ladies," "Mother Lode," "Two Blind Mice," "The Bird Cage," "Glad Tidings," "Time Out For Ginger," "Inherit The Wind," "Waltz of The Toreadors," "Juno," "The Gang's All Here," "The Best Man," "Spofford."

DOWD, M'EL. Born Feb. 2 in Chicago. Studied at Goodman Theatre. Appeared Off-Bdwy in "Macbeth," "A Midsummer Night's Dream," "Romeo and Juliet," and "Julius Caesar" before Bdwy debut in 1958 in "Methuselah," followed by "Royal Gambit" (OB), "Sweet Bird of Youth," "Camelot," "The Emperor" (OB), "A Case of Libel," "Right Honourable Gentleman," "The Sound of Music" (CC), with LCRep. Co. in "The Unknown Soldier and His Wife" and "Tiger At The Gates," "Everything In The Garden."

DOWLING, VINCENT. Born Dec. 22, 1922 in NYC. Has appeared Off-Bdwy in "Come Back, Little Sheba," "Mister Roberts," "Billy Budd," "Passion of Gross," and "Mary Stuart," and on Bdwy in "Red Roses For Me," "Sunrise At Campobello," and "More Stately Mansions."

DOWNING, DAVID. Born July 21, 1943 in NYC. Has appeared in Bdwy in "Green Pastures," "The Cool World," and Off-Bdwy in "Day of Absence," "Happy Ending," and "Song of The Lusitanian Bogey."

DRAKE, ALFRED. Born Oct. 7, 1914 in NYC. Graduate of Brooklyn College. Made Bdwy bow in 1935 in "The Mikado," followed by "White Horse Inn," "Babes In Arms," "Two Bouquets," "One For The Money," "Two For The Show," "Straw Hat Revue," "Out Of The Frying Pan," "As You Like It," "Yesterday's Magic," "Oklahoma!," "Sing Out, Sweet Land," "Beggar's Holiday," "The Cradle Will Rock," "Joy To The World," "Kiss Me, Kate," "The Liar," "The Gambler," "The King and I," "Kismet," "Kean," "Lorenzo," "Hamlet," "Those That Play The Clowns," "Song of The Grasshopper."

DRAPER, ANNE. Born Sept. 1, 1938 in NYC. Has appeared with American Shakespeare Festival, Off-Bdwy in "Between Two Thieves," "Posterity For Sale," "Caricknabauna," "Phedra," and "Magic Prison," with Natl. Repertory Theatre, and on Bdwy in "A Gift of Time."

DRAPER, MARGARET. Born Nov. 20, 1922 in Salt Lake City. Made Bdwy debut in 1948 in "For Heaven's Sake, Mother," followed by Off-Bdwy roles in "The Cherry Orchard," "Time of The Cuckoo," "Edward II," "The Cocktail Party," "Duchess of Malfi," and on Bdwy in "The Gambler," "A Minor Adjustment."

DREMAK, W. P. Born Aug. 2 in Akron, O. Graduate of Carnegie Tech. Made NY debut Off-Bdwy in "Jonah" in 1967.

DRISCHELL, RALPH. Born Nov. 26, 1927 in Baldwin, L.I., N.Y. Attended Carnegie Tech. Has appeared Off-Bdwy in "Playboy of The Western World," "The Crucible," "The Balcony," "Time of Vengeance," "Barroom Monks," "Portrait of The Artist As A Young Man," "Abe Lincoln In Illinois," "The Caretaker," "A Slight Ache," and "The Room," and on Bdwy in "Rhinoceros," "All In Good Time," "Rosencrantz and Guildenstern Are Dead."

DUELL, WILLIAM. Born Aug. 30, 1923 in Corinth, N.Y. Attended Ill. Wesleyan, and Yale. Appeared Off-Bdwy in "Threepenny Opera," "Portrait of The Artist As A Young Man," "Barroom Monks," "A Midsummer Night's Dream," "Henry IV," "Taming of The Shrew," and "The Memorandum," on Bdwy in "A Cook For Mr. General," "Ballad of The Sad Cafe," "Illya, Darling."

DUKAS, JAMES. Born June 6, 1926 in Portsmouth, O. Graduate of W.Va.U., and American Theatre Wing. Has appeared Off-Bdwy in "Man With The Golden Arm," "Brothers Karamazov," "Threepenny Opera," "Incident At Vichy," "After The Fall," "Condemned of Altona," on Bdwy in "The Visit," "The Last Analysis," "Nobody Loves An Albatross," "Don't Drink The Water."

DULLEA, KEIR. Born May 30, 1936 in Cleveland, N.J. Attended San Francisco College, and Neighborhood Playhouse. Made Off-Bdwy debut in 1959 in "Season of Choice," and Bdwy bow in 1967 in "Dr. Cook's Garden."

DUNCAN, SANDY. Born Feb. 20, 1946 in Henderson, Tex. Attended Lon Morris College. Made NY debut in 1966-67 City Center revival of "Music Man," followed by "Carousel," "Finian's Rainbow," "Sound of Music," "Wonderful Town," "Life With Father," and Off-Bdwy in "Ceremony of Innocence" for which she received a THEATRE WORLD Award.

DUNFEE, ETHELYNE. Born Dec. 9, 1937 in Jersey City. Attended Columbia. Made Bdwy debut in 1956 in "Silk Stockings," followed by "Body Beautiful," "West Side Story," "Greenwillow," "Cactus Flower."

DURNING, CHARLES. Born Feb. 28, 1933 in Highland Falls, N.Y. Attended Columbia, Hunter, and NYU. Has appeared Off-Bdwy in NY Shakespeare Festival productions, in "Two By Saroyan," "The Child Buyer," and "An Album of Gunter Grass," on Bdwy in "Poor Bitos," "Drat! The Cat!," "Pousse Cafe," "The Happy Time."

DURRELL, MICHAEL. Has appeared Off-Bdwy in "Worm In The Horseradish," "The Butterfly Dream," "Phedre," and "MacBird," and with APA in "The Cherry Orchard."

DYBAS, JAMES. Born Feb. 7, 1944 in Chicago. Made Bdwy debut in 1965 in "Do I Hear A Waltz?," followed by "George M!"

EASTON, RICHARD. Born Mar. 22, 1933 in Montreal, Can. Appeared in Canada and Eng. before making US debut with Am. Shakespeare Festival in 1957, and Bdwy bow in "The Country Wife" for which he received a THEATRE WORLD Award, followed by "Back To Methuselah," "Salad Days" (IB), "School For Scandal," and APA productions of "Anatol," "Man and Superman," "The Seagull," "Exit The King," "Pantagleize," and "The Cherry Orchard."

ELKINS, FLORA. Born in NYC on July 28. Studied at Neighborhood Playhouse. Made Bdwy debut in 1961 in "Rhinoceros," and appeared Off-Bdwy in "Ardele," "Geranium Hat," "Othello," "Troilus and Cressida," "Baal," and "Stephen D."

| nes Dybas | Ed Ericksen | Rex Everhart | Erica Fitz | Judy Frank |

ELLIN, DAVID. Born in Montreal, Jan. 10, 1925. Attended AADA. Has appeared in "Swan Song," "West Side Story," "The Education of Hyman Kaplan."

ELLIOT, JANE. Born in NYC, Jan. 17, 1947. Made Bdwy debut in 1965 in "The Impossible Years."

ELSTON, ROBERT. Born in NYC, May 29, 1934. Graduate of Hunter and CCNY. Has appeared in "Maybe Tuesday," "Tall Story," "Golden Fleecing," "Spoon River Anthology," Off-Bdwy in "Undercover Man," and "Conditioned Reflex," on tour in "You Know I Can't Hear You When The Water's Running.",

ENSERRO, MICHAEL. Born Oct. 5, 1918 in Soldier, Pa. Attended Allegheny College and Pasadena Playhouse. Has appeared in "Molly and Me," "The Passion of Josef D.," Off-Bdwy in "Penny Change," "The Fantasticks," "The Miracle," and "The Kitchen," "Song of The Grasshopper," "Mike Downstairs."

ENSSLEN, DICK. Born Dec. 19, 1926 in Reading, Pa. Attended Musical Theatre Academy. Has appeared in "Anyone Can Whistle," "Bajour," "The Education of Hyman Kaplan."

ERICKSEN, ED. Born in Brooklyn, June 14, 1931. Attended L.I. Art Inst. and Mannes College of Music. Has appeared in "Donnybrook," "Kean," "On A Clear Day You Can See Forever," "A Time For Singing," "Apple Tree," "I'm Solomon."

EVANS, ALICE. Born Sept. 4, 1939 in Deposit, N.Y. Attended Juilliard. Made Bdwy debut in 1961 in "Sound of Music," followed by "Tovarich," "How To Succeed In Business," "Pleasures and Palaces," "Sweet Charity," "I'm Solomon."

EVANS, WILBUR. Born in Philadelphia, Aug. 5, 1905. Attended Curtis Inst. Has appeared in "The Merry Widow," "New Moon," "La Vie Parisienne," "Mexican Hayride," "Up In Central Park," "South Pacific," "By The Beautiful Sea," "Man of La Mancha."

EVERHART, REX. Born June 13, 1920 in Watseka, Ill. Graduate of U.Mo. and NYU. Made Bdwy bow in 1955 in "No Time For Sergeants," followed by "Tall Story," "Moonbirds," "Tenderloin," "Matter of Position," "Rainy Day In Newark," "Skyscraper," 1960 season with Phoenix Theatre, 5 seasons with American Shakespeare Festival, "How Now, Dow Jones?"

FAIRMAN, MICHAEL. Born Feb. 25, 1934 in NYC. Made NY bow Off-Bdwy in "Red Roses For Me," and Bdwy debut in 1965 in "Cactus Flower."

FAY, BRENDAN. Born in NYC, and attended NY State Maritime Academy. Made NY bow Off-Bdwy in 1958 in "Heloise," followed by "Threepenny Opera," "Donogoo," "King of The Whole Damned World," "Wretched The Lion-Hearted," "Time of The Key," "Thistle In My Bed," "Posterity For Sale," and "Stephen D.," and on Bdwy in "Legend of Lizzie," "First Love."

FELDMAN, SHELLIE. Born in NYC. Attended Brooklyn College. Made Bdwy bow in 1966 in "Marat/DeSade," followed by "Comedy of Errors" (NY Shakespeare Festival).

FERRER, JOSE. Born in Santurce, P.R., Jan. 8, 1912. Graduate of Princeton. Has appeared in "A Slight Case of Murder," "Brother Rat," "In Clover," "Missouri Legend," "Mamba's Daughters," "Key Largo," "Charley's Aunt," "Vickie," "Let's Face It," "Othello," "Cyrano de Bergerac," "The Silver Whistle," "20th Century," "Volpone," "The Shrike," "Angel Street" (CC), "Richard III," "Edwin Booth," "The Girl Who Came To Supper," "Man of La Mancha."

FERRIS, BARBARA. Born in London in 1943, where she appeared on stage before making Bdwy debut in 1967 in "There's A Girl In My Soup."

FINNEY, ALBERT. Born in Salford, Eng., May 9, 1936. Attended RADA. Made Bdwy debut in 1963 in "Luther," followed by "A Day In The Death of Joe Egg."

FITZ, ERICA. Born in Chicago, May 25, 1942. Graduate of Northwestern. Made Bdwy debut in 1967 in "There's I Girl In My Soup."

FLANAGAN, WALTER. Born Oct. 4, 1928 in Ponta, Tex. Graduate of U. Houston. Has appeared Off-Bdwy in "Bedtime Story," "Coffee and Windows," "The Opening of A Window," "The Moon Is Blue," "Laughwind," and "The Dodo Bird," and on Bdwy in "Once For The Asking."

FLETCHER, JACK. Born Apr. 21, 1921 in Forest Hills, L.I. Attended Yale. Has appeared Off-Bdwy in "Comic Strip," "The Way of The World," "Thieves' Carnival," and "The Amorous Flea," in City Center revivals of "Can-Can," "Cyrano de Bergerac," and "Wonderful Town," on Bdwy in "Trial Honeymoon," "She Stoops To Conquer," "Romeo and Juliet," "Ben Franklin In Paris," "Drat! The Cat!"

FORBES, BRENDA. Born in London, Jan. 14, 1909. Made Bdwy debut in 1931 in "The Barretts of Wimpole Street," followed by "Candida," "Lucrece," "Flowers of The Forest," "Pride and Prejudice," "Storm Over Patsy," "Heartbreak House," "One For The Money," "Two For The Show," "Three To Make Ready," "Yesterday's Magic," "Morning Star," "Suds In Your Eyes," "Quadrille," "The Reluctant" Debutante", "Loves of Cass McGuire," "Darling of The Day."

FORD, PAUL. Born in Baltimore, Nov. 2, 1901. Attended Dartmouth. Made Bdwy bow in 1944 in "Decision," followed by "Lower North," "Kiss Them For Me," "Flamingo Road," "Oh Whitman Avenue," "Another Part of The Forest," "Command Decision," "Teahouse of The August Moon," "Whoop-Up," "Music Man," "Thurber Carnival," "Never Too Late," "3 Bags Full," "What Did We Do Wrong?"

FORD, RUTH. Born July 7, 1915 in Hazelhurst, Miss. Attended U. Miss. Made NY debut in 1937 in "Shoemaker's Holiday," followed by "Swinging The Dream," "No Exit," "This Time Tomorrow," "Clutterbuck," "House of Bernarda Alba," "Island of Goats," "Phoenix revivals of "Miss Julie" and "The Stronger," "Requiem For A Nun," "Dinner At 8" (1966), "90 Day Mistress."

FORSYTHE, HENDERSON. Born Sept. 11, 1917 in Macon, Mo. Attended Iowa U. Has appeared in "The Cellar and The Well," "Miss Lonelyhearts," "The Iceman Cometh" (OB), "Who's Afraid of Virginia Woolf?," Off-Bdwy in "The Collection," "The Room" and "A Slight Ache," "Malcolm," "Right Honourable Gentleman," "A Delicate Balance," "The Birthday Party."

FORSYTHE, JOHN. Born Jan. 29, 1918 in Penn's Grove, N.J. Made Bdwy bow in 1942 in "Yankee Point," followed by "Vickie," "Winged Victory," "Yellow Jack," "It Takes Two," "All My Sons," Mister Roberts," "Teahouse of The August Moon," "Weekend."

FOWKES, CONARD. Born Jan. 4, 1933 in Washington, D.C. Graduate of Yale. Made Bdwy bow in 1958 in "Howie," followed by "The Wall," "Minor Miracle," and Off-Bdwy in "Look Back In Anger," "That Thing At The Cherry Lane," and "America Hurrah."

Morgan Freeman

Ray Fry

Igors Gavon

Jay Gerber

John Gerst

FRANK, JUDY. Born Nov. 26, 1936 in Cincinnati. Graduate of Indiana U. and Yale. Made Bdwy debut in "Mary, Mary," followed by "Xmas In Las Vegas," "Spoon River Anthology," Off-Bdwy in "Six Characters in Search of An Author," and "Now Is The Time For All Good Men."

FRANKLIN, HUGH. Born Aug. 24, 1916 in Muskogee, Okla. Attended Northwestern. Made Bdwy bow in 1938 in "Gloriana," followed by "Harriet," "Alice In Wonderland," "Medea," "The Best Man," "Luther," "A Shot In The Dark," "Arturo Ui," "The Devils," "What Did We Do Wrong?"

FREEMAN, ANN. Born in Portsmouth, Eng. Made NY debut in 1967 City Center revival of "Life With Father."

FREEMAN, ARNY. Born Aug. 28, 1908 in Chicago. Made Bdwy bow in 1949 in "A Streetcar Named Desire," followed by City Center revivals of "Dream Girl" and "The Shrike," "The Great Sebastians," "Tall Story," "Hot Spot," "The Gay Divorcee" (OB), "What Makes Sammy Run?," "Cactus Flower."

FREEMAN, MORGAN. Born June 1, 1937 in Memphis, Tenn. Attended LA City College. Appeared Off-Bdwy in "Ostrich Feathers," and "The Niggerlovers," before Bdwy bow in 1967 in "Hello, Dolly!"

FRENCH, ARTHUR. Born in NYC. Attended Brooklyn College. He appeared Off-Bdwy in "Raisin' Hell In The Sun," "Ballad of Bimshire," "Day of Absence," "Happy Ending," and "Jonah."

FREUND, KIM. Born Dec. 15, 1955 in Houston, Tex. Made Bdwy debut in 1968 in "The Happy Time."

FREY, NATHANIEL. Born Aug. 3, 1918 in NYC. Attended NYU, American Theatre Wing. Made Bdwy bow in 1947 in "Barefoot Boy With Cheek," followed by "High Button Shoes," "Touch and Go," "Call Me Madam," "A Tree Grows In Brooklyn," "Wonderful Town," "Damn Yankees," "Goldilocks," "Harold," "She Loves Me," "The Odd Couple," "The Education of Hyman Kaplan."

FRY, RAY. Born Feb. 22, 1923, in Hebron, Ind. Graduate of San Francisco State College and Northwestern. Made Bdwy bow in 1944 in "Hickory Stick," followed by "Cyrano de Bergerac," "The Cradle Will Rock," and with LCRep. Theater in "Danton's Death," "The Country Wife," "Caucasian Chalk Circle," "The Alchemist," "Galileo," "St. Joan," "Tiger At The Gates," and "Cyrano de Bergerac."

FUDGE, ALAN. Born Feb. 27, 1944 in Wichita, Kan. Attended U. Ariz. Has appeared with APA in "School For Scandal," "The Wild Duck," "War and Peace," "Escurial," "The Show-Off," "Pantagleize," and "The Cherry Orchard."

GALLAGHER, HELEN. Born in Brooklyn in 1926. Studied at American Ballet School. Made Bdwy debut in 1947 in "Seven Lively Arts," followed by "Mr. Strauss Goes To Boston," "Billion Dollar Baby," "Brigadoon," "High Button Shoes," "Touch and Go," "Make A Wish," "Pal Joey," "Hazel Flagg," CC revivals of "Guys and Dolls," "Finian's Rainbow" and "Oklahoma!," "Pajama Game," "Bus Stop," "Portofino," "Sweet Charity," "Mame."

GALLISON, JOSEPH. Born Mar. 9, 1939 in Boston. Graduate of Northwestern. Made Bdwy debut in 1967 in "Mame."

GALVIN, GENE. Born Nov. 30, 1917 in Seattle. Graduate of U. Wash. and Seattle U. Made Bdwy debut in 1946 in "Lute Song," followed by "Temporary Island," "Flight From Fear," "Othello," "Tiger At The Gates," and Off-Bdwy in "Born Yesterday," "White Steed," "God's of The Lightning," "Lorenzo's Folly," and "Curley McDimple."

GAM, RITA. Born in Pittsburgh, Apr. 2, 1928. Attended Columbia, and Actors Studio. Made Bdwy debut in 1946 in "A Flag Is Born," followed by "Temporary Island," "Insect Comedy" (CC), "The Young and The Fair," "Montserrat," "There's A Girl In My Soup."

GARDE, BETTY. Born Sept. 19, 1905 in Philadelphia. Has appeared in "Easy Come, Easy Go," "The Primrose Path," "Oklahoma!," "Agatha Sue, I Love You," "Stephen D." (OB).

GARY, HAROLD. Born in NYC, May 7, 1910. Made Bdwy bow in 1928 in "Diamond Lil," followed by "Crazy With The Heat," "A Flag Is Born," "Guys and Dolls," "Oklahoma!," "Arsenic and Old Lace," "Billion Dollar Baby," "Fiesta," "The World We Make," "Born Yesterday," "Will Success Spoil Rock Hunter?," "Let It Ride," "The Counting House," "Arturo Ui," "A Thousand Clowns," "Enter Laughing," "Illya, Darling," "The Price."

GASSELL, SYLVIA. Born in NYC, July 1, 1923. Attended Hunter and New School. Made Bdwy debut in 1952 in "The Time of The Cuckoo," followed by "Sunday Breakfast," "Fair Game For Lovers," and Off-Bdwy in "U.S.A.," "Romeo and Juliet," "A Darker Flower," "Electra," "Fragments," and "Goa."

GATES, LARRY. Born Sept. 24, 1915 in St. Paul, Minn. Attended U. Minn. Made Bdwy bow in 1939 in "Speak of The Devil," followed by "Twelfth Night," "Bell, Book and Candle," "Taming of The Shrew," "The Love of Four Colonels," "Teahouse of The August Moon," "Sing Me No Lullaby" and "Carefree Tree" at the Phoenix, "A Case of Libel," "Carving A Statue" (OB).

GAVON, IGORS. Born in Latvia, Nov. 14, 1937. Made Bdwy bow in 1961 in "Carnival," followed by "Hello, Dolly!," "Marat/deSade," "Your Own Thing" (OB).

GENN, LEO. Born in London, Aug. 9, 1905. Trained with Old Vic. Has appeared on Bdwy in "The Flashing Stream" (1939), "Another Part of The Forest" (1946), "Small War On Murray Hill" (1957), "The Devil's Advocate" (1961), "Fair Game For Lovers" (1964), "The Only Game In Town" (1968).

GERBER, JAY. Born Apr. 18, 1929 in The Bronx. Graduate of NYU. Made Bdwy bow in 1956 in "Tamburlaine The Great," followed by "49th Cousin," and Off-Bdwy in "Endgame," "Half-Past Wednesday," "Toys for The Clowns," "Wretched The Lion-Hearted," and "Jonah."

GERSTAD, JOHN. Born Sept. 3, 1925 in Boston. Attended Harvard. Made Bdwy bow in 1943 in "Othello," followed by "Dark of The Moon," "Joy To The World," "Not For Children," "The Male Animal" (CC1952), "The Golden Fleecing," "Trial of Lee Harvey Oswald."

GESSNER, ADRIENNE. Born in Vienna. Came to U.S. during WWII, and appeared on Bdwy in "Another Sun," "Claudia," "Thank You, Svoboda," and "I Remember Mama" before returning to Vienna Burgtheater. Appeared with them for season of repertory in 1968 at City Center.

GIFTOS, ELAINE. Born Jan. 24, 1945 in Pittsfield, Mass. Studied at School of American Ballet. Made Bdwy debut in 1966 in "Pousse Cafe," followed by "New Faces of 1968."

| David Gold | Bob Gorman | Gawn Grainger | Robert Gray | Howard Green |

GILFORD, JACK. Born in NYC, July 25. Made Bdwy bow in 1940 in "Meet The People," followed by "They Should Have Stood In Bed," "Count Me In," "The Live Wire," "Alive and Kicking," "Once Over Lightly," "Diary of Anne Frank," "Romanoff and Juliet," "The Tenth Man," "A Funny Thing Happened On The Way To The Forum," "Cabaret."

GILLETTE, ANITA. Born in Baltimore, Aug. 16, 1938. Made NY debut Off-Bdwy in 1960 in "Russell Patterson's Sketchbook" for which she received a THEATRE WORLD Award, followed by "Carnival," "All American," "Mr. President," "Guys and Dolls" (CC1965), "Don't Drink The Water."

GISH, LILLIAN. Born Oct. 14, 1896 in Springfield, O. Made stage debut at 6. After eminent career in films, made Bdwy debut in 1930 in "Uncle Vanya," followed by "Camille," "Nine Pine Street," "The Joyous Season," "Hamlet," "The Star Wagon," "Dear Octopus," "Life With Father," "Mr. Sycamore," "Crime and Punishment," "The Curious Savage," "The Trip To Bountiful," "Family Reunion" (OB), "All The Way Home," "Too True To Be Good," American Shakespeare Festival (1965), "Anya," "I Never Sang For My Father."

GLENN, SCOTT. Born Jan. 26, 1942 in Pittsburgh. Graduate of William & Mary College. Made Bdwy debut in 1965 in "The Impossible Years," followed by "Collision Course" (OB).

GOLD, DAVID. Born in NYC, Feb. 2, 1929. Attended Antioch College. Appeared with Martha Graham Dance Co. before Bdwy bow in 1955 in "Red Roses For Me," followed by "Copper and Brass," "New Girl In Town," "Redhead," "Greenwillow," "Do Re Mi," "We Take The Town," "Little Me," "Pleasures and Palaces," "Drat! The Cat!," "Sweet Charity," "The Education of Hyman Kaplan."

GOLDSMITH, MERWIN. Born Aug. 7, 1937 in Detroit. Graduate of UCLA. Trained and appeared with Bristol, Eng., Old Vic before making Off-Bdwy bow in 1967 in "Hamlet As A Happening."

GORMAN, BOB. Born Dec. 30, 1928 in Peoria, Tenn. Gradute of Ill. Wesleyan U. and Columbia. Made Bdwy bow in 1957 in "Li'l Abner," followed by "Music Man," "Subways Are For Sleeping," "Half A Sixpence," "Breakfast At Tiffany's," "Sweet Charity," "How Now, Dow Jones."

GORMAN, CLIFF. Born Oct. 13, 1936 in NYC. Attended NYU, UCLA, U.N. Mex. Has appeared Off-Bdwy in "Hogan's Goat," "The Boys In The Band," "Ergo."

GORMAN, MARI. Born Sept. 1, 1944 in NYC. Made debut Off-Bdwy in 1966 in "The Kitchen," followed by "Walking To Waldheim" (LC), "The Memorandum."

GORME, EYDIE. Born in the Bronx, and attended CCNY. After successful tv, recording, and nightclub career, made Bdwy debut in 1968 in "Golden Rainbow."

GOSSETT, LOUIS. Born May 27, 1936 in Brooklyn. Graduate of NYU. Made Bdwy bow in 1953 in "Take A Giant Step," followed by "The Desk Set," "Lost In The Stars" (CC), "A Raisin In The Sun," "Tambourines To Glory," Off-Bdwy in "The Blacks," "Telemachus Clay," and "The Bloodknot," "The Zulu and The Zayda," "My Sweet Charlie," "Carry Me Back To Morningside Heights."

GOULD, GORDON. Born May 4, 1930 in Chicago. Graduate of Yale, and Cambridge, Eng. Has appeared with APA since 1963 in "Man and Superman," "War and Peace," "Judith," "Lower Depths," "Right You Are," "Scapin," "Impromptu At Versailles," "You Can't Take It With You," "The Hostage," "The Tavern," "A Midsummer Night's Dream," "Merchant of Venice," "Richard II," "Much Ado About Nothing," "The Wild Duck," "The Show-Off," "Pantagleize."

GOULET, ROBERT. Born Nov. 36, 1933 in Lawrence, Mass. Attended Toronto's Royal Conservatory of Music. Made Bdwy debut in 1960 in "Camelot" for which he received a THEATRE WORLD Award, followed by "The Happy Time."

GRABLE, BETTY. Born Dec. 18, 1916 in St. Louis. Made Bdwy debut in 1939 in "DuBarry Was A Lady," and after many years in films returned in "Hello, Dolly!"

GRAINGER, GAWN. Born Oct. 12, 1940 in Holywood, Ire. Made NY bow with Bristol Old Vic in 1967 in "Romeo and Juliet," "Measure For Measure," and "Hamlet," followed by "There's A Girl In My Soup."

GRAVES, ERNEST. Born May 5, 1919 in Chicago. Studied at Goodman Theatre. Made Bdwy bow in 1941 in "Macbeth," followed by "The Russian People," "Cyrano de Bergerac," "Eastward In Eden," "Venus Is," "Ceremony of Innocence" (OB).

GRAY, ROBERT. Born July 2, 1940 in Detroit. Graduate of U. Detroit. Studied at Dramatic Workshop. Made NY debut Off-Bdwy in 1967 in "Nighthawks."

GREEN, HOWARD. Born Mar. 9, 1936 in Detroit. Graduate of U. Mich. Has appeared Off-Bdwy in "Darkness At Noon," "Cyrano de Bergerac" (LCRep), and "Ceremony of Innocence."

GREEN, MARTYN. Born in London, Apr. 22, 1899. Attended Royal College of Music. Appeared with D'Oyly Carte Co. (1934-51), with Chartok's Gilbert and Sullivan Co., and in "Misalliance," "Shangri-La," "Child of Fortune," "A Visit To A Small Planet," Off-Bdwy in "Drums Under The Windows," "Red Roses For Me," and "Carricknabauna," "Black Comedy."

GREENE, JAMES. Born Dec. 1, 1926 in Lawrence, Mass. Graduate of Emerson College. Appeared Off-Bdwy in "The Iceman Cometh," "American Gothic," "The King and The Duke," "The Hostage," "Plays For Bleecker Street," "Moon In The Yellow River," and "Misalliance," with LC Rep. for 2 years, on Bdwy in "Romeo and Juliet," "Girl On The Via Flaminia," "Compulsion," "Inherit The Wind," "Shadow of A Gunman," "Andersonville Trial," "Night Life," with APA in "You Can't Take It With You," "School For Scandal," "The Wild Duck," "Right You Are," "The Show-Off."

GREENE, MAXINE. Born July 28, 1945 in Philadelphia. Graduate of Temple U. Made NY debut Off-Bdwy in 1968 in "Ergo," followed by Bdwy bow in 1968 in "Leda Had A Little Swan."

GREENE, REUBEN. Born Nov. 24, 1938 in Philadelphia. Appeared Off-Bdwy in "Jericho-Jim Crow" and "Happy Ending," and with APA in "War and Peace," "You Can't Take It With You," and "Pantagleize," and in "The Boys In The Band" (OB).

GREGG, JULIE. Born Jan. 24, 1944 in Niagara Falls, N.Y. Attended US Cal. Made Bdwy debut Jan. 18, 1968 in "The Happy Time" for which she received a THEATRE WORLD Award.

| Danny Guerrero | Marian Hailey | Eric Hamilton | Roger Hamilton | Michael Hawkir |

GREY, JOEL. Born Apr. 11, 1932 in Cleveland, O. Attended Cleveland Playhouse, Neighborhood Playhouse. Made NY bow Off-Bdwy in "The Littlest Revue," followed by "Borscht Capades," "Come Blow Your Horn," "Stop The World—I Want To Get Off," "Half A Sixpence," "Harry, Noon and Night" (OB), "Cabaret," "George M!"

GRICE, WAYNE. Born Feb. 24, 1942 in NYC. Attended New School, Actors Studio. Has appeared on Bdwy in "Blues For Mr. Charlie" (1965), and Off-bdwy in "Moon On A Rainbow Shawl," "Walk In Darkness," "Bohikee Creek," "A Son Comes Home," and "The Electronic Nigger."

GRIMES, TAMMY. Born Jan. 30, 1934 in Lynn, Mass. Attended Stephens College, and Neighborhood Playhouse. Appeared Off-Bdwy in "The Littlest Revue," and "Clerambard," and made Bdwy debut in 1959 in "Look After Lulu" for which she received a THEATRE WORLD Award, followed by "The Unsinkable Molly Brown," "Rattle Of A Simple Man," "High Spirits," "The Only Game In Town."

GRIZZARD, GEORGE. Born Apr. 1, 1928 in Roanoke Rapids, NC. Graduate of UNC. Made Bdwy bow in 1954 in "All Summer Long," followed by "The Desperate Hours," "The Happiest Millionaire" and for which he received a THEATRE WORLD Award, "The Disenchanted," "Big Fish, Little Fish," with APA (1961-62), "Who's Afraid of Virginia Woolf?," "The Glass Menagerie" (1965), "You Know I Can't Hear You When The Water's Running."

GROSS, GENE. Born Feb. 17, 1920, in NYC. Attended American Theatre Wing. Made debut Off-Bdwy in 1957 in "Career," followed by "Handful of Fire," "J.B.," "The Passion of Josef D," "The Tenth Man" (CC1967).

GROSSMANN, SUZANNE. Born in Switzerland. Graduate of McGill U., Canada. Appeared with American Shakespeare Festival before making Bdwy debut in 1966 in "The Lion In Winter," followed by "Cyrano de Bergerac" with LC Rep. Co.

GROVER, STANLEY. Born Mar. 28, 1926 in Woodstock, Ill. Attended U. Mo. Appeared in "Seventeen," "Wish You Were Here," "Time Remember'd," "Candide," "13 Daughters," "Mr. President," City Center revivals of "South Pacific," "Finian's Rainbow," and "The King and I."

GUARDINO, HARRY. Born in NYC, Dec. 23, 1925. Attended Dramatic Workshop. Has appeared in "End As A Man," "A Hatful of Rain," "Natural Affection," "Anyone Can Whistle," "The Rose Tattoo" (1966), "The Seven Descents of Myrtle."

GUERRERO, DANNY. Born Oct. 14, 1945 in Tucson, Ariz. Attended UCLA, and Pasadena Playhouse. Has appeared Off-Bdwy in "Hello, Tourista," "Two Gentlemen of Verona," "The Devil's Disciple," and "Who's Who, Baby."

GUNN, MOSES. Born Oct. 2, 1929 in St. Louis. Graduate of Tenn. A & I U., and U. Kan. Has appeared Off-Bdwy in "Measure For Measure," "Bohikee Creek," "Day of Absence," "Happy Ending," "Baal," "Hard Travelin'," "Lonesome Train," "In White America," and "The Blacks," with NY Shakespeare Festival in "Titus Andronicus," on Bdwy in "A Hand Is On The Gate," with NEC in "Song of The Lusitanian Bogey," "Summer of The 17th Doll," and "Kongi's Harvest" and "Daddy Goodness."

HACKETT, BUDDY. Born Aug. 31, 1924 in Brooklyn. Appeared in nightclubs, films and tv before making Bdwy bow in 1954 in "Lunatics and Lovers," followed by "Viva Madison Avenue," "I Had A Ball," and with Eddie Fisher "At The Palace."

HACKMAN, GENE. Born in San Bernardino, Calif. Made Bdwy bow in 1963 in "Children From Their Games," followed by "A Rainy Day In Newark," "Any Wednesday," "Poor Richard," "The Natural Look," "Fragments" (OB).

HADGE, MICHAEL. Born June 6, 1932 in Greensboro, N.C. Made Bdwy debut in 1958 in "The Cold Wind and The Warm," followed by "Lady of The Camellias," "The Impossible Years."

HAGEN, UTA. Born June 11, 1919 in Goettingen, Ger. Made NY debut in 1938 in "The Seagull," followed by "The Happiest Years," "Key Largo," "Vickie," "Othello," "A Streetcar Named Desire," "Country Girl," "St. Joan," "The Whole World Over," "In Any Language," "The Magic and The Loss," City Center revivals of "Angel Street" and "Tovarich," "A Month In The Country" and "Good Woman of Setzuan" at Phoenix, "Who's Afraid of Virginia Woolf?," with APA in "The Cherry Orchard."

HAIGH, KENNETH. Born in Yorkshire, Eng., Mar. 25, 1930. Attended Central School of Dramatic Art, London. Made Bdwy bow in 1957 in "Look Back In Anger," followed by "Caligula," "Endecott and The Red Cross" (OB).

HAILEY, MARION. Born Feb. 1, 1941 in Portland, Ore. Graduate of U. Wash. Made Bdwy debut in 1965 in "Mating Dance," followed by "Any Wednesday," "Best Laid Plans," Off-Bdwy in "Under The Yum Yum Tree" and "Thornton Wilder's Triple Bill," "Keep It In The Family."

HALL, GEORGE. Born Nov. 19, 1916 in Toronto, Can. Attended Neighborhood Playhouse. Appeared in "Call Me Mister," "Lend An Ear," "Touch and Go," "The Live Wire," "The Boy Friend," Off-Bdwy in "The Balcony" and "Ernest In Love," "There's A Girl In My Soup."

HALL, MARGARET. Born in Richmond, Va., Graduate of William and Mary College. Made Bdwy debut in 1960 in "Becket" after appearing Off-Bdwy in "The Boy Friend," "Fallout," "U.S.A.," "A Midsummer Night's Dream," and "Little Mary Sunshine," "High Spirits," "Mame."

HALLOW, JOHN. Born in NYC. Nov. 28, 1924. Attended Neighborhood Playhouse. Made Bdwy bow in 1954 in "Anastasia," followed by "Ross," "Visit To A Small Planet," "Foxy," "Oh, Dad, Poor Dad . . .," "Ben Franklin In Paris," "3 Bags Full," "Don't Drink The Water."

HAMILTON, ERIC. Born Dec. 27, 1954 in Bridgeport, Conn. Appeared in City Center revivals of "The Sound of Music" and "The King and I," and in "The Happy Time."

HAMILTON, ROGER. Born May 2, 1928 in San Diego. Attended San Diego State College, and RADA. Appeared Off-Bdwy in "Merchant of Venice," "Hamlet," "Live Like Pigs," "Hotel Passionato," and "Sgt. Musgrove's Dance," on Bdwy in "Someone Waiting," "Separate Tables," "Little Moon of Alban," "Luther," "The Deputy," "Rosencrantz and Guildenstern Are Dead."

HANNAFIN, DANIEL P. Born Feb. 8, 1933 in NYC. Attended Juilliard. Has appeared on Bdwy in "Camelot," "Flora The Red Menace," "Baker Street," and City Center revivals of "South Pacific," "Wonderful Town," "Brigadoon," "Oklahoma!," and "The Tenth Man."

| Tom Helmore | Bette Henritze | William Herter | Holly Hill | Judd Hirsch |

HARE, WILL. Born Mar. 30, 1919 in Elkins, W.Va. Attended American Actors Theatre. Has appeared in "The Eternal Road," "The Moon Is Down," "Suds In Your Eye," "Only The Heart," "The Visitor," "Trip To Bountiful," "Witness For The Prosecution," "Marathon '33," Off-Bdwy in "The Viewing" and "Winter Journey."

HARRIS, BARBARA. Born in Evanston, Ill. Made Bdwy debut in 1961 in "From The Second City," followed Off-Bdwy by "Seacoast of Bohemia," "Alarums and Excursions," "Oh, Dad, Poor Dad, . . .," for which she received a THEATRE WORLD Award, "Mother Courage and Her Children," and "Dynamite Tonight," "On A Clear Day You Can See Forever," "The Apple Tree."

HARTMAN, ELEK. Born Ipr. 26, 1922 in Canton, O. Graduate of Carnegie Tech. Has appeared Off-Bdwy in "Where People Gather," and "Goa."

HASSO, SIGNE. Born in Stockholm. Aug. 15, 1915. Attended Swedish Academy of Dramatic Arts. Has appeared in "Golden Wings," "Edwina Black,", "Glad Tidings," "Uncle Vanya" (OB), "The Apple Cart," "Mary Stuart" (OB), "Cabaret."

HAWKINS, MICHAEL. Born in NYC. Attended Carnegie Tech. Has appeared Off-Bdwy in "MacBird" and "Love and Let Love," and with American Shakespeare Festival.

HAYES, BARBARA. Born in NYC. Graduate of Syracuse U. Made Bdwy debut in 1961 in "Invitation To A March," followed by "Daughter of Silence," "In The Counting House," Off-Bdwy in "Clearing In The Woods," "U.S.A.," "The Way of The World," "Hey You, Lightman," "Big Man," and "Four Seasons."

HAYES, BILL. Born June 5, 1925 in Harvey, Ill. Attended DePauw and Northwestern. Made Bdwy bow in 1953 in "Me and Juliet," followed by "Brigadoom" (CC1967).

HAYES, HELEN. Born Oct. 10, 1900 in Washington, D.C. Graduate of Sacred Heart Convent Academy. Made Bdwy debut in 1909 in "Old Dutch," followed by "The Summer Widowers," "Penrod," "Dear Brutus," "Clarence," "To The Ladies," "We Moderns," "Dancing Mothers," "Caesar and Cleopatra," "What Every Woman Knows," "Coquette," "Mary of Scotland," "Victoria Regina," "Twelfth Night," "Candle In The Wind," "Happy Birthday," "Wisteria Trees," "Mrs. McThing," "The Glass Menagerie" (CC), "The Skin of Our Teeth," "Time Remember'd," "Touch of The Poet," "The White House," and with APA in "School For Scandal," "Right You Are," "We Comrades Three," and "The Show-Off."

HECHT, PAUL. Born in London, Aug. 16, 1941. Attended McGill U. Appeared Off-Bdwy with NY Shakespeare Festival in "Sgt. Musgrave's Dance" and "MacBird," on Bdwy in "Rosencrantz and Guildenstern Are Dead."

HECKART, EILEEN. Born May 29, 1919 in Columbus, O. Graduate of Ohio State U. Made NY debut Off-Bdwy in "Tinker's Dam," followed by "Our Town" (CC), "They Knew What They Wanted," "The Traitor," "Hilde Crane," "In Any Language," "Picnic" for which she received a THEATRE WORLD Award, "The Bad Seed," "A View From The Bridge," "The Dark At The Top of The Stairs," "Invitation To A March," "Pal Joey" (CC), "Everybody Loves Opal," "A Family Affair," "Too True To Be Good," "And Things That Go Bump In The Night," "Barefoot In The Park," "You Know I Can't Hear You When The Water's Running."

HEFFERNAN, JOHN. Born May 30, 1934 in NYC. Attended City College, Columbia, Boston U. Made Off-Bdwy bow in "The Judge," followed by "Julius Caesar," "Great God Brown," "Lysistrata," "Peer Gynt," "Henry IV," "Taming of The Shrew," "She Stoops To Conquer," "The Plough and The Stars," "The Octoroon," "Hamlet," "Androcles and The Lion," "A Man's A Man," "Winter's Tale," "Luther," "Tiny Alice," "Postmark Zero," "Arms and The Man (OB), "St. Joan" (LCRep), "The Memorandum" (OB).

HEFLIN, MARTA. Born Mar. 29, 1945 in Washington, D.C. Attended Northwestern, Carnegie Tech. Made NY debut in 1967 City Center revival of "Life With Father."

HEIT, MICHAEL. Born in NYC, Sept. 9, 1943. Attended NYU, U. Alaska, Neighborhood Playhouse. Has appeared Off-Bdwy in "The Party on Greenwich Avenue" and "Hamlet."

HELMORE, TOM. Born in London, Jan. 4, 1912. Made Bdwy bow in 1939 in "No Time For Comedy," followed by "Day Before Spring," "Clutterbuck," "Legend of Sarah," "Love and Let Love," "The High Ground," "The Winner," "One Eye Closed," "The Dark Is Light Enough," "Debut," "Mary, Mary," "The Playroom," "House of Flowers" (OB).

HENRITZE, BETTE. Born May 3 in Betsy Layne, Ky. Graduate of U. Tenn. Appeared Off-Bdwy with Phoenix Rep., NY Shakespeare Festival, "Lion In Love," "Abe Lincoln In Illinois," "Othello," "Baal," "Long Christmas Dinner," "Queens of France," "Rimers of Eldritch," and "The Displaced Person," on Bdwy in "Jenny Kissed Me," "Pictures In The Hallway," "Giants, Sons of Giants," "Ballad of The Sad Cafe," "The White House," "Dr. Cook's Garden," "Here's Where I Belong."

HERLIE, EILEEN. Born Mar. 8, 1920 in Glasgow, Scot. Made Bdwy debut in 1955 in "The Matchmaker," followed by "The Makropoulos Secret" (OB), "Epitaph For George Dillon," "Take Me Along," "All American," "Photo Finish," "Hamlet" (1964), "Halfway Up The Tree."

HERLIHY, ED. Born in Boston. After wide experience on radio and tv, made Bdwy bow April 1, 1968 in "Mame."

HERTER, WILLIAM. Born Sept. 17, 1947 in Philadelphia. Attended Temple U. Has appeared with Am. Shakespeare Festival, Off-Bdwy in "Antigone," and "Hair."

HILARY, JENNIFER. Born Dec. 14, 1942 in Frimley, Eng. Attended RADA. Made Bdwy debut in 1963 in "The Rehearsal," followed by "Ivanov" (1966), "Avantil"

HILL ARTHUR. Born Aug. 1, 1922 in Melfort, Can. Attended U. British Col. Made Bdwy bow in 1955 in "The Matchmaker," followed by "Look Homeward, Angel," "The Gang's All Here," "All The Way Home," "Who's Afraid of Virginia Woolf?," "Something More," "The Porcelain Year," "More Stately Mansions."

HILL, HOLLY. Born Nov. 16 in Cleveland, O. Graduate of Stanford U. Made Bdwy debut in 1966 in "3 Bags Full," followed by "Where People Gather" (OB).

HILLMAN, GEORGE. Born Sept. 21, 1906 in NYC. Attended Lincoln U. After 35 years with Hillman Brothers Dance Team, made NY bow Off-Bdwy in "Curley McDimple."

| Gail Honig | Beth Howland | Barnard Hughes | Charles Hull | Carl Jacobs |

HINGLE, PAT. Born July 19, 1923 in Denver. Graduate of Tex. U. Member of Actors Studio. Made Bdwy bow in 1953 in "End As A Man," followed by "Festival," "Cat On A Hot Tin Roof," "Girls of Summer," "The Dark At The Top Of The Stairs," "J.B.," "Deadly Game," "Strange Interlude" (1963), "Blues For Mr. Charlie," "A Girl Could Get Lucky," "The Glass Menagerie" (1965), "Johnny No Trump," "The Price."

HINNANT, BILL. Born Aug. 28, 1935 in Chincoteague Island, Va. Graduate of Yale. Has appeared in "No Time For Sergeants," "All Kinds of Giants," "Put It In Writing" (OB), "Here's Love," "You're A Good Man, Charlie Brown" (OB).

HINNANT, SKIP. Born Sept. 12, 1940 in Chincoteague Island, Va. Graduate of Yale. Made NY bow Off-Bdwy in 1964 in "The Knack," followed by "You're A Good Man, Charlie Brown" (OB).

HIRSCH, JUDD. Born Mar. 15, 1935 in NYC. Attended AADA. Made Bdwy bow in 1966 in "Barefoot In The Park," and appeared Off-Bdwy in "On The Necessity of Being Polygamous," and "Scuba Duba."

HOLBROOK, HAL. Born Feb. 17, 1925 in Cleveland, O. Graduate of Denison U. Made Bdwy bow in 1961 in "Do You Know The Milky Way?," followed by "Henry IV" and "Richard II" with Am. Shakespeare Festival, "Abe Lincoln In Illinois" (OB), LC Rep. Co. productions of "Marco Millions," "Incident At Vichy," "Tartuffe," and "After The Fall," in 1965 revival of "The Glass Menagerie," toured world in one man show "Mark Twain Tonight!" and presented it on Bdwy in 1966, followed by "The Apple Tree," "I Never Sang For My Father."

HOLLANDER, JACK. Born Jan. 29, 1918 in Chicago. Graduate of Goodman Theatre School. Made Bdwy bow in 1959 in "The Miracle Worker," followed by "All The Way Home," "Gideon," Off-Bdwy in "Girl of The Golden West," "The Dybbuk," and "Journey To The Day," "The Impossible Years," and with NY Shakespeare Festival in "Titus Andronicus" and "Comedy of Errors," "Ergo" (OB).

HOLM, CELESTE. Born Apr. 29, 1919 in NYC. Made Bdwy debut in 1938 in "Glorianna," followed by "The Time of Your Life," "Another Sun," "The Return of The Vagabond," "Papa Is All," "Damask Cheek," "Oklahoma!," "She Stoops To Conquer," "Bloomer Girl," "Affairs of State," "Anna Christie" (1951), "His and Hers," "Interlock," "Third Best Sport," "Invitation To A March," "A Month In The Country" (OB), "Mame."

HONIG, GAIL. Born May 3, 1956 in The Bronx. Made NY debut with Lincoln Center Rep. Co. in "Tiger At The Gates" and "Cyrano de Bergerac."

HOOKS, ROBERT. Born Apr. 18, 1937 in Washington, D.C. Attended Temple U. Made Bdwy bow in "A Raisin In The Sun," followed by "A Taste of Honey," "Tiger, Tiger Burning Bright," "Arturo Ui," "The Milk Train Doesn't Stop Here Anymore," "Where's Daddy?" for which he received a THEATRE WORLD Award, and "Hallelujah Baby," Off-Bdwy in "Henry V," "Ballad of Bimshire," "The Blacks," "Dutchman," "Happy Ending," "Day of Absence," with Negro Ensemble Co. that he co-founded in "Kongi's Harvest."

HORTON, RUSSELL. Born Nov. 11, 1941 in Los Angeles. Graduate of UCLA. Has appeared in "The Displaced Person" (OB), "How's The World Treating You?," "Galileo" (LCRep), "What Did We Do Wrong?"

HOWARD, ALAN. Born Mar. 21, 1951 in Rockville Centre, L.I. Made Bdwy bow in 1960 in "The Wall," followed by "Garden of Sweets," "A Gift of Time," Off-Bdwy in "King of The Whole Damn World" and "Square In The Eye," "The Playroom," "Titus Andronicus" (NY Shake), "A Certain Young Man" (OB).

HOWELL, ERIK. Born in Dathan, Ala. Attended William & Mary College. Made NY debut Off-Bdwy in 1966 in "The Fantasticks," followed by "Who's Who, Baby?" (OB).

HOWLAND, BETH. Born May 28, 1941 in Boston. Made NY debut Off-Bdwy in 1960 in "Once Upon A Mattress," followed by Bdwy roles in "Bye, Bye Birdie," "High Spirits," "Drat! The Cat!," "Darling of The Day."

HUBBARD, ELIZABETH. Born Dec. 22 in NYC. Graduate of Radcliffe College, and RADA. Made Bdwy debut in 1960 in "The Affair," followed by "Threepenny Opera," and "Boys From Syracuse" Off-Bdwy, "The Passion of Josef D," "The Physicists," "A Time For Singing," "A Day In The Death of Joe Egg."

HUGHES, BARNARD. Born July 16, 1915 in Bedford Hills, N.Y. Attended Manhattan College. Appeared Off-Bdwy in "Rosmersholm," "A Doll's House," and "Hogan's Goat," made Bdwy bow in 1949 in "The Ivy Green," followed by "Dinosaur Wharf," "Teahouse of The August Moon" (1956CC), "A Majority of One," "Advise and Consent," "The Advocate," "Hamlet" (1964), "I Was Dancing," "Generation," "How Now, Dow Jones."

HUGHES, TRESA. Born Sept. 17, 1929 in Washington, D.C. Attended Wayne U. Has appeared Off-Bdwy in "Electra," "The Crucible," "Hogan's Goat," "Party On Greenwich Avenue," and "Fragments," on Bdwy in "The Miracle Worker," "The Devil's Advocate," "Dear Me, The Sky Is Falling," "The Last Analysis," "Spofford."

HUGO, LAURENCE. Born Dec. 22, 1917 in Berkeley, Calif. Attended U. Cal., Neighborhood Playhouse. Made Bdwy bow in 1941 in "The Distant City," followed by "The Skin of Our Teeth," "I'll Take The High Road," "Decision," "Born Yesterday," "Stalag 17," "Double In Hearts," "U.S.A." (OB), "There's A Girl In My Soup."

HULL, CHARLES. Born Mar. 3, 1936 in Vienna, Aust. Graduate of Lehigh U. Made Bdwy bow in 1960 in "The Story of Mary Surratt," followed by Off-Bdwy roles in "Abe Lincoln In Illinois" and "A Certain Young Man."

HUMPHREY, CAVADA. Born June 17 in Atlantic City. Graduate of Smith College. Made NY debut Off-Bdwy in "A Man's House," followed by "The House In Paris," "The Cherry Orchard," "Song of Bernadette," "As The Girls Go," "The Devil's Disciple," "Moon In Capricorn," "Richard II," "The Taming of The Shrew," "Love's Labour's Lost," "Richard III," "Othello," "Henry IV," "Girl of The Golden West," "Time Remember'd," "Dear Liar," "Life Is A Dream," "You Can't Take It With You" (APA), "King John" (CP).

HUNTER, JAMES. Born Aug. 16, 1943 in London. Attended London Academy of Music and Dramatic Art. Made Bdwy debut in 1968 in "Loot."

| William Jay | Page Johnson | Lauren Jones | John Joy | Raul Julia |

HUNTER, KIM. Born Nov. 12, 1922 in Detroit. Member of Actors Studio. Made Bdwy debut in 1947 in "A Streetcar Named Desire," followed by "Darkness At Noon," "The Chase," "The Children's Hour" (1952), "The Tender Trap," "Come Slowly, Eden" (OB) with Am. Shakespeare Festival in 1961, "Write Me A Murder," "Weekend."

HUOT, DENISE. Born Oct. 13, 1936 in Pittsburgh. Graduate of Carnegie Tech and London Academy of Music and Drama. Made Bdwy debut in 1966 in "How's The World Treating You?," followed by "Carricknabauna" (OB), "The Prime of Miss Jean Brodie."

HUTT, WILLIAM. Born May 2, 1920 in Toronto, Can. Graduate of Trinity College, U. Toronto. Made Bdwy bow in 1956 in "Tamburlaine The Great," followed by "Mary Stuart" (OB), "The Makropoulos Secret" (Phoenix), "Tiny Alice," "St. Joan" (LCRep.).

HYMAN, EARLE. Born Oct. 11, 1926 in Rocky Mt., N.C. Attended New School, and Am. Theatre Wing. Made Bdwy bow in 1943 in "Run, Little Chillun," followed by "Anna Lucasta," "The Climate of Eden," "Merchant of Venice," "Othello," "Julius Caesar," "The Tempest," "No Time For Sergeants," "Mr. Johnson" for which he received a THEATRE WORLD Award, "St. Joan," "Hamlet," "Waiting For Godot," Am. Shakespeare Festival, "The Duchess of Malfi," "The White Rose and The Red," "The Worlds of Shakespeare," "Jonah," "St. Joan" (LCRep.).

IRVING, GEORGE S. Born Nov. 1, 1922 in Springfield, Mass. Attended Leland Powers School. Made Bdwy bow in 1943 in "Oklahoma!," followed by "Call Me Mister," "Along Fifth Avenue," "Two's Company," "Me and Juliet," "Can-Can," "Shinbone Alley," "Bells Are Ringing," "The Good Soup," "Tovarich," "A Murderer Among Us," "Alfie," "Sanya," "Galileo" (LC), "The Happy Time."

IVES, BURL. Born June 14, 1909 in Hunt City Township, Ill. Attended Eastern Ill. State Teachers College, Juilliard. Made Bdwy debut in 1938 in "The Boys From Syracuse," followed by "This Is The Army," "Sing Out, Sweet Land!," "She Stoops To Conquer," "Show Boat" (1954CC), "Cat On A Hot Tin Roof," "Dr. Cook's Garden."

JACKSON, ANNE. Born Sept. 3, 1926 in Allegheny, Pa. Attended Neighborhood Playhouse, New School, Actors Studio. Made Bdwy debut in 1945 in "Signature," followed by "Yellow Jack," "John Gabriel Borkman," "The Last Dance," "Summer and Smoke," "Magnolia Alley," "Love Me Long," "Lady From The Sea," "Never Say Never," "Oh, Men! Oh, Women!," "Rhinoceros," Off-Bdwy in "Brecht On Brecht," "The Tiger," and "The Typists," "Luv," "The Exercise."

JACOBI, LOU. Born in Toronto, Can., Dec. 28, 1913. Made Bdwy bow in 1955 in "The Diary of Anne Frank," followed by "The Tenth Man," "Come Blow Your Horn," "Fade Out—Fade In," "Don't Drink The Water."

JACOBS, CARL. Born Nov. 29, 1916 in Cincinnati. Graduate of New School. Appeared Off-Bdwy in "The Father," "Coriolanus," and "The White Rose and The Red," before making Bdwy bow in 1967 in "Rosencrantz and Guildenstern Are Dead."

JACOBY, SCOTT. Born Nov. 26, 1955 in Chicago. Appeared in "Oliver" on tour, and on "Dandelion Wine" (LC), before making Bdwy bow in 1968 in "Golden Rainbow."

JAMES, CLIFTON. Born May 29, 1921 in Spokane, Wash. Attended Ore. U., Actors Studio. Has appeared in "The Time of Your Life" (CC), "The Cave Dwellers," "Great Day In The Morning," "Andorra," "And Things That Go Bump In The Night," "The Coop" (OB), "Trial of Lee Harvey Oswald."

JAMESON, HOUSE. Born Dec. 17, 1902 in Austin, Tex. Graduate of Columbia. Made Bdwy bow in 1923 in "St. Joan," followed by "Goat Song," "Grand Street Follies," "Garrick Gaieties," "An American Tragedy," "The Dark Hours," "We, The People," "Judgement Day," "In Time To Come," "The Patriots," "Requiem For a Nun," "Never Too Late," "The Great Indoors," "Don't Drink The Water."

JARVIS, GRAHAM. Born Aug. 25, 1930 in Toronto, Can. Attended Williams College, American Theatre Wing. Made Bdwy bow in 1957 in "Orpheus Descending," followed by "The Egghead," "Man In The Dog Suit," "Much Ado About Nothing," "The Best Man," "Romulus," LCRep. Co. productions, "The Investigation," "Halfway Up The Tree."

JASPER, ZINA. Born Jan. 29, 1939 in The Bronx, N.Y. Attended CCNY. Made Bdwy debut in 1967 in "Something Different," followed by Off-Bdwy's "Saturday Night."

JAY, WILLIAM. Born May 15, 1935 in Baxter Springs, Kan. Attended Omaha U. Made NY bow Off-Bdwy in 1963 in "Utopia," followed by "The Blacks," "Loop The Loop On The Moebius Strip," "Happy Ending," "Day of Absence," NY Shakespeare's "Hamlet" and "Othello," NEC's "Song of The Lusitanian Bogey."

JENS, SALOME. Born in Milwaukee, May 8, 1935. Attended Northwestern, and U. Wis. Made Bdwy debut in 1956 in "Sixth Finger In A Five Finger Glove," followed Off-Bdwy in "The Bald Soprano," "Jack," "Deidre Of The Sorrows," "U.S.A.," "The Balcony," "Desire Under The Elms," and "Posterity For Sale," LCRep. Col.'s "After The Fall," "But For Whom, Charlie," and "Tartuffe," "The Disenchanted," "A Far Country," "Night Life," "I'm Solomon."

JOHANN, DALLAS. Born June 15, 1944 in Madison, Wisc. Made Bdwy debut Jan. 18, 1968 in "The Happy Time."

JOHNS, ANDREW. Born Dec. 12, 1935 in Martinez, Calif. Has appeared Off-Bdwy in "The Wood Demon," and made Bdwy bow in 1967 in "The Unknown Soldier and His Wife."

JOHNSON, BAYN. Born Nov. 4, 1958 in New Orleans. Made NY debut Off-Bdwy in 1967 in "Curley McDimple."

JOHNSON, PAGE. Born Aug. 25, 1930 in Welch, W. Va. Graduate of Ithaca College. Made Bdwy bow in 1951 in DeHavilland's "Romeo and Juliet," followed by "Electra," "Oedipus," "Camino Real," "In April Once" for which he received a THEATRE WORLD Award, "Red Roses For Me," "The Lovers," Off-Bdwy in "Military Taps," "The Enchanted," "Guitar," "4 In 1," "Journey of The Fifth Horse," and "Yucca Trail," with APA in "School For Scandal," "The Tavern," and "The Seagull," "The Odd Couple."

JONES, CHARLOTTE. Born Jan. 1 in Chicago. Attended Loyola and DePaul U. Appeared Off-Bdwy in "False Confessions," "Sign of Jonah," "Girl on The Via Flaminia," "Red Roses For Me," "Night Is Black Bottles," "Camino Real," "Plays For Bleecker Street," "Pigeons," "Great Scot!," and "Sgt. Musgrave's Dance," and on Bdwy in "Camino Real," "Buttrio Square," "Mame," "How Now, Dow Jones."

| Michael Kapec | Rita Karin | Lynn Kellogg | Ken Kercheval | Glenn Keze |

JONES, LAUREN. Born Sept. 7, 1942 in Boston. Made Bdwy debut in 1964 in "Ben Franklin In Paris," followed by "Skyscraper," and Off-Bdwy in "Ballad of Bimshire," and "Trials of Brother Jero."

JONES, NEIL. Born May 6, 1942 in Boston. Attended Boston Conservatory. Has appeared in "The Music Man," "Hello, Dolly!"

JOY, JOHN. Born May 31, 1937 in Fredonia, N.Y. Graduate of Dartmouth. Attended American Theatre Wing. Made Bdwy bow in 1967 in "How Now, Dow Jones."

JOYCE, STEPHEN. Born in NYC, Mar. 7, 1933. Attended Fordham U. Appeared in Am. Shakespeare Festival productions before Bdwy bow in 1966 in "Those That Play The Clowns," followed by "Three Hand Reel," LCRep. Co.'s "Galileo" and "St. Joan," "Stephen D" for which he received a THEATRE WORLD Award, and on Bdwy in "The Exercise."

JULIA, RAUL. Born Mar. 9, 1940 in San Juan, P.R. Graduate of U.P.R. Appeared with NY Shakespeare Festival in "Macbeth," "Titus Andronicus," and "Theatre In The Street," Off-Bdwy in "Life Is A Dream," "Blood Wedding," "The Ox Cart," "No Exit," and "The Memorandum."

KAGAN, DIANE. Born in Maplewood, N.J. Graduate of Fla. State U. Made NY debut Off-Bdwy in 1963 in "Asylum," followed by "Days and Nights of Bebe Fenstermaker," and "Death of The Well-loved Boy," and Bdwy roles in "Chinese Prime Minister," "Never Too Late," "Any Wednesday," "Venus Is," and with LCRep. Co. in "Tiger At The Gates."

KAHL, HOWARD. Born Sept. 17, 1930 in New Albany, Ind. Graduate of Ind. U. Made Bdwy bow in 1962 in "Camelot," followed by "Hot Spot," "Fade Out—Fade In," "Pleasures and Palaces," "Anya," "On A Clear Day You Can See Forever," "Cabaret."

KAHN, MADELINE. Born Sept. 29, 1942 in Boston. Graduate of Hofstra U. Made Bdwy debut in "New Faces of 1968."

KAMINSKA, IDA. Born Sept. 4, 1899 in Odessa, USSR. Made Broadway debut Oct. 19, 1967 with Jewish State Theatre of Poland in "Mirele Efros," followed by "Mother Courage."

KAPEC, MICHAEL. Born Jan. 1, 1944 in Allentown, Pa. Member of Actors Studio. Made NY bow Off-Bdwy in 1967 in "Where People Gather."

KAPLAN, JEANNE. Born in Brooklyn. Has appeared Off-Bdwy in "A View From The Bridge," "The Ox Cart," and "The Electronic Nigger."

KARATY, TOMMY. Born Mar. 25, 1940 in Paterson, N.J. Graduate of Notre Dame and Catholic U. Made Bdwy bow in 1960 in "West Side Story," followed by "Cindy" (OB), "Pousse Cafe," "Mame."

KARIN, RITA. Born Oct. 24, 1919 in Warsaw, Poland. Made Bdwy debut in 1960 in "The Wall," followed by "A Call On Kuprin," and Off-Bdwy in "The Pocket Watch" and "Scuba Duba."

KARNILOVA, MARIA. Born Aug. 3, 1920 in Hartford, Conn. Attended Met Opera Ballet School. Appeared with Ballet Theatre before making Bdwy debut in 1938 in "Stars In Your Eyes," followed by "Call Me Mister," "High Button Shoes," "Two's Company," "Hollywood Pinafore," "Beggar's Opera," (CC), "Kaleidoscope" (OB), "Ballets USA," "Gypsy," "Miss Liberty," "Out Of This World," "Bravo Giovanni," "Fiddler On The Roof."

KAYE, ANNE. Born Sept. 6, 1942 in New Haven, Conn. Attended Emerson College, and AMDA. Has appeared Off-Bdwy in "Now Is The Time For All Good Men," "Have I Got One For You," and "The Fantasticks."

KAYE, GLORIA. Born Feb. 11, 1944 in NYC. Made Bdwy debut in 1963 in "Happiest Girl In The World," followed by City Center revivals of "Most Happy Fella" and "West Side Story," and Off-Bdwy in "Who's Who, Baby."

KEISER, KRIS. Born Apr. 16 in Philadelphia. Attended Central State U. Has appeared with Theatre in The Street, and Off-Bdwy in "Clara's Ole Man."

KELLIN, MIKE. Born Apr. 26, 1922 in Hartford, Conn. Attended Trinity College, and Yale. Made Bdwy bow in 1949 in "At War With The Army," followed by "The Bird Cage," "Stalag 17," "The Emperor's Clothes," "The Time of Your Life," "Pipe Dream," Off-Bdwy in "Taming of The Shrew," "Diary of A Scoundrel," "Purple Dust," "Tevya and His Daughters," and "Winkelberg," "God and Kate Murphy," "Mother Courage and Her Children," "The Odd Couple."

KELLOGG, LYNN. Born in Appleton, Wisc., in 1945. Made Bdwy debut Apr. 19, 1968 in "Hair."

KELTON, PERT. Born in Great Falls, Mont. Began career in vaudeville at 3. Made Bdwy debut in 1925 in "Sunny," followed by "Five O'Clock Girl," "The DuBarry," "Guest In The House," "The Bad Seed," "The Music Man," "Greenwillow," "Come Blow Your Horn," "I Was Dancing," "A Minor Miracle," "Spofford."

KEMP, ROGER. Born May 15, 1931 in Bristol, Eng. Attended Bristol U. Made Bdwy debut Oct. 16, 1967 in "Rosencrantz and Guildenstern Are Dead."

KENNEDY, ARTHUR. Born Feb. 1, 1914 in Worcester, Mass. Attended Carnegie Tech. Has appeared in "Henry IV," "Richard II," "All My Sons," "Death Of A Salesman," "See The Jaguar," "The Crucible," "Time Limit!," "The Loud Red Patrick," "The Price."

KERCHEVAL, KEN. Born July 15, 1935 in Indiana. Attended Pacific U., and Neighborhood Playhouse. Appeared Off-Bdwy in 1959 in "Dead End" followed by "Young Abe Lincoln," "Black Monday," "A Man's A Man," "23 Pat O'Brien Movies," and "Father Uxbridge Wants To Marry," on Bdwy in "Something About A Soldier," "Fiddler On The Roof," "Happily Never After," "The Apple Tree."

KERMOYAN, MICHAEL. Born Nov. 29, 1925 in Fresno, Calif. Attended Stanford, USC, and Los Angeles Conservatory. Made Bdwy bow in 1954 in "The Girl In Pink Tights," followed by "Sandhog" (OB), "Whoop-Up," "Happy Town," "Camelot," "Happiest Girl In The World," "Fly Blackbird," "Ross," "Angels of Anadarko" (OB), "Tovarich," "Anya," "The Guide," and City Center revivals of "Carousel," and "The King and I" (1968).

KERR, JOHN. Born Nov. 15, 1931 in NYC. Graduate of Harvard, and Columbia. Made Bdwy bow in 1952 in "Bernardine" for which he received a THEATRE WORLD Award, followed by "Tea and Sympathy," "All Summer Long," "The Infernal Machine" (OB), "Cue For Passion," "The Tenth Man" (CC1967).

KEYES, DANIEL. Born Mar. 6, 1914 in Concord, Mass. Attended Harvard, Am. Theatre Wing. Made Bdwy bow in 1954 in "The Remarkable Mr. Pennypacker," followed by "Bus Stop," Off-Bdwy roles in "Our Town," "Epitaph For George Dillon," "Plays For Bleecker Street," "Hooray! It's A Glorious Day," "Six Characters in Search of An Author," "Sgt. Musgrave's Dance," and "Arms and The Man," "Only In America," "Christine," "First Love," "Take Her, She's Mine," "Baker Street," "Dinner At 8," "I Never Sang For My Father."

| ally Kirkland | Samuel Kressen | Jerry Lanning | Dino Laudicina | Lee Lawson |

KEZER, GLENN. Born Apr. 2, 1923 in Okemah, Okla. Graduate of U. Okla. Made Bdwy bow in 1956 in "My Fair Lady," followed by "Camelot," "Walk In Darkness" (OB), "Fade Out—Fade In," "Half A Sixpence," "Little Murders," "Brigadoon" (CC1964), "The Trial of Lee Harvey Oswald," "The Other Man" and "Oh, Say Can You See L.A." (OB).

KILEY, RICHARD. Born Mar. 31, 1922 in Chicago. Attended Loyola U., and Barnum Drama School. Made Bdwy bow in 1953 in "Misalliance" for which he received a THEATRE WORLD Award, followed by "Kismet," "Sing Me No Lullaby," "Time Limit," "Redhead," "Advise and Consent," "No Strings," "Here's Love," "I Had A Ball," "Man of La Mancha."

KING, DENNIS. Born Nov. 2, 1897 in Coventry, Eng. Made Bdwy bow in 1921 in "Claire de Lune," followed by "Romeo and Juliet," "Antony and Cleopatra," "Vagabond King," "Three Musketeers," "I Married An Angel," "A Doll's House," "Three Sisters," "Dunnigan's Daughter," "He Who Gets Slapped," "Medea," "Edward, My Son," "The Devil's Disciple," "Billy Budd," "Music In The Air," "The Strong Are Lonely," "Lunatics and Lovers," "A Day By The Sea," "Affair of Honor," "Shangri-La," "Hidden River," "The Greatest Man Alive," "Love and Libel," "Photo Finish," "Minor Miracle," "Loves of Cass McGuire," "Portrait Of A Queen."

KING, JOHN MICHAEL. Born May 13, 1926 in NYC. Attended AADA. Appeared in "Inside U.S.A.," "Courtin' Time," "Music In The Air," "Of Thee I Sing," "Buttrio Square," "Me and Juliet," "Ankles Aweigh," "Hit The Trail," "Fanny," "My Fair Lady" for which he received a THEATRE WORLD Award, "Anya," "On A Clear Day You Can See Forever," "Have I Got One For You" (OB).

KINGSTON, KAYE. Born Sept. 5, 1924 in Youngstown, O. Graduate of U. Chicago. Studied at Goodman Theatre. Made Bdwy debut in 1955 in "Catch A Star," followed by "A Midsummer Night's Dream," "As You Like It," "Call It Virtue," "Tiger At The Gates," "The Trial," "Mating Dance," "The Victims."

KIRKHAM, SAM. Born Apr. 28, 1923 in Gainesville, Tex. Attended Chicago U., St. John's, N. Tex. State, and SMU. Made Bdwy bow in 1946 in "Cyrano de Bergerac," followed by "Alive and Kicking," "That's The Ticket," "Stalag 17," "Marat/deSade," "Don't Drink The Water," "The King and I" (CC1968).

KIRKLAND, SALLY. Born Oct. 31, 1944 in NYC. Member of Actors Studio. Made Bdwy debut in 1961 in "Step On A Crack," followed by "The Love Nest" (OB), "Bicycle Ride To Nevada," "Marathon '33," Off-Bdwy in "A Midsummer Night's Dream," "Fitz," "The Bitch of Waverly Place," and "Tom Paine."

KISER, TERRY. Born Aug. 1, 1939 in Omaha, Neb. Graduate of U. Kan. Made NY bow Off-Bdwy in "Night of The Dunce," followed by "Fortune and Men's Eyes" for which he received a THEATRE WORLD Award.

KLEIN, REID. Born Nov. 15, 1938 in Saginaw, Mich. Attended U. Mich. Leading tenor with American Savoyards before making Bdwy bow in 1964 in "Half A Sixpence," followed by "A Time For Singing," "Darling Of The Day."

KLEIN, ROBERT. Born Feb. 8, 1942 in NYC. Graduate of Alfred U., Yale Drama School. Has appeared Off-Bdwy in "Six Characters In Search Of An Author," "Second City Returns," "Upstairs At The Downstairs," and on Bdwy in "The Apple Tree," "New Faces of 1968."

KLENOSKY, WILLIAM J. Born May 28, 1922 in Jamaica, N.Y. Attended CCNY. Author, composer, producer, and actor in "Utopia!," and "Against The Slings and Arrows."

KLUNIS, TOM. Has appeared on Bdwy in "Gideon" and "The Devils," Off-Bdwy in "The Immoralist," "Hamlet," "Arms and The Man," "The Potting Shed," "Measure For Measure," "Henry V," "Romeo and Juliet," "The Balcony," "Our Town," "The Man Who Never Died," "God Is My Ram," "Rise, Marlowe," "Iphigenia In Aulis."

KOURKOULOS, NIKOS. Born in Athens, Greece, Dec. 5, 1934. Attended U. Greece, National Theatre. Made Bdwy bow in 1967 in "Illya, Darling."

KRAWFORD, GARY. Born Mar. 23, 1941 in Kitchener, Can. Made NY bow Off-Bdwy in "The Fantasticks," followed by Bdwy roles in "Pousse Cafe," "The Education of Hyman Kaplan."

KRESSEN, SAMUEL. Born Oct. 5, 1918 in Philadelphia. Made NY bow in 1961 in "Two By Saroyan" Off-Bdwy, followed by "Golden Rainbow."

KUHNER, JOHN. Born Dec. 27, 1942 in Cleveland, O. Graduate of Denison U. Made NY bow Off-Bdwy Jan. 13, 1968 in "Your Own Thing."

LACY, TOM. Born in NYC, Aug. 30, 1933. Made debut Off-Bdwy in 1965 in "The Fourth Pig," followed by "The Fantasticks," "Shoemaker's Holiday," and "Love and Let Love."

LaMOTTA, JOHNNY. Born Jan. 8, 1939 in Brooklyn. Has appeared in "Dead Survivors" (OB), "Illya, Darling," "I'm Solomon."

LANCASTER, LUCIE. Born Oct. 15, 1907 in Chicago. Educated in Europe. Made Bdwy debut in 1947 in "Heads or Tails," followed by "Mr. Pickwick," "The Girl Who Came To Supper," "Bajour," "How Now, Dow Jones."

LANDIS, JESSIE ROYCE. Born in Chicago, Nov. 25, 1904. Made Bdwy debut in 1926 in "The Honor Of The Family," followed by "Solid South," "Merrily We Roll Along," "Love From A Stranger," "Brown Danube," "Dame Nature," "Love's Old Sweet Song," "Papa Is All," "Kiss and Tell," "The Winter's Tale," "The Last Dance," "Little A," "Magnolia Alley," "Richard III," "Sing Me No Lullaby," "Someone Waiting," Off-Bdwy in "I Knock At The Door" and "The Club Bedroom."

LANGDON, SUE ANE. Born March 8 in Patterson, N.J. Attended North Tex. State Teachers College, Idaho State, Montana State. Made Bdwy debut in 1967 in "The Apple Tree."

LANGTON, BASIL. Born Jan. 9, 1912 in Clifton, Bristol, Eng. Has appeared in NY Off-Bdwy in "Macbeth" and "Hedda Gabler," and on Bdwy in "Camelot," "The Affair," "Soldiers."

LANNING, JERRY. Born May 17, 1943 in Miami, Fla. Graduate of US Cal. Made Bdwy debut in 1966 in "Mame" for which he received a THEATRE WORLD Award.

LANSBURY, ANGELA. Born Oct. 16, 1925 in London. Attended Feagin School of Drama. Made Bdwy debut in 1957 in "Hotel Paradiso," followed by "A Taste of Honey," "Anyone Can Whistle," "Mame."

LARSEN, WILLIAM. Born Nov. 20, 1927 in Lake Charles, La. Attended U. Tex. Appeared Off-Bdwy in "The Crucible," "The Fantasticks," "Legend of Lovers," "Twelfth Night," "Troilus and Cressida," and with APA in "The Tavern," "Lower Depths," and "School For Scandal," on Bdwy in "Ballad of The Sad Cafe," "Half A Sixpence," "Funny Girl," "Halfway Up The Tree."

| Abby Lewis | Leo Leyden | Margaret Linn | Ryan Listman | Jody Locker |

LAUDICINA, DINO. Born Dec. 22, 1939 in Brooklyn. Made Bdwy bow in 1960 in "Christine," followed by "King of The Dark Chamber" (OB), "Rosencrantz and Guildenstern Are Dead."

LAVERENZ, MARY GAIL. Born Dec. 28, 1948 in Moline, Ill. Was Radio City Music Hall Rockette before Bdwy debut Jan. 18, 1968 in "The Happy Time."

LAVIN, LINDA. Born Oct. 15, 1939 in Portland, Me. Graduate of William & Mary College. Made Bdwy debut in 1962 in "A Family Affair," followed by "The Riot Act," "Wet Paint (OB) for which she received a THEATRE WORLD Award, "The Game Is Up," "Hotel Passionato," "The Mad Show," "It's A Bird . . . It's A Plane . . . It's Superman!," "On A Clear Day You Can See Forever," "Something Different."

LAWRENCE, STEVE. Born July 8, 1935 in Brooklyn. Made Bdwy debut in 1964 in "What Makes Sammy Run?," followed by "Golden Rainbow."

LAWSON, LEE. Born Oct. 14, 1941 in NYC. Attended Boston U. and Columbia. Appeared Off-Bdwy in "Firebugs," and "The Knack," before Bdwy debut in 1966 in "Agatha Sue, I Love You," followed by "Cactus Flower."

LEE, SONDRA. Born Sept. 30, 1930 in Newark, N.J. Studied at Met Opera Ballet School. Made Bdwy debut in 1947 in "High Button Shoes," followed by "Peter Pan," "Hotel Paradiso," "Sunday In New York," "Hello, Dolly!"

LeGALLIENNE, EVA. Born Jan. 11, 1899, in London. Attended RADA. Made Bdwy debut in 1915 in "Mrs. Boltay's Daughters," followed by "Bunny," "The Melody of Youth," "Mr. Lazarus," "Saturday To Monday," "Lord and Lady Algy," "The Off Chance," "Elsie Janis and Her Gang," "Not So Long Ago," "Liliom," "The Rivals," "The Swan," "The Call of Life," "The Master Builder," "John Gabriel Borkman." Founded Civic Repertory Theatre in 1926, directed, and appeared in many of its notable productions until it disbanded in 1933. Subsequently appeared in "L'Aiglon," "Hedda Gabler," "Cradle Song," "Rosmersholm," "The Women Have Their Way," "A Sunny Morning," "Prelude to Exile," "Madame Capet," "The Rivals," "Uncle Harry," "The Cherry Orchard," "Therese," co-founded and performed with Am. Rep. Theatre, "Ghosts," "The Corn Is Green" (CC1950), "The Starcross Story," "Southwest Corner," "Mary Stuart" (OB), directed and toured with Natl. Rep. Theatre, and with APA appeared in "Exit The King."

LEIGH-HUNT, BARBARA. Born Dec. 14, 1935 in Bath, Eng. Has appeared in NY with London Old Vic in 1959, and with Bristol Old Vic at City Center in 1967.

LEIGHTON, MARGARET. Born Feb. 26, 1922 in Barnt Gree, Eng. Made Bdwy debut in 1946 with Old Vic, subsequently appearing in "Separate Tables," "Much Ado About Nothing," "Night of The Iguana," "Tchin-Tchin," "The Chinese Prime Minister," "Homage To Shakespeare," "Slapstick Tragedy," "The Little Foxes."

LeMASSENA, WILLIAM. Born May 23, 1916 in Glen Ridge, N.J. Attended NYU. Made Bdwy bow in 1940 in "The Taming of The Shrew," followed by "There Shall Be No Night," "The Pirate," "Hamlet," "Call Me Mister," "Inside U.S.A.," "I Know, My Love," "Dream Girl," "Nina," "Ondine," "Fallen Angels," "Redhead," "The Conquering Hero," "The Beauty Part," "The Coop" (OB), City Center revivals of "Brigadoon" and "Life With Father."

LENN, ROBERT. Born June 13, 1914 in Cortland, N.Y. Appeared in "Star and Garter," "The Girl From Nantucket," "Ballet Ballads," "The King and I" (CC1968).

LENYA, LOTTE. Born Oct. 18, 1900 in Vienna, Aust. Made Bdwy debut in 1941 in "Candle In The Wind," followed by "Firebrand of Florence," "Barefoot In Athens," "The Threepenny Opera" (OB), "Cabaret."

LENZ, RICK. Born Nov. 21, 1939 in Springfield, Ill. Graduate of U. Mich. Made Bdwy bow in 1965 in "The Mating Dance," followed by "The Infantry" (OB), "Cactus Flower."

LEVENE, SAM. Born Aug. 28, 1905. Attended AADA. Made Bdwy bow in 1927 in "Wall Street," followed by "Three Men On A Horse," "Dinner At 8," "Room Service," "Margin For Error," "A Sound of Hunting," "Light Up The Sky," "Guys and Dolls," "The Hot Corner," "Fair Game," "Make A Million," "Heartbreak House," "The Good Soup," "The Devil's Advocate," "Let It Ride," "Seidman and Son," "Cafe Crown," "The Last Analysis," "Nathan Weinstein, Mystic, Conn.," "The Impossible Years."

LEWIS, ABBY. Born Jan. 14, 1910 in Mesilla Park, N. Mex. Graduate of N. Mex. U. Made Bdwy debut in 1934 in "Richard III," followed by "You Can't Take It With You," "Macbeth," "Willow and I," "The Chase," "Four Winds," "Howie," "The Riot Act," "Life With Father" (CC1967).

LEWIS, CAROLE ANN. Born New Year's Eve, 1939 in Shaker Heights, O. Graduate of Sarah Lawrence College. Appeared Off-Bdwy in "Faust," "Port Royale," "This Side of Paradise," "The Parasite," and "The Butter and Egg Man," before making Bdwy debut in 1967 in "Spofford."

LEWIS, MICHAEL. Born June 20, 1930 in NYC. Attended Chicago U., and RADA. Made Bdwy bow in 1954 in "Quadrille," followed by "Small War On Murray Hill," "Once There Was A Russian," "The Visit," "Little Moon of Alban," "A Man For All Seasons," "On A Clear Day You Can See Forever," "Darling of The Day," "Soldiers."

LEYDEN, LEO. Born Jan. 28, 1929 in Dublin, Ire. Attended Abbey Theatre School. Has appeared on Bdwy in "Love and Libel" (1960) and "Darling of The Day" (1968).

LICHTERMAN, MARVIN. Born May 12, 1938 in Brooklyn. Graduate of Bklyn. College, and Yale. Appeared Off-Bdwy in "Anthology of Love" and "Saturday Night" before Bdwy bow in 1968 in "Happiness Is Just A Little Thing Called A Rolls Royce."

LINDEN, HAL. Born Mar. 20, 1931 in NYC. Attended CCNY, Queens College, Am. Theatre Wing. Appeared in "Strip For Action," "Bells Are Ringing," "Wildcat," "Subways Are For Sleeping," "Anything Goes" (OB), "Something More," "The Apple Tree," "The Education of Hyman Kaplan."

LINDFORS, VIVECA. Born Dec. 29, 1920 in Upsala, Sweden. Attended Stockholm Royal Dramatic Theatre School. Made Bdwy debut in 1952 in "I've Got Sixpence," followed by "Anastasia," "King Lear" (CC), Off-Bdwy in "Miss Julie," "The Golden Six," "Brecht On Brecht," and "The Niggerlovers," "Pal Joey" (CC), "Postmark Zero."

LINDLEY, AUDRA. Born Sept. 24 in Los Angeles. Studied with Max Reinhardt. Appeared in "Comes The Revolution," "Heads or Tails," "Hear That Trumpet," "The Young and Fair," "Venus Is," "Spofford."

eorge Loros   Roy Lozano   Regina Lynn   William MacAdam   Winifred Mann

LINN, MARGARET. Born Aug. 21, 1934, in Richmond, Ind. Attended Northwestern, and Denver U. Appeared Off-Bdwy in "Pale Horse, Pale Rider," "The Room," and "Billy Liar," before Bdwy debut in 1966 in "How's The World Treating You?," followed by "Halfway Up The Tree."

LINVILLE, LAWRENCE. Born Sept. 29, 1939 in Ojai, Calif. Attended U. Colo., RADA. Appeared for 4 seasons with APA before making Bdwy debut in 1967 in "More Stately Mansions."

LISTMAN, RYAN. Born Dec. 30, 1939 in Newark, N.J. Appeared Off-Bdwy in "Utopia," "Until The Monkey Comes," and "Fortune and Men's Eyes," and with LCRep. Co. in "St. Joan," "Tiger At The Gates," and "Cyrano de Bergerac."

LIPTON, MICHAEL. Born Apr. 27, 1925 in NYC. Attended Queens College. Has appeared in "Caesar and Cleopatra" (1949), "The Moon Is Blue," "Sing Me No Lullaby," "Wake Up, Darling," "The Tenth Man," "Separate Tables," Off-Bdwy in "The Lover," "Trigon," "Long Christmas Dinner," and "Hamp."

LoBIANCO, TONY. Born Oct. 19, 1936 in NYC. Appeared Off-Bdwy in "Threepenny Opera," "Answered The Flute," "Camino Real," "Oh, Dad, Poor Dad . . .," "Journey To The Day," "Zoo Story," with LCRep. Co. in "Incident At Vichy," and "Tartuffe," on Bdwy in "The Office," "Royal Hunt of The Sun," "The Rose Tattoo," "90 Day Mistress."

LOCKER, JODY. Born Apr. 1, 1944 in NYC. Attended Briarcliff, and Yale. Has appeared Off-Bdwy in "A Certain Young Man" and "Goa."

LODEN, BARBARA. Born July 8, in Marion, N.C. Made Bdwy debut in 1957 in "Compulsion," followed by "Look After Lulu," "The Long Dream," "After The Fall" for which she received a THEATRE WORLD Award, "Winter Journey" (OB).

LOROS, GEORGE. Born Jan. 9, 1944 in NYC. Attended Neighborhood Playhouse. Made stage debut Off-Bdwy in 1967 in "The Nighthawks."

LOZANO, ROY. Born Oct. 18, 1943 in San Antonio, Tex. Attended San Antonio College, Nat. Conserv. of Music, AADA. Has appeared on Bdwy in "High Spirits," "Royal Hunt of The Sun," "Rosencrantz and Guildenstern Are Dead."

LUCKINBILL, LAURENCE. Born Nov. 21, 1938 in Ft. Smith, Ark. Graduate of U. Ark., Catholic U. Made Bdwy bow in "A Man For All Seasons," followed by "Beekman Place," Off-Bdwy in "Oedipus Rex," "There Is A Play Tonight," "The Fantasticks," "Tartuffe," and "The Boys In The Band."

LUISI, JAMES. Born Nov. 11, 1928 in NYC. Attended St. Francis College, and AADA. Appeared Off-Bdwy in "The Crucible," "Threepenny Opera," "Between Two Thieves," and "Detective Story," on Bdwy in "Alfie," "Do I Hear A Waltz?," "Sweet Charity," "Soldiers."

LYNN, REGINA. Born July 12, 1938 in Orangeburg, SC. Attended Wesleyan College. Has appeared Off-Bdwy with American Savoyards, "Autumn's Here," "Now Is The Time For All Good Men."

MacADAM, WILLIAM. Born Mar. 29, 1943 in East Hempstead, L.I., N.Y. Appeared with American Shakespeare Festival before making Bdwy debut Mar. 18, 1968 in "Loot."

MACKENZIE, WILL. Born July 24, 1938 in Providence, R.I. Graduate of Brown U. Appeared with Am. Shakespeare Festival, Off-Bdwy in "Wonderful Town" (CC), "Put It In Writing," "Morning Sun," and "Brigadoon" (CC), on Bdwy in "Half A Sixpence," "Hello, Dolly!"

MacMAHON, ALINE. Born May, 1899 in McKeesport, Pa. Attended Barnard College. Made Bdwy debut in 1921 in "The Madras House," followed by "The Green Ring," "The Exciters," "Grand Street Follies," "Beyond The Horizon," "Maya," "Once In A Lifetime," "Heavenly Express," "Eve of St. Mark," "Confidential Clerk," "A Day By The Sea," "I Knock At The Door" and "Pictures In The Hallway" (OB), "All The Way Home," LCRep. Co.'s "The Alchemist," "Yerma," "East Wind," "Galileo," "Walking To Waldheim," "Tiger At The Gates," and "Cyrano de Bergerac."

MACOLLOM, BARRY. Born in Ireland. Made Bdwy debut in 1912 in "Kismet," followed by "Moon In The Yellow River," "S.S. Tenacity," "Loggerheads," "Juno and The Paycock," "Elizabeth The Queen," "Mr. Gilhooley," "John Ferguson," "Within The Gates," "Love On The Dole," "Parnell," "Happily Ever After," "The Quare Fellow" (OB), "Red Roses For Me," "More Stately Mansions."

MACY, WILLIAM. Born May 18, 1922 in Revere, Mass. Graduate of NYU. Made Bdwy bow in 1959 in "Once More With Feeling," followed by Off-Bdwy's "Threepenny Opera," "Machinal," "The Balcony," and "America Hurrah."

MADDEN, DONALD. Born Nov. 5, 1933 in NYC. Attended CCNY. Made Bdwy bow in 1958 in "Look Back In Anger," followed by "First Impressions," "Julius Caesar" (NY Shake.) for which he received a THEATRE WORLD Award, Off-Bdwy in "Lysistrata," "Pictures In A Hallway," "Henry IV," "She Stoops To Conquer," "Octoroon," "Hamlet," and "Ceremony of Innocence," "Step On A Crack," "One By One," "White Lies," "Black Comedy."

MAGGART, BRANDON. Born Dec. 12, 1933 in Carthage, Tenn. Graduate of U. Tenn. Appeared Off-Bdwy in "Sing, Muse!," "Like Other People," and "Put It In Writing" for which he received a THEATRE WORLD Award, before making Bdwy bow in 1965 in "Kelly," followed by "New Faces of 1968."

MAGGIORE, CHARLES. Born Mar. 19, 1936 in Valley Stream, L.I., N.Y. Attended Bates College, Adelphi U., and Neighborhood Playhouse. Appeared Off-Bdwy in "Six Characters In Search of An Author," "The Rivals," "The Iceman Cometh," and "Othello," before Bdwy bow in 1967 in "Spofford."

MAHER, JOSEPH. Born Dec. 29, 1933 in Westport, Ire. Made Bdwy bow in 1964 in "The Chinese Prime Minister," followed by Off-Bdwy roles in "The Hostage," "Live Like Pigs," "The Importance of Being Earnest," and "Eh?," "The Prime of Miss Jean Brodie."

MANN, WINIFRED. Born July 20 in Brooklyn. Attended Actors Lab, Hollywood. Appeared with NY Shakespeare Festival in "King John," with LC Rep. Co. in "Tiger At The Gates," and "Cyrano de Bergerac."

MANNING, DAVID. Born Feb. 20, 1958 in Brooklyn. Made Bdwy debut in 1966 in "Annie Get Your Gun" revival, followed by "Mame."

| Jared Martin | Tom Matsusaka | Jacqueline Mayro | James McDonald | Maeve McGuir |

MANSON, ALAN. Born in NYC. Made Bdwy bow in 1940 in "Journey To Jerusalem," followed by "This Is The Army," "Call Me Mister," "Southern Exposure," "Angels Kiss Me," "The Ponder Heart," "Maybe Tuesday," "The Tenth Man," "Gideon," "Nobody Loves An Albatross," "Funny Girl," Off-Bdwy in "Dr. Jekyll and Mr. Hyde," "Midsummer Night's Dream," "Oh, Say Can You See L.A.," and "The Other Man."

MARCHAND, NANCY. Born June 19, 1928 in Buffalo, N.Y. Graduate of Carnegie Tech. Made NY debut in "The Taming of The Shrew" (CC), followed by "Merchant of Venice," Am. Shakespeare Festival productions, "Much Ado About Nothing," "The Balcony" (OB), APA repertory, "Three Bags Full," "After The Rain," LCRep. Co.'s "The Alchemist," "Yerma," and "Cyrano de Bergerac."

MARIA, LISA. Born Sept. 9, 1948 in Poland. Attended AADA, Harkness Ballet School. Made NY debut Off-Bdwy in 1968 in "The Memorandum."

MARIANO, PATTI. Born June 12, 1945 in Philadelphia. Made Bdwy debut in 1957 in "The Music Man," followed by "Bye Bye Birdie," "Sail Away," "I Had A Ball," "Country Girl" (OB), "George M!"

MARICLE, MARIJANE. Born Jan. 13, 1922 in Wichita Falls, Tex. Graduate of U. Tex., and Juilliard. Made Bdwy debut in 1951 in "Paint Your Wagon," followed by "Finian's Rainbow," "Bye Bye Birdie," "The Sound of Music," "Hello, Dolly!," and "Hair" (OB).

MARIE, JULIENNE. Born in 1943 in Toledo, O. Attended Juilliard. Has appeared in "The King and I," "Whoop-Up!," "Gypsy," "Foxy," "Do I Hear A Waltz?," Off-Bdwy in "The Boys From Syracuse" for which she received a THEATRE WORLD Award, "Othello," and "Comedy of Errors."

MARKEY, ENID. Born Feb. 22 in Dillon, Colo. Made Bdwy debut in 1919 in "Up In Mabel's Room," followed by "Barnum Was Right," "The Women," "Morning's At Seven," "Ah, Wilderness," "Mr. Sycamore," "Beverly Hills," "Snafu," "Happy Birthday," "The Silver Whistle," "Buy Me Blue Ribbons," "Mrs. McThing," "Mrs. Patterson," "Southwest Corner," "Only In America," "Ballad of The Sad Cafe," "What Did We Do Wrong?"

MARKS, JOE E. Born in NYC, June 15, 1891. Made Bdwy bow in 1909 in "The Girl From Rector's," followed by "High Kickers," "Count Me In," "Bloomer Girl," "Topaze," "The Vigil," "The Enchanted," "Peter Pan," "Li'l Abner," "My Mother, My Father and Me," "Flora, The Red Menace," "Illya, Darling."

MARLOWE, HUGH. Born Jan. 30, 1911 in Philadelphia. Attended Pasadena Playhouse. Made Bdwy bow in 1936 in "Arrest That Woman," followed by "Kiss The Boys Goodbye," "Young Couple Wanted," "The Land Is Bright," "Lady In The Dark," "It Takes Two," "Laura," "Duet For Two Hands," "The Rabbit Habit," Off-Bdwy in "Deer Park" and "Postcards."

MARLOWE, MARION. Born Mar. 7, 1930 in St. Louis. Attended Wash. U., London Conservatory of Music. Made Bdwy debut in 1959 in "The Sound of Music," followed by "The Athenian Touch" (OB), "Man of La Mancha."

MARRIOTT, JOHN. Born Sept. 30, 1900 in Boley, Okla. Attended Wilberforce U. Made Bdwy bow in 1934 in "Too Many Boats," followed by "Sweet River," "Chalked Out," "The Little Foxes," "Janie," "No Way Out," "The Iceman Cometh," "How I Wonder," "The Respectful Prostitute," "The Ponder Heart," "Season of Choice" (OB), "More Stately Mansions," "Weekend."

MARSHALL, E.G. Born June 18, 1910, in Owatonna, Minn. Attended Minn. U. Made Bdwy debut in 1938 in "Prelude To Glory," followed by "Jason," "The Skin of Our Teeth," "Petrified Forest," "Jacobowsky and The Colonel," "The Iceman Cometh," "Hope's The Thing," "The Survivors," "The Crucible," "Red Roses For Me," "Waiting For Godot," "The Gang's All Here," "The Little Foxes" (1967).

MARTIN, ANGELA. Appeared Off-Bdwy in "Miss Emily Adams" before making Bdwy debut in 1968 in "George M!"

MARTIN, JARED. Born Dec. 21, 1943 in NYC. Graduate of Columbia. Made stage debut Off-Bdwy in 1967 in "Hamlet as A Happening."

MARTIN, JOY. Born Aug. 2, 1944 in Seattle. Appeared Off-Bdwy in "The Kitchen" and "The Experiment."

MARTIN, MARY. Born Dec. 1, 1913 in Weatherford, Tex. Attended Ward-Belmont College. Made Bdwy debut in 1938 in "Leave It To Me," followed by "One Touch of Venus," "Lute Song," "Annie Get Your Gun," "South Pacific," "Kind Sir," "Peter Pan," "The Skin of Our Teeth," "The Sound of Music," "Jennie," "Hello, Dolly!," "I Do! I Do!"

MARTIN, NICHOLAS. Born June 10, 1938 in Brooklyn. Graduate of Carnegie Tech. Appeared with Am. Shakespeare Festival before Bdwy bow with APA in "The Wild Duck," "You Can't Take It With You," "Right You Are," "School For Scandal," and "Pantagleize."

MARVEL, PAULINE. (formerly Pauline Anton) Born Dec. 3, 1918. Graduate of Columbia. Appeared Off-Bdwy in "Uncle Vanya," "Waters of The Moon," "Don't Destroy Me," "Marriage Proposal," "Blood Wedding," "Pocket Watch" and "Nighthawks."

MASON, MARLYN. Born Aug. 7, 1940 in San Fernando, Calif. Made Bdwy debut Dec. 7, 1967 in "How Now, Dow Jones,"

MASON, MARSHA. Born Apr. 3, 1942 in St. Louis. Made NY debut Off-Bdwy in 1967 in "The Deer Park," followed by "It's Called The Sugar Plum."

MASSI, BERNICE. Born Aug. 23 in Camden, N.J. Made Bdwy debut in 1952 in "South Pacific," followed by "Wish You Were Here," "By The Beautiful Sea," "Can-Can," "The Vamp," "Two For The Seesaw," "Beg, Borrow or Steal," "No Strings," "What Makes Sammy Run?," "Man of La Mancha."

MASTERSON, PETER. Born June 1, 1936 in Houston, Tex. Graduate of Rice U. Member of Actors Studio. Made NY debut in 1961 in "Call Me By My Rightful Name" (OB) before Bdwy bow in 1963 in "Marathon '33," followed by "Blues For Mr. Charlie," "The Trial of Lee Harvey Oswald."

MATHEWS, CARMEN. Born May 8, 1918 in Philadelphia. Graduate of Bennett College, and RADA. Made Bdwy debut in 1938 in "Henry IV," followed by "Hamlet," "Richard II," "Harriet," "The Cherry Orchard," "The Assassin," "Man and Superman," "The Ivy Green," "Courtin' Time," "My Three Angels," "Holiday For Lovers," "Night Life," "Lorenzo," "The Yearling," "A Delicate Balance," "I'm Solomon."

MATSUSAKA, TOM. Born Aug. 8 in Wahiawa, Hawaii. Graduate of Mich. State U. Made Bdwy bow in 1968 in "Mame."

MATTHEWS, ART. Born in NYC. Attended Columbia, Northwestern. Made NY bow Off-Bdwy with American Savoyards, followed by "Leave It To Jane" (OB), "Mame."

chell McGuire   Susan McMullen   Constance Meng   Dutch Miller   June Miller

MATTHEWS, GERRY. Born Apr. 12, 1936 in San Antonio, Tex. Attended U. Tex. Made Bdwy bow in 1965 in "On A Clear Day You Can See Forever," followed by "Nathan Weinstein, Mystic, Conn.," "Don't Drink The Water."

MAYER, JERRY. Born May 12, 1941 in Waterloo, Iowa. Graduate of NYU. Made NY bow with LC Rep. Co. in 1968 in "Cyrano de Bergerac."

MAYRO, JACQUELINE. Born Apr. 2, 1948 in Philadelphia. Made Bdwy debut in 1959 in "Gypsy," followed by "Bye Bye Birdie," "Cindy" (OB), "Ben Franklin In Paris," "Who's Who, Baby" (OB).

McCARTY, EDDIE. Born Aug. 25, 1940 in Argenta, Ill. Attended Millikin U. Appeared Off-Bdwy in 1967 in "Kitchenette," followed by "Two Camps By Koutoukas."

McCOWEN, ALEC. Born May 26 in Tunbridge Wells, Eng. Attended RADA. Made NY debut in 1952 in "Antony and Cleopatra" and "Caesar and Cleopatra," followed by "King Lear," and "Comedy of Errors" (LC 1964), "After The Rain."

McDONALD, EARL. Born Nov. 15, 1905 in Chicago. Graduate of U. Ill. Made Bdwy bow in 1926 in "White Wings," followed by "Merchant of Venice," "Fredrika," "Three Waltzes," "Two On An Island," "Three's A Family," "Made In Heaven," "Dream Girl," "Regina," "Brigadoon" (CC).

McDONALD, JAMES. Born June 23 in Jersey City, N.J. Attended Rutgers U. Appeared with Am. Shakespeare Festival, and Off-Bdwy in "The Trojan Women," "The White Devil," "Fortune and Men's Eyes."

McGIVER, JOHN. Born Nov. 5, 1913 in NYC. Attended Fordham, Columbia, and Catholic U. Made Bdwy bow in 1956 in "Little Glass Clock," followed by "Cloud 7," "Drink To Me Only," "God and Kate Murphy," "A Thurber Carnival," "A Cook For Mr. General," "Happiness Is Just A Little Thing Called A Rolls Royce."

McGUIRE, MAEVE. Born in Cleveland, O. Graduate of Sarah Lawrence College. Attended Cleveland Playhouse, and Perry-Mansfield School of Theatre. Made NY stage debut in 1968 with Lincoln Center Rep. Co. in "Cyrano de Bergerac."

McGUIRE, MITCHELL. (formerly Michael) Born Dec. 26, 1936 in Chicago. Attended Goodman Theatre School, Santa Monica City College. Appeared Off-Bdwy in "The Rapists," "Go, Go, Go, God Is Dead," "Waiting For Lefty," and "The Bond."

McKAY, SCOTT. Born May 28, 1917 in Pleasantville, Iowa. Attended U. Colo. Made Bdwy bow in 1938 in "Good Hunting," followed by "The American Way," "The Three Sisters," "The Night Before Christmas," "Letters To Lucerne," "The Moon Is Down," "The Eve of St. Mark," "Dark Eyes," "Pillar To Post," "Swan Song," "The Live Wire," "Another Part of The Forest," "Born Yesterday," "Bell, Book and Candle," "Sabrina Fair," "Teahouse of The August Moon," "Brigadoon" (CC1957), "Nature's Way," "Mary, Mary," "Once For The Asking," "Requiem For A Nun," "The Little Foxes" (1967).

McKELLEN, IAN. Born in Burnley, Eng. Attended St. Catherine's College. Made Bdwy debut in 1967 in "The Promise."

McMARTIN, JOHN. Born in Warsaw, Ind. Attended Columbia. Made NY debut Off-Bdwy in "Little Mary Sunshine" for which he received a THEATRE WORLD Award, followed by Bdwy bow in 1961 in "The Conquering Hero," followed by "Blood, Sweat and Stanley Poole," "Children From Their Games," "A Rainy Day In Newark," "Too Much Johnson," (OB), "Sweet Charity."

McMULLEN, SUSAN. Born Nov. 17, 1944 in Knoxville, Tenn. Attended Boston U. Made NY debut Off-Bdwy in "No Exit" and "The Little Private World of Arthur Morton Fenwick."

McNEIL, CLAUDIA. Born Aug. 13, 1917 in Baltimore. Made Bdwy debut in 1952 in "The Crucible," followed by "Simply Heavenly," "A Raisin In The Sun," "Tiger, Tiger Burning Bright," "Something Different."

McPHILLIPS, EDWARD. Born July 23, 1925 in England. Attended Webber-Douglas School of Drama, London. Made NY debut Off-Bdwy in "Stephen D," followed by "The Victims."

McQUEEN, BUTTERFLY. Born Jan. 8, 1911 in Tampa, Fla. Attended CCLA, Queens College, and UCLA. Made Bdwy debut in 1937 in "Brother Rat," followed by "What A Life," "Swingin' The Dream," Off-Bdwy in "School For Wives," "The World's My Oyster," "The Athenian Touch" and "Curley McDimple."

MEACHAM, ANNE. Born July 21, 1925 in Chicago. Attended Rochester U., Yale, Neighborhood Playhouse. Made Bdwy debut in 1952 in "The Long Watch," followed by "Ondine," "The Immortal Husband," "Eugenia," "A Legend of Lizzie," "A Passage To India," Off-Bdwy in "Suddenly Last Summer," and "Hedda Gabler," "Elizabeth The Queen" (CC1966), "Rosencrantz and Guildenstern Are Dead."

MEDFORD, KAY. Born Sept. 14, 1920 in NYC. Made Bdwy debut in 1951 in "Paint Your Wagon," followed by "Two's Company," "John Murray Anderson's Almanac," "Lullaby" for which she received a THEATRE WORLD Award, "Black-Eyed Susan," "Almost Crazy," "Wake Up, Darling," "Mr. Wonderful," "A Hole In The Head," "Carousel" and "Pal Joey" at City Center, "Handful of Fire," "Bye Bye Birdie," "In The Counting House," "The Heroine," "Funny Girl," "Don't Drink The Water."

MELVIN, DONNIE. Born Aug. 22, 1955 in NYC. Made theatre debut in 1967 with LCRep. Co. "Galileo" followed by "Summertree" and "Cyrano de Bergerac."

MENG, CONSTANCE. Born May 12, 1939, in Potsdam, N.Y. Graduate of St. Lawrence U. Made Bdwy debut in 1964 in "Foxy," followed by Off-Bdwy roles in "Money" and "A Certain Young Man."

MERCER, MARIAN. Born Nov. 26, 1935 in Akron, O. Graduate of Mich. U. Made Bdwy debut in 1960 in "Greenwillow," followed by "Fiorello!," Off-Bdwy in "Little Mary Sunshine," "Hotel Passionato," and "Your Own Thing."

MERRIMAN, DAN. Born July 10, 1929 in Ft. Worth, Tex. Attended N. Tex.U., Tex. Christian, and Juilliard. Appeared in "The Saint of Bleecker Street," Off-Bdwy in "Pirates of Penzance," "Ransom of Red Chief," and "All In Love," Hello, Dolly!"

MEYERS, MARTIN. Born Dec. 26, 1934 in NYC. Attended Am. Theatre Wing. Made Bdwy bow in 1961 in "Mandingo," followed by "Lady of The Camellias," "The Guide."

MIDDLETON, RAY. Born Feb. 8, 1907 in Chicago. Graduate of U. Ill., and Juilliard. Made Bdwy bow in 1933 in "Roberta," followed by "Knickerbocker Holiday," "George White's Scandals," "Annie Get Your Gun," "Love Life," "South Pacific," "Too Good To Be True," "Man of La Mancha."

Bill Moor   Edward Moore   Lynda Myles   Claudette Nevins   Mary Ann N

MILLER, BETTY. Born Mar. 27, 1925 in Boston. Attended CCLA and Dramatic Workshop. Appeared Off-Bdwy in "Summer and Smoke," "Cradle Song," "La Ronde," "Plays For Bleecker Street," "Desire Under The Elms," "The Balcony," "The Power and The Glory," "Beaux Stratagem," NY Shakespeare Festival. Made Bdwy debut in 1954 in "Girl On The Via Flaminia," followed by APA's "You Can't Take It With You," "Right You Are," "The Wild Duck," and "The Cherry Orchard."

MILLER, DUTCH. Born Mar. 16, 1927 in Jersey City, N.J. Attended Theatre School of Dramatic Arts. Made Bdwy bow in 1967 in "Fiddler On The Roof" after Off-Bdwy roles in "The Adding Machine," "Poppa Is Home," "The Fantasticks," "Taming of The Shrew," "Gogo Loves You," "Colombe," "Hotel Passionato," and "Ergo."

MILLER, JUNE. Born June 10, 1934 in West Lawn, Pa. Graduate of Penn State. Appeared Off-Bdwy in "The Flies," "Sunday Night Music Hall," "While The Iron's Hot," "Streets of Confusion," "The Boy Friend," "The Caller," "Black Roses," "The Crucible," "Where People Gather."

MILLS, DONNA. Born Dec. 11, 1943 in Chicago. Attended U. Ill. Made Bdwy debut in 1966 in "Don't Drink The Water."

MILNE, LENNOX. Born In Edinburgh, Scot. Attended U. Edinburgh, RADA. Made Bdwy debut in 1968 in "The Prime of Miss Jean Brodie."

MILNER, MARTIN. Born Dec. 28, 1931 in Detroit, Mich. Attended US Calif. Made Bdwy debut in 1967 in "90 Day Mistress."

MIXON, ALAN. Born Mar. 15, 1933 in Miami, Fla. Attended Miami U. Appeared Off-Bdwy in "Suddenly Last Summer," "Desire Under The Elms," "The Trojan Women," "The Alchemist," "The Child Buyer," "Mr. and Mrs. Lyman," "A Whitman Portrait," and "Iphigenia In Aulis. Bdwy bow in 1962 in "Something About A Soldier," followed by "The Sign In Sidney Brustein's Window," "The Devils," "Unknown Soldier and His Wife."

MOFFAT, DONALD. Born Dec. 26, 1930 in Plymouth, Eng. Attended RADA. Made Bdwy bow in 1957 in "Under Milk Wood," followed by "Much Ado About Nothing," "The Tumbler," "Duel of Angels," "A Passage To India," and "The Affair," Off-Bdwy in "The Bald Soprano," "Jack," "The Caretaker," and "Misalliance," roles with APA in "You Can't Take It With You," "War and Peace," "Right You Are," "The Wild Duck," and "The Cherry Orchard."

MOHYEDDIN, ZIA. Born June 20, 1931 in Lyallpur, Pakistan. Attended RADA. Made Bdwy debut in 1962 in "A Passage To India," followed by "The Guide" (1968).

MONTGOMERY, EARL. Born Apr. 17, 1921 in Memphis, Tenn. Graduate of Harvard. Made NY bow in 1947 in "Galileo," followed by "Summer and Smoke," "The Relapse," "Mr. Pickwick," "Love's Labour's Lost," "The Merchant of Venice," "The Strong Are Lonely," "Heavenly Twins," "A Visit To A Small Planet," "Look After Lulu," "Lady of The Camellias," "Tovarich," "The Rehearsal," LCRep. Co.'s "Caucasian Chalk Circle," "The Alchemist," "East Wind," "Galileo," "St. Joan," "Tiger At The Gates," "Cyrano de Bergerac."

MOOR, BILL. Born July 13, 1931 in Toldeo, O. Attended Northwestern, and Denison U. Made Bdwy bow in 1964 in "Blues For Mr. Charlie." Off-Bdwy credits: "Dandy Dick," "The Love Nest," "Days and Nights of Bebe Fenstermaker," "The Collection," "The Owl Answers," "Long Christmas Dinner," "Fortune and Men's Eyes."

MOORE, CHARLES. Born May 22 in Cleveland, O. Appeared on Bdwy in "Jamaica," "Kwamina," "The Zulu and The Zayda," Off-Bdwy in "Ballad For Bimshire," "House of Flowers."

MOORE, EDWARD. Born June 2, 1935 in Chicago. Graduate of Goodman Theatre School. Made Bdwy bow in 1967 in "After The Rain."

MOORE, LAURENS. Born Dec. 2, 1919 in Gaffney, SC. Attended Wofford College. Made NY Off-Bdwy in 1957 in "Nightmare," followed by "Our Town," "The County Seat," "Nordis and The Ark," and "Jonah!." Made Bdwy debut in 1960 in "Only In America."

MOORE, MICHAEL. Born Sept. 15, 1942 in New Jersey. Attended U. Maryland, Hunter College. Made NY bow Off-Bdwy in 1967 in "No Exit."

MOORE, ROBERT. Born Aug. 7, 1930 in Washington, D.C. Attended Catholic U. Made Bdwy bow in 1948 in "Jenny Kissed Me," followed by "The Owl and The Pussycat," "Cactus Flower," "Everything In The Garden."

MORAN, DON. Born in Wilkes-Barre, Pa. Graduate of Emerson College. Appeared Off-Bdwy in "The Drunkard," "The Firebugs," "Brides of Dracula," and "Love and Let Love."

MORROW, KAREN. Born Dec. 15, 1936 in Chicago. Attended Clarke College. Made NY debut Off-Bdwy in 1961 in "Sing, Muse!" for which she received a THEATRE WORLD Award, followed by "The Boys From Syracuse," City Center revivals of "Oklahoma!," "Most Happy Fella" and "Brigadoon," on Bdwy in "I Had A Ball," "A Joyful Noise," "I'm Solomon."

MORSE, RICHARD. Born May 31, 1927 in Brookline, Mass. Attended Principia College, Neighborhood Playhouse. Made NY bow Off-Bdwy in "Teach Me How To Cry" (1955), followed by "Thor With Angels," "The Makropoulos Secret," and "All Kinds of Giants," on Bdwy in "Mother Courage," "Fiddler On The Roof."

MOSER, MARGOT. Born Aug. 15, 1930 in Reading, Pa. Attended Juilliard. Made Bdwy debut in 1947 in "Oklahoma!," followed by "Carousel" (CC1949), "Candide," "Triad" (OB), "Regina" (CC1959), "My Fair Lady," "Brigadoon" (CC1967).

MURDOCK, KERMIT. Born Mar. 20, 1908 in Pittsburgh. Graduate of Harvard. Made NY bow Off-Bdwy in "No More Frontier," followed by "Lamp At Midnight," "The Sun and I," "Bruno and Sidney," "The Man Who Never Died," and "The Idiot," on Bdwy "Merry-Go-Round," "The Strong Are Lonely," "More Stately Mansions."

MURPHY, ROSEMARY. Born Jan. 13, 1927 in Munich, Ger. Attended Neighborhood Playhouse, Actors Studio. Made Bdwy debut in 1950 in "Tower Beyond Tragedy," followed by "Look Homeward, Angel," "Period of Adjustment," "Any Wednesday," "A Delicate Balance," "Weekend."

| eather North | Sam Nudell | David O'Brien | Ken Olfson | Dick O'Neill |

MURRAY, PEG. Born in Denver, Colo. Attended Western Reserve U. Appeared Off-Bdwy in "Children of Darkness," "A Midsummer Night's Dream," and "O, Dad, Poor Dad . . .," on Bdwy in "The Great Sebastians," "Gypsy," "Blood, Sweat and Stanley Poole," "She Loves Me," "Anyone Can Whistle," "The Subject Was Roses," "Something More," "Cabaret."

MYLES, LYNDA. Attended Michigan State and Columbia. Appeared Off-Bdwy in "Two Gentlemen of Verona," "The Trojan Women," "Rocking Chair," "No Exit," and "Iphigenia In Aulis."

NASTASI, FRANK. Born Jan. 7, 1923 in Detroit. Graduate of Wayne State, and NYU. Appeared Off-Bdwy in "Bonds of Interest," "One Day More," "Nathan The Wise," "The Chief Thing," "Cindy," "Escurial," and "MacBird," on Bdwy in "Lorenzo," "Avanti-"

NeJAME, GEORGE. Born Nov. 30, 1953 in Poughkeepsie, N.Y. Made Bdwy debut Oct. 23, 1967 in "Henry, Sweet Henry."

NELSON, BARRY. Born in Oakland, Calif. Graduate of U. Cal. Made Bdwy debut in 1943 in "Winged Victory," followed by "Light Up The Sky," "The Moon Is Blue," "Wake Up, Darling," "The Rat Race," "Mary, Mary," "Nobody Loves An Albatross," "Cactus Flower," "Everything In The Garden," "The Only Game In Town."

NELSON, KENNETH. Born Mar. 24, 1930 in Rocky Mt., N.C. Attended Baylor U. Made Bdwy bow in 1951 in "Seventeen," followed by "The Fantasticks" (OB), "Stop The World—I Want To Get Off," "Half A Sixpence," "The Boys In The Band" (OB).

NEVINS, CLAUDETTE. Born in Wilkes-Barre, Pa. Graduate of NYU. Appeared Off-Bdwy in "The Emperor" and "In White America," LCRep. Co.'s "Danton's Death," on Bdwy in "The Wall," "Wait Until Dark," "Plaza Suite."

NEWMAN, PHYLLIS. Born Mar. 19, 1936 in Jersey City, N.J. Attended Western Reserve U., Columbia. Appeared in "Wish You Were Here," "Bells Are Ringing," "I Feel Wonderful" (OB), "First Impressions," "Subways Are For Sleeping," "The Apple Tree."

NICHOLAS, DENISE. Born July 12, 1944 in Detroit. Attended U. Mich. Appeared Off-Bdwy in "Viet Rock," and in Negro Ensemble Co. productions.

NILES, MARY ANN. Born May 2, 1933 in NYC. Attended Miss Finchley's School and Ballet Academy. Made Bdwy debut in 1945 in "Girl From Nantucket," followed by "Dance Me A Song," "Call Me Mister," "Make Mine Manhattan," "La Plume de Ma Tante," "Carnival," Off-Bdwy in "The Boys From Syracuse," "Little Brown Road," "The Big Spender," and "Your Sister Rose," "Flora, The Red Menace," "Wonderful Town" (CC1967), "Sweet Charity."

NILLO, DAVID. Born July 13, 1918 in Goldsboro, N.C. Attended Baltimore City College. With Ballet Theatre and Ballet Caravan before Bdwy bow in 1946 in "Call Me Mister," followed by "Great To Be Alive," "Out Of This World," "Two On The Aisle," "Goldilocks," "The Bench" (OB).

NOLEN, JOYCE. Born Oct. 5, 1949 in Philadelphia. Made NY debut Off-Bdwy in 1967 in "Curley McDimple."

NORRIS, RUTH ANN. Born in Ada, Okla. Graduate of U. Okla. Made NY debut Off-Bdwy in 1967 in "Where People Gather."

NORTH, ALAN. Born Dec. 23, 1927 in NYC. Attended Columbia. Made Bdwy bow in 1955 in "Plain and Fancy," followed by "South Pacific" (CC), "Summer of the 17th Doll," "Requiem For A Nun," "Never Live Over A Pretzel Factory," "Dylan," "Spofford."

NORTH, HEATHER. Born Dec. 13, 1945 in Pasadena, Calif. Made Bdwy debut in 1967 in "Girl In The Freudian Slip."

NUDELL, SAM. Appeared in "Sunset," "Come Blow Your Horn," "World of Sholom Aleichem," "Comic Strip," "Girl Crazy," "Courageous One," "A View From The Bridge," "Detective Story," "Born Yesterday," "Light Up The Sky," "Picnic," "Our Town," "Enter Laughing," "Merchant of Venice," "Hamlet," "The Tenth Man" (CC).

NYPE, RUSSELL. Born Apr. 26, 1924 in Zion, Ill. Attended Lake Forest College. Made Bdwy bow in 1949 in "Regina," followed by "Call Me Madam" for which he received a THEATRE WORLD Award, "Tender Trap," "Tunnel of Love," "Wake Up, Darling," City Center revivals of "Carousel" and "Brigadoon," "Goldilocks," "Brouhaha" (OB), "The Owl and The Pussycat," "Girl In The Freudian Slip," "Private Lives" (OB).

O'BRIAN, HUGH. Born Apr. 19, 1925 in Rochester, NY. Attended U. Cincinnati. Made Bdwy bow in "Destry Rides Again," followed by "First Love," "Guys and Dolls" (CC 1966), "Cactus Flower."

O'BRIEN, DAVID. Born Oct. 1, 1935 in Chicago. Graduate of Stanford, London Academy of Music and Dramatic Art. Appeared Off-Bdwy in "Under Milk Wood," and "A Month In The Country," on Bdwy in "A Passage To India," "Arturo Ui," "A Time For Singing," "King John" (NYShake.).

OCASIO, JOSE. Born July 13, 1938 in Morovis, P.R. Attended U.P.R., Am. Theatre Wing. Appeared with NY Shakespeare Festival (1965), Off-Bdwy in "The Ox Cart," before Bdwy bow in 1968 in "Plaza Suite."

O'CONNOR, KEVIN. Born May 7, 1938 in Honolulu. Attended Hawaii U., U. Cal., San Francisco State, Neighborhood Playhouse. Appeared Off-Bdwy in "Up To Thursday," "Six From La Mama," "Rimers of Eldritch," "Tom Paine."

O'HARA, JILL. Born Aug. 23, 1947 in Warren, Pa. Attended Edinburgh State Teachers College. Appeared Off-Bdwy in "Hang Down Your Head and Die" and "Hair" before Bdwy debut in 1968 in "George M."

OLFSON, KEN. Born Apr. 2, 1937 in Dorchester, Mass. Attended Syracuse U., Am. Theatre Wing. Made stage debut Off-Bdwy in 1967 in "Scuba Duba."

OLIVER, ANTHONY. Born July 4, 1924 in Abersychan, Wales. Made Bdwy debut in 1953 in "Gently Does It," followed by "After The Rain" (1967).

OLSON, MURRAY. Born Aug. 6, 1932 in Langdon, ND. Attended Hamline U. Appeared Off-Bdwy in "The Pirates of Penzance," and "Now Is The Time For All Good Men."

O'NEILL, DICK. Born Aug. 29, 1928 in The Bronx. Attended Utica College. Made Bdwy bow in 1961 in "The Unsinkable Molly Brown," followed by "Skyscraper," "Have I Got One For You" (OB).

| Emily Peden | Tom Pedi | Robert Phalen | Randy Phillips | Warren Pincus |

ORBACH, JERRY. Born Oct. 20, 1935 in NYC. Attended U. Ill., Northwestern. Made Bdwy bow in 1961 in "Carnival," followed by "Guys and Dolls" (CC), LC's revivals of "Carousel" and "Annie Get Your Gun," "The Natural Look," Off-Bdwy in "Threepenny Opera," "The Fantasticks," "The Cradle Will Rock," and "Scuba Duba."

ORFALY, ALEXANDER. Born Oct. 10, 1935 in Brooklyn. Appeared in 1967 LC revival of "South Pacific" before Bdwy bow in "How Now, Dow Jones."

ORMISTON, GEORGE. Born Nov. 18, 1939 in Providence, R.I. Attended Ga. Inst. of Tech., and HB Studio. Made Bdwy debut in "New Faces of 1968."

O'SHEA, MILO. Born June 2, 1926 in Dublin, Ire. Made Bdwy debut Jan. 10, 1968 in "Staircase."

O'SULLIVAN, MAUREEN. Born May 17, 1911 in Roscommon, Ire. After film career, made Bdwy debut in 1962 in "Never Too Late," followed by "The Subject Was Roses," "Keep It In The Family."

O'SULLIVAN, MICHAEL. Born Mar. 4, 1934 in Phoenix, Ariz. Attended Regis College, Denver U., Goodman Theatre School. Appeared Off-Bdwy in "Six Characters In Search of An Author," "In White America," with LC Rep. Co. in "Tartuffe" for which he received a THEATRE WORLD Award, and "The Alchemist." Made Bdwy bow in 1964 in "The White House," followed by "It's A Bird . . . It's A Plane . . . It's Superman!," "Love and Let Love" and "The Bench" Off-Bdwy.

OSUNA, JESS. Born May 28, 1933 in Oakland, Calif. Appeared Off-Bdwy in "Blood Wedding," "Come Share My House," "This Side of Paradise," "Bugs and Veronica," "Monopoly," "The Infantry," "Hamp."

OYSTER, JIM. Born May 3, 1930 in Washington, D.C. Appeared Off-Bdwy in "Coriolanus," "The Cretan Woman," and "Man and Superman," on Bdwy in "The Cool World," "Hostile Witness," "Sound of Music" (CC1967), "The Prime of Miss Jean Brodie."

PACINO, AL. Born Apr. 25, 1940 in NYC. Member of Actors Studio. Appeared Off-Bdwy in "Why Is A Crooked Letter," "The Peace Creeps," and "The Indian Wants The Bronx."

PAGE, GERALDINE. Born Nov. 22, 1924 in Kirksville, Mo. Attended Goodman Theatre School. Appeared Off-Bdwy in "Seven Mirrors" and "Summer and Smoke" before Bdwy debut in 1953 in "Midsummer" for which she received a THEATRE WORLD Award, followed by "The Immoralist," "The Rainmaker," "The Innkeepers," "Separate Tables," "Sweet Bird of Youth," "Strange Interlude" (1963), "The Three Sisters" (1964), "P.S. I Love You," "The Great Indoors," "White Lies," "Black Comedy," "The Little Foxes" (1968).

PAIGE, JANIS. Born Sept. 16, 1922 in Tacoma, Wash. Made Bdwy debut in 1951 in "Remains To Be Seen," followed by "Pajama Game," "Mame."

PALMIERI, JOSEPH. Born Aug. 1, 1939, in Brooklyn. Attended Catholic U. Has appeared with Natl. Rep. Theatre (1965-66), NY Shakespeare Festival (1965, 1966), "The Butter and Egg Man" (OB), LC Rep. Co.'s "Cyrano de Bergerac."

PARSONS, ESTELLE. Born Nov. 20, 1927 in Lynn, Mass. Attended Conn. College, Boston U., Actors Studio. Made Bdwy debut in 1956 in "Happy Hunting," followed by "Whoop-Up!," "Beg, Borrow or Steal," Off-Bdwy in "Threepenny Opera," "Automobile Graveyard," "Mrs. Dally Has A Lover" for which she received a THEATRE WORLD Award, "In The Summer House," and "Monopoly," "Ready When You Are C.B.," "Malcolm," LC Rep.'s "East Wind" and "Galileo," "The Seven Descents of Myrtle."

PATTERSON, JAMES. Born June 29, 1932 in Derry, Pa. Appeared Off-Bdwy in "Brothers Karamazov," "Epitaph For George Dillon," "Zoo Story," "The Collection," and "Benito Cereno." Made Bdwy bow in 1964 in "Conversation At Midnight," followed by "Inadmissible Evidence," "The Birthday Party."

PAUL, ELLIOT. Born Sept. 4, 1942 in Boston. Attended Idaho State U. Made NY debut Off-Bdwy in 1968 in "Goa."

PAYTON-WRIGHT, PAMELA. Born Nov. 1, 1941 in Pittsburgh. Graduate of Birmingham Southern College, and RADA. Made Bdwy debut in 1967 with APA in "The Show-Off," "Exit The King," and "The Cherry Orchard."

PEARL, IRWIN. Born Oct. 14, 1945 in Brooklyn. Graduate of Hofstra U. Appeared Off-Bdwy in "Big Hotel," and "Ergo."

PEDEN, EMILY. Born Nov. 12, 1944 in El Paso, Tex. Attended SMU, AADA. Made NY debut in 1967 City Center revival of "Life With Father."

PEDERSON, MICHAEL. Born Sept. 2, 1947 in Milwaukee. Attended School of The Actors Co. Made NY debut Off-Bdwy in 1967 in "Beyond Desire."

PEDI, TOM. Born Sept. 29, 1913 in Brooklyn. Made Bdwy bow in 1941 in "Brooklyn, U.S.A.," followed by "Pins and Needles," "Comic Strip," "King of The Whole Damned World," "Kiss Me, Kate," "Pal Joey," "Beggars Are Coming To Town," "Death of A Salesman," "The Iceman Cometh," "A Hole In The Head," "A View From The Bridge," "My Mother, My Father and Me," "Arturo Ui," "The Investigation," "Mike Downstairs."

PELLOW, CLIFFORD. Born Nov. 13, 1928 in Windsor, Can. Graduate of Wayne State. Made Bdwy bow in 1966 in "Royal Hunt of The Sun," Off-Bdwy in "Desire Under The Elms," "Pullman Car Hiawatha," "Matty, The Moron, and The Madonna," "Paths of Glory," "Fortune and Men's Eyes."

PENDLETON, AUSTIN. Born Mar. 27, 1940 in Warren, O. Attended Yale. Appeared with LC Rep. Co. (1962-3), in "Oh, Dad, Poor Dad . . .," "Fiddler On The Roof," "Hail Scrawdyke," "The Little Foxes" (1967).

PENTECOST, GEORGE. Born July 15, 1939 in Detroit. Graduate of Wayne State, U. Mich. With APA since 1964 in "Scapin," "Lower Depths," "The Tavern," "School For Scandal," "Right You Are," "War and Peace," "The Wild Duck," "The Show-Off," "Pantagleize," and "The Cherry Orchard."

PERKINS, ANTHONY. Born Apr. 4, 1932 in NYC. Attended Rollins College, and Columbia. Made Bdwy bow in 1954 in "Tea and Sympathy" for which he received a THEATRE WORLD Award, followed by "Look Homeward, Angel," "Greenwillow," "Harold," "The Star Spangled Girl."

240

oe Ponazecki   Bernard Poulain   Bernie Rachelle   Walter Raines   Charles Randall

PERRY, JOHN BENNETT. Born Jan. 4, 1941 in Williamston, Mass. Graduate of St. Lawrence U. Made NY stage bow Off-Bdwy in 1967 in "Now Is The Time For All Good Men."

PERTWEE, JOHN. Born July 7, 1919 in London. Attended RADA. Made Bdwy debut in 1967 in "There's A Girl In My Soup."

PETERS, BERNADETTE. Born Feb. 28, 1948 in Jamaica, N.Y. Appeared Off-Bdwy in "Penny Friend" and "Curley McDimple," "Most Happy Fella" (CC), made Bdwy debut in 1967 in "The Girl In The Freudian Slip," followed by "Johnny No Trump," "George M!" for which she received a THEATRE WORLD Award.

PHALEN, ROBERT. Born May 10, 1937 in San Francisco. Attended CCSF, U. Cal. Appeared with LC Rep. Co. in "Danton's Death," "The Country Wife," "Caucasian Chalk Circle," "The Alchemist," "Yerma," "Galileo," "St. Joan," "Tiger At The Gates," and "Cyrano de Bergerac."

PHILLIPS, MARGARET. Born July 6, 1923 in Cwmgwrach, Wales. Made Bdwy debut in 1942 in "Proof Through The Night," followed by "The Late George Apley" for which she received a THEATRE WORLD Award, "Another Part of The Forest," "Summer and Smoke," "The Cocktail Party," "The Heiress," "Merchant of Venice," "Second Threshold," "Dial 'M' For Murder," "Fallen Angels," Am. Shakespeare Festival productions, Off-Bdwy in "The Lady's Not For Burning," "Under The Sycamore Tree" and "The Ginger Man," "White Lies," "Black Comedy," "Lion In Winter."

PHILLIPS, RANDY. Born Jan. 22, 1926 in NYC. Attended Juilliard. Appeared Off-Bdwy in "H.M.S. Pinafore," and on Bdwy in "How To Succeed," "Hello, Dolly!," "Skyscraper," "Mame."

PIAZZA, BEN. Born July 30, 1934 in Little Rock, Ark. Attended Princeton, and Actors Studio. Made Bdwy bow in 1958 in "Winesburg, Ohio," followed by "Kataki" for which he received a THEATRE WORLD Award, "A Second String," Off-Bdwy in "American Dream," "Zoo Story," and "Deathwatch," "The Fun Couple," "Who's Afraid of Virginia Woolf?," "Song of The Grasshopper."

PICON, MOLLY. Born June 1, 1898. International Yiddish theatre star. Has appeared on Bdwy in "Morning Star," "For Heaven's Sake, Mother," "Milk and Honey," "How To Be A Jewish Mother."

PIERCE, RIK. Born Jan. 21, 1939 in NYC. Attended U. Pittsburgh. Appeared Off-Bdwy in "Call It Virtue" and "The Experiment" before Bdwy bow in 1968 in "Avanti!"

PINCUS, WARREN. Born Apr. 13, 1938 in Brooklyn. Attended CCNY. Appeared Off-Bdwy in "Miss Nepertiti Regrets," "The Circus," "The Magician," "Boxcars," "Demented World," "Give My Regards," and "The Electronic Nigger."

PLAYTEN, ALICE. Born Aug. 28, 1947 in NYC. Attended NYU and Bklyn College. Made stage debut in 1959 in Metropolitan Opera's "Wozzeck," and Bdwy bow in 1960 in "Gypsy," followed by "Oliver," "Hello, Dolly!," "Henry, Sweet Henry" for which she received a THEATRE WORLD Award.

PLESHETTE, JOHN. Born July 27, 1942 in NYC. Attended Brown U. Made Bdwy debut in 1966 in "The Zulu and The Zayda," appeared Off-Bdwy in "A Sound of Silence," with NY Shakespeare Festival, "MacBird," and "It's Called The Sugar Plum."

POINTER, PRISCILLA. Born in NYC. Appeared with San Francisco Actors Workshop from 1952-65, and Lincoln Center Repertory Co. from 1965-69, and in "Summertree."

POLAN, LOU. Born in Russia, June 15, 1904. Appeared in "All The Living," "Night Music," "Liberty Jones," "Cafe Crown," "The Whole World Over," "Gentleman From Athens," "Bus Stop," "The Seagull" (OB), "The Golden State," "Desire Under The Elms," "Drink To Me Only," "Legend of Lizzie," "Hamlet" (CP), "The Tenth Man" (CC1967).

POLLOCK, NANCY R. Born Feb. 10, 1905 in Brooklyn. Attended U. Cuba, Columbia, U. Mex., NYU. Made Bdwy debut in 1950 in "Diamond Lil," followed by "One Bright Day," "In The Summer House," "Middle of The Night," "Period of Adjustment," "Come Blow Your Horn," "In The Counting House," "Have I Got A Girl For You," "Ceremony of Innocence," "A Day In The Death of Joe Egg."

PONAZECKI, JOE. Born Jan. 7, 1934 in Rochester, N.Y. Attended Rochester U., Columbia. Made Bdwy bow in 1959 in "Much Ado About Nothing," followed by "Send Me No Flowers," "A Call On Kuprin," "Take Her, She's Mine," "The Dragon" (OB), "Fiddler On The Roof," "Xmas In Las Vegas," "3 Bags Full," "Love In E-Flat," "90 Day Mistress," "Muzeeka" (OB).

PONTERIO, ROBIN. Born May 10, 1957 in St. Petersburg, Fla. Made Bdwy debut Sept. 28, 1967 in "Song of The Grasshopper."

POPE, PEGGY. Born May 15, 1929 in Montclair, N.J. Attended Smith College. Appeared in "The Doctor's Dilemma" (1955), "Volpone" (1957), "The Rose Tattoo" (1966), "Muzeeka" (OB).

POULAIN, BERNARD. Born Sept. 4, 1934 in Amiens, France. Appeared with Comedie Francaise in Paris before making NY bow Off-Bdwy in 1967 in "Scuba Duba."

POWERS, ED. Born Jan. 23, 1938 in Brooklyn. Attended U. Fla., Pasadena Playhouse, Dramatic Workshop. Appeared Off-Bdwy in "The Bear" and "Nighthawks."

PREMICE, JOSEPHINE. Born July 21, 1926 in Brooklyn. Graduate of Columbia, Cornell. Made Bdwy debut in 1945 in "Blue Holidy," followed by "Caribbean Carnival," "Mister Johnson," "Jamaica," "A Hand Is On The Gate," "House of Flowers" (OB1968).

PRESTON, ROBERT. Born June 8, 1918 in Newton Highland, Mass. Attended Pasadena Playhouse. Made Bdwy bow in 1951 in "20th Century," followed by "The Male Animal," "Men of Distinction," "His and Hers," "The Magic and The Loss," "Tender Trap," "Janus," "Hidden River," "The Music Man," "Too True To Be Good," "Nobody Loves An Albatross," "Ben Franklin In Paris," "The Lion In Winter," I Do! I Do!"

PRICE, VINCENT. Born May 27, 1911 in St. Louis. Attended Yale, and U. London. Made Bdwy bow in 1935 in "Victoria Regina," followed by "Shoemaker's Holiday," "Heartbreak House," "The Lady Has A Heart," "Outward Bound," "Angel Street," "Richard III," "Black-Eyed Susan," "Darling of The Day."

PRIEST, DAN. Born Feb. 29, 1924 in Altus, Okla. Attended West Tex. State Teachers College. Appeared Off-Bdwy in "The Crucible," "Deep Are The Roots," and "A View From The Bridge," on Bdwy in "The Investigation," "The Trial of Lee Harvey Oswald."

241

| Nancy Reardon | George Reeder | Eugene Roche | Sandy Rochelle | Patricia R |

PRINCE, WILLIAM. Born Jan. 26, 1913 in Nicholas, N.Y. Attended Cornell. Appeared in "Richard II," "Hamlet," "Ah, Wilderness," "Guest In The House," "Across The Board On Tomorrow Morning," "Eve of St. Mark," "John Loves Mary," "Forward The Heart," "As You Like It," "I Am A Camera," "Affair of Honor," "Third Best Sport," "The Highest Tree," "Venus At Large," "Strange Interlude" (1963), "Ballad of The Sad Cafe," "Stephen D." (OB), "The Little Foxes" (1967).

PRYOR, MAUREEN. Born May 23, 1924 in Limerick, Eng. Attended London Theatre School. Made Bdwy debut in 1965 in "Boeing, Boeing," followed by "After The Rain".

PUGH, TED. Born Apr. 24, 1937 in Anadarko, Okla. Graduate of U. Okla. Appeared Off-Bdwy in "In The Nick of Time" and "Have I Got One For You."

QUAM, MYLO. Born June 1, 1942 in Fargo, N.D. Attended Brandeis U., LIU, Boston U., and NYU. Made Bdwy debut in 1965 in "Royal Hunt of The Sun." Off-Bdwy credits: "Deathwatch," "The Killers," "Picnic On The Battlefield," "Collision Course."

QUAYLE, ANTHONY. Born Sept. 7, 1913 in Ainsdale, Eng. Attended RADA. Made Bdwy debut in 1936 in "The Country Wife," followed by "Tamburlaine The Great" (1956), "The First Born" (1958), "Galileo" (LC1967), "Halfway Up The Tree" (1967).

RABB, ELLIS. Born June 20, 1930 in Memphis, Tenn. Attended Carnegie Tech. Appeared with Am. Shakespeare Festival, Off-Bdwy in "Le Misanthrope" and "Mary Stuart," made Bdwy bow in 1959 in "Look After Lulu," organized and remains artistic director of APA Repertory Co. with whom he has acted in "School For Scandal" and "Pantagleize."

RACHELLE, BERNIE. Born Oct. 7, 1939 in NYC. Graduate of Yeshiva U., Hunter College. Appeared Off-Bdwy in "Winterset," "Golden Boy," "Street Scene," "World of Sholom Aleichem," "Diary of Anne Frank," "Electra," and "Nighthawks."

RACHINS, ALAN. Born Oct. 3, 1942 in Brookline, Mass. Attended U. Pa. Made Bdwy debut Oct. 9, 1967 in "After The Rain."

RAINES, WALTER. Born Aug. 16, 1940 in Braddock, Pa. Attended Carnegie Tech., Juilliard. Appeared with Penna. and John Cranko Ballet Cos., and in German Plays, Films, and tv before NY bow Off-Bdwy in 1968 revival of "House of Flowers."

RAITT, JOHN. Born Jan. 29, 1917 in Santa Ana, Calif. Graduate of Redlands U. Made Bdwy bow in 1945 in "Carousel" for which he received a THEATRE WORLD Award, followed by "Magdalena," "Three Wishes For Jamie," "Pajama Game," "Carousel" (1965), "A Joyful Noise," "On A Clear Day You Can See Forever."

RAM, JERRY. Born Oct. 5, 1946 in New Delhi, India. Attended Delhi U. Made Bdwy debut Mar. 6, 1968 in "The Guide."

RANDALL, CHARLES. Born Mar. 15, 1923 in Chicago. Attended Columbia. Appeared Off-Bdwy in "The Adding Machine," "The Cherry Orchard," "Brothers Karamazov," "Susan Slept Here" and "Two For Fun," made Bdwy bow in 1953 in "Anastasia," followed by "Enter Laughing," "The Trial of Lee Harvey Oswald."

RANDOLPH, JOHN. Born June 1, 1915 in The Bronx. Attended CCNY, Am. Theatre Wing, Actors Studio. Made Bdwy bow in 1937 in "Revolt of The Beavers," followed by "The Emperor's New Clothes," "Capt. Jinks," "No More Peace," "Coriolanus," "Medicine Show," "Hold On To Your Hats," "Native Son," "Command Decision," "Come Back, Little Sheba," "Golden State," "Peer Gynt," "Paint Your Wagon," "Seagulls Over Sorrento," "The Grey-Eyed People," "Room Service," "All Summer Long," "House of Flowers," "The Visit," "Mother Courage and Her Children," "A Sound of Music," "A Case of Libel," "Conversation At Midnight," "An Evening's Frost" (OB), "My Sweet Charlie," "The Peddler and The Dodo Bird" (OB).

RAPHAEL, GERRIANNE. Born Feb. 23, 1935 in NYC. Attended New School and Columbia. Appeared in "Solitaire," "Guest In The House," "Violet," "Goodbye, My Fancy," "Seventh Heaven," "Li'l Abner," "Saratoga," Off-Bdwy in "Threepenny Opera," "The Boy Friend," "Ernest In Love," "Man of La Mancha."

RAWLS, EUGENIA. Born Sept. 11, 1916, in Macon, Ga. Attended U.N.C. Made Bdwy debut in 1934 in "The Children's Hour," followed by "To Quinto and Back," "Journeyman," "The Little Foxes," "Guest In The House," "The Man Who Had All The Luck," "Strange Fruit," "The Shrike," "The Great Sebastians," "First Love," "A Case of Libel," "The Poker Session" (OB).

REARDON, NANCY. Born June 28, 1942, in NYC. Made Bdwy debut in 1964 in "Poor Bitos," followed by "Right Honourable Gentleman," "The Odd Couple," "Black Comedy," "The Unknown Soldier and His Wife."

REDFIELD, WILLIAM. Born Jan. 26, 1927 in NYC. Made Bdwy bow in 1936 in "Swing Your Lady," followed by "Excursion," "Virginia," "Stop-Over," "Our Town," "Second Helping," "Junior Miss," "Snafu," "Barefoot Boy With Cheek," "Montserrat," "Miss Liberty," "Out of This World," "Misalliance," "Double In Hearts," "The Making of Moo" (OB), "A Man For All Seasons," "Minor Adjustment."

REDFORD, LESLIE. Born Sept. 18, 1929 in Bolton, Eng. Attended Manchester U. Made Bdwy bow in 1963 in "Rattle of A Simple Man," followed by "Bicycle Ride To Nevada," "The Zulu and The Zayda," Off-Bdwy in "Squat Betty," "Sponge Room," "Play With A Tiger," and "Hamp."

REDMOND, LIAM. Born July 27, 1913 in Ireland. Attended Natl. U. Made Bdwy debut in 1939 in "The White Steed," followed by "The Wayward Saint," "The Loves of Cass McGuire," "Loot."

REEDER, GEORGE. Born July 15, 1931 in Pomona, Calif. Made Bdwy bow in 1952 in "Buttrio Square," followed by "Hazel Flagg," "John Murray Anderson's Almanac," "Li'l Abner," "Destry Rides Again," "A Funny Thing Happened On The Way To The Forum," "Funny Girl."

REID, KATE. Born Nov. 4, 1930 in London. Attended Toronto U. Made Bdwy debut in 1962 in "Who's Afraid of Virginia Woolf?," followed by "Dylan," "Slapstick Tragedy," "The Price."

REINHOLT, GEORGE. Born Aug. 22, 1940 in Philadelphia. Appeared Off-Bdwy in "Misalliance," "The Bald Soprano" and "Colombe" before Bdwy bow in 1967 in "Cabaret."

| bert Ronan | Martin Ross | Robert Salvio | Honey Sanders | Alfred Sandor |

REYNOLDS, JONATHAN. Born in 1942. Graduate of RADA. Appeared with NY Shakespeare Festival before making Bdwy debut in 1967 in "Rosencrantz and Guildenstern Are Dead."

RICHARDS, BEAH. Born in Vicksburg, Miss. Attended Dillard U. Appeared Off-Bdwy in 1956 in "Take A Giant Step," on Bdwy in 1959 in "A Raisin In The Sun," followed by "The Miracle Worker," "Purlie Victorious," "The Amen Corner" for which she received a THEATRE WORLD Award, "The Little Foxes" (1967).

ROBBINS, JANE MARLA. Born Nov. 2, 1943 in NYC. Attended Bryn Mawr. Appeared in 1967 Off-Bdwy in "The Bear" and "Beyond Desire."

ROBERTS, ANTHONY. Born Oct. 22, 1939 in NYC. Graduate of Northwestern. Made Bdwy bow in 1962 in "Something About A Soldier," followed by "Take Her, She's Mine," "The Last Analysis," "The Cradle Will Rock" (OB), "Never Too Late," "Barefoot In The Park," "Don't Drink The Water," "How Now, Dow Jones."

ROBERTS, MARILYN. Born Oct. 30, 1939 in San Francisco. Graduate of SF State College. Made NY debut Off-Bdwy in "Telemachus Clay" in 1963, followed by "The Maids," "The Class," "Gabriella," "Futz" and "Tom Paine."

ROBINSON, ROGER. Born May 2, 1941 in Seattle, Wash. Attended USCal. Appeared Off-Bdwy in "Walk In Darkness," "Does A Tiger Wear A Necktie?," with Am. Shakespeare Festival in 1965, "Jerico-Jim Crow," "Who's Got His Own," "Trials of Brother Jero."

ROCHE, EUGENE. Born Sept. 22, 1928 in Boston. Attended Emerson College. Appeared Off-Bdwy in "Waiting For Godot," "Under Milkwood," "Between Two Thieves," "Valmouth," "Laughwind," and "Father Uxbridge Wants To Marry," on Bdwy in "Blood, Sweat and Stanley Poole," "All In Good Time," "The White House," "Mother Courage and Her Children," "Great Day In The Morning," "The Millionairess," "Time of The Barracudas."

ROCHELLE, SANDY. Born May 17, 1942 in Boston. Attended AADA, Pasadena Playhouse, Actors Workshop. Appeared Off-Bdwy in "Dracula" and with LC Rep. Co. in "Tiger At The Gates" and "Cyrano de Bergerac."

RODD, MARCIA. Born July 8, in Lyons, Kan. Attended Northwestern and Yale. Made Bdwy debut in 1964 in "Oh What A Lovely War," followed by "Love In E Flat," and appeared Off-Bdwy in "Oh Say Can You See," "Cambridge Circus," "The Mad Show," "Madame Mousse," "Love and Let Love," and "Your Own Thing."

RODGERS, LOU. Born Oct. 15, 1935 in London. Graduate of New Eng. Conservatory. Made Bdwy bow in 1967 in "Illya, Darling."

RODGERS, SHEV. Born Apr. 9, 1928 in Holister, Cal. Attended San Francisco State College. Made Bdwy bow in 1959 in "Redhead," followed by "The Music Man," "Man of La Mancha."

ROE, PATRICIA. Born Sept. 18, 1932 in NYC Attended US Cal., Columbia, Am. Theatre Wing, Actors Studio. Made Bdwy debut in 1951 in "Romeo and Juliet," followed by "Cat On A Hot Tin Roof," "Compulsion," "The Beautiful Sea," "Night Circus," "A Distant Bell," "Look After Lulu," "Night of The Iguana," "The Collection" (OB), LC Rep. Co.'s "After The Fall" and "But For Whom Charlie," "The Homecoming."

ROEBLING, PAUL. Born Mar. 1, 1934 in Philadelphia. Attended Columbia, HB Studio. Made Bdwy bow in 1953 in "A Girl Can Tell," followed by "The Dark Is Light Enough," "The Lark," "A Desert Incident" for which he received a THEATRE WORLD Award, "Romeo and Juliet," "This Side of Paradise" (OB), "The Milk Train Doesn't Stop Here Anymore," "The Four Seasons' (OB).

ROERICK, WILLIAM. Born Dec. 17, 1912 in NYC. Attended Hamilton College. Made Bdwy bow in 1935 in "Romeo and Juliet," followed by "St. Joan," "Hamlet," "Our Town," "The Importance of Being Earnest," "The Land Is Bright," "Autumn Hill," "This Is The Army," "The Magnificent Yankee," "Tonight At 8:30," "Madam, Will You Walk" (OB), "The Burning Glass," "Right Honourable Gentleman," "Come Slowly, Eden" (OB), "Elizabeth The Queen" (1966CC), "Marat/DeSade," "The Homecoming."

ROGERS, GINGER. Born July 16, 1911 in Independence, Mo. Made Bdwy debut in 1929 in "Top Speed," followed by "Girl Crazy." Made 71 films before returning to Bdwy in 1951 in "Love and Let Love," then "Hello, Dolly!" (1965-67).

ROGERS, PAUL. Born Mar. 22, 1917 in Plympton, Eng. Attended Michael Chekhov Theatre Studio. Made Bdwy debut with Old Vic (1956-7) in "Macbeth," "Romeo and Juliet," "Troilus and Cressida," and "Richard II," subsequently in "Photo Finish" (1963), "The Homecoming" (1967), "Here's Where I Belong" (1968).

RONAN, ROBERT. Born Feb. 17, 1938 in Richmond Hill, N.Y. Attended Hostra U. Made Off-Bdwy in 1964 in "Doctor Faustus," "followed by "Colombe," NY Shakespeare Festival's "Love's Labor's Lost," "All's Well That Ends Well," and "Comedy of Errors," "The Memorandum."

ROSE, GEORGE. Born Feb. 19, 1920 in Bicester, Eng. Attended Central School of Drama, London. Made NY bow with Old Vic in 1946 in "Henry IV," followed by "Much Ado About Nothing," "A Man For All Seasons," "Hamlet" (1964), "Royal Hunt of The Sun," "Walking Happy," "Loot."

ROSE, JANE. Born in Spokane, Wash. Graduate of U. Wash. Made Bdwy debut in 1952 in "The Time of The Cuckoo," followed by "The Wooden Dish," "Orpheus Descending," "The Gazebo," N.Y Shakespeare Festival (1966, 1967), "Arms and The Man" (OB).

ROSE, REVA. Born July 30, 1940 in Chicago. Attended Goodman Theatre School. Made Bdwy debut in 1960 in "Look After Lulu," followed by Off-Bdwy roles in "The Time of The Cuckoo" and "You're A Good Man, Charlie Brown" for which she received a THEATRE WORLD Award.

ROSQUI, TOM. Born June 12, 1928 in Oakland, Cal. Graduate of College of Pacific. With LC Rep. Co. since 1965 in "Danton's Death," "The Condemned of Altona," "The Country Wife," "Caucasian Chalk Circle," "The Alchemist," "Yerma" and "The East Wind," Off-Bdwy in "Collision Course."

ROSS, MARTIN. Born July 9, 1938 in NYC. Appeared Off-Bdwy in "We're Civilized" before Bdwy bow in 1963 in "Milk and Honey," followed by "Once For The Asking," "The Yearling," "Pousse Cafe," "Cabaret."

Patricia Sauers	John Scanlan	Muni Seroff	Ellen Shade	Barbara Shar

ROUNSEVILLE, ROBERT. Born Mar. 25, 1919 in Attleboro, Mass. Attended Tufts U. Made Bdwy bow in 1937 in "Babes In Arms," followed by "Two Bouquets," "Knickerbocker Holiday," "Higher and Higher," "Up In Central Park," 1952 Gilbert & Sullivan revivals, "Show Boat" (1954), "The Merry Widow," "Candide," "Brigadoon" (CC), "Man of La Mancha."

ROUTLEDGE, PATRICIA. Born in Birkenhead, Eng. Graduate of U. Liverpool. Made Bdwy debut in 1966 in "How's The World Treating You?," followed by "Darling of The Day" (1968).

ROWLES, POLLY. Born Jan. 10 in Philadelphia. Graduate of Carnegie Tech. Made Bdwy debut in 1938 in "Julius Caesar," followed by "Richard III," "Anne of The Thousand Days," "Golden State," "The Small Hours," "Gertie," "Time Out For Ginger," "Wooden Dish," "Goodbye Again," "Auntie Mame," "Look After Lulu," "A Mighty Man Is He," "No Strings," "The Killing of Sister George."

ROZAKIS, GREGORY. Born Jan. 30, 1943 in NYC. Made Bdwy bow in 1963 in "Natural Affection," followed by "Royal Hunt of The Sun," "What Did We Do Wrong?"

RULE, CHARLES. Born Aug. 4, 1928 in Springfield, Mo. Made Bdwy bow in 1951 in "Courtin' Time," followed by "Happy Hunting," "Oh, Captain!," "The Conquering Hero," "Donnybrook," "Bye Bye Birdie," "Fiddler On The Roof," "Henry, Sweet Henry."

RUPERT, MIKE. Born Oct. 23, 1951 in Denver, Colo. Made Bdwy debut Jan. 18, 1968 in "The Happy Time" for which he received a THEATRE WORLD Award.

RYLAND, JACK. Born July 2, 1935 in Lancaster, Pa. Attended AFDA, Philadelphia. Appeared Off-Bdwy in "Palm Tree In A Rose Garden," "Lysistrata," "The White Rose and The Red," "The Old Glory," with NY Shakespeare Festival, on Bdwy in "The World of Suzie Wong" (1959), "A Very Rich Woman," with LC Rep. Co. in "Cyrano de Bergerac."

SABIN, DAVID. Born Apr. 24, 1937 in Washington, D.C. Graduate of Catholic U. Made NY bow in 1965 in "The Fantasticks" (OB), followed by Bdwy roles "The Yearling," "Slapstick Tragedy," "Now Is The Time For All Good Men" (OB).

ST. JOHN, MARCO. Born May 7, 1939 in New Orleans. Graduate of Fordham. Appeared Off-Bdwy in "Angels of Anadarko," and "Man of Destiny," on Bdwy in "Poor Bitos," "And Things That Go Bump In The Night," with APA in "We Comrades Three" and "War and Peace," "The Unknown Soldier and His Wife," "Weekend."

SALMON, SCOTTY. Born Jan. 13, 1943 in Wichita Falls, Tex. Made Bdwy bow in 1966 in "Pousse Cafe," followed by "Mame," "George M!"

SALVIO, ROBERT. Born Feb. 14, 1942 in NYC. Graduate of UCLA. Appeared Off-Bdwy in "The Awakening of Spring," "Night of The Dunce," and "Hamp" for which he received a THEATRE WORLD Award, "Cabaret."

SANCHEZ, JAIME. Born Dec. 19, 1938 in Rincon, P.R. Attended Actors Studio. Made Bdwy bow in 1957 in "West Side Story," followed by "Oh, Dad, Poor Dad . . .," "A Midsummer Night's Dream" and "Othello" (NYShakeF), Off-Bdwy in "The Toilet," "Conerico Was Here To Stay" for which he received a THEATRE WORLD Award, and "The Ox Cart."

SANDERS, HONEY. Born Dec. 24, 1928 in Brooklyn. Attended Hofstra U. Appeared Off-Bdwy in "She Shall Have Music" and "Tobacco Road" before Bdwy debut in 1961 in "13 Daughters," followed by "South Pacific" (CC1965), "Rose Tattoo" (1966), "Mame," "The Education of Hyman Kaplan."

SANDOR, ALFRED. Born Nov. 5, 1918 in Budapest, Hungary. Attended U.PA., AADA. Made Bdwy bow in 1952 in "Wish You Were Here," followed by "No Time For Sergeants," "Time Limit," "Third Best Sport," "Gypsy," "On An Open Roof" (OB), "My Mother, My Father and Me," "Tchin-Tchin," "Luther," "The Odd Couple," "Plaza Suite."

SANDS, DIANA. Born Aug. 22, 1934 in NYC. Appeared Off-Bdwy in "An Evening With Will Shakespeare," "The World of Sholem Aleichem," "Major Barbara," "Man With The Golden Arm," "A Land Beyond The River," "The Egg and I," "Another Evening With Harry Stoones," "Black Monday," "Brecht On Brecht," "The Living Premise," made Bdwy debut in "A Raisin In The Sun," followed by "Tiger, Tiger, Burning Bright" for which she received a THEATRE WORLD Award, "Blues For Mr. Charlie," "The Owl and The Pussycat," with LCRep. Co. in "St. Joan" and "Tiger At The Gates."

SANDS, DOROTHY. Born Mar. 5, 1900 in Cambridge, Mass. Attended Radcliffe College. Appeared in "Grand Street Follies," "The Seagull," "The Stairs," "All The Comforts of Home," "Papa Is All," "Tomorrow The World," "A Joy Forever," "Bell, Book and Candle," "Misalliance," "Quadrille," "First Gentleman," "Moonbirds," "Once For The Asking," Off-Bdwy in "Mary Stuart," "Whisper To Me" and "The Club Bedroom."

SAPPINGTON, FAY. Born May 22, 1906. Attended U. Tex., Pasadena Playhouse. Appeared in "Southern Exposure," "The Cellar and The Well," "Glad Tidings," "J.B.," "The Yearling," "The Campbells of Boston" (OB), "Golden Rainbow."

SAUERS, PATRICIA. Born Apr. 25, 1941 in Glendale, Cal. Attended UCLA, Pasadena Playhouse. Made Bdwy debut in 1967 in "Hello, Dolly!" after touring with Natl. Co.

SCAMMELL, TERENCE. Born Mar. 1, 1937 in London. Attended RADA. Appeared with Am. Shakespeare Festival, Off-Bdwy in "The Mousetrap," and "The Giants' Dance," toured with Natl. Rep. Co.

SCANLAN, JOHN. Born Apr. 3, 1924 in Milwaukee. Graduate of Columbia. Attended AADA. Appeared Off-Bdwy in "The Plow and The Stars," "The Mousetrap," "To Bury A Cousin," "A Christmas Carol," and "Beyond Desire."

SCARLETT, KATHLEEN. Born Apr. 7, 1943 in Perpignan, France. Attended U Cal., Neighborhood Playhouse. Appeared Off-Bdwy in "Enemy of The People," "Marching Song," "The Boy Friend," and "Scarlet Lullaby."

SCHAFER, NATALIE. Born Nov. 5, 1912 in Red Bank, N.J. Attended Merrill School. Made NY debut in 1927 in "Trigger," followed by "March Hares," "These Few Ashes," "The Nut Farm," "Rhapsody," "The Great Barrington," "Perfectly Scandalous," "New York To Cherbourg," "So Many Paths," "Lady Precious Stream," "Susan and God," "Lady In The Dark," "The Doughgirls," "A Joy Forever," "Forward The Heart," "Six Characters In Search of An Author" (OB), "Romanoff and Juliet," "The Highest Tree," "The Killing of Sister George."

| bert Shattuck | April Shawhan | Sloane Shelton | Stanley Simmonds | Joseph Sirola |

SCHROEDER, MICHAEL. Born June 7, 1943 in Sydney, Aust. Attended AMDA. Toured in "Hello, Dolly!" before NY bow Off-Bdwy in 1968 in "Have I Got One For You."

SCOTT, GEORGE C. Born Oct. 18, 1927 in Wise, Va. Attended U. Mo. Appeared Off-Bdwy in "Richard II" for which he received a THEATRE WORLD Award, "As You Like It," "Children of Darkness," and "Desire Under The Elms." Made Bdwy bow in 1958 in "Comes A Day," followed by "The Andersonville Trial," "The Wall," "General Seeger," "The Little Foxes" (1967), "Plaza Suite."

SCOTT, HAROLD. Born Sept. 6, 1935 in Morristown, N.J. Graduate of Harvard. Made NY bow in 1957 Off-Bdwy in "A Land Beyond The River," followed by "I, Too, Have Lived In Arcadia," "The Egg and I," "Deathwatch," "God's Trombones," "The Jackass," "Program One," "The Death of Bessie Smith," "The Blacks," "The Trials of Brother Jero," "The Strong Breed," with LC Rep. Co. in "After The Fall," "Marco Millions," "But For Whom Charlie," "The Changeling," and "Incident At Vichy," on Bdwy in "The Cool World."

SELDES, MARIAN. Born in NYC, Aug. 23, 1928. Attended Neighborhood Playhouse. Made Bdwy debut in 1947 in "Medea," followed by "Crime and Punishment," "That Lady," "Tower Beyond Tragedy," "Ondine," "The High Ground," "Come of Age," "The Chalk Garden," "The Milk Train Doesn't Stop Here Anymore," "The Wall," "A Gift of Time," Off-Bdwy in "Diff'rent," and "The Ginger Man," "A Delicate Balance," "Before You Go."

SEROFF, MUNI. Born in Russia, Jan. 8, 1905. Attended U. Odessa. Made Bdwy bow in 1960 in "The Wall," appeared Off-Bdwy in "Between Two Thieves," "Shadow of Heroes," "Corruption In The Palace of Justice," "The Day The Whores Came Out To Play Tennis," "The Kitchen," and "Javelin," "The Tenth Man" (CC1967), "Soldiers."

SETTIMIO, AL. Born Feb. 16, 1945 in Philadelphia. Attended Temple U. Made NY debut in 1967 Off-Bdwy in "The Poker Session."

SEYMOUR, JOHN D. Born Oct. 24, 1897 in Boston. Attended Colgate U. Made NY bow in 1918 in "Out There," followed by "Richard III," "Dearest Enemy," "Blood Money," "The Barretts of Wimpole Street," "Sweet Adeline," "Cyrano de Bergerac," "Pride and Prejudice," "Susan and God," "The Moon Is Down," "Eastward In Eden," "The Vigil," "Light Up The Sky," "The Sacred Flame," City Center revivals of "Pal Joey," "The King and I" and "Life With Father."

SHADE, ELLEN. Born Feb. 17, 1945 in NYC. Graduate of Hunter College and Juilliard. Appeared with American Savoyards, in "The Sound of Music" (CC1967), "Have I Got One For You" (OB).

SHARMA, BARBARA. Born Sept. 14, 1942. Appeared Off-Bdwy in "The Boy Friend," "Italian Straw Hat," "In Your Hat," and "Cole Porter Revisited," on Bdwy in "Fiorello!," "Little Me," "Sweet Charity," "Hallelujah, Baby."

SHARPE, JOHN. Born Oct. 2, 1932 in Chicago. Attended Northwestern. Appeared in "Seventeen," "Shoestring Revue" (OB), "The Most Happy Fella," "Sweet Charity."

SHATTUCK, ROBERT. Born in Vermont, Apr. 26, 1940. Graduate of Hiram College. Made NY debut Off-Bdwy in 1967 in "The Ceremony of Innocence."

SHAW, G. TITO. Born Feb. 1, 1943 in Chicago. Graduate of Columbia. Appeared Off-Bdwy in "Barabas," "The Intellectual Ladies," and "The Trials of Brother Jero."

SHAW, JOSEPH. Born in Lancashire, Eng. Graduate of Central School of Speech and Drama, London. Made Bdwy debut May 1, 1968 in "Soldiers."

SHAWHAN, APRIL. Born Apr. 10, 1940 in Chicago. Attended AADA. Made NY debut Off-Bdwy in 1964 in "Jo" and Bdwy bow in 1965 in "Race of Hairy Men," followed by "3 Bags Full" for which she received a THEATRE WORLD Award, "Dinner At 8" (1966), "Hamlet" (OB).

SHAWN, DICK. Born Dec. 1, in Buffalo, NY. Attended U. Miami. Made Bdwy debut in 1948 in "For Heaven's Sake, Mother," followed by "A Funny Thing Happened On The Way To The Forum," "The Egg," "Peterpat," "Fade Out—Fade In," "I'm Solomon."

SHEEN, MARTIN. Born Aug. 3, 1940 in Dayton, O. Appeared Off-Bdwy in "The Connection," "Many Loves," and "The Jungle of Cities," made Bdwy bow in 1964 in "Never Live Over A Pretzel Factory," followed by "The Subject Was Roses," "The Wicked Cooks" (OB), "Hamlet" (OB).

SHELLEY, CAROLE. Born Aug. 16, 1939 in London. Made Bdwy debut in 1965 in "The Odd Couple," followed by "The Astrakhan Coat," "Loot."

SHELTON, SLOANE. Born Mar. 17, 1934 in Ashville, N.C. Attended Bearea College and RADA. Appeared Off-Bdwy in "Androcles and The Lion," "The Maids," "Way of The World," and "Dark of The Moon," and Bdwy debut in 1967 with Natl. Rep. Theatre in "The Imaginary Invalid," "A Touch of The Poet," and "Tonight At 8:30," followed by "I Never Sang For My Father."

SHERMAN, HIRAM. Born Feb. 11, 1908 in Boston. Attended U. Ill., and Goodman Theatre. Made Bdwy bow in 1936 in "Horse Eats Hat," followed by "Shoemaker's Holiday," "Sing Out The News," "Very Warm For May," "The Talley Method," "Cyrano de Bergerac," "The Alchemist," "4 Twelves Are 48," "The Moon Is Blue," "Two's Company," "Frogs of Spring," "3 For Tonight," "Goodbye Again," "Measure For Measure," "International Soiree," "Mary, Mary, "Where's Daddy?," "How Now, Dow Jones."

SHOWALTER, MAX (formerly Casey Adams) Born June 2, 1917 in Caldwell, Kan. Attended Pasadena Playhouse. Made Bdwy bow in 1938 in "Knights of Song," followed by "Very Warm For May," "My Sister Eileen," "Show Boat," "John Loves Mary," "Make Mine Manhattan," "Hello, Dolly!"

SICARI, JOSEPH R. Born Apr. 29, 1939 in Boston. Graduate of Catholic U. Appeared Off-Bdwy in "The Parasite," "Comedy of Errors" (NYShakeF), and "Love and Let Love."

SIDNEY, SYLVIA. Born Aug. 10, 1910, in NYC. Attended Theatre Guild School. Made Bdwy debut in 1926 in "Prunella," followed by "The Squall," "Crime," "Mirrors," "The Breaks," "Nice Women," "Cross Roads," "Many A Slip," "Bad Girl," "To Quito and Back," "The Gentle People," "A Very Special Baby," "Auntie Mame," "Enter Laughing," "Riverside Drive" (OB), with Nat. Rep. Theatre, "Barefoot In The Park."

SIGGINS, JEFF. Born Sept. 22, 1943 in Warren, Pa. Appeared Off-Bdwy in "Anything Goes," "Ginger Man," "All Women Are One," and "Biscuit," before 1965 Bdwy bow in "The Impossible Years," followed by "Keep It In The Family."

Rufus Smith	Sarah Jane Smith	Sheila Smith	Robert Stattel	Barton Stone

SILBER, DON. Born Dec. 11, 1936 in Utica, N.Y. Attended Utica College, Colgate, and Syracuse U. Made Bdwy bow in 1965 in "Royal Hunt of The Sun" followed by "Hamp" (OB).

SILLMAN, LEONARD. Born May 9, 1908 in Detroit, Mich. Appeared in vaudeville, "Loud Speaker," "Merry-Go-Round Revue," "Polly," "Lady Be Good," "Greenwich Village Follies," and "New Faces of 1968," which is the eleventh edition he has produced in addition to 13 other plays and musicals.

SILVER, JOE. Born Sept. 28, 1922 in Chicago. Attended U. Wisc., Am. Theatre Wing. Made Bdwy bow in 1942 in "Tobacco Road," followed by "The Doughgirls," "Heads or Tails," Off-Bdwy in "Blood Wedding," "Lamp At Midnight," "Joseph and His Brethren," and "The Victors," "Nature's Way," "Gypsy," "The Heroine," "The Zulu and The Zayda," "You Know I Can't Hear You When The Water's Running."

SIMMONDS, STANLEY. Born July 13, 1907 in Brooklyn. Attended Roosevelt College. Appeared in vaudeville before Bdwy bow in 1927 in "My Maryland," followed by "Castles In The Air," "Simple Simon," "If The Shoe Fits," "Brigadoon" (CC), "Call Me Madam," "Silk Stockings," "Li'l Abner," "Fiorello!," "Let It Ride," "I Can Get It For You Wholesale," "How To Succeed," "Pickwick," "Kelly," "Half A Sixpence," "How Now, Dow Jones."

SIMMONS, CONNIE. Born Dec. 25, 1952 in Douglas, Ga. Made Bdwy debut Jan. 18, 1968 in "The Happy Time."

SIMMONS, NAT. Born Nov. 17, 1936 in Richmond, Va. Attended Columbia. Appeared Off-Bdwy in "The Baptism," "Hatful of Rain," "Moon On A Rainbow Shawl," "Flowers For The Dead," "with NY Shakespeare Festival, and since 1965 has appeared on Bdwy with APA in "You Can't Take It With You," "School For Scandal," and "Pantagleize."

SIROLA, JOSEPH. Born Oct. 7, 1929 in Carteret, N.J. Graduate of Columbia. Appeared Off-Bdwy in "Child of The Morning," "Song For A Certain Midnight" and "Phaedra," before Bdwy bow in 1960 in "The Unsinkable Molly Brown," followed by "Golden Rainbow."

SKILES, STEVE. Born Sept. 10, 1945 in Augusta, Ga. Attended U.N.C., AADA. Made NY bow Off-Bdwy in 1967 in "Now Is The Time For All Good Men," and Bdwy debut in 1967 in "Everything In The Garden," followed by "The Fantasticks" (OB).

SLOAN, MIMI. Born in Aug. 18, in Brooklyn. Made Bdwy debut in 1967 in "Hello, Dolly!," followed by "The Education of Hyman Kaplan."

SMALL, NEVA. Born Nov. 17, 1952 in NYC. Made Bdwy debut in 1964 in "Something More," followed by "The Impossible Years," "Henry, Sweet Henry."

SMILEY, BRENDA. Born in 1947 in Indiana. Attended Ind. U, NYU. Made NY debut in 1966 Off-Bdwy in "America Hurrah," followed by "Scuba Duba" for which she received a THEATRE WORLD Award.

SMITH, DELOS V., JR. Born June 2, 1906 in Hutchinson, Kan. Attended Harvard, Actors Studio. Appeared Off-Bdwy in "The Making of Moo," "When We Dead Awaken," "Tiger Rag," "In The First Place," "Do You Know The Milky Way?," and "Winter Journey," on Bdwy in "The Fun Couple," followed by "The Three Sisters" (1964).

SMITH, NICHOLAS. Born Mar. 5, 1934 in Banstead, Eng. Graduate of RADA. Made Bdwy debut in 1968 in "Portrait Of A Queen."

SMITH, RUFUS. Born July 11, 1917, in Smithfield, Va. Attended U. Va. Made Bdwy bow in 1938 in "Knickerbocker Holiday," followed by "Queen of Spades," "Park Avenue," "Street Scene," "Allegro," Mr. Roberts," "Paint Your Wagon," "Pipe Dream," "Goldilocks," "Fiorello!," "A Gift of Time," "Come On Strong," "The Advocate," "3 Bags Full," "Annie Get Your Gun" (LC), "Halfway Up The Tree," "The Education of Hyman Kaplan."

SMITH, SARAH JANE. Born in Ithaca, N.Y. Graduate of Butler U. Made N Ydebut in 1967 City Center revival of "Brigadoon."

SMITH, SHEILA. Born Apr. 3, 1933 in Conneaut, O. Attended Kent U., Cleveland Playhouse. Made Bdwy debut in 1963 in "Hot Spot," followed by roles Off-Bdwy in "Taboo Revue," "Anything Goes," and "Sweet Miani," "Fiorello!" (CC1962), "Mame" for which she received a THEATRE WORLD Award.

SOBOLOFF, ARNOLD. Born Nov. 11, 1930 in NYC. Attended Cooper Union. Appeared Off-Bdwy in "Threepenny Opera," "Career," "Brothers Karamazov," and "Vincent," on Bdwy in "Mandingo," "The Egg," "The Beauty Part," "One Flew Over The Cuckoo's Nest," "Anyone Can Whistle," "Bravo Giovanni," "Sweet Charity," "Mike Downstairs."

SPEYSER, PAUL J., III. Born Oct. 23, 1941 in Buffalo, N.Y. Attended AADA. Made NY bow in 1967 Off-Bdwy in Public Theater's "Hamlet."

SQUIBB, JUNE. Born Nov. 6 in Vandalia, Ill. Attended Cleveland Playhouse. Appeared Off-Bdwy in "The Sable Brush," "The Boy Friend" and "Lend An Ear," before Bdwy debut in 1960 in "Gypsy" followed by "The Happy Time."

STANDER, HOLLICE. Born Aug. 30, 1944 in Brooklyn. Made debut Off-Bdwy in 1967 in "Nighthawks."

STAPLETON, MAUREEN. Born June 21, 1925 in Troy, N.Y. Attended HB Studio. Made Bdwy debut in 1946 in "The Playboy of The Western World," followed by "Antony and Cleopatra," "Detective Story," "The Bird Cage," "The Rose Tattoo" for which she received a THEATRE WORLD Award, "The Emperor's Clothes," "The Crucible," "Richard III," "The Seagull," "27 Wagons Full of Cotton," "Orpheus Descending," "The Cold Wind and The Warm," "Toys In The Attic," "The Glass Menagerie" (1965), "Plaza Suite."

STARK, DOUGLAS. Born Aug. 4, 1916. Attended U. Va. Made Bdwy bow in 1938 in "Everywhere I Roam," followed by "Three Sisters," "The Man Who Killed Lincoln," "The Trial of Lee Harvey Oswald."

STATTEL, ROBERT. Born Nov. 20, 1937 in Floral Park, N.Y. Graduate of Manhattan College. Made debut Off-Bdwy in 1958 in "Heloise," followed by "When I Was A Child," "Man and Superman," "The Storm," "Don Carlos," "The Taming of The Shrew," with LC Rep. Co. in "Danton's Death," "The Country Wife," and "Caucasian Chalk Circle," "Titus Andronicus" (CP), "Iphigenia In Aulis" and "Ergo" Off-Bdwy.

STERLING, PHILLIP. Born Oct. 9, 1922 in NYC. Graduate of U. Pa. Made Bdwy bow in 1955 in "Silk Stockings," followed by "Interlock," NY Shakespeare Festival productions, Off-Bdwy in "Victims of Duty," "The Opening of A Window," "The Trojan Women," "A Party For Divorce," "The Party On Greenwich Avenue," "The Peddler," and "Summertree."

| irdre Sullivan | Florence Tarlow | Maggie Task | Holland Taylor | Caryl Jeanne Tenney |

STERNE, RICHARD. Born Feb. 26, 1942 in Philadelphia. Graduate of Northwestern. Made Bdwy bow in 1964 in Burton's "Hamlet," followed by "Beyond Desire" (OB).

STEVENS, FRAN. Born March 8 in Washington, D.C. Attended Notre Dame, Maryland Art Inst., and Cleveland Playhouse. Appeared in "Pousse Cafe," "Most Happy Fella," "A Funny Thing Happened On The Way To The Forum," "How Now, Dow Jones."

STEVENS, PAUL. Born June 17, 1924 in Los Angeles. Graduate of UCLA, Pasadena Playhouse. Appeared Off-Bdwy in "The Crucible," "Romeo and Juliet," "Two Gentlemen From Verona," "As You Like It," "Much Ado About Nothing," "Ivanov," "The White Devil," and "The Memorandum," made Bdwy bow in 1957 in "Compulsion," followed by "Girls of Summer," "General Seeger," "Andorra," "The Advocate."

STEWART, FRED. Born Dec. 7, 1906 in Atlanta, Ga. Graduate of Oglethorpe U. Made Bdwy bow in 1931 in "Ladies of Creation," followed by "Experience Unneccessary," "20 Were Chosen," "Excursion," "Robin Landing," "Washington Jitters," "The Devil and Daniel Webster," "Night Music," "Retreat To Pleasure," "Land's End," "The Whole World Over," "Brigadoon," "The Crucible," "Cat On A Hot Tin Roof," "The Girls In 509," "Romulus," "Strange Interlude" (1963), "Galileo" (LC), "More Stately Mansions."

STEWART, RAY. Born Apr. 21, 1932 in San Benito, Tex. Graduate of U. Tex., Neighborhood Playhouse. Appeared Off-Bdwy in "Black Monday," "Conerico Was Here To Stay," "Second City," "Play," "The Experiment," and "The Fantasticks."

STICKNEY, DOROTHY. Born June 21, 1900 in Dickinson, S.D. Attended Northwestern. Made Bdwy debut in 1926 in "The Squall," followed by "Chicago," "March Hares," "The Beaux Strategem," "The Front Page," "Philip Goes Forth," "Another Language," "On Borrowed Time," "Life With Father" (original and 1967 CC revival), "Life With Mother," "The Small Hours," "To Be Continued," "Kind Sir," "The Honeys," "The Riot Act," "A Lovely Light" (solo show).

STONE, BARTON. Born Dec. 6, 1920 in Nashville, Tenn. Attended Peabody, U. Fla. Made Bdwy bow in 1944 in "For Keeps," followed by "Show Boat" (LC), "The Trial of Lee Harvey Oswald."

STRAIGHT, BEATRICE. Born Aug. 2, 1916 in Old Westbury, N.Y. Attended Dartington Hall, Eng. Made Bdwy debut in 1934 in "Bitter Oleander," followed by "Twelfth Night," "Land of Fame," "Wanhope Building," "Eastward In Eden," "Macbeth," "The Heiress," "The Innocents," "The Grand Tour," "The Crucible," "Sing Me No Lullaby" (OB), "The River Line" (OB), "Everything In The Garden."

STRICKLER, JERRY. Born Dec. 4, 1939 in Goose Creek, Tex. Attended Southwestern U., Am. Theatre Wing. Made Bdwy bow in 1962 in "Mr. President," followed by "Venus Is," "Love and Kisses," "Rate Of Exchange" (OB).

STRITCH, ELAINE. Born Feb. 2, 1925 in Detroit. Graduate of Sacred Heart Convent. Made Bdwy debut in 1946 in "Loco," followed by "Made In Heaven," "Angel In The Wings," "Call Me Madam," "Pal Joey," "On Your Toes," "Bus Stop," "The Sin of Pat Muldoon," "Goldilocks," "Sail Away," "Who's Afraid Of Virginia Woolf?," "Wonderful Town" (CC 1967), "Private Lives" (OB).

SULLIVAN, DEIRDRE. Born Dec. 7, 1925 in Newark, N.J. Graduate of Hunter College. Made debut Off-Bdwy in 1967 in "Beyond Desire."

SULLIVAN, JOSEPH. Born Nov. 29, 1918 in NYC. Attended Fordham, Am. Theatre Wing. Appeared in "Sundown Beach," "Command Decision," "The Live Wire," "The Country Girl," "Oh, Men! Oh, Women!," "The Rainmaker," "The Best Man," "Fiddler On The Roof."

SULLIVAN, LIAM. Born May, 18, 1923 in Jacksonville, Ill. Attended Harvard. Made Bdwy bow in 1951 in "The Constant Wife," followed by "The Little Foxes" (1967).

SWEET, DOLPH. Born July 18, 1920 in NYC. Graduate of Columbia. Made Bdwy bow in 1961 in "Rhinoceros," followed by "Romulus," "The Advocate," "The Sign In Sidney Brustein's Window," Off-Bdwy in "The Dragon," "Too Much Johnson," and "Sgt. Musgrave's Dance," "The Great Indoors," "The Natural Look," "Ceremony of Innocence."

SYMINGTON, DONALD. Born Aug. 30, 1925 in Baltimore. Made NY bow in 1947 in "Galileo," followed by "Caesar and Cleopatra," "Dream Girl" and "Lute Song" revivals at City Center, "A Girl Can Tell," Off-Bdwy in "Suddenly Last Summer," "Lady Windermere's Fan," and "Rate Of Exchange."

SYMONDS, ROBERT. Born Dec. 1, 1926 in Bristow, Okla. Attended Tex. U., U. Mo. Made NY bow with Lincoln Center Rep. Co. in "Danton's Death," "The Country Wife," "The Alchemist," "Galileo," "St. Joan," "Tiger At The Gates," and "Cyrano de Bergerac."

TARLOW, FLORENCE. Born Jan. 19, 1929 in Philadelphia. Graduate of Hunter College. Attended Piscator's Workshop. Appeared Off-Bdwy in "Beautiful Day," "Istanboul," "Gorilla Queen," "America Hurrah," and "Red Cross."

TASK, MAGGIE. Born July 4 in Marion, O. Attended Wright Jr. College. Made Bdwy debut in 1960 in "Greenwillow," followed by "Family Affair," "Tovarich," City Center revivals of "Most Happy Fella" and "Carousel," "Funny Girl," "Kelly," "Anya," "A Time For Singing," "Darling Of The Day," "The Education of Hyman Kaplan."

TATE, DENNIS. Born Aug. 31, 1938 in Iowa City, Iowa. Attended Iowa U. Appeared Off-Bdwy in "Black Monday," "The Blacks," "The Hostage," "Bohikee Creek," "The Happy Bar," "Trials of Brother Jero," "The Strong Breed," "Goa," "The Electronic Nigger."

TAUBIN, AMY. Born Sept. 10, 1939 in NYC. Graduate of Sarah Lawrence College. Appeared Off-Bdwy in "Apollo Of Bellac," "Double Talk," "Measure For Measure" and "Rimers of Eldritch" before Bdwy debut in 1968 in "The Prime Of Miss Jean Brodie."

TAYLOR, HOLLAND. Born Jan. 14, 1943 in Philadelphia. Graduate of Bennington College. Made Bdwy debut in 1965 in "The Devils," followed by "The Poker Session" (OB).

TEITEL, CAROL. Born Aug. 1, 1929 in NYC. Attended Am. Theatre Wing. Appeared on Bdwy in "The Country Wife," "The Entertainer," "Hamlet" (1964), "Marat/DeSade," and Off-Bdwy in "The Way of The World," "The Plough and The Stars," "The Anatomist," "A Country Scandal," "Under Milkwood," and "The Bench."

| Jennifer Tilston | John A. Topa | Mimi Turque | Dan Tyra | Cicely Tyso |

TENNEY, CARYL. Born July 11 in Thatcher, Ariz. Made Bdwy debut Apr. 23, 1968 in "I'm Solomon."

THACKER, RUSTY. Born June 23, 1946 in Washington, D.C. Attended Montgomery, and East Caroline Colleges. Made NY debut in 1967 City Center revival of "Life With Father," followed by Off-Bdwy's "Your Own Thing" for which he received a THEATRE WORLD Award.

THOMAS, EVAN. Born Feb. 17, 1891, in Vancouver, Can. Attended RADA. Among his NY appearances are "Golden Wings," "Rebecca," "Lady Windermere's Fan," "Brigadoon," "All In Love" (OB).

THOMAS, RICHARD. Born June 13, 1951 in NYC. Made Bdwy bow in 1958 in "Sunrise At Campobello," followed by "Member of The Wedding," "Strange Interlude" (1963), "The Playroom," "Richard III" (CP), "Everything In The Garden."

THOMPSON, SADA. Born Sept. 27 in Des Moines, Iowa. Graduate of Carnegie Tech. Made NY debut Off-Bdwy in "Under Milk Wood," followed by "The Clandestine Marriage," "Murder In The Cathedral," "The White Devil," "The Carefree Tree," "The Misanthrope," "U.S.A.," "The River Line," "Ivanov," "The Last Minstrel," with Am. Shakespeare Festival, and on Bdwy in "Festival," "Juno," "Johnny No Trump."

THOMPSON, TAZEWELL. Born May 27, 1948 in NYC. Attended School of The Actors Co. Made debut Off-Bdwy in 1968 in "Goa."

TILLINGER, JOHN. Born June 28, 1938 in Tabriz, Iran. Attended U. Rome. Appeared with Bristol Old Vic before Bdwy debut in 1966 in "How's The World Treating You?," followed by "Halfway Up The Tree!"

TILSTON, JENNIFER. Born Mar. 29, 1947 in Tilston, Eng. Attended Tulane U., AADA. Made Bdwy debut in 1967 in "Black Comedy."

TONE, FRANCHOT. Born Feb. 27, 1906 in Niagara Falls, N.Y. Attended Cornell U. Made Bdwy bow in 1928 in "The Age of Innocence," followed by "Cross Roads," "Red Dust," "Hotel Universe," "Green Grow The Lilacs," "Pagan Lady," "Night Over Taos," "The Gentle People," "Success Story," "The Fifth Column," "Hope For The Best," "Oh, Men! Oh, Women!," "Moon For The Misbegotten," "Mandingo," "Strange Interlude" (1963), "Bicycle Ride To Nevada," Off-Bdwy in "Uncle Vanya," "The Dirty Old Man," and "Beyond Desire."

TOPA, JOHN A. Born Nov. 25, 1909 in Atlantic City. Graduate of Pacific U. Made Bdwy bow in 1955 in "No Time For Sergeants," followed by "Mandingo," and Off-Bdwy in "House of Satan," "Vincent," "Come Share My House," "Walk-Up," "Anything Goes," "The Little Private World of Arthur Morton Fenwick."

TORMEY, JOHN. Born Aug. 4, 1937 in Willimantic, Conn. Graduate of Boston U. Made Bdwy bow in 1960 in "Beg, Borrow or Steal," followed by "Bajour," "Marat/DeSade," "Mike Downstairs."

TOWBIN, BERYL. Born June 14, 1938 in NYC. Made Bdwy debut in 1951 in "The King and I," followed by "Hazel Flagg," "The Girl In Pink Tights," "Ziegfeld Follies," "Plain and Fancy," "A To Z," "Bells Are Ringing," "A Family Affair," "Hallelujah, Baby," "The Education of Hyman Kaplan."

TOWERS, CONSTANCE. Born May 20, 1933 in Whitefish, Mont. Attended Juilliard, AADA. Made Bdwy debut in 1965 in "Anya," followed by "Show Boat" (LC), and City Center revivals of "Carousel," "Sound of Music," and "The King and I."

TROOBNICK, GENE. Born Aug. 23, 1926 in Boston. Attended Ithaca Cillege, Columbia, U. Chicago. Made Bdwy bow in 1960 in "Second City," followed by "The Odd Couple," "Dynamite Tonight" (OB), "Before You Go."

TRUEMAN, PAULA. Born Apr. 25, 1907 in NYC. Graduate of Hunter, Neighborhood Playhouse. Made Bdwy debut in 1922 in "Thunderbird," followed by "Grand Street Follies," "Sweet and Low," "Grand Hotel," "You Can't Take It With You," "George Washington Slept Here," "Kiss and Tell," "Violet," "For Love Or Money," "Gentlemen Prefer Blondes," "Solid Gold Cadillac," "Mrs. McThing," "Wake Up, Darling," "A Family Affair," "Wonderful Town" (CC1963), "Sherry," Off-Bdwy in "The Sunday Man," "Wilder's Triple Bill" and "Postcards."

TUCCI, MARIA. Born June 19, 1941 in Florence, Italy. Attended Actors Studio. Appeared Off-Bdwy in "Corruption In The Palace of Justice," "Five Evenings," "The Trojan Women" and "The White Devil," in NY and Am. Shakespeare Festival productions, with LC.Rep. Co. in "Yerma," on Bdwy in "The Milk Train Doesn't Stop Here Anymore," "The Rose Tattoo" (1966), "The Little Foxes" (1967).

TUMARIN, BORIS. Born Apr. 4, 1910 in Riga, Latvia. Attended Acad. of Arts, Riga, Berlin Acad. of Arts, Actors Workshop. Appeared in "The Emperor's New Clothes," "The Family," "The Victors," "The Prescott Proposals," "Anastasia," "The Innkeepers," "The Three Sisters," "The Devil's Advocate," "Garden of Sweets," "Venus At Large," "Merchant of Venice," "Whisper Into My Good Ear," "The Firebugs," "Traveller Without Luggage," "The Giants' Dance," "Caucasian Chalk Circle," "The Tenth Man" (CC1967).

TURNER, DOUGLAS. Born May 5, 1930 in Burnside, La. Attended U. Mich. Made Bdwy bow in 1959 in "A Raisin In The Sun," followed by "One Flew Over The Cuckoo's Nest," and Off-Bdwy in "The Iceman Cometh," "The Blacks," "Pullman Car Hiawatha," "Bloodknot," "Happy Ending," "Day Of Absence," "Kongi's Harvest" with NEC which he co-founded.

TURQUE, MIMI. Born Sept. 30, 1939 in Brooklyn. Graduate of Bklyn College. Made Bdwy bow in 1945 in "Carousel," followed by "Seeds In The Wind," "The Enchanted," Off-Bdwy in "Johnny Summit," "The Dybbuk," "Romeo and Juliet," and "The Happy Journey," "Cry of The Peacock," "Anniversary Waltz," "Carnival," "Man of La Mancha."

TUTIN, DOROTHY. Born Apr. 8, 1931 in London. Attended RADA. Made Bdwy debut in 1963 in "The Hollow Crown," followed by "Portrait of A Queen" (1968).

TYRA, DAN. Born Oct. 17, 1936, in Campton, Ky. Attended U. Dayton, U. Ky. Made NY bow Off-Bdwy in 1967 in "Hogan's Goat," followed by "Where People Gather."

TYSON, CICELY. Born in NYC. Appeared Off-Bdwy in "Dark of The Moon," "The Blacks," "Moon On A Rainbow Shawl," and "Blue Boy In Black," on Bdwy in "Trumpets Of The Lord," "A Hand Is On The Gate," "Carry Me Back To Morningside Heights."

| ?anne Murray Vanderbilt | Glory Van Scott | Heidi Vaughn | Virginia Vestoff | David Vilner |

UGGAMS, LESLIE. Born in NYC May 25, 1943. After tv and nightclubs, made Bdwy debut Apr. 26, 1967 in "Hallelujah, Baby" for which she received a THEATRE WORLD Award.

VACCARO, BRENDA. Born Nov. 18, 1939 in Brooklyn. Attended Neighborhood Playhouse. Made Bdwy debut in 1961 in "Everybody Loves Opal" for which she received a THEATRE WORLD Award, followed by "The Affair," "Children From Their Games," "The Cactus Flower," "The Natural Look," "How Now, Dow Jones."

VALE, MICHAEL. Born June 28, 1922 in Brooklyn. Attended New School. Made Bdwy debut in 1961 in "The Egg," followed by "Cafe Crown," "The Last Analysis," "The Impossible Years."

VALENTI, MICHAEL. Born Nov. 21, 1943 in NYC. Attended Juilliard. Made Bdwy bow in "How To Succeed," and appeared Off-Bdwy in "Leave It To Jane," and "Your Own Thing."

VANDERBILT, JEANNE MURRAY. Born in Brooklyn. Attended Cleveland Playhouse. Made stage debut in 1967 City Center revival of "Brigadoon."

VANDIS, TITOS. Born Nov. 7, 1917 in Athens, Greece. Attended Natl. Theatre Dramatic School. Made Bdwy debut in 1965 in "On A Clear Day You Can See Forever," followed by "Illya, Darling," "The Guide."

VAN SCOTT, GLORY. Attended Goddard College, and Ballet Arts School. Appeared in City Center revivals of "Carmen Jones," "Porgy and Bess," and "Show Boat," on Bdwy in "House of Flowers," "Kwamina," with Am. Ballet Theatre (1965-66), Off-Bdwy in "Fly Blackbird," "Prodigal Son," and "Who's Who, Baby?"

VAUGHN, HEIDI. Born Oct. 12 in Berkley, Calif. Attended Scripps College, Cal. Coll. of Arts and Crafts, Honolulu Academy of Arts. Made NY debut Off-Bdwy in 1964 in "Once In A Lifetime," and Bdwy bow in 1967 in "What Did We Do Wrong?"

VELIE, JAY. Born May 16, 1892 in Denver, Colo. Attended Fealy Drama School. Made Bdwy bow in 1923 in "Little Jessie James," followed by "The Fabulous Invalid," "Carousel," "Call Me Madam," "Happy Hunting," "A Sound of Music," "Jennie," "Beyond Desire" (OB).

VESTOFF, VIRGINIA. Born Dec. 9, 1940 in NYC. Appeared Off-Bdwy in "The Boy Friend," "The Crystal Heart" and "Fall Out," before Bdwy debut in 1960 in "From A To Z," followed by "Irma La Duce," "Baker Street," and Off-Bdwy in "New Cole Porter Revue," "Man With A Load Of Mischief," and "Love and Let Love."

VILLELLA, EDWARD. Born Oct. 1, 1936 in Bayside, N.Y. Graduate of NYU. Joined NYC Ballet in 1956. Appeared in City Center revivals of "Brigadoon."

VILNER, DAVID. Born June 4, 1941 in San Francisco. Graduate of U. Calif. Member of Actors Workshop. Made NY debut in 1968 with LC Rep. Co. in "Cyrano de Bergerac."

VON FURSTENBERG, BETSY. Born Aug. 16, 1931 in Westphalia, Ger. Made Bdwy debut in 1951 in "Second Threshold," followed by "Dear Barbarians," "Oh, Men! Oh, Women!," "The Chalk Garden," "Child of Fortune," "Nature's Way," "Wonderful Town" (CC), Off-Bdwy in "The Making of Moc," "Season of Choice," "Measure For Measure," "Beyond Desire," and "Private Lives," "Mary, Mary," "The Paisley Convertible," "Avanti!"

VON SCHERLER, SASHA. Born Dec. 12 in NYC. Made Bdwy debut in 1959 in "Look After Lulu," followed by "Rape of The Belt," "The Good Soup," "The Great God Brown," "First Love," "Alfie," Off-Bdwy in "The Admirable Bashville," "The Comedian," "Conversation Piece," "Good King Charles Golden Days," "Under Milk Wood," "Plays For Bleecker Street," "Ludlow Fair," "Harold," "Sondra," "Cyrano de Bergerac" (LCRep.)

VOSKOVEC, GEORGE. Born June 19, 1905 in Sazava, Czech. Graduate of Dijon U. Made NY bow in 1945 in "The Tempest," followed by "The Love of Four Colonels," "His and Hers," "The Seagull," "Festival," "Uncle Vanya" (OB), "A Call On Kuprin," "The Tenth Man," "Big Fish, Little Fish," "Do You Know The Milky Way?," "Hamlet," "Brecht on Brecht" (OB), "The Physicists," "The World of Ray Bradbury" (OB), LCRep.'s "The Alchemist," "East Wind," and "Galileo," "Oh, Say Can You See L.A." (OB).

WALKEN, CHRISTOPHER. Born Mar. 31, 1943 in Astoria, N.Y. Attended Hofstra U. Made Bdwy debut in 1958 in "J.B.," followed by "Best Foot Forward" (OB), "High Spirits," "Baker Street," "The Lion In Winter," "Measure For Measure" (CP), "The Rose Tattoo" (1966) for which he received a THEATRE WORLD Award, "The Unknown Soldier and His Wife," "Iphigenia In Aulis" (OB).

WALKER, DIANA. Born June 28, 1942 in NYC. Appeared Off-Bdwy in "The Fourth Pig," and "The Cat and The Canary," before Bdwy debut in 1966 in "Mame."

WALKER, NANCY. Born May 10, 1921 in Philadelphia. Appeared in "Best Foot Forward," "On The Town," "Barefoot Boy With Cheek," "Look, Ma, I'm Dancin'," "Along Fifth Avenue," "Phoenix '55," "Fallen Angels," "Copper and Brass," "Wonderful Town" (CC), "The Boys Against The Girls," "Do Re Mi," "The Cherry Orchard" (APA).

WALKER, SIDNEY. Born May 4, 1921 in Philadelphia. Attended Conservatoire Nationale de Musique, Paris. Made Bdwy bow in 1960 in "Becket," appeared Off-Bdwy in "Volpone," "Julius Caesar," "King Lear," "The Collection," and repertory with APA since 1963 in "You Can't Take It With You," "War and Peace," "Right You Are," "School for Scandal," "We Comrades Three," "The Wild Duck," "Pantagleize," and "The Cherry Orchard."

WALKER, ZENA. Born March 7 in Birmingham, Eng. Attended RADA. Made Bdwy debut Feb. 1, 1968 in "A Day In The Death Of Joe Egg."

WALLACE, ART. Born Sept. 21, 1935 in Oklahoma City. Attended Ill. Wesleyan, and Wash. U. Made bdwy bow in 1962 in "Nowhere To Go But Up," followed by "A Joyful Noise," and Off-Bdwy in "Hotel Passionato," "Music Man" (CC), and "Now Is The Time For All Good Men."

Vernon Washington

Willard Waterman

Mary K. Wells

Joan White

James Whittl

WALLACH, ELI. Born Dec. 7, 1915 in Brooklyn. Graduate of U. Tex., CCNY. Attended Neighborhood Playhouse, Actors Studio. Made Bdwy bow in 1945 in "Skydrift," followed by "Henry VIII," "Androcles and The Lion," "Alice In Wonderland," "Yellow Jack," "What Every Woman Knows," "Antony and Cleopatra," "Mister Roberts," "The Lady From The Sea," "The Rose Tattoo" for which he received a THEATRE WORLD Award, "Mlle. Colombe," "The Teahouse of The August Moon," "Major Barbara," "The Chairs" (OB), "The Cold Wind and The Warm," "Rhinoceros," "The Tiger" and "The Typists" (OB), "Luv," "The Staircase."

WARING, RICHARD. Born May 27, 1912 in Buckinghamshire, Eng. Appeared with Civic Rep. Co., and in "Romeo and Juliet," "Camille," "Cradle Song," "Boy Meets Girl," "The Corn Is Green," "Henry VIII," "Androcles and The Lion," "What Every Woman Knows," "Alice In Wonderland," "Gramercy Ghost," "Measure For Measure," "Edwin Booth," Am. Shakespeare Festival, "The Cherry Orchard" (OB), "Portrait Of A Queen."

WARREN, JOSEPH. Born June 5, 1916 in Boston. Graduate of Denver U., Powers School of Drama. Made Bdwy bow in 1951 in "Barefoot In Athens," followed by "One Bright Day," "The Love of Four Colonels," "Hidden River," "The Advocate," "Brecht On Brecht" (OB), "Philadelphia, Here I Come," "Jonah" (OB).

WARRINER, FREDERIC. Born June 2, 1916 in Pasadena, Calif. Attended Pasadena City College and Playhouse. Appeared in "King Lear," "Taming of The Shrew," "Getting Married," "St. Joan," "The Clandestine Marriage," "The Doctor's Dilemma," "Wayward Saint," "The Carefree Tree" (OB), "Major Barbara," "Time Remember'd," Am. Shakespeare Festival, "The White Devil," (OB), "Royal Hunt of The Sun," "Hamlet" (OB), "Portrait of A Queen."

WASHINGTON, VERNON. Born Aug. 10, 1927, in Hartford, Conn. Attended Wholter School of Drama. Appeared Off-Bdwy in 1964 "Cabin In The Sky," followed by "The Strong Breed," and "The Trials of Brother Jero."

WATERMAN, WILLARD. Born Aug. 29, 1914 in Madison, Wisc. Attended U. Wisc. Made Bdwy debut in 1966 in "Mame."

WATERSTON, SAM. Born Nov. 15, 1940 in Cambridge, Mass. Graduate of Yale. Made Bdwy bow in 1963 in "Oh, Dad, Poor Dad . . .," followed by "First One Asleep Whistle," "Halfway Up The Tree," Off-Bdwy in "As You Like It," "Thistle In My Bed," "The Knack," "Fitz and Biscuit," "La Turista," "Posterity For Sale," "Ergo," "Muzeeka," and "Red Cross."

WATSON, DOUGLAS. Born Feb. 24, 1921 in Jackson, Ga. Graduate of UNC. Made Bdwy bow in 1947 in "The Iceman Cometh," followed by "Antony and Cleopatra" for which he received a THEATRE WORLD Award, "Leading Lady," "Richard III," "The Happiest Years," "That Lady," "Wisteria Trees," "Romeo and Juliet," "Desire Under The Elms," "Sunday Breakfast," "Cyrano de Bergerac," "The Confidential Clerk," "Portrait of A Lady," "The Miser," "The Young and Beautiful," "Little Glass Clock," "The Country Wife," "A Man For All Seasons," "The Chinese Prime Minister," Am. Shakespeare Festival productions, "Marat/DeSade," "The Prime of Miss Jean Brodie," "The Pirates of Penzance" (CC1968).

WAYNE, DAVID. Born Jan. 31, 1916 in Traverse City, Mich. Attended Western Mich. U. Made Bdwy bow in 1938 in "Escape This Night," followed by "Dance Night," "The American Way," "Scene of The Crime," "The Merry Widow," "Peepshow," "Park Avenue," "Finian's Rainbow" for which he received a THEATRE WORLD Award, "Mister Roberts," "Teahouse of The August Moon," "The Ponder Heart," "The Loud Red Patrick," "Say, Darling," "Send Me No Flowers," "Venus At Large," "Too True To Be Good," with LCRep. Co. in "Marco Millions," "But For Whom Charlie," and "Incident At Vichy," "The Yearling," "Show Boat" (LC), "The Happy Time."

WEBB, ALAN. Born July 2, 1906 in York, Eng. Attended Royal Navy College. Made Bdwy debut in 1936 in "Tonight At 8:30," followed by "George and Margaret," "The Winslow Boy," "Nina," "The Deep Blue Sea," "The Genius and The Goddess," "The Night of The Iguana," "The Chinese Prime Minister," "UTBU," "We Have Always Lived In The Castle," "I Never Sang For My Father."

WELCH, CHARLES. Born Feb. 2, 1921 in New Britain, Conn. Attended Randall School of Fine Arts, Am. Theatre Wing. Made Bdwy debut in 1958 in "Cloud 7," followed by "Make A Million," "Donnybrook," "Golden Boy," "Breakfast At Tiffany's," "Married Alive," "Darling of The Day."

WELLS, MARY K. Born in Omaha, Neb. Attended BH Studio. Made Bdwy debut in 1958 in "Interlock," followed by many tv serials, "Any Wednesday," "Everything In The Garden."

WEST, JENNIFER. Born Sept. 22, 1939 in Ft. Smith, Ark. Attended CCLA. Made NY debut Off-Bdwy in "Dutchman" for which she received a THEATRE WORLD Award, followed by "After The Fall" (LCRep), "Diamond Orchid," "Malcolm," "Harold" and "Sondra" (OB), "Hemingway Hero," "Tiger At The Gates" (LCRep).

WEYAND, RONALD. Born Feb. 28, 1929 in Quincy, Mass. Attended Boston College. Appeared in "Inherit The Wind," "Threepenny Opera" (OB), "The Cave Dwellers," "Becket," Off-Bdwy in "A Country Scandal," "The Lesson," "The Firebugs," "The Dumbwaiter," with LCRep. in "Danton's Death," "Caucasian Chalk Circle," "The Alchemist," "East Wind," "Galileo," "St. Joan," "Tiger At The Gates," and "Cyrano de Bergerac."

WHEEL, PATRICIA. Born in NYC. Appeared in "Cyrano de Bergerac," "The Tempest," "Arms and The Man," "Little Brown Jug," "The Stars Weep," "The Browning Version," "Cry of The Peacock," "Gertie," "The Sacred Flame," "Soldiers."

WHITE, JOAN. Born Dec. 3 in Alexandria, Egypt. Attended RADA. Made Bdwy debut in 1962 in "A Passage To India," followed by "Stephen D." (OB).

WHITE, RUTH. Born in Perth Amboy, N.J. Graduate of Douglass College. Made Bdwy debut in 1956 in "The Ponder Heart," followed by "The Happiest Millionaire," "Rashomon," "The Warm Peninsula," "Whisper To Me" (OB), "Big Fish, Little Fish," "Happy Days" (OB), "Lord Pengo," "Absence of A Cello," "Malcolm," "Little Murders," "The Birthday Party."

Dee Williams   Clarence Williams III   Susan Willis   Andre Womble   Victoria Zussin

WHITTLE, JAMES. Born Oct. 25, 1939 in Bisbee, Ariz. Attended Pasadena Jr. College, and Pasadena Playhouse. Made NY bow in 1964 Off-Bdwy in "The Long Voyage Home," and appeared since 1967 with APA in "War and Peace," "The Wild Duck," "You Can't Take It With You," and "Pantagleize."

WICKWIRE, NANCY. Born Nov. 29, 1925 in Harrisburg, Pa. Attended Carnegie Tech, and Old Vic, London. Appeared in "Jane," "Dial 'M' For Murder," "St. Joan," "The Grand Prize," Off-Bdwy in "The Way of The World," "The Cherry Orchard," "Measure For Measure," "Girl of The Golden West," "As You Like It," "A Clearing In The Woods," and "Rosmersholm," "Seidman & Son," "The Golden Age," "Abraham Cochrane," "Traveller Without Luggage," "Here's Where I Belong."

WILKERSON, ARNOLD. Born Apr. 6, 1943 in San Francisco. Attended RADA. Made NY bow in 1967 Off-Bdwy in "Hair."

WILLIAMS, BILLY DEE. Born Apr. 6, 1938 in NYC. Attended Natl. Academy Fine Arts. Has appeared in "The Firebrand of Florence," "The Cool World," "A Taste of Honey," "Blue Boy In Black" (OB), "Hallelujah, Baby!"

WILLIAMS, C. LEONARD. Born Mar. 4, 1943 in Philadelphia. Attended Hedgerow Drama School. Made NY bow in 1967 with Shakespeare Festival in "Volpone," followed by "Ergo" (OB).

WILLIAMS, CLARENCE III. Born Aug. 21, 1939 in NYC. Made Bdwy bow in 1960 in "The Long Dream," followed Off-Bdwy in "The Egg and I," "Walk In Darkness," "Double Talk," "Sarah and The Sax." and "Party On Greenwich Avenue," "Slow Dance On The Killing Ground" for which he received a THEATRE WORLD Award, "The Great Indoors," "King John" (CP).

WILLIS, SUSAN. Born in Tiffin, O. Attended Carnegie Tech, Cleveland Playhouse. Appeared in 1953 Off-Bdwy in "Little Clay Cart," before Bdwy debut in 1960 in "Take Me Along," followed by "Gypsy," "Dylan," "Come Live With Me," "Love and Let Love" (OB).

WILSON, ELEANOR. Born in Chester, Pa. Attended Hollins College, Pasadena and Cleveland Playhouses. Made Bdwy debut in 1956 in "The Eagle Has Two Heads," followed by "The Silver Whistle," "The Wayward Saint," "Weekend."

WILSON, LISLE. Born Sept. 2, 1943 in Brooklyn. Attended Am. Theatre Wing, AADA. Appeared with NY Shakespeare Festival in "Coriolanus," "Troilus and Cressida," and "Volpone," Off-Bdwy in "Blues For Mr. Charlie," "The Niggerlovers," "Hamlet."

WILSON, URAL. Born Dec. 25, 1930 in Tampa, Fla. Appeared as lead dancer-singer for many seasons on Bdwy with Katherine Dunham, including "Caribbean Rhapsody" and "Bambouche," Off-Bdwy in "Ballad For Bimshire," and "Who's Who, Baby."

WINDUST, PENELOPE. Born in NYC. Attended Carnegie Tech. Made Bdwy debut Dec. 14, 1967 in "Spofford."

WINSTON, HATTIE. Born Mar. 3, 1945 in Greenville, Miss. Attended Howard U. Appeared Off-Bdwy in "Prodigal Son," "Day of Absence," "Pins and Needles," "Weary Blues," and with Negro Ensemble Co.

WINTER, EDWARD. Born June 3, 1937 in Roseburg, Ore. Attended U. Ore. Appeared with LCRep. Co. in "The Country Wife," "The Condemned of Altona," and "The Caucasian Chalk Circle," on Bdwy in "Cabaret," "The Birthday Party."

WOMBLE, ANDRE. Born Feb. 11, 1940 in Brooklyn. Attended NYU, HB Studio. Appeared in "Miss Julie" (OB), "Slow Dance On The Killing Ground," "The Zulu and The Zayda," "The Little Foxes" (1967).

WOOD, PEGGY. Born Feb. 9, 1894 in Brooklyn. Made Bdwy deyut in 1910 in "Naughty Marietta," followed by "Lady Of The Slipper," "Love O' Mike," "Maytime," "Candida," "Trelawney of The Wells," "Merchant of Venice," "Bitter Sweet," "Old Acquaintance," "Blithe Spirit," "The Happiest Years," "Getting Married," "Charley's Aunt" (CC1954), "Girls In 509," Off-Bdwy in "Transposed Heads," "Opening Night," "Pictures In The Hallway" and "A Madrigal For Shakespeare."

WOODS, RICHARD. Born May 9, 1930 in Buffalo, N.Y. Graduate of Ithaca College. Appeared in "Beg, Borrow and Steal," "Capt. Brassbound's Conversion," "Sail Away," Off-Bdwy in "The Crucible," "Summer and Smoke," "American Gothic," "Four-In-One," "My Heart's In The Highlands," "Eastward In Eden," "The Long Gallery," "The Little Hut, with Am. Shakespeare Festival, and with APA since 1962 in "You Can't Take It With You," "War and Peace," "School For Scandal," "Right You Are," "The Wild Duck," "Pantagleize," "Exit The King," and "The Cherry Orchard."

WRIGHT, TERESA. Born Oct. 27, 1918 in NYC. Made Bdwy debut in 1938 in "Our Town," followed by "Life With Father," "The Dark At The Top of The Stairs," "Mary, Mary," I Never Sang For My Father."

YOUNG, GIG. Born Nov. 4, 1917 in St. Cloud, Minn. Attended Pasadena Playhouse. Made Bdwy bow in 1953 in "Oh, Men! Oh, Women!," followed by "Teahouse of The August Moon" (1956CC), "Under The Yum-Yum Tree," "There's A Girl In My Soup."

YOUNG, JANIS. Born March 28 in Grand Rapids, Mich. Attended Carnegie Tech, London Academy of Music and Dramatic Art. Appeared Off-Bdwy in "Don Carlos," "Plays For Bleecker Street," and "Where People Gather."

YOUNG, RONALD. Born June 11, 1941 in Tulsa, Okla. Graduate of Tulsa U. Made Bdwy bow in "Hello, Dolly!," followed by "Mame," "George M!"

ZANG, EDWARD. Born Aug. 19, 1934 in NYC. Graduate of Boston U. Made Off-Bdwy bow in 1963 in "The Good Soldier Schweik," followed by "St. Joan" (LCRep).

ZIMMERMANN, ED. Born Mar. 30, 1935 in NYC. Graduate of Columbia. Appeared Off-Bdwy in "20 Poems of E. E. Cummings," and "Hamlet," on Bdwy in "Luther," "The Right Honourable Gentleman," "Venus Is," "A Day In The Death of Joe Egg."

ZUSSIN, VICTORIA. Born Oct. 10, 1927 in Rock Island, Ill. Graduate of Bethany College. Made NY debut Off-Bdwy in 1965 in "The New Pinter Plays," followed by Bdwy bow in 1967 in "Something Different."

OBITUARIES

ADKINS, GILBERT, musical comedy actor and gospel singer, died May 26, 1967 on Fire Island, N.Y. Came to NY from Chicago in 1937 to appear with Ethel Waters at the Cotton Club. Subsequently appeared in several editions of the "Blackbird" revues, "Show Boat" (1947), Jones Beach shows, and in "Black Nativity." His wife survives.

ANDREWS, LOIS, 44, former showgirl and stage and screen actress, died of lung cancer in Encino, Calif. on Apr. 5, 1968. She appeared in Earl Carroll's "Vanities," George White's "Scandals," "Starlets" revue, and on tour in "Gentlemen Prefer Blondes" and "Blind Alley," and also in a number of films. She is survived by her fourth husband Col. Leonard Kleckner, a daughter by her first husband George Jessel, whom she married at 16, and three other children.

AYERS, SHIRLEY OSBORN, 50, actress, producer, and costume designer, died of viral pneumonia in a NY hospital on June 19, 1967. She appeared in the original production of "Our Town," assisted with the production of the 1957 revival of "Girl of The Golden West," and recently had been designing costumes for City Center productions. She was the widow of scene designer and producer Lemuel Ayers. A son and daughter survive.

BAINTER, FAY, 74, stage and film star, died April 16, 1968 in Beverly Hills after a long illness. She made her stage debut at 4 in "The Jewess," and Bdwy debut in 1912 in the musical "The Rose of Panama," followed by many long-running hits such as "Arms and The Girl," "The Willow Tree," "The Kiss Burglar," "East Is West," "First Love," "The Dream Girl," "The Enemy," "The Two Orphans," "Fallen Angels," "She Stoops To Conquer," "Beaux Stratagem," "The Admirable Crichton," "Lysistrata," "Jealousy," "Dodsworth," "Uncle Tom's Cabin," "The Next Half Hour," "Gayden," and her last in the 1957 touring company of "Long Day's Journey Into Night." Went to Hollywood in 1934 and appeared in 39 films, winning an Academy Award in 1939 for her portrayal in "Jezebel." Interment was in Arlington National Cemetery beside her husband of 42 years, Lt. Cmdr. Reginald Venable, who died in 1964. A son Reginald, Jr. survives.

BAIRD, CORA, 55, actress and puppeteer, died in a NY hospital Dec. 7, 1967 after a long illness. As Cora Burlar, had appeared in "Valley Forge," "Noah," "Winterset," and "Dr. Faustus" where she met and married Bil Baird in 1937. Together they formed the Bil and Cora Baird Marionettes that have appeared in "Ziegfeld Follies," "Nelly Bly," "Falhooley," "Ali Baba and The 40 Thieves," "Davy Jones' Locker," and "Man In The Moon," and many tv shows. In addition to her husband, a son and daughter survive.

BARBOUR, OLIVER, 63, actor, director, producer, and advertising man, died in a Bronx hospital Apr. 11, 1968. Appeared in such plays as "John Brown," "The Body Beautiful," and "Ethan Frome," and directed for several summer stock companies. He produced many popular radio and tv shows, and was a vice-president of Benton and Bowles. Surviving are his widow and 2 sons.

BARNES, HOWARD, 64, former drama and motion picture critic of the NY Herald Tribune, died in a NY hospital Mar. 12, 1968. After his retirement in 1951 he became a writer of television plays. His second wife and a daughter survive.

BARNES, MARGARET A., 81, playwright and 1930 Pulitzer Prize novelist, died in Cambridge, Mass., Oct. 25, 1967. She dramatized Edith Wharton's "Age of Innocence," and with Edward Sheldon wrote the plays "Jenny" that starred Jane Cowl, and "Dishonored Lady" in which Katharine Cornell appeared. "Years of Grace" won her the Pulitzer Prize. Surviving are 3 sons.

BARR, JEANNE, 35, actress, died in NYC Aug. 10, 1967. She had appeared on Bdwy in "The Waltz of The Toreadors," "Lady of The Camellias," "Handful of Fire," in several films, and as a regular in the tv series "The Nurses," and "Kitty Foyle." Her parents and sister survive.

BENNETT, JOE, 78, vaudeville headliner and eccentric dancer, died in Amityville, L.I., on Aug. 31, 1967. Born Joseph Bennett Aldert, he had appeared in minstrels, vaudeville, and on Bdwy before going to Hollywood to appear in several films. A daughter survives.

BENNETT, WILDA, 73, star of many Bdwy musicals, died Dec. 20, 1967 at her home in Winnemucca, Nev. After making her debut in 1911 in "Everyman," she appeared in "The Good Little Devil," "The Only Girl," "Riviera Girl," "The Girl Behind The Gun," "Lady In Ermine," "Apple Blossoms," "The Music Box Revue," and "Mme. Pompadour." She had lived alone since the death of her fourth husband in 1960.

BEVANS, PHILLIPA, 55, character actress, died in a NYC hospital on May 10, 1968. Her Bdwy debut was in 1930 in "The Stepdaughters of The War," followed by roles in "Ah, Wilderness," "Harriet," "Dream Girl," "Harvest of Years," "Temporary Island," "Afternoon Storm," "The Long Voyage Home," "The Relapse," "Buy Me Blue Ribbons," "Mr. Pickwick," "Starcross Story," "My Fair Lady," "Look After Lulu," and her last in this season's "What Did We Do Wrong?" She also appeared on tv and in films. She was the daughter of actress Viola Roache who died in 1961.

BICKFORD, CHARLES, 77, stage, film and tv actor, died of a blood stream infection in UCLA Medical Center, Los Angeles, on Nov. 9, 1967. First appeared in burlesque and stock before making Bdwy bow in 1919 in "Dark Rosaleen," followed by "Houses of Sand," "Outside Looking In," "Glory Hallelujah," "No More Women," "Chicago," "Bless You, Sister," "The Cyclone Lover," "Gods of The Lightning," and "Casey Jones," his last in 1938. Made his first film in 1929, and from then on became a familiar screen favorite. He was in his second year as star of tv's "The Virginian." A son and daughter survive.

BINGHAM, GEORGE, 74, stage, burlesque, and vaudeville actor and singer, died of leukemia in Los Angeles on Aug. 4, 1967. He appeared in many Oscar Hammerstein productions and in the original "Show Boat" and "George White's Scandals." He was born Gus Bing. Surviving are his widow and son.

BREIT, HARVEY, 58, playwright, novelist, poet, newspaperman, died of a heart attack in his NY home on Apr. 9, 1968. His last play, "The Guide," in collaboration with his former wife, was produced this season. He also collaborated with Budd Schulberg on "The Disenchanted." Surviving are 2 sons and 2 daughters.

BRYNER, VERA, 51, lyric soprano, died of cancer in her NY home on Dec. 13, 1967. She had appeared with the NYC Opera Co., on tv, and won acclaim as the alternate in the 1950 production of Menotti's "The Consul." Her husband, Roy Raymond, a daughter, and actor-brother Yul Brynner survive.

BUSH, FRANCES CLEVELAND, 78, musical comedy singer, died of a stroke in Sierra Madre, Calif. on Nov. 21, 1967. She had appeared in numerous musical comedies and Gilbert and Sullivan operettas. She was the widow of Lon Chaney. A son, Lon Chaney, Jr., and a daughter survive.

CADELL, JEAN, 83, actress, died in London, Sept. 24, 1967. She had appeared on the British and American stage for more than 50 years before her retirement in 1959. Made Bdwy debut in 1911 in "Bunty Pulls The Strings," followed by "At Mrs. Beam's," "Spring Meeting," and the 1947 "Importance of Being Earnest." She also appeared in films. A son survives.

CALDWELL, ORVILLE, stage and film actor, died in Los Angeles on Sept. 24, 1967. Before going to Hollywood, he had starred in such productions as "Mecca" and "The Miracle." His widow, former actress Audrey Anderson, and a son survive.

CARLO, MONTE, 83, musical comedy composer and songwriter, died in Houston, Tex., on June 9, 1967. With his wife, Alma Sanders, he wrote for numerous Bdwy shows including "Tangerine," "Elsie," "The Chiffon Girl," "Princess April," "Bye Bye Barbara," "The Voice of McConnell," "Oh! Oh! Oh! Nurse," "Houseboat On The Styx," and "Louisiana Lady." He also composed for films. A son survives.

Fay Bainter   Charles Bickford   Albert Dekker   Bert Lahr   Vivien Leigh

CHAMBERS, RALPH, 76, actor, died in NY March 16, 1968. Before his retirement several years ago, he had appeared in "Clash By Night," "Arsenic and Old Lace," "Snafu," "Something For The Boys," "Show Boat" (1946), "John Loves Mary," "Diamond Lil" (1949), "Call Me Madam," "The Pajama Game," and "The Gazebo."

CHERRY, JOHN L., 80, retired musical comedy actor, died in West Palm Beach, Fla., Jan. 11, 1968. In addition to many Gilbert and Sullivan operettas, he appeared in "The Chimes of Normandy," "Nobody Home," "So Long, Letty," "Poppy," "Glory," "Excursion," "A Connecticut Yankee," and "Violet" in 1944. A daughter survives.

COCHRANE, JUNE, 64, musical comedy actress, died in Forest Hills, N.Y., Dec. 30, 1967. Among the shows in which she sang and danced were "A Connecticut Yankee," "Queen High," and the first "Garrick Gaieties." Her husband, John Ortgies, survives.

COLEMAN, WARREN R., 67, stage, film, and radio actor and singer, died at his home on Martha's Vineyard, Mass., Jan. 13, 1968. He had appeared on Bdwy in "Porgy and Bess" (original and 1942 revival), "Anna Lucasta," "Sing out The News," "Roll, Sweet Chariot," "Swinging The Dream," "John Henry," "Scarlet Sister Mary," and on radio for several years appeared on "Amos 'n' Andy." He also wrote and directed films. His widow survives.

CRANDALL, EDWARD, 64, former actor, died in his Palm Beach home on May 9, 1968. Before retirement he had appeared in "Young Woodley," "The Play's The Thing," "Heavy Traffic," "Our Betters," "Lady of The Orchids," "Give Me Yesterday," "Absent Father," "A Party," "Small Miracle," and "Kiss Them For Me." His mother and two sisters survive.

CUMMING, RUTH, 63, retired actress and singer, died in NYC of a gastric hemorrhage on Aug. 11, 1967. She had appeared on Bdwy in many Gilbert and Sullivan operettas, and toured with Katharine Cornell. She had also appeared in films. Her husband, actor James C. Rodis, survives.

CUNNINGHAM, ZAMAH, 74, an actress for more than 50 years, died in a NYC hospital on June 2, 1967. On Bdwy she had appeared in such plays as "Hitchy-Koo," "Post Road," "Are You Decent?," "Tanyard Street," "Gentlewoman," "The Trojan Women," "On The Town," "Shadow of A Gunman," "Watch On The Rhine," "The Beggar's Opera," and "Minor Miracle." For 7 years she was a regular on the Jackie Gleason tv show. She also appeared in several films. A brother and 3 sisters survive.

DARWELL, JANE, 87, stage and film actress, died of a heart attack in the Motion Picture Country Home on Aug. 13, 1967. Her career began on stage in 1906, but she devoted most of her life to making more than 300 films. After going to Hollywood in 1914, she returned to the stage only twice: in 1944 in "Suds In Your Eye," and in 1959 in "Saratoga." She had also appeared frequently on television. There were no survivors.

DEKKER, ALBERT, 62, stage and screen actor, was found dead in his Hollywood apartment May 5, 1968. He began his career on stage in 1927 as Albert Van Dekker, subsequently dropping the Van, and appearing in "Marco Millions," "Volpone," "Conflict," "Troika," "Sisters of The Chorus," "Grand Hotel," "Napi," "Brittle Heaven," "Fly Away Home," "Johnny Johnson," "An Enemy of The People," "Death of A Salesman," "Gertie," "The Andersonville Trial," "Face of A Hero," "A Man For All Seasons," and "The Devils." He also appeared in more than 30 films. His widow, actress Esther Guernini, a son and daughter survive.

DENNY, REGINALD, 75, stage and screen actor, died June 16, 1967 of a stroke while visiting relatives in England. After appearing on London stage, made Bdwy debut in 1911 in "The Quaker Girl," and subsequently appeared in such musicals and plays as "Kitty McKay," "Twin Beds," "Rosalind," "Paganini," "Great Katherine," "The Professor's Love Story," "Friend Martha," "The Passing Show of 1919," "Richard III," "All Men Are Alike," "Blithe Spirit," "The Cocktail Party," and "My Fair Lady." He also appeared in over 200 films and on tv. His widow, actress Isobel Stiefel, a son and 2 daughters survive.

DE SILVA, FRANK, 78, stage, film, and tv actor, died March 20, 1968 in NYC. Made his stage debut in 1923 in "White Cargo," followed by such plays as "Rain," "Sadie Thompson," "The Rugged Path," and "He Who Gets Slapped." Since 1954 he had worked for the Actor's Fund.

DICKENS, C. STAFFORD, 71, actor, playwright, and film writer, died in NYC Oct. 12, 1967. He had appeared on stage in "Bulldog Drummond," "The Bat," "The Green Goddess," "Old English," "Freddy," "Hostile Witness," "Sail Away," and "The Affair." His plays include "Freddy" and "Command Performance." Surviving are his widow, a son, and 3 daughters.

DONATH. LUDWIG, 67, Austrian-born stage and screen actor, died of leukemia in NYC on Sept. 29, 1967. He fled Austria in 1940 and made his Bdwy debut in 1951 in "4 Twelves Are 48," subsequently appearing in "Abie's Irish Rose" (1954 revival), "The Dybbuk," "The Marriage of Figaro," "The Threepenny Opera," "The Seagull," "Only In America," "The Deadly Game," "A Far Country," "She Loves Me." He appeared in many films, on radio and tv. His widow survives.

DOWLING, EDWARD DURYEA, theatrical director and producer, died in a NYC hospital on Dec. 18, 1967. Among his many Bdwy productions were "Hellzapoppin'," and "An Evening With Beatrice Lillie." He was divorced from Betty Compton and Irene Vernon. His third wife survives.

DUNN, JAMES, 61, stage and film actor, died in Santa Monica, Calif., Sept. 3, 1967, after a long illness. After roles on Bdwy in "Nightstick," and "Sweet Adeline," he went to Hollywood to make films, and returned only for "Panama Hattie" (1940) and "Harvey" in 1948. He appeared in tv series "It's a Great Life." His second wife, former singer Edna Rush, survives.

ERWIN, STUART, 64, stage and screen actor, died of a heart attack in his Beverly Hills home on Dec. 21, 1967. His career began on stage in 1924 in Calif. His Bdwy debut was in 1942 in "Mr. Sycamore," followed by "Good Night, Ladies," and "Great To Be Alive." He appeared in 115 films and on tv in "The Trouble With Father" series that became "The Stu Erwin Show." His widow, actress June Collyer, a son and daughter survive.

EVANS, REYNOLDS, 72, actor, died in his home in Branford, Conn., on July 27, 1967. Began his career with Sothern and Marlowe, subsequently appearing in "Cyrano de Bergerac," "Richard III," "Henry IV," "The Doughgirls," "The Late George Apley," "Metropole," "Fancy Meeting You Again," "The Solid Gold Cadillac," "Eugenia," "Compulsion," "First Love," "Lord Pengo," and "The Deputy" in 1964.

FERBER, EDNA, 82, playwright and novelist, died in her NYC home on Apr. 16, 1968 after a long illness. Plays on which she collaborated were "Our Mrs. McChesney," "Minick," "The Royal Family," "Dinner At Eight," "Stage Door," "The Land Is Bright," and "Bravo!" Her novel "So Big" won the 1924 Pulitzer Prize. Several of her novels were made into films and "Show Boat" became a Broadway hit. A spinster, she is survived by a sister.

FLAVIN, MARTIN, 84, playwright and novelist, died of complications following a fall in Carmel, Calif. on Dec. 27, 1967. His plays include "Children of The Moon," "Lady of The Rose," "Service For Two," "The Criminal Code," "Broken Dishes," "Crossroads," "Achilles Had A Heel," "Tapestry In Grey," and "Around The Corner." He received the 1944 Pulitzer Prize for his novel "Journey In The Dark." A son and daughter survive.

FLINT, HELEN, 69, stage and screen actress, died Sept. 9, 1967 after being struck by a car in Washington, D.C. After beginning her career in the chorus of the "Ziegfeld Follies," she went on to leads in such plays as "The Nest," "Gentlemen of The Press," "The Demi-Virgin," "The Man Who Came To Dinner," "Ah, Wilderness," and her last "The Dancer" in 1946. She also appeared in 18 films. Several cousins survive.

FOX, FRANKLYN, 73, stage, radio, and tv actor, died of a heart attack in Wantagh, L.I., N.Y., on Nov. 2, 1967. Born in England, he made his NY bow in 1919 in "Lord and Lady Algy," subsequently appearing in such plays as "Declasse," "Hooray For What," "Desert Song," "Student Prince," "Maytime," "Proposals," "Gypsy Fires, "Carnival," "Riddle Me This," "Pre-Honeymoon," "Pillar To Post," "Calculated Risk," and "Pajama Game." Surviving are his widow and daughter.

FREEMAN, HOWARD, stage, screen and tv actor, died in a NYC hospital on Dec. 11, 1967 after a short illness. His career began in "Irene" in 1919, and included roles in such plays as "A Serpent's Tooth," "Battling Buttler," "All Wet," "Clouds," "The Butter and Egg Man," "Cock Robin," "Climax," "The Star Wagon," "Knickerbocker Holiday," "Liliom," "Suzannah and The Elders," "Liberty Jones," "Sunny River," "The Seven Year Itch," "No Time For Sergeants," and "Hot Spot." On tv he appeared as a regular in "The Baileys of Balboa," "Car 54," and the Jackie Gleason series. His widow and son survive.

FRIEDLANDER, WILLIAM B., 83, producer-director, died in a NYC hospital on Jan. 1, 1968. Became a producer in 1926 and was connected with such productions as "The Shelf," "Cain and Mabel," "The Winged Messenger," "Speakeasy," "Separate Rooms," and "Good Morning Corporal.". He also wrote music and lyrics for several productions including "Frivolities of 1920" and "Cry Baby." His widow survives.

HACKETT, HAL, 44, actor, died in NYC Dec. 4, 1967 after a long illness. He had appeared in "Lend An Ear," "Kismet," "The Lady's Not For Burning," "Bonanza Bound," and "To Broadway With Love" at the NY World's Fair. He had roles in several films, and for 14 years played Bob Lyle in the "Ma Perkins" radio serial. Surviving are his parents and 3 sisters.

HALL, JUANITA, 66, singer-actress, died of diabetic complications in a Bayshore, L.I., hospital on Feb. 28, 1968. She was probably best known for her portrayal of Bloody Mary in "South Pacific" on stage, for which she received a "Tony," and in film. She also appeared in "Show Boat," "The Green Pastures," "The Pirate," "Sing Out, Sweet Land," "St. Louis Woman," "Deep Are The Roots," "Street Scene," "House of Flowers," "The Ponder Heart," "Flower Drum Song," and "Mardi Gras" at Jones Beach. She organized and sang with the Juanita Hall Choir. She had been ill for several years.

HAMILTON, JOHN F., 73, stage and film actor, died July 11, 1967 in a Paramus, N.J., hospital. He had been in retirement since 1962. He began his career in 1916 in vaudeville, but later appeared in many plays, including "Lushmore," "Shore Leave," "Hell-Bent-Fer-Heaven," "The Mongrel," "The Dagger," "Rockbound," "The Silver Tassie," "The Black Tower," "Ceiling Zero," "Iron Men," "Of Mice and Men," "Clash By Night," "The Day Will Come," and "Therese." He also had roles in several films and on tv. Surviving are 3 brothers and 3 sisters.

HOLT, STELLA, 50, Off-Broadway producer, died of a heart attack in a NYC hospital on Aug. 28, 1967. In the last 15 years, she had produced 38 plays, mostly at the Greenwich Mews Theatre, including "Monday's Heroes," "Red Roses For Me," "Orpheus Descending," "Me Candido!," "Simply Heavenly," "The Long Gallery," "All In Love," "Jerico-Jim Crow," "The Ox Cart," and her last "Carricknabauna" last season. A brother and 2 sisters survive.

JOHNSON, ALBERT, 57, scenic designer, died of a vascular ailment in a NYC hospital on Dec. 21, 1967. He had designed the sets for more than 100 shows, including "The Skin of Our Teeth," "Of Thee I Sing," "George White's Scandals," "Ziegfeld Follies of 1934," "As Thousands Cheer," "Let 'Em Eat Cake," "The Band Wagon," "The Great Waltz," "Leave It To Me," "My Dear Public," "Two Blind Mice," and his last "What Did We Do Wrong" during this season. His wife survives.

KESSELRING, JOSEPH, 65, playwright, died in Kingston, N.Y., Nov. 5, 1967. He was author of "Arsenic and Old Lace" that ran for 1444 performances on Bdwy. He also wrote "Aggie Appleby, Maker of Men," "There's Wisdom In Women," "Cross-Town," "Maggie McGilligan," "Identically Yours," "Solomon's Mother," "4 Twelves Are 48," "Surgery Is Indicated," "Accidental Angel," "A Frog In His Pocket," and "Mother of That Wisdom." His widow survives.

KRIEGER, LEE, 48, stage and screen actor, died in his Van Nuys, Calif., home Dec. 22, 1967. Before moving to Calif., he appeared on Bdwy in "Mister Roberts," "Along Fifth Avenue," and "Viva Madison Avenue." In addition to films, he appeared in such tv series as "Big Valley," "Gunsmoke," "The Andy Griffith Show," and "The FBI." Surviving are his widow and 2 sons.

LAHR, BERT, 72, one of the truly great stage and film comedians, died in a NYC hospital Dec. 4, 1967 of massive internal hemorrhage after having been critically ill with pneumonia that developed while filming "The Night They Raided Minsky's." His career of more than 50 years began in vaudeville and burlesque at 15. His Bdwy debut was in "Harry Delmar's Revels" in 1927, followed by "Hold Everything," "Flying High," "Hot-Cha!," "George White's Scandals," "The Show Is On," "Du Barry Was A Lady," "The Seven Lively Arts," "Burlesque" (1946), "Two On The Aisle," "Waiting For Godot," "Hotel Paradiso," "The Girls Against The Boys," "A Midsummer Night's Dream," "The Winter's Tale," "The Beauty Part," and "Foxy." He appeared in several films but was best known for his Cowardly Lion in "The Wizard of Oz." He made many guest appearances on tv. He is survived by his second wife, former actress Mildred Schroeder, 2 sons and a daughter.

LAWRENCE, REGINALD, 67, playwright, died following a heart attack suffered while teaching a class in City College of NY on Nov. 20, 1967. He was the co-author of "Men Must Fight," "Hervey House," "If This Be Treason," "Feathers In A Gale," and "Out Of This World." He also wrote "Dream of Fair Women," "The Thread That Runs So True," "The Legend of Lizzie," and "Heaven Come Wednesday." Two sisters survive.

LEIGH, VIVIAN, 53, one of England's most beautiful and renowned stage and screen actresses, was found dead of natural causes in her London home on July 8, 1967. She had been ill for some months from a recurrence of tuberculosis. After a successful career in London, and marriage to Laurence Olivier, she made her Bdwy debut with him in "Romeo and Juliet," and subsequently in the U.S. in "Caesar and Cleopatra," "Antony and Cleopatra," "Duel of Angels," the musical version of "Tovarich" for which she received a "Tony" Award, and "Ivanov" in 1966. At her death, she was rehearsing for the London production of "A Delicate Balance" by Edward Albee. She reserved most of her time for the stage, but gave many memorable performances on film. She received "Oscars" for "Gone With The Wind" and "A Streetcar Named Desire." Surviving is a daughter by her first marriage to barrister Herbert Leigh Holman, whose middle name she used professionally, having been born Vivian Mary Hartley.

| Howard Lindsay | Paul Muni | Basil Rathbone | Florence Reed | Spencer Tracy |

LEVEY, HAROLD A., 73, composer, died of a heart attack in NYC, June 18, 1967. He composed the scores for "Lady Billy," "The Clinging Vine," "Greenwich Village Follies," "Rainbow Rose," and "Lovely Lady." He was musical director for several radio and tv shows. His widow and daughter survive.

LINDSAY, HOWARD, 78, playwright, director, producer, and actor, died of leukemia in his NY home on Feb. 11, 1968, after an illness of 2 years. His acting career began in 1909, and in 1921 made his successful directorial debut with "Dulcy." With the late Russel Crouse he collaborated on "Anything Goes," "Red, Hot and Blue," "Hooray For What!," "Life With Father" that had a record-breaking run in which he co-starred with his wife Dorothy Stickney, "Strip For Action," "State of The Union" that won the 1946 Pulitzer Prize, "Life With Mother" in which he and Mrs. Lindsay repeated their successful characterizations of Mr. and Mrs. Day, "Call Me Madam," "Remains To Be Seen," "The Prescott Proposals," "The Great Sebastians," "Happy Hunting," "Tall Story," "The Sound of Music" that won him a "Tony" Award, and "Mr. President." They co-produced, among others, "Arsenic and Old Lace" and "Detective Story." He also wrote several screenplays. Surviving is his second wife of 40 years, Miss Stickney.

LORNE, MARION, 80, character actress, died of a heart attack in her NYC home on May 9, 1968. Her career began as a serious actress, but she became better known in later years for her comedy roles in such tv series as "The Garry Moore Show," "Mr. Peepers," and "Bewitched." On stage she had appeared in "Mrs. Temple's Telegram," "The Devil," "The Florist Shop," "Don't Weaken," "Harvey," and "Dance Me A Song." After her marriage to the late actor-manager-producer Walter Hackett lived and appeared in many plays in London. There are no immediate survivors.

MacCAULAY, JOSEPH, 76, a musical and dramatic actor for 50 years, collapsed on a NYC street and died Oct. 6, 1967. His Bdwy debut was in 1919 in "The Lost Leader," followed by many Gilbert and Sullivan operettas, and "The Music Box Revue of 1924," "A Bit Of Love," "The Wild Rose," "Kiss Me," "Rapid Transit," "The Lottery Bridge," "The Show Is On," "St. Helena," "Sea Dogs," and his last performance was in "Funny Girl." He was a founder of the Episcopal Actors Guild. His wife and son were deceased. A brother survives.

MacFARLANE, BRUCE, 57, stage and screen actor, died in Hollywood, Nov. 25, 1967. He made his stage debut in "Front Page," followed by "Weekend," "The Last Mile," "Five Star Final," "Wonder Boy," "Wild Waves," "Page Miss Glory," "Sailor, Beware!," "Geraniums In My Window," "Behind Red Lights," "My Sister Eileen," "The Odds On Mrs. Oakley," and "A Bell For Adano." During his 20 years in Hollywood he appeared in many films and on tv.

MARION, GEORGE F., JR., 68, librettist and actor, died in his NYC home on Feb. 25, 1968 after a long illness. He wrote such musicals as "Too Many Girls" in which he acted, "Beat The Band," "Early To Bed," "Allah Be Praised," "Marinka," "Toplitzsky of Notre Dame," and "Arabian Nights" which was produced at Jones Beach. He also wrote for films. His widow and daughter survive.

MARSHALOV, BORIS, 65, actor, and for 30 years director of the acting school that bore his name, died of a heart ailment in a NYC hospital on Oct. 16, 1967. Born in Russia, he came to the U.S. in 1923, subsequently appearing in such plays as "This One Man," "Brief Moment," "Libel," "Flight To The West," "Innocent Voyage," "Julia, Jake and Uncle Joe." Survivors include his widow and daughter.

McCULLERS, CARSON, 50, novelist, playwright, and short story writer, died Sept. 29, 1967 in Nyack, N.Y., hospital after having suffered a stroke in her home several weeks previous. Her adaptation of "The Member of The Wedding" won the Critics Circle Award for the best play of 1950, and wrote "The Square Root of Wonderful" produced in 1957. Edward Albee adapted "The Ballad of The Sad Cafe" that was produced in 1963. Her "Reflections In A Golden Eye," and "The Heart Is A Lonely Hunter" were recently filmed. A brother and sister survive.

MERLIN, FRANK, 76, retired actor, author, director, and producer, died in a Bay Shore, L.I., N.Y., hospital on Mar. 1, 1968. Born in Ireland, he came to the U.S. in 1910 and produced, directed, and acted in plays from 1912 until 1963. He also taught at the American Theatre Wing, and was influential in the organizing of Actors Equity. There are no immediate survivors.

MORROW, DORETTA, 40, former musical comedy singer, died of cancer in London, Feb. 28, 1968. She had appeared in "The Red Mill" (1945) "The Chocolate Soldier," "Where's Charley?," "The King and I," and "Kismet." She appeared opposite Mario Lanza in the film "Because You're Mine," and in several tv specials. She retired before her marriage eight years ago to Albert Hardman of London. They had a daughter.

MOULDER, WALTER, 34, stage and tv actor, died of a heart attack in NYC June 24, 1967. He had appeared on stage in "Romeo and Juliet," "What Every Woman Knows," and "Take Her She's Mine." Surviving are his mother and sister.

MUNI, PAUL, 71, Austrian-born stage and film actor, died Aug. 25, 1967 in his Santa Barbara, Calif. home after a lengthy illness. One of the most talented and versatile actors of this century, began his career in vaudeville, and the Yiddish Art Theatre. His Bdwy appearances began with "We Americans," followed by "Four Walls," "This One Man," "Rock Me, Julie," "Counsellor-at-Law," "Key Largo," "Yesterday's Magic," "A Flag Is Born," "They Knew What They Wanted," and his last performance in "Inherit The Wind" won a Tony Award. He appeared in many films and won an Oscar for "The Story of Louis Pasteur." His widow, former actress Bella Finkel, survives.

POST, GUY BATES, 92, retired stage star whose career spanned 50 years, died in a Los Angeles Hospital Jan. 16, 1968. Made his first professional appearance in 1893 in "Charlotte Corday," followed by starring roles in such plays as "My Lady Dainty," "Hamlet," "The Bridge," "The Nigger," "Bird of Paradise," "Omar, The Tentmaker" that played 959 performances, "The Masquerader" that ran 1500 performances, "The Play's The Thing," "The Shattered Lamp," and his last "Good Morning, My Son" in Los Angeles in 1945. Surviving is his widow, actress Lily Kemble-Cooper.

PRUD'HOMME, CAMERON, 75, stage, film, radio, and tv actor, died Nov. 27, 1967 in a Pompton Plains, N.J., hospital after a long illness. His career began in San Francisco on stage and radio before moving to NY where he made his Bdwy bow in 1936 in "Tide Rising," followed by "See The Jaguar," "By The Beautiful Sea," "The Rainmaker," "New Girl In Town," "A Desert Incident," "Drink To Me Only," and his last "The Unsinkable Molly Brown." He played the title role in radio's "David Harum" for 6 years, and appeared in numerous tv dramatic shows, and in several films. His actress daughter, June Prud'homme survives.

RANDOLPH, AMANDA, 65, actress, died after a stroke in Duarte, Calif., Aug. 24, 1967. After appearing in night clubs and musical comedies, she became the meddling mother-in-law in the "Amos 'n' Andy" series on both radio and tv, and the maid on "The Danny Thomas Show." A son and daughter survive.

RASCH, ALBERTINA, 76, ballerina and choreographer, died after a long illness in the Motion Picture Country Hospital, Woodland Hills, Calif., on Oct. 2, 1967. She was premiere danseuse with several companies before beginning a noted career as choreographer for such productions as "George White's Scandals," "Show Girl," "Rio Rita," "The Three Musketeers," "The Band Wagon," "The Cat and The Fiddle," "Bally-hoo of 1932," "The Great Waltz," "Very Warm For May," "Boys and Girls Together," "Lady In The Dark," and "Marinka." After marrying film composer Dimitri Tiomkin, she moved to California and choreographed several films. Her husband survives.

RATHBONE, BASIL, 75, stage and film actor, died of a heart attack in his NYC home on July 21, 1967. Born in Johannesburg, S.A., he made his NY debut in 1912 with Benson's Shakespearean Co., followed by roles in "The Czarina," "R.U.R.," "The Swan," "The Grand Duchess and The Waiter," "The Captive," "Julius Caesar," "Romeo and Juliet," "Obsession," "The Heiress," "The Gioconda Smile," "Jane," "Sherlock Holmes," "Hide and Seek," and his last "J.B." in 1959. He appeared in over 100 films but is probably best known for the 16 he made portraying Sherlock Holmes. Surviving is his second wife, actress-writer-designer Ouida Bergere, a daughter and a son.

REED, FLORENCE, 84, veteran Broadway actress, died in the Percy Williams Home, East Islip, L.I., on Nov. 21, 1967 after a long illness. After her Bdwy debut in 1901 she appeared in "Hamlet," "If I Were King," "Don Quixote," "Girls," "Seven Days," "The Typhoon," "Master of The House," "Painted Woman," "The Girl and The Pennant," "The Yellow Ticket," "A Celebrated Case," "The Wanderer," "Chu Chin Chow," "Roads of Destiny," "The Mirage," "East of Suez," "Hail and Farewell," "The Lullaby," "Ashes," "Shanghai Gesture," "Macbeth," "Purity," "Mourning Becomes Electra," "Criminal At Large," "Thoroughbred," "Madame X," "Romeo and Juliet," "A Point of Honor," "Outward Bound," "The Flying Gerardos," "The Skin of Our Teeth," and "The Family Reunion," her last in 1958. She had appeared in movies and tv but preferred the stage. She was the widow of actor Malcolm Williams.

SEYMOUR, MAY DAVENPORT, 83, a fifth generation actress who founded and was curator of the theatre collection of the Museum of the City of NY, died in her home, Oct. 5, 1967. She appeared in "The Lady of Lyons," "The Little Princess," "The Best of Friends," "The Triumph of Love," "The Ruling Power," "Brother Jacques," "A Doll's House," "Beauty and The Barge," "The Marriage of William Ashe," "Alice Sit-By-The-Fire," and "The Evangelist." She retired in 1908 when she married William Eckert, but came out of retirement to appear with her daughter, Anne Seymour, for 9 years on radio's "Against The Storm." Surviving are her daughter and a son.

SHERWOOD, HENRY, 83, veteran Broadway actor, died in NYC of a heart ailment on June 8, 1967. Among the many plays in which he had appeared are "Arsenic and Old Lace,' "Front Page," "On The Town," "Twentieth Century," "A Tree Grows In Brooklyn," "Call Me Madam," and "Witness For The Prosecution." His widow, former opera singer Carmen Baruch, and a son survive.

SHURR, LOUIS, one of the best known theatrical agents of New York and Hollywood, died in Los Angeles on Nov. 2, 1967. He was in his eighties. Four Brothers and two sisters survive.

SMITH, HOWARD, 73, actor for more than 50 years in all fields of entertainment, died of a heart attack in a Hollywood hospital on Jan. 10, 1968. Made Bdwy bow in 1915 in "The Eternal Magdalene," and subsequently appeared in "Miss Quis," "Solitaire," "Manhattan Nocturne," "Decision," "Dear Ruth," "Mr. Peebles and Mr. Hooker," "Magic Touch," "Death Of A Salesman," "Midsummer," "The Pink Elephant," "A Red Rainbow," "Anniversary Waltz," "The Gang's All Here," "Here's Love," and his last appearance in 1967 City Center revival of "Finian's Rainbow." He played Mr. Griffen in the "Hazel" tv series. He left no survivors.

STANWYCK, JAY, 58, Off-Broadway producer, died in a NYC hospital on Sept. 15, 1967. She was associated with such productions as "Six Characters In Search Of An Author," "Here Come The Clowns," "Trumpets of The Lord," "Medea," "Serjeant Musgrave's Dance," and "Hamp." Surviving are her mother and sister.

SYDNEY, BASIL, 73, British actor, and popular Bdwy performer, died in his London home of pleurisy on Jan 10, 1968. In the U.S. he had appeared in "Fanny's First Play," "Romance," "He Who Gets Slapped," "R.U.R.," "Romeo and Juliet," "Sandro Botticelli," "The Devil's Disciple," "She Stoops To Conquer," "Peer Gynt," "Hamlet," "The Jest," "Henry IV," "The Humble," "The Crown Prince," "Taming of The Shrew," "Twelve Thousand," "Meet The Prince," "Becky Sharp," "Children of Darkness," "Jewel Robbery," "The Dark Tower," and "Wife Insurance." He also appeared in many films. His three marriages ended in divorce.

TORREY, SUSAN, 61, actress, died in NYC after a lengthy illness on April 15, 1968. She had appeared in several editions of the Ziegfeld Follies, "Rio Rita," "Little Accident," "Heigh, Ho, Everybody," and "Look Homeward, Angel." Her husband, 2 daughters, and 3 sons survive.

TRACY, SPENCER, 67, stage and Academy Award screen actor, died of a massive heart attack in his West Hollywood home on June 10, 1967. His career began with his 1922 Bdwy debut in "R.U.R.," followed by "A Royal Fandango," "Yellow," "The Baby Cyclone," "Conflict," "Nigger Rich," "Veneer," "The Last Mile," and "The Rugged Path" in 1945. He made more han 60 films, was nominated for 8 Academy Awards, and received two. Surviving are his estranged wife, former actress Louise Treadwell, a son and daughter.

VAN, GUS, 80, veteran vaudeville and musical comedy star, died in Miami Beach on March 12, 1968 of injuries sustained when he was hit by a car. With his late partner Joe Schenck, they won national fame as vaudeville, nightclub, and musical comedy headliners for over 20 years until Schenck's death in 1930. They appeared in several editions of the Ziegfeld Follies. Van continued as a single and made his last appearance at the Palace in 1954. He also served as president of AGVA. His second wife survives.

WATTS, ELIZABETH, 79, actress and singer, died in NYC July 27, 1967. Her stage career began in 1940 after concert appearances in Paris for a number of years. She had roles in many operettas and musicals, including "Anything Goes," "Firefly," "Bitter Sweet," "The Wizard of Oz," "The Italian Straw Hat," "Destry Rides Again," and "Miss Liberty." Twice divorced, three sisters survive.

WEEKS, MARION, 81, stage and film singer-actress, died in her NYC home on Apr. 20, 1968. Her career began in vaudeville. Her Bdwy credits include roles in "The Student Prince," "Blossom Time," "The Women," "Strange Bedfellows," "Gentlemen Prefer Blondes," and "Two Blind Mice." A son survives.

WHITEMAN, PAUL, 77, band-leader known as "The King of Jazz," died of a heart attack in a Doylestown, Pa., hospital on Dec. 29, 1967. He appeared in "George White's Scandals," "Ziegfeld Follies," and "Jumbo," in addition to several movies, and regularly on radio with his band. Surviving are his fourth wife, actress Margaret Livingston, a son, and 3 daughters.

WHEELER, BERT, 72, star of vaudeville, stage, and films for more than 50 years, died of emphysema in a NYC hospital on Jan. 18, 1968. After headlining in vaudeville and several editions of "Ziegfeld Follies," he appeared in "Rio Rita," "New Priorities of 1943," "Laugh Time," "Harvey," "All For Love," "Three Wishes For Jamie," and "The Gang's All Here." In 1929 he went to Hollywood to film "Rio Rita," and teamed with Robert Woolsey, and together they became a successful movie team, appearing in over 30 films. In 1966 an Off-Broadway theatre was named for him. He was married and divorced 4 times, and his only child, a daughter, preceded him in death by 2 weeks.

WOLFIT, DONALD, 65, British stage and film actor-manager, died of heart trouble in a London hospital on Feb. 17, 1968. He appeared on Bdwy in repertory in 1947 in "King Lear," "Hamlet," "Merchant Of Venice," "As You Like It," and "Volpone," and in 1965 in "All In Good Time." He was knighted in 1957. His third wife, actress Rosalind Iden, a son and daughter survive.

INDEX

261

268

Schneider, Schorling, 170
Schnitzler, Arthur, 90
Schoen, Judy, 207
Schofield, Frank, 189
Schoming, David, 140
Schon, Bonnie, 69
Schor, Myrna Barbara, 134
Schrank, Joseph, 98
Schratt, Peter, 90, 91
Schreiber, Avery, 34
Schroeder, Michael, 122, 245
Schroeder, William, 190
Schuck, John, 186
Schulman, Arnold, 43
Schultz, Gloria, 148
Schultz, Michael, 146, 148, 149, 184
Schulz, Charles M., 96, 182
Schulz, Eva, 90
Schuman, Wilfred, 88
Schwartz, Harold, 153, 154
Schwartz, Risa, 87
Schwartz, Sylvia, 28, 32, 38, 53, 69, 72, 76, 166, 180, 183, 185
Schwinn, Ron, 32
Scimonelli, Don, 187
Scooler, Zvee, 70
Scotlin, Michael, 155, 155, 158
Scott, Adam, 172
Scott, Charles, 166
Scott, Clifford, 49
Scott, George C., 4, 6, 46, 79, 214, 245
Scott, Harold, 6, 114, 245
Scott, Henry E., III, 125
Scott, Hutchinson, 20
Scott, James, 202
Scott, Kenneth, 57
Scott, Marc, 70
Scott, Pippa, 21
Scott, Steven, 20
Scott, Tom, 144
Scuba Duba, 6, 108, 213
Sea Gull, The, 196
Seader, Richard, 21, 29, 64, 181
Seagraves, Fred, 80, 81, 82
Seals, Charles, 152, 153, 154
Seamon, Helen, 189
Searle, Judith, 20
Seattle Repertory Theatre, 204
Seay, Betti, 108
Second Shepherd's Pageant, The, 198
Seff Associates Ltd., 139
Seff, Manuel, 9
Segal, David F., 145, 204
Segal, Linda, 194
Seger, Richard, 192
Seibert, Jeannette, 40
Seidelman, Arthur A., 119, 135
Seiden, Stan, 168, 172
Seig, John, 186
Seitz, John, 190
Selbert, Mariannne, 74
Selden, Albert W., 48, 71, 168
Seldes, Marian, 6, 36, 135, 245
Sell, David, 93, 171
Sell, Janie, 55, 121
Selman, Linda, 75
Semenni, David, 116
Senn, Herbert, 117, 145, 171
Serbagi, Roger Omar, 121, 197
Serchio, Tony, 139
Sergejev, Barbara, 104
Serio, Joy, 49
Serlin, Sol, 87, 97
Seroff, Muni, 60, 87, 245
Serva, David, 168
Servant Of Two Masters, 188
Servello, Joe, 206
Setrakian, Ed, 201
Settimio, Al, 103, 245
Seven Descents Of Myrtle, The, 6. 53
Sewell, Danny, 180
Seymour, May Davenport, 256
Seymour, John D., 86, 245
Shade, Ellen, 92, 93, 122, 244, 245
Shafer, Reuben, 151
Shaffer, Louise, 10
Shaffer, Peter, 178

Shakespeare, William, 100, 120, 122, 123, 150, 152, 153, 154, 155, 157, 158, 159, 160, 161, 162, 163, 164, 165, 179
Shaler, Anna, 187
Shalhoub, Susan, 207
Shalom, Belle, 73
Shangri-La Salon, 118
Shankar, Ravi, 50
Shankewitz, Sandra, 187
Shannon, Nancy, 198
Shanstrom, David, 106, 130
Shapiro, Anita, 184
Shapiro, Herman, 86, 87, 88, 89
Shapiro, Nat, 125
Sharaff, Irene, 89, 169, 185
Sharkey, Jack, 61
Sharma, Barbara, 244, 245
Sharp, Archie, 189
Sharp, Robert, 74
Sharp, Saundra, 28
Sharp, William, 205
Sharpe, John, 245
Shatner, William, 214
Shattuck, Robert, 119, 245
Shaughnessy, Kathleen, 101
Shaw, G. Tito, 114, 245
Shaw, George Bernard, 16, 80, 99
Shaw, Joseph, 60, 164, 195, 245
Shaw, Paula, 182
Shaw, Steven, 131, 152
Shaw, Sydney, 61
Shawhan, April, 6, 120, 214, 245
Shawn, Dick, 57, 245
Shawn, Jeffrey, 57
Shawn, Michael, 43
Shawn, Peter, 201
She Stoops To Conquer, 179
Shea, Joan, 166
Shea, Joe, 167
Shearer, Jack, 104
Shearer, John, 104
Sheen, Martin, 6, 120, 245
Sheffer, Isaiah, 102
Shelle, Lori, 134
Shelley, Carole, 52, 245
Shelly, Norman, 26, 57, 101
Shelton, Reid, 201
Shelton, Sloane, 39, 245
Shelton, Timothy, 161, 162
Shenar, Paul, 186
Shepard, Linda, 133
Shepard, Sam, 143
Shepard, Wendy, 154
Shephard, William, 152, 153, 154
Shepis, Nicholas, 133
Sheppard, Stephanie, 37
Shepperd, Drey, 121
Sheraton, Ted, 203
Sherin, Edwin, 187, 195
Sherman, George L., 50, 84, 154
Sherman, Hiram, 6, 32, 245
Sherr, Thelma, 43
Sherven, Judith, 172
Sherwood, Henry, 256
Shevalow, Allan, 114
Shevlin, Rosemary, 161, 162, 178
Shield, Gina, 179
Shields, James E., 22
Shimizu, Dana, 77, 89
Shimizu, Keenan, 77, 89
Shimono, Sab, 73, 173
Shinall, Vern, 93
Shire, David, 61, 78
Shlosberg, Lee, 187
Shock Of Recognition, The, 75, 175
Shoctor. Ioseph H., 23
Shorr, William, 102, 200
Shorte, Dino, 207
Show, Danny, 73
Show Management Inc., 97
Showalter, Max, 69, 245
Show-Off, The, 6, 66
Shrewsbury, Anne, 25
Shropshire, Anne, 25
Shubert, Roberta, 140
Shumlin, Diana, 60
Shumlin, Herman, 33, 60
Shumlin, Lola, 33
Shull, Richard B., 197
Shulman, Max, 32
Shuman, Mort, 125
Shumska, Bettiane, 69
Shumsky, Oscar, 163

Shurr, Louis, 256
Shwartz, Martin, 8, 13, 34, 49, 55, 77, 122
Shyer, Brian, 38
Sica, Louis, 23
Sicari, Joseph R., 122, 152, 245
Sidney, Sylvia, 179, 245
Siebert, Charles, 208
Siegel, Arthur, 61
Siegel, Doris Einstein, 91
Sierra, Gregory, 26, 140, 153
Sieveking, Alejandro, 127
Siggins, Jeff, 10, 245
Sigrist, Susan, 38
Silber, Don, 246
Siletti, Mario, 191
Silju, Erik, 132
Sille, Carlos, 154
Sillman, Leonard, 61, 246
Sills, Stephanie, 95
Silo, Jon, 87
Silver, Fred, 133
Silver, Joe, 75, 246
Silver, Raphael, 60
Silver, Robert, 102
Silverman, Stanley, 80, 81, 163
Silvia, Leslie, 70
Simmonds, Stanley, 32, 245, 246
Simmons, Connie, 38, 246
Simmons, James, 202
Simmons, Michele, 49, 177
Simmons, Nancy, 34
Simmons, Nat, 65, 246
Simmons, Stanley, 20, 88
Simon, Avivah, 117, 126
Simon, Bernard, 62, 112, 117, 126, 170, 173
Simon, Danny, 192
Simon, Elizabeth, 202
Simon, Gerald, 202
Simon, Linda, 115
Simon, Mayo, 84
Simon, Neil, 46, 168, 169, 177
Simon, Roger Hendricks, 154, 210
Simone, 101
Simons, Ted, 61, 121
Simonson, Jon, 38
Simpson, Sean, 96
Sincere, Jean, 86
Sinclair, Betty, 196
Sinclair, Eric, 214
Sinclair, Michael, 40
Singer, Margaret, 110
Singer, Raymond, 208
Singleton, Carole, 187
Sinnott, Patricia, 181
Siré, Augustin, 127
Siretta, Fred, 40
Sirola, Joseph, 43, 245, 246
Sisson, Bill, 176
Sissov, William, 166
Six Characters In Search Of An Author, 202
Six, Robert, 186
Skeete, Yolande, 140
Skelton, Thomas, 56, 123
Skiles, Steve, 31, 94, 106, 246
Sklar, Roberta, 122
Skolnik, Peter, 12, 39
Skolnik, Walter, 119
Slaiman, Marjorie, 187, 246
Slater, Herbert, 134
Slattery, Kerry, 168
Slaughter, Harriet, 168
Slezak, Erika, 199
Slezak, Walter, 183
Slivnick, Charlene, 83, 84
Sloan, Mimi, 54, 246
Sloan, Walter K., 198
Slocum, Richard, 193
Sloninger, Lana, 172
Sloyan, James J., 120, 153
Small, Danette, 187
Small, Neva, 23, 246
Smalls, Samuel, 177
Smelko, Albert L., 188
Smiley, Brenda, 6, 95, 105, 213, 246
Smith, Archie, 204
Smith, Bill, 8
Smith, Buddy, 193
Smith, C. W., 141
Smith, Carol, 174
Smith, Cedric, 163, 164, 165
Smith, David Rae, 206
Smith, Delos V., Jr., 135, 246
Smith, Donegan, 187
Smith, E. B., 28
Smith, Ed, 151
Smith, Elise, 102

Smith, Ethel, 109
Smith, Francesca, 32
Smith, Garnett, 18
Smith, Hale, 83
Smith, Holly, 174
Smith, Howard, 256
Smith, Izetta, 186
Smith, Jack E., 204
Smith, Kirby, 168
Smith, Michael, 190
Smith, Nicholas, 48, 246
Smith, Oliver, 11, 28, 32, 40, 46, 51, 58, 69, 72, 76, 88, 105, 107, 121, 144, 166, 168, 176, 180, 183
Smith, Ross D., 201
Smith, Roy, 173
Smith, Rufus, 27, 54, 246
Smith, Sammy, 32
Smith, Sandra, 214
Smith, Sarah Jane, 88, 246
Smith, Sheila, 73, 214, 246
Smith, Stephen, 188
Smith, Sydney, 195
Smith, Verdelle, 151
Smith, Viola, 74
Smithers, William, 214
Smithies, Richard H. R., 103
Smuckler, Ruth D., 126, 133
Smythe, John, 164
Snell, David, 191
Snell, Eugenie, 11
Snook, Robert, 191
Snow, Danny, 73
Snow, Mary Ann, 23, 69
Snow, Virginia, 23, 59
Snyder, Arlan Dean, 195
Soble, Stanley, 167
Soboloff, Arnold, 56, 246
Sofaer, Abraham, 189
Soffer, Sheldon, 115
Sokol, Marilyn, 168
Soldiers, 60
Solen, Paul, 176
Solms, Kenny, 61, 121
Solomon, Artie, 16, 40, 64, 139, 144
Soloway, Leonard, 101
Solters, Lee, 9, 10, 17, 18, 20, 23, 28, 32, 38, 39, 46, 47, 50, 51, 53, 54, 69, 72, 76, 79, 166, 173, 175, 176, 180, 183, 185
Somack, Jack, 151
Somers, Donald, 209
Something Different, 30
Somlyo, Roy A., 16, 27, 78, 178, 180
Sommer, Josef, 159, 160, 204
Somner, Pearl, 26
Son, Come Home, A, 129
Sondheimer, Hans, 92, 93
Song Of The Grasshopper, 11
Song Of The Lusitanian Bogey, 146
Sonnichsen, Ingrid, 197
Sontag, Hedy, 129
Soper, Felicia, 208
Sorel, Theodore, 99, 204
Sorrows Of Frederick, The, 189
Sotoconi, Ruben, 127
Souchon, Janine, 139
Soules, Dale, 122
South Pacific, 77
Soyinka, Wole, 114, 148
Spaic, Kosta, 193
Spalding, Ioan E., 105, 121, 127
Spalding. Thomas, 202
Sparer, Paul, 15, 45
Spark, Muriel, 37
Sparks, Dennis, 161, 162
Spaull, Guy, 208
Spearman, James A., 39
Specter, Edward, 23
Spector, Arnold, 101
Spencer, Bud, 88
Spencer, T. J., 104
Speransky, Nicholai G., 187
Sperber, Milo, 196
Speyser, Paul, 120, 246
Spicer, Graham, 165
Spiegel, Richard, 190
Spielberg, David, 184
Spierer, Terry, 49
Spina, John, 167
Spinetti, Victor, 214
Spingler, Doug, 32
Spinner, Helene, 57
Spitzer, Dionis, 198
Spofford, 6. 33
Spohn, Patrick, 169
Spoon River Anthology, 193

Springer, John, 16, 111, 119, 129, 140, 179
Spruill, James, 107, 114, 208
Squarzina, Luigi, 64
Squibb, June, 38, 246
Stack, Richard, 171
Stadlen, Lewis, 167
Staff, Frank, 169
Staircase, 35
Stallman, Charles, 157, 158
Stamm, Lisa, 58, 144
Stanczak, Marian, 21
Stander, Holice, 121, 246
Stanford Repertory Theater, 205
Stanley, Florence, 70
Stanley, Kim, 214
Stanovitch, Anna, 100
Stanton, Bill, 71
Stanton, Thomas F., 109
Stanwyck, Jay, 256
Stapleton, Maureen, 4, 6, 46, 214, 246
Stark, Bruce W., 135, 184
Stark, Douglas, 25, 246
Stark, Joy, 23
Stark, Leslie J., 58
Stark, Sally, 151
Starkman, 30
Star-Spangled Girl, The, 76, 177, 192
State Theater of Florida, The, 188
Statler, Vernon, 161, 162
Staton, Mary, 205
Stattell, Robert, 115, 131, 154, 246
Stavjanik, Edd, 90, 91
Stearns, James Hart, 27, 82
Stearns, Michael, 38
Steele, Robert L., 171
Steelman, Ronald, 198
Steenberg, Patricia, 163, 164, 165
Steere, Clifton, 169
Stein, Gertrude, 113
Stein, Howard, 210
Stein, Joseph, 70, 167
Stein, Julian, 34, 54, 94, 174, 175
Steinbeck, John, 49
Steinbeck, Ron L., 32
Steinberg, Bilee, 39
Steinberg, David, 47
Steinberg, Deborah, 83
Steinberg, Harold, 25
Steinberg, Robert, 111, 181
Steinbock, Rudolf, 91
Steinbrecher, Alexander, 9
Steiner, Eileen, 144
Stella, Leo, 134
Stepanek, Lilly, 91
Stephanie Sills Productions, Inc., 95
Stephen D., 6, 105, 212
Stephens, Harold, 5
Stephens, Peter, 196
Sterling, Jay Theodore, 161, 162
Sterling, Philip, 85,1 17, 246
Stern, Lenny, 97
Stern, Leo, 10, 28, 54
Stern, Peter, 4
Stern, Rudi, 135
Sterne, Richard, 109, 246
Sternhagen, Frances, 75
Stevens, Adam, 125
Stevens, Cari, 133
Stevens. Connie. 214
Stevens, Fran, 32, 247
Stevens, John Wright, 202
Stevens, Paul, 142, 189, 247
Stevens, Susan, 98, 118
Stevens, Tony, 166
Stevenson, Robert, 200
Steward, Ron, 145
Stewart, Dixie, 32, 101
Stewart, Fred, 24, 154, 247
Stewart, John, 92, 93, 172, 214
Stewart, Michael, 28,55, 69, 166, 176
Stewart, Nancy, 191
Stewart, Narcellus G., 157
Stewart, Ray, 94, 247
Stewart, Susan, 171
Stewart, William, 200
Stickney, Dorothy, 86, 247
Stites, Julane, 38
Stockdale, Joseph, 201
Stockfisch, Thomas, 205
Stoddard, Haila, 12, 145
Stoddard, Michael, 53
StomsVik, Don, 185